Future of Business and Finance

The Future of Business and Finance book series features professional works aimed at defining, describing and charting the future trends in these fields. The focus is mainly on strategic directions, technological advances, and challenges and solutions which will affect the way we do business tomorrow. We also encourage books which focus on the future of sustainability and governance. Mainly written by practitioners, consultants and academic thinkers, the books are intended to spark and inform further discussions and developments.

More information about this series at http://www.springer.com/series/16360

Armin Trost

Human Resources Strategies

Balancing Stability and Agility
in Times of Digitization

Armin Trost
Furtwangen University
Villingen-Schwenningen, Germany

ISSN 2662-2467   ISSN 2662-2475 (electronic)
Future of Business and Finance
ISBN 978-3-030-30594-9   ISBN 978-3-030-30592-5 (eBook)
https://doi.org/10.1007/978-3-030-30592-5

Original German edition published by Springer-Verlag GmbH Deutschland, Wiesbaden, Germany, 2018

© Springer Nature Switzerland AG 2020
This work is subject to copyright. All rights are reserved by the Publisher, whether the whole or part of the material is concerned, specifically the rights of translation, reprinting, reuse of illustrations, recitation, broadcasting, reproduction on microfilms or in any other physical way, and transmission or information storage and retrieval, electronic adaptation, computer software, or by similar or dissimilar methodology now known or hereafter developed.
The use of general descriptive names, registered names, trademarks, service marks, etc. in this publication does not imply, even in the absence of a specific statement, that such names are exempt from the relevant protective laws and regulations and therefore free for general use.
The publisher, the authors, and the editors are safe to assume that the advice and information in this book are believed to be true and accurate at the date of publication. Neither the publisher nor the authors or the editors give a warranty, express or implied, with respect to the material contained herein or for any errors or omissions that may have been made. The publisher remains neutral with regard to jurisdictional claims in published maps and institutional affiliations.

This Springer imprint is published by the registered company Springer Nature Switzerland AG.
The registered company address is: Gewerbestrasse 11, 6330 Cham, Switzerland

To my dear parents
Edith and Ernst Trost

Preface

When I started studying psychology about 30 years ago, my goal was to become a family therapist. At that time I had already 2 years behind me in which I had learned to work intensively with people in a small psychiatric clinic. That was a wonderful, instructive time. At some point during my studies, I turned to industrial and organizational psychology and ended up where many of my fellow students ended up: in the training and development department of a large corporation. My career as a HR professional took its course. I implemented performance appraisal systems without ever having to ask myself what performance, on the part of the people concerned, actually means in concrete terms. I conducted employee surveys without having to take a personal interest in an employee's experience. I introduced applicant tracking systems without meeting an applicant personally. In contrast to my work in a psychiatric environment, it became clear to me at some point that HR in large corporations means above all setting up processes, instruments, systems, and programs and keeping them running. All this has very little to do with working with people.

Basically, that is fine. One quickly learns and accepts that one should not be an HR professional or HR manager if one likes working with people. However, over the years my inner dislike, which somehow became silently apparent from the beginning, became ever clearer. It is not the systems themselves that turned out to be more and more unbearable for me, but the attitude with which these systems were developed and kept alive. You will find descriptions of these systems in most common textbooks about human resources management—the annual performance appraisal, change management, competence management, talent management, etc. And I have to admit that during my studies I hated books on personnel management. There is nothing creepier than a classic textbook on human resources management. To this day, hardly anything has changed, neither in my reaction, nor in the books themselves. What is described in all these books, and mostly lived in practice, has something patronizing, not infrequently even something contemptuous of people. The employee, the human resource, is not treated as a subject here but as an object. It is measured, judged, developed ("upskilled"), promoted, transferred, terminated, rewarded, retained, etc. You do something with the human resource. "You" is the superordinate, corporate system, represented by the human resources department as the executive body. All this is done under the premise of putting the employee at the centre. What an illusion. The operator of a laying battery also puts his 10,000 chickens at the centre.

Then I, of all people, became a professor of human resources management. Looking back, this was the ideal time. Companies slowly woke up and began to rethink. In the beginning, there was a shortage of skilled workers, and suddenly we had to learn to value applicants and candidates, to be interested in their preferences, and to apply to them and not vice versa. My first book appeared: *Employer Branding*. How can we convince as an employer? Then followed the book *Talent Relationship Management*. After writing other books, I started to work on a particularly incapacitating HR instrument, namely the annual performance appraisal. The book *The End of Performance Appraisal* appeared and nothing pleased me more than the great irritation, coupled with broad, positive resonance, that it brought. I've been really lucky over the past few years because a gradual awakening in the HR community has become more and more visible. New generations of HR people took the helm, supported by new generations of executives. Throughout the years I found it a wonderful task to throw coals into the blazing fire again and again, critically, provocatively but always constructively, and close to practice. It seemed as if my attitude and the zeitgeist had met, and I was allowed to play an active role in this development.

How very much I now welcome the growing debate on the subject of agility. For me, agility is much more than just a buzzword. It symbolizes a long overdue development towards a changing attitude: the employee as a mature human being. My great role model, Douglas McGregor, is being turned to again, and rarely was his juxtaposition of the Theory X—humans are lazy by nature and have to be kept on a short leash—and the humanistic opposite, of Theory Y, more important and alive than now. In the course of this development, it was my great dream to finally write a comprehensive book that would deal with HR from the point of view of Theory X versus Theory Y. What does HR look like in a traditional, hierarchical, and stable enterprise, and how are things presented in a more agile context? What an exciting question! Writing this book was a matter of real concern to me. Here we are talking about much more than just the image of a mature human being. It is ultimately a question of the competitiveness of many proud companies. I share the view that agility is a prerequisite for the majority of companies to survive in current and future markets. And human resources management plays a key role in this.

When I started this book in 2017, I had great respect for this task. I was filled with ideas, an attitude, and a blurry picture of what I would write. In the end, writing this book was a long journey into something uncertain. First you start writing a book. But then the book writes you. The fact that such a book has a static character, i.e. one is forced to fix thoughts in black and white and with finality, is difficult for me to bear. Because the journey continues, and everything I write in this book is just a snapshot. Agility also means never really arriving at a final destination.

This journey did not take place in a quiet room, but in a constant exchange with numerous forward-thinking, open-minded people and companies who were willing to contribute constructively to the uncertainty. At this point, we usually thank all those who contributed to the success of this book. I can not even name them all.

They are the many HR managers, HR professionals, executives, and also students with whom I have spent hours, even days, discussing and struggling for solutions. They are the many impulses in the infinite number of books, articles, blogs, and TED talks that have continuously irritated me. But it is also my family who had to endure a father and husband for 1 year, who was mentally absent at times. In particular I'd like to thank Iliana Haro, who supported me so wonderfully with this English version of this book. Thank you, thank you, thank you. I look forward to the long journey that lies ahead of us.

Tübingen, Germany Armin Trost
July 31, 2019

Contents

1	**HR in the Context of Digitization**		1
	References		5
2	**Agility and Stability**		7
	2.1	From Attitude to Management Systems	7
		The Founder and His or Her Personal Attitude	8
		A Corporate Culture Emerges and Remains	8
		Rules and Structures	8
		Strategic Management Systems	9
		Hierarchical and Agile Development	10
		The Hierarchical Hemisphere	10
		The Agile Hemisphere	13
		Connected Markets Require Connected Organizations	14
	2.2	Types of HR	15
		Hire & Pay and Darwinism	16
		Institutionalization and the HR Amplitude	16
		Central Planning and Control	17
		People-Centered Enablement	20
		Painful Transformation	21
		The Digital Dehumanization of Human Resources Management	23
	References		24
3	**Building an HR Strategy**		25
	3.1	HR Strategy: An Overview	25
		HR Strategy	26
		Building Blocks of an HR Strategy	26
		All Relevant Questions at a Glance	28
	3.2	Corporate Strategy as the Basis	28
		The Ultimate Business Purpose	29
		The Positioning of the Company in the Market	31
		Strategic Challenges and Opportunities	32
		A Different Understanding of Leadership and Organization	33

	3.3	Critical Functions and Roles	34
		Roles and Functions with High Strategic Relevance	34
		Hard to Fill Functions and Roles	36
		The Volume of Needs	37
		Key and Bottleneck Functions	37
	3.4	HR-Relevant Strategic Challenges	38
		Why Are You Doing This?	39
		Stakeholders, Dynamics and Limited Resources	40
		Three Times "Why?"	41
		The Pragmatic Approach	42
		Possible HR-Related Challenges	42
	3.5	Key HR Topics and Their Strategic Alignment	43
		From Challenge to Key HR Topics	43
		Possible Key HR Topics	44
		The Third Level	45
		Strong Strategic Statements	46
		Strategic Statements in HR	46
		The Relevance of Stability Versus Agility	47
		Outlook on the Following Chapters	47
	3.6	International HR Strategies	48
		Ethnocentric World View in an International Setting	49
		Local Differentiation in a Multinational Setting	49
		Global Integration	50
		Clarify How the Company Operates	50
	References	51
4	**The Structural and Cultural Context**	53
	4.1	The Context and Its Relevance for HR	53
		Structural and Cultural Framework Conditions	54
		Stability in a Traditional, Hierarchical World	55
		Agility and the Connected World	56
	4.2	The Employees	57
		Individuality, Diversity and Work-Life Balance	57
		The Focus Is on the Employee: Really?	59
		The Idea of Man: X or Y?	60
		Who Dependents on Whom?	61
	4.3	The Tasks	63
		David Against Goliath	64
		Certainty of Process and Outcome	66
		Short Cycles, Long Cycles	68
	4.4	The Dominant Understanding of Leadership	69
		General Knowledge, Expert Knowledge	69
		Boss, Coach, Partner or Enabler	71
		Autonomy and Trust	73

	4.5	Organization, Dynamics and Commitment	75
		Division of Labour and Task Dynamics	75
		Consequences and Commitment	76
	4.6	Current and Future Status	78
	References		80
5	**Talent Acquisition and Selection**		**81**
	5.1	Employer Branding	81
		Focus on Candidate or on Requirements	82
		The Employee Value Proposition as the Core of any Employer Brand	83
		Reach	83
		The Degree of Differentiation	85
		The Right Amplitude	86
		Pure Advertising?	87
		Employer Branding from the Inside	88
		The Role of Social Media	88
		Employer Branding Strategy	90
	5.2	Sourcing, Approaching and Retaining Candidates	90
		The Passive, Vacancy-Focused Scenario	91
		The Active, Candidate Focused Scenario	93
		Fun or Networking?	94
		Current and Possible Sourcing Strategies	95
		The Right Strategy Depending on the Target Function	96
		Simple (Operational) Hiring	97
		Difficult Mass Hiring	98
		Specialist Hiring	99
		Strategic Search	99
		Talent Acquisition Strategy	100
	5.3	Selection and Fit	101
		Short-Term and Long-Term Fit	102
		Potential for Future Development or Current Suitability?	103
		Efficiency Versus Effectiveness	104
		Who Is Supposed to Benefit from Aptitude Testing?	105
		The Positive Candidate Experience	106
		Who Is Supposed to Convince Whom?	108
		Artificially Intelligent Selection Procedures	109
		Bear the Consequences of the Selection Decision	110
		Long-Term Candidate and Team Orientation	111
	5.4	Onboarding	111
		Two Opposing Testimonials	111
		When Does Onboarding Start?	113
		The Hard and Soft Side of Onboarding	114

		Babysitting or Cold Water	115
		Responsibility for Onboarding	115
		Compatibility and Implementation	117
	References		118
6	**Goals, Assessment and Feedback**		119
	6.1	Objective Settings and Performance Expectations	119
		The Classic, Strategic Alignment	120
		The General Problem with "Smart" Objectives	120
		Toxic Effects of Individual Goals in Connected Organizations	121
		What Do You Do for Whom and Why?	122
		Goal Agreement Versus Goal Setting	123
		Personal Responsibility and Openness	124
		Target Transparency Versus Drawer	125
		Target Agreement in Agile Working Environments	125
	6.2	Feedback	127
		Feedback Rules and Processes	128
		Openness to Feedback	128
		Situational and Institutional Framework Conditions	130
		Responsibility for Feedback	131
		Relevant Feedback Providers	132
		The Right Time for Feedback	133
		Check-in and Feedback Apps	134
		Whose Feedback Is This?	135
		A Matter for the Company or the Feedback Recipient	136
	6.3	Formal Judgement	137
		The Special Nature of Formal Appraisals	137
		The Boss as Judge	138
		Forced Distribution	139
		Performance or Performer?	141
		The Right Time to Deal with Weak Performance	143
		Continuous and Qualitative Review of Performance and Behaviour in the Team	143
	References		145
7	**Learning and Knowledge**		147
	7.1	Vocational Training	147
		Cool and Not So Cool Training	148
		Learning Opportunities, Trust and Cold Water	148
		Diversity and Co-design Versus Conformity and Standards	149
		Learning by Teaching	151
		Buddies and Reversed Mentoring	152
		Treating Trainees as Adults	152

	7.2	Executive Development................................	153
		The Separation of Strategy, Business Context and Learning Context..	154
		MBA Light..	155
		Strategically Derived Leadership Competencies at Different Levels...	155
		Strategic Tasks.......................................	157
		Teachers and Learners.................................	157
		Hotels, Business Schools, Corporate Universities and Academies......................................	158
		The Responsibility Lies with the HR Department...........	158
		Strategy Development = Executive Development...........	159
		Leadership Role, Leadership Expectations, Leadership Effectiveness...	160
		Critical Leadership Situations...........................	161
		Peer Counselling......................................	162
		Who Are You? How Do You Want to Be? What Do You Stand for?...	163
		Leadership Feedback or Assessment.....................	164
		A Matter of Responsibility..............................	165
	7.3	Continuous Learning...................................	166
		Continuous Learning in a Hierarchical and Stable Setting.....	167
		A Simple Model of Agile Learning.......................	170
		Irritation and Relevant Uncertainty.......................	170
		Learning = Work, Work = Learning, Learning = Conscious Reflection..	172
		Informal Learning.....................................	173
		Social Learning.......................................	174
		Internalization: From Explicit to Implicit..................	175
		Externalization: From Implicit to Explicit..................	175
		Be Careful About Filter Bubble..........................	177
		Socialization...	178
		What Has Always Existed..............................	178
	7.4	Knowledge Management................................	180
		Retaining, Identification and Transferring Knowledge........	180
		Knowledge Management, for Whom?.....................	181
		Humans Versus Database...............................	181
		Obligation or Incentive.................................	183
		References...	185
8	**Development and Career**.................................		187
	8.1	Talent Identification....................................	187
		Finding the Personal Vocation...........................	188
		The Responsibility of the Company.......................	189
		Employee Responsibility................................	190

		To Have Talent or to Be Talent	190
		High Potentials: Right Potentials	191
		Who Needs to Be Convinced?	192
		Transparency Versus Discretion	193
		Digital Talent Identification	194
		External and Personal Understanding of Talent	196
	8.2	Talent Development	196
		Three Variants of Talent Development	197
		Normative and Descriptive Career Paths	199
		The 70-20-10 Rule of Talent Development	200
		Mentors and Mentoring	202
		Career Coaching	203
		Action Learning	204
		Where Do Strategic Challenges and Learning Projects Come from?	205
		Formal and Interpersonal Approaches	207
		Formal Fit and Trust	208
		The Independent Talent in Its Natural Environment	210
	8.3	Expert Career	212
		The Internal Positioning of the Expert Career	213
		Top-Class Sport Versus Mass Sport	213
		Four Basic Types of Expert Careers	214
		Organizational Integration and Reporting Lines	215
		Equal Treatment of Managers and Experts	216
		How Experts Work	217
		When Is an Expert an Expert?	218
		Nerds as Experts?	219
	References		220
9	**Remuneration**		223
	9.1	Compensation Policy	223
		Work as a Prerequisite for Salary	224
		Salary as a Prerequisite for Work	224
		Reward Versus Profit	226
		Equity or Fairness	226
		Complexity and Simplicity	227
		Pay Transparency	229
		Motivation	230
		Talking about Money	232
		Social Dynamics	233
		Acquisition and Loyalty	235
		A Question of Leadership and Attitude	235
	9.2	Base Pay	235
		Flexible Versus Static Grouping	236
		Narrow and Broad Pay Bands	238

		Top and Bottom	240
		Does it Cost What it Takes?	241
		Little Room for Manoeuvre	242
	9.3	Pay for Performance	243
		Money Motivates: But Only when Paid for Doing Boring Tasks	243
		Tasks for which One Gets Money Must Be Unattractive	244
		Contingent Reward Kills Motivation and Cooperation	245
		One-Time Bonuses	246
		Sharing Profit Among Employees	247
		Active Involvement	249
		Fewer Bonuses, More Participation	250
	References		250
10	**Engagement and Retention**		253
	10.1	Working Conditions and Employer Attractiveness	253
		Garbage Men, Soldiers and Mountaineers	254
		Objective and Subjective Attractiveness	255
		Place and Time	257
		Regulation of First Order	258
		Regulation of Second Order	260
		Why Agile Organizations Do Not Win HR Awards	262
		Work-Life Balance	263
		Work-Life Balance = Diversity, Diversity = Work-Life Balance	264
		Structure Versus Individuality	265
	10.2	Employee Survey	266
		The Classic Approach of an Employee Survey	267
		Only What Was Important Before Is also Important Afterwards	269
		Who Is the Customer?	271
		Pulse Surveys	272
		Fast and Minimally Invasive	272
		On-Going Feedback	273
		Talk to Each Other	273
		Compatible Questions	274
		Dinosaurs and Minimally Invasive Measures	275
	10.3	Employee Retention	275
		Individual and Universal Preferences	277
		The Analysis Versus Forecast of Voluntary Fluctuation	278
		Is Voluntary Fluctuation Really a Problem?	281
		Retain Employees by Letting Them Go	282
		Threat to the Company Versus Interpersonal Confrontation	283
	References		285

11 HR Operation 287
11.1 HR Organization 287
Personnel Department 287
Dave Ulrich and the Three-Pillar Model 288
On the Way to Global HR 290
The Leap to Global HR 290
Obligated to the Head of HR 291
HR Organization in Agile Companies 292
Social Dynamics 293
Factual Complexity 294
Roles in an Agile HR Organization 295
People Over Processes 297
Simplicity 298
No Internal Monopolies 298
Bear the Consequences of Your Own Actions 299
As Little Central as Possible 300
Back to the Business Line 301
11.2 Key Figures and Control 302
What You Can't Measure, You Can't Manage: Really? 303
In the End, It Is All About Trust 305
Feedback or Control 306
Interesting and Relevant Key Figures 307
Investment Calculations in HR Management 309
Evidence-Based Management 310
A Profound Debate 311
Pre-mortem Analysis 311
Strategic Decisions at 30-Minute Intervals 312
Experimenting, Trying, Piloting 314
Digitization = More Data and Key Figures? 315
11.3 Digital HR and People Analytics 315
Making Life Easier for HR Professionals 316
Mobile, BYOD, Social and Cloud 317
Big Data and Artificial Intelligence 318
Human and Algorithmic Decisions 321
Employee Experience 322
People Over Systems 323
What Is the Best HR Solution on the Market? 324
The Hierarchical Heritage 325
People Over Data and Analytics 326
References 327

12 Managing Change and Transformation 329
12.1 Three Different Scenarios 329
Two Levels 331
12.2 Change Management: Classic Thinking 332
From Stability to Stability 332

		Change in Hierarchical Organizations	333
		Top Management as the Driving Force	333
		Change Management from a Hierarchical Perspective	334
		Communication: As Late as Possible	336
	12.3	Change in an Agile Setting	336
		The Diffusion of a Traditional Concept	336
		Early Involvement	337
		Corporate Democracy and Grassroots Movements	338
		Iterative Change	340
		Evolution or Revolution	341
		Internal and External Locus of Control	341
		Change as a Normal State	344
		Change and Change Management in an Agile Context	345
	References	347
13	**Transformation into an Agile Future**	349
	13.1	Challenges and Hurdles	350
		Integration and Interfaces	350
		Internalized Thinking and Acting	350
		Proven Behavioral Patterns in Difficult Times	350
		Reproduction of the Same	351
		Hierarchization of Agile Efforts	351
		External Regulation	351
		When Employees Request the Boss	351
	13.2	Principles of Agile Transformation	352
		Agility Is Not an End in Itself	352
		Self-Critical Status Review and Realistic Expectations of the Future	353
		The CEO Must Really Want it	353
		Coaching by Externals with Experience	354
		Agile Principles in Transformation	355
		You Do Not Change the Culture by Changing the Culture	356
		Personal Experience Instead of Only Theoretical Teaching	358
		One Stone at a Time	358
		Allowing Failure and Learning from it	359
		Green Meadow as an Option	360
		Be Bold, Be Right	361
	References	362
Index			363

About the Author

Armin Trost has for many years been regarded as one of the best-known and leading thought leaders in human resources management. He has been teaching and researching at the Business School of Furtwangen University in Germany since 2005. For many years, he has successfully advised companies of all sizes and industries on strategic human resource management issues. Dr. Armin Trost is not only known as an author of numerous specialist articles and books but also as an internationally sought-after speaker at renowned congresses.

Contact
Homepage: www.armintrost.de
Mail: mail@armintrost.de
Twitter: @armintrost
LinkedIn: www.linkedin.com/in/armintrost/

HR in the Context of Digitization

Human resources management (HR) does not seem to come to rest. In the late nineties, we had to learn from Dave Ulrich (1997) not only to be administratively but also strategically positioned. As a result, administrative tasks were bundled and often relocated to low-wage countries. This saved time for strategic, value-adding activities in HR. The HR generalist became the "HR Business Partner" with a claim to eye level with the line management. All this cost a lot of energy and effort. At the beginning of the new century the nervousness about a growing talent shortage increased. Employer branding had to be done suddenly and also talent management, active sourcing, talent communities and eventually candidate experience. In addition, the young generation Y seemed to be pushing for new themes: Work-Life-Balance and an innovative, flexible working environment. At the end of the day, we discovered that at the beginning of the twenty-first century, HR hardly had anything in common with the kind HR that had been preached ten or 20 years earlier and had been written about in the usual textbooks. We experienced an almost overwhelming development towards modernization and professionalization with the aim of competitiveness in both business and labour markets.

Digitization and Agilization
What about today? Today we deal with the topics *digitization* and *agilization*. We are talking about a completely different HR, more flexible, faster, less technocratic, less bureaucratic. The employee must again be more at the centre of attention. In great number, companies are abolishing HR processes that were initiated with a lot of effort and pain. Think here of the annual performance appraisal (Trost 2017). Some "thought leaders" are already talking about the abolition of HR as a whole. "HR needs to get back to business. Everything else can be outsourced". A certain restlessness is spreading. It is hard to find a company nowadays that does not have digitization as part of its strategic agenda. This is accompanied by an increasing number of companies asking themselves whether traditional forms of organization and leadership are still viable for the future. The topics of speed, connectivity, proximity to customers and users are omnipresent. HR cannot be left out of the

equation. Not infrequently I hear HR managers say: "We now also have a digitization strategy. Our executive board wants us to look at what this has to do with HR". What do you do as a human resources manager when you have received an order of this particular kind?

First, you Google: "Digitization HR". This will not help. You will find half-baked, superficial and even more dogmatic views. What the search provides, rarely helps for your own special case. Then you would go to a convention or conference on the subject. What you take home along with a folder with event documents and new LinkedIn contacts is at least the comforting feeling that you are not alone with your own insecurity. The likelihood of leaving a congress with more than just new contacts and congress-material is frighteningly low. Then you do the right thing right away. You take money into your hands and bring a consultant into the house. Here the probability is very high of finding consultants who, only a few years or even months ago, generated revenue with (complicated, technocratic) concepts from the past. There are no consultants who can look back on several years of experience in the context of digitization and HR. The topic appeared too quickly, also in the eyes of the consultants.

HR in the Context of Digitization

First, it shall be clear at what level HR and digitization must relate in order to resolve the confusion of languages in a very first stage. This in turn concerns the role HR wants to play in this context. Six roles can be distinguished here: Administrators, supporters, companions, creator, enablers and entrepreneurs.

- The *administrator* optimizes existing HR processes through digital technology. We've always done that. Think about the digitization of the recruiting processes (applicant tracking systems), the electronic tracking of the working hours or of the digital personnel file.
- The *supporter* provides employees and managers with useful assistance for HR-related tasks in electronic form. This has also been around for a long time in the form of Employee Self Services (ESS), e-learning, employee referral apps, internal yellow pages, etc.
- The *companion* supports the company in the course of the digital transformation with all HR-relevant challenges. What do we do with certain groups of employees when their jobs become obsolete due to digitization? How do we secure the necessary competencies in the company that are critical to succeed in the context of digital transformation or will be in the future?
- The *creator* changes the way employees work using digital technology. This can also mean that HR actively contributes to replacing jobs and tasks with appropriate technology, or it at least makes them simpler and more effective. This role is hardly anchored in HR today, but is conceivable as a matter of course.
- The *enabler* changes structural (and thus also cultural) framework conditions in order to strengthen the overall competitiveness of the company in times of digitization. How do we have to adapt HR in the context of a changing

understanding of organization and leadership in order to achieve a high degree of innovation and change capability? This role directly affects the aspect of agilization.
- The *entrepreneur deals with the* question of how the company has to position itself in the course of the digital transformation and with regard to its products and relevant partnerships. Traditionally, this role would not be attributed to HR. But to assume this categorically would be a mistake. Because this does not always have to be the case. Why should an HR executive not get involved in strategic positioning issues to the same extent as his or her colleagues from Marketing, Research and Development have always done?

To the six roles, from administrator to entrepreneur, there is an underlying dimension. While the administrator deals primarily with HR itself (HR for HR), the entrepreneur deals with the company and its markets (From the company for markets). The first question is therefore what role HR would like to occupy or at least strive for in a company (see Fig. 1.1).

This book primarily deals with the role of the *enabler*. At best, all other roles are affected if they appear to be relevant for further discussion. Why is this role chosen for this book? There are several reasons for this. On the one hand, according to my own observations, there is a great need for action here. Hardly any role is more affected by current developments than this one. This is not only about the question of *what* we do in HR, but above all about *how* and *why* we will do things in the future. Here in particular, we will probably observe considerable upheavals in the coming years. On the other hand, this role seems to be under strong pressure. CEOs, but also employees and managers, demand a different kind of HR in times of a drastically changing environment. The lack of compatibility between a modern understanding of leadership and organization on one side and traditional HR processes, systems and instruments on the other is becoming increasingly apparent. At the same time, this is where the greatest uncertainty lies. HR bashing alone, the one-sided hitting on HR does not help. The HR community has enough of that anyway. The pressure is on the development of alternative approaches and solutions at a time when it is difficult to look back on the experience of other companies.

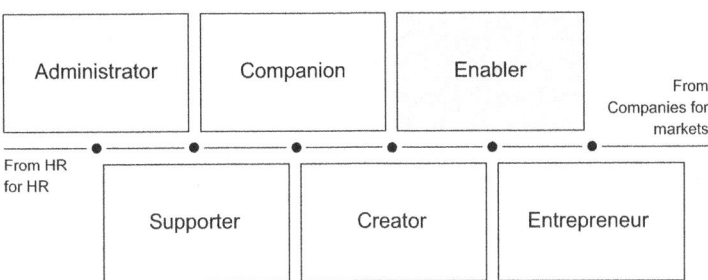

Fig. 1.1 Possible roles of HR in the context of digitization

Promise of this Book
This book is intended to provide orientation. If you are looking for a new HR strategy in times of digitization you will find a practical guide in this book. That is my promise as an author to the reader. Of course, no finished HR strategy will be proposed in the further course of this book. This would only be possible with the greatest possible ignorance of company-specific challenges and framework conditions. This book does not provide the ultimate solution, but leads step-by-step through questions paired with practical orientation. The aim of this book is to be undogmatic. There is no ultimate right or wrong. This is intended to set this book apart from many other sources, which, in my view, too often and too hastily bring one-sided views to the fore as prophecies.

One thing this book does *not* promise. Hopefully inspired, and with better orientation, one will ask oneself again and again when reading, how strategic orientations could be put into practice. In this book, the practitioner will reflect on considerations in the light of his given framework conditions and try to translate these into as concrete processes, instruments or responsibilities as possible. Now I have tried to make numerous thoughts tangible in this book with practical examples and ideas. However, this book cannot afford to provide a concrete solution to everything. There are at least two reasons for this. Firstly, solutions always look different, depending on the given framework conditions, and it would be presumptuous to highlight certain approaches as particularly suitable here. Secondly, this book would have a much larger scope if I wanted to discuss all the strategies presented here at the same time as the operative design. Then this work would have become a comprehensive textbook or practice manual, which was not the intention from the beginning.

Outlook on the Contents of this Book
This book essentially consists of two segments, a general, strategic part and one, in which the most important fields of action and HR topics are described according to hierarchical and agile aspects. The first part covers Chaps. 2–4. It sets out basic considerations for the development of an HR strategy. This segment provides a practical guide. What are the steps to take in developing an HR strategy? How do the different steps build on each other? An essential component of this section are the different varieties of HR. It describes a model that became my mantra in HR. It shows the area between the three poles, either deliberately doing nothing, planning centrally or empowering employees. There is hardly a keynote in which I do not show this model. In this book it forms the guard rails of all considerations. Already here the spectrum between agility and stability becomes clear. The central thesis of this book is that in an agile context HR functions according to different rules than it is the case in a company striving for stability. Chapter 4 therefore explains in detail what the differences are between a hierarchical world based on stability and a more agile world. Here, too, this book provides practical orientation. Step by step, relevant factors and criteria are illustrated, which enable each company to classify itself. Where are we today, and where are we going? Chapter 4 hardly deals at all with HR. It is only about the internal structural and cultural context within a company.

Up to this point it becomes clear that the definition of strategically important HR topics—we call them key HR topics—should be a central component of any HR strategy. In the following Chaps. 5–12, a broad spectrum of possible HR topics will be discussed in the light of agile but also stable framework conditions. An attempt has been made here to treat HR comprehensively. It is about employer branding, candidate sourcing and retention, selection, onboarding, objective setting, performance review, feedback, training, leadership development, learning, knowledge management, talent identification and development, expert careers, working hours, architecture, work flexibility, employee surveys, employee retention, remuneration policy, base pay and variable pay, almost everything we deal with in the context of HR. After that, it is about topics that could rather be assigned to infrastructure: HR organization, technology, people analytics and the big topic of change management. In this sense, this book has the character of a textbook because it covers a very wide range of common HR topics, although it does not address the basics. Rather, the focus is on the strategic options related to the topics discussed in this book. While it is recommended to read Chaps. 2–12, and even the respective subchapters can be read independently. The order is also arbitrary, more or less.

This book has to close with a chapter that explores how a transformation from a stable to an agile world can succeed. This concluding Chap. 13, does not deal with HR in the narrower sense but with the company context as a whole. But if HR is to contribute to not only taking part in this agile change but to actively shaping it, then this topic should not be missing from a book like this.

References

Trost A (2017) The end of performance appraisal. A practitioners' guide to alternatives in agile organizations. Springer, Heidelberg

Ulrich D (1997) Human resource champions. The next agenda for adding value and delivering results. Harvard Business School Press, Boston, MA

Agility and Stability 2

Of course, companies and their leaders want stability or predictability. No serious CEO would voluntarily want to do without it. Especially in today's complex, dynamic, uncertain and rapidly changing times, the call for more security is more than understandable. Now it is the same CEOs who want a high degree of adaptability, flexibility and resilience too. Today we are also talking about agility, an entrepreneurial flexibility in turbulent times. However, the problem is that both are not possible at the same time. Companies that focus on stability will inevitably show a different understanding of leadership and organization than those that focus on agility. This dilemma shapes the discussion about leadership and organization especially in these times of digitization. Therefore an approach is first made to these two worlds: stability versus agility. Building on these, this chapter presents basic types of HR in terms of the role of the HR function and its self-understandings. These different types of HR form an essential basis for the rest of this book.

2.1 From Attitude to Management Systems

You can only grasp the future if you understand its origin and take it seriously. Hardly any company develops an HR strategy on the much-cited greenfield. Why are we the way we are today? Why do we now have an HR that is the way it is? These are crucial questions, which must be at the beginning of the development of a new HR strategy. Only on the basis of their answers can one turn to the question: How do we want to be, and what does this mean for our HR strategy? The following is therefore a simple story of how companies and their understanding of leadership and organization develop. All this has little to do with HR in itself, but is important for further understanding. We start at the very beginning.

The Founder and His or Her Personal Attitude

At the beginning of a company there is usually a founder and his or her idea. Even if these may have been founding teams, the term 'the founder' will be used here. This founder has a personal *attitude*, a complex construct of personality, self-image, values, beliefs, world view, image of man. This attitude shapes the cooperation in the young company. There are patriarchal founders, founders who lead their young team paternally or maternally. Some want control, others trust. Some see themselves, their idea itself as the centre. Others put the employees or customers at the centre. Often the attitude of the founder can still be felt in the company after many decades. This even applies in cases where the young plant has grown to become a global player. You can still feel the spirit of Bill Hewlett and Dave Packard, of Robert Bosch, of Richard Branson of Dietmar Hopp and Hasso Plattner (SAP) when you walk through the corridors not only of the respective headquarters.

This attitude of the founder has a lasting influence on the cooperation and leadership in the company. Especially in the early days this attitude is reflected in how decisions are made, who makes them, what is important and what is not.

A Corporate Culture Emerges and Remains

This attitude of the founder is reproduced in the thinking and behaviour of the increasing number of colleagues. A *corporate culture* emerges. It is basically the reproduced version of the company's original DNA, which was implanted into the company by the founders at the very beginning. It reflects the collective understanding of what is desirable or undesirable in the company. It does not stop at anything and not only shapes the way decisions are made but also what type of humour is allowed or desired, what clothes you wear.

Already in this early phase culture has an important coordinating function. It creates mutual understanding and trust in daily actions, because surprises in behaviour and thus complexity are reduced. Culture also has an important selection function. Only those who can cope with the respective culture feel attracted to a company, or they are repelled in the event of a lack of cultural fit. The special thing about culture is that it is very consistent. Because it is based on unwritten rules and merges into the unconscious of the employees, it hardly seems accessible to targeted change or conscious reflection.

Rules and Structures

While in an early phase of the company's development the attitude of the founder and the resulting culture are absolutely sufficient to make quick and reliable decisions and set priorities, this is no longer enough from a certain company size on. The bigger the company, the less can the attitude of the founder be experienced by all individuals. In addition, with increasing company size, the probability of

2.1 From Attitude to Management Systems

situations calling for an official regulation grows. Fast, interpersonal coordination processes require more and more general clarification. Rules and structures will be created.

Unlike implicit norms of a culture, *rules* are explicit. They may be documented. They are officially valid and must leave as little room for interpretation as possible as far as their meaning is concerned. You can even post them on walls or communicate them on the intranet. Rules describe how employees and managers should behave in a certain situation. They can affect working time, travel expenses, hiring processes, external purchases, and much more. Rules reduce complexity because they minimize possible options in decision-making processes. You do not always have to discuss everything over and over again. This reduces the potential for interpersonal conflicts.

Rules in themselves are rules of first order. Second order rules deal, on a meta-level, with the question of how rules are created or changed. Who sets the rules? Who determines their field of application? What do you have to do to adapt rules? Who controls compliance with rules and how?

Rules also reproduce the culture and thus the attitude of the founder. How one regulates travel expenses, working hours, or the acquisition of resources, is usually the signature of the culture. This will be discussed in more detail later in this chapter. At least since the works of Talcott Parsons (1951), the translation of culture into rules has been called *institutionalization*. Conversely, new employees learn the culture by learning and adhering to existing rules. The latter is then called *internalization*.

Structures, on the other hand, clarify responsibilities within the company. While in the early days of the company's history responsibilities are often clarified on demand and on the basis of personal availability, this becomes more and more difficult with increasing company size. Clear responsibilities reduce complexity to the extent that it is always clear who bears which responsibility today and tomorrow. Structures are formed horizontally between the employees. The possible consequences are functional or product-related departments, teams, roles, clusters or even silos, depending on organizational understanding. In addition, vertical structures with corresponding management levels are formed. That does not say anything about how leadership turns out. Even in highly agile organizations there are hierarchies, as we will see later.

Strategic Management Systems

For some organizations it is sufficient for successful functioning to have rules and structures and to adhere to them accordingly. Think, for example, of public institutions, schools or associations. However, as soon as a company has to assert itself in a dynamic market environment, mere compliance with rules and structures will no longer be enough. And this probably applies to all companies today. Even small companies find themselves in a dynamic and competitive environment, often experiencing it even more intensively than their large competitors. But they can act faster and more directly, not least because of the presence of the founder. Larger companies in a dynamic environment, on the other hand, add another level to existing (mostly static) rules and structures. *Strategic management systems* emerge.

For many years, personnel administration, for example, was able to withdraw to compliance with rules and structures. Pure administration—that was fine. And because compliance with rules often has to do with legality, executive positions in HR were mostly filled by lawyers. Comprehensive management systems, such as talent management or talent relationship management, emerged at the latest stage with the advent of competition for talent. That is not all. Today we have competence management, performance management, diversity management, change management and health management. For many years students of business studied "Business Administration". Today we prefer to talk about "Business Management" and, alongside the classics, such as accounting, students learn customer relationship management, supply chain management, strategic management, etc. Strategic Management deals with the question of how a company must position itself in a dynamic market and how it can successfully implement and control its strategic priorities in a goal-oriented manner. The conceptual orientation of the strategic management systems also follows the cultural values of the company. In this respect, an institutionalization also takes place on this level, in which culture is reproduced in a certain way. A company based on control and mistrust will design its management systems differently than a company based on trust.

Hierarchical and Agile Development

The quality of the development described above varies from company to company. Founders differ in their attitude. Accordingly, cultures develop differently in companies that are institutionalized in rules, structures and management systems. In addition to the already known phases of the company's development, Fig. 2.1 shows two different hemispheres within which the development of a company can take place, the hierarchical and the agile hemisphere.

The upper hemisphere points to a traditional organization striving for stability. This is about bundling responsibility at top management level. Probably the majority of the companies will find themselves on this side. The lower hemisphere indicates an agile organization. Here, responsibility is shared in networks. This distinction will be highly relevant in the further course of the book.

The Hierarchical Hemisphere

Hierarchical organizations often have a patriarchal founder. Right from the start, the attitude is that the boss is in charge. The employees know this and have already learned it in the first days of their employment. Accordingly, decisions are always made at the top, either by the direct superior, the next higher manager, or at even higher levels of the hierarchy. As soon as rules and structures are created, they have a

2.1 From Attitude to Management Systems

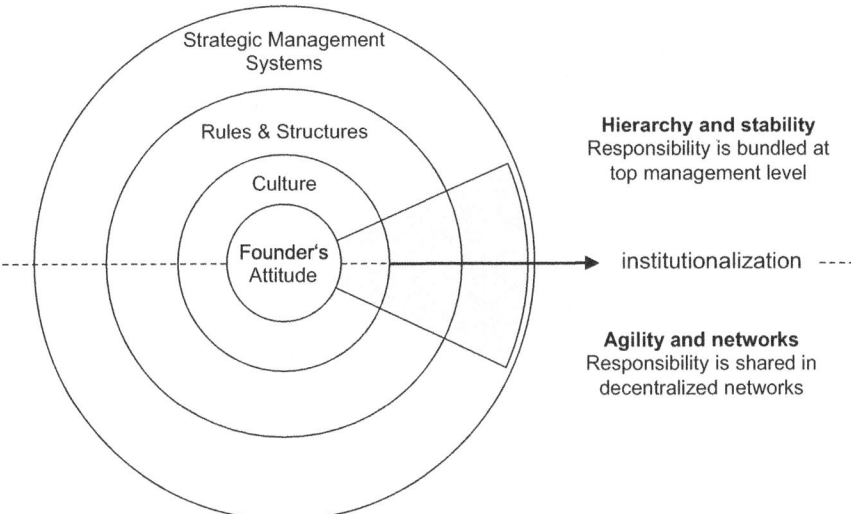

Fig. 2.1 The phases of business development within two opposing hemispheres

certain character. Rules take responsibility away from the employees and communicate unmistakably how to act in a certain situation. "Travel expenses must be approved by the line manager." "Presence is required from nine to five". "Holidays are approved by the next level manager." The principles that Max Weber described in his bureaucracy model almost a 100 years ago dominate here: Division of labour, authority of command, hierarchy, rule binding and compliance with documents (Morgan 1997).

In hierarchical organizations the principle of division of labour applies. Employees are encouraged to concentrate on their assigned tasks. An orientation to the left or right within the value chain is explicitly not planned. The terms "department" or "division" are meant literally. In addition to this horizontal division of responsibilities, we find a vertical division of powers in established companies. Anything that exceeds the responsibility of a unit or organizational unit is passed on to the next higher management level. If, for example, an employee in the marketing department is about to decide whether to place an ad the publication of which costs 20,000 euros and the employee is only allowed to decide up to 500 euros, then this employee passes this decision on to the next level. If the next level can only decide up to 5000 euros, the matter goes one level higher. This continues until the severity of a decision corresponds to the authority of an executive level. All duties, responsibilities and authorities are sorted and structured in a hierarchy according to the principle of superiority and subordination.

Hierarchical organizations try to bundle power and responsibility as high up in the pyramid as possible. The executive board is the head of the company. Rules are there to carry top management's ideas about correct conduct downwards and to secure its own powers. "Why are we doing this? Because I say so!". The same

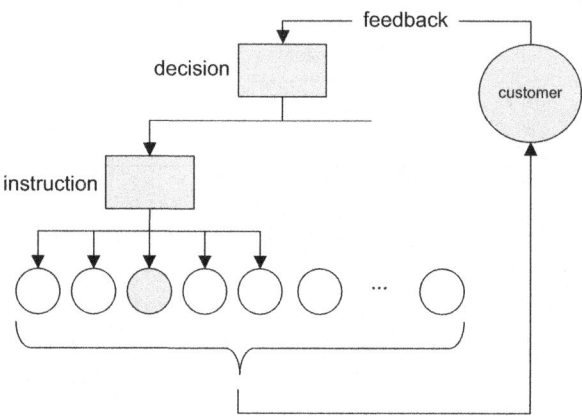

Fig. 2.2 Cycle of decision, instruction and feedback in hierarchical organizations (first published in Trost 2017, Unter den Erwartungen. Wiley. p. 1251)

applies to management systems. They are there to empower executives. Through management systems, the upper management of the company gains access to the organization. At the same time, management systems provide the information that is required at higher levels for further decisions. Decisions are then cascaded to the bottom, where employees organized according to the division of labour receive their instructions. The sum of the individual work results in those products or services, which are then delivered to the customers. Using appropriate feedback systems, such as customer surveys or the development of sales, top decision-makers receive feedback, which in turn could induce them to make adaptable, sometimes strategic decisions. A simplified representation of this hierarchical cycle of decision, instruction and feedback is provided in Fig. 2.2.

Direct cooperation between employees from different departments is not explicitly provided for in hierarchical organizations, even though it may take place informally. The same applies to direct contact and exchange with the company's customers. Employees, teams and departments are more committed to higher authorities than to neighbouring departments.

Companies that develop within the hierarchical hemisphere have a central advantage. Decisions at the top of the company can be implemented quickly and their progress monitored. The word of the CEO has weight and is the trigger for appropriate behaviour throughout the company. On the other hand, the increasing complexity inside and outside the company forces hierarchically thinking companies to set up even more complex rules, structures and management systems. In some companies, the impression is increasingly being given that employees and managers spend more energy on feeding existing management systems than on looking after customers' interests and needs. Maintaining or operating management reports, balanced scorecards, KPIs in management cockpits, internal and external audits, annual performance appraisals, budget meetings, planning meetings, and the like is a lot of effort and time consuming. However, it is actually not work. Work is only work if it leads to added value that is rewarded, demanded and paid for by the customer.

The Agile Hemisphere

Companies developing in the agile hemisphere have completely different rules, structures and management systems. Here, too, the development goes back to the underlying attitude of the founder and the corporate culture. In practice, however, they lead to different practices. One of the central principles of this hemisphere is to leave as much responsibility as possible to employees and teams. Institutionalization not only demands but also strengthens this level of responsibility. In hierarchical companies, employees must ask the manager for approval before travelling. This removes responsibility from employees. Their only responsibility is to respect the rule itself. However, in agile organizations, employees decide for themselves. In order to strengthen personal responsibility, for example, employees have to pay 5% of their travel expenses out of their own pocket (for which they receive a higher fixed salary). Alternatively, all travel expenses are displayed in an internal portal to be seen by everybody. Wasteful behaviour can then certainly lead to social conflicts. Either you stand through the conflicts or you adapt your behaviour. Agility does not mean that there are no rules. The opposite is true. The difference is in how the rules are designed and what they ultimately do. Scrum, for example, is an agile method of running projects based on very clear, comprehensive rules. It seems important to point this out explicitly, because from a hierarchical point of view agile organizations are often interpreted as anarchic or chaotic.

Second order rules (the handling of rules themselves) are usually simple in hierarchical companies: In case of uncertainty, the boss decides. In agile organizations, second-order rules usually describe democratic processes. Employees decide for themselves, and often after exhausting discussions, how they want to deal with certain situations in the future. Here, too, a widespread myth must be pointed out. Hierarchically socialized people often interpret dealing with people in agile organizations as a "cuddling course", because there is no "hard hand" that takes action from time to time. Here, too, things behave exactly the other way round. To fight things out, to represent opinions, to resolve conflicts is interpreted in agile organizations as part of intelligence and motivation. That is sometimes hard and not everyone's cup of tea. Those who can not stand it or have too little backbone could be better off in hierarchical organizations.

Agile organizations also have structures. However, they function according to different principles. While in hierarchical organizations the employees and teams feel primarily committed to the next higher level, employees and teams in agile companies see themselves as, above all, committed to their colleagues, to neighbouring teams and customers. Accordingly, they are more permeable with regard to lateral cooperation and communication. Instead of hard and statically defined positions and silos that are separated from each other, agile organizations have overlapping roles, clusters and projects that adapt to given requirements over time. Even if there are so-called departments, they are more open to neighbouring units along the value chain. Correspondingly, much effort is made in such companies to offer all people at any time the transparency necessary to understand who is currently involved in what.

When developing management systems, agile companies are guided by the question of what connected teams and their employees need to be successful. The aim of institutionalization is to empower everyone, not just executives.

Connected Markets Require Connected Organizations

Fish are viable because the quality of their fins and scales reflects the nature of the water. Birds can fly because their wings and feathers are a perfect reflection of the nature of the air. The eye can see because its structure corresponds to the nature of light. These examples from nature show how, in the sense of evolutionary theory, natural beings became viable because they adapted to the nature of their immediate environment. They became a reflection of their environment.

If this analogy is taken up, it can be assumed that companies are and remain competitive above all if they adapt to the nature of the markets. These markets, in turn, are experiencing what we call *digital transformation*. Digital transformation is not something that someone does or drives forward. Nor can digital transformation be equated with internal company changes that take place in the course of digitization. Digital transformation is a global change in markets and societies as a result of digital technologies and new business models. It comes over us, so to speak, like the Industrial Revolution over a 100 years ago. Almost all players in business, politics and society are involved. No one controls this development. Rather, it is a phenomenon that simply happens.

A central aspect of this digital transformation—the corporate environment—is the increasing connectivity of almost everything, people, things, machines, companies, suppliers, institutions, paired with distributed and decentralized artificial intelligence. In fact, according to my own conversations and observations, a growing number of traditional companies are becoming nervous. "Are we still well prepared in the way we lead and cooperate to keep up with the digital transformation?" is a question that is being discussed more and more loudly and seriously on numerous upper floors. I suppose it is right to ask yourself that question. Doubts about traditional, hierarchical rules, structures and management systems are becoming increasingly noticeable. As a hierarchical company, you are very quick to make strategic decisions. However, operational implementation often proves to be inconceivably slow and alien to the customer due to endless decision-making processes. In addition, you pay the high price of low employee satisfaction, limited commitment, unclear purpose and lack of learning opportunities. These traditional approaches may no longer be able to cope with the complex and dynamic reality.

So, should companies not respond to the changing external reality with an internal one? Connected markets probably also require connected organizations. This does not only mean the connection between organizations, but above all the internal connection of distributed intelligence within companies. Nothing else is meant by what is today understood by the agile organization.

Up to this point in the book, the focus was on the one hand on the development of companies and on the other hand on the hierarchical and agile hemisphere. HR was hardly touched upon, because first some basics of the organizational environment had to be pointed out. In the following section, the previous considerations are transferred to HR.

2.2 Types of HR

The various phases of the company's development as well as the two hemispheres have been graphically depicted already in Fig. 2.1. In the same figure there is a (grey shaded) triangle that is sufficient for further reflection, because it includes all relevant dimensions, namely the degree of institutionalization as well as the agile and hierarchical hemisphere. Applied to HR, this results in the so-called *HR playing field* shown in Fig. 2.3, which I often refer to as the *HR triangle*.

This HR triangle reflects a central concept throughout this book. In addition to the already known phases of institutionalization, the HR playing field consists of three extreme cornerstones. These symbolize three extreme *varieties of HR* on the basis of previous considerations. A version (A) without any form of institutionalization is here called *hire & pay*, a very simple form of HR, which could also be described as "HR Darwinism". Type (B) *central planning and control* stands for a version of HR with a strongly institutionalized, hierarchical character. This approach could also be described as a "HR planned economy", which will be explained below. This is contrasted by (C), *people-centered enablement* that is compatible with an agile understanding of organization. In the following, the three extremes of the HR

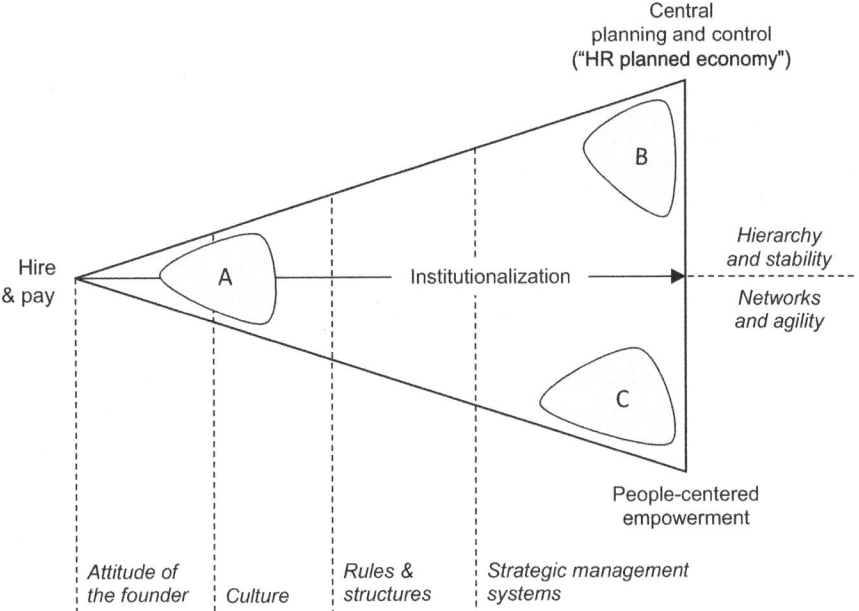

Fig. 2.3 Types of HR within the HR playing field (HR triangle)

playing field are described in more detail. It is assumed that the current but also the desired type HR of every company can be located somewhere in this playing field.

Hire & Pay and Darwinism

Particularly in small and medium-sized enterprises (SMEs) you can find an HR version in which employees are somehow hired (hire) and then paid fairly (pay). No more, no less. CEOs of these companies like to report that they simply do not need all the modern approaches to HR that exist today. You do not need performance appraisals; after all, people talk to each other every day and especially when it is necessary. There is no need for systematic training and development. When employees are faced with challenging tasks, learning cannot be avoided anyway. You do not need variable pay systems. This only leads to unnecessary friction. And as long as you treat your employees properly, you do not need an employer brand. Why talent management? The best will find their way by themselves, otherwise they are not the best anyway—the cream always comes to the top. Why rules, as long as you can talk to each other and people act in the interest of the company? Problematic situations, such as poor performance or bad behaviour, are discussed on a case-by-case basis and personally when they occur. That is what it sounds like when hire & pay as a version of HR dominates.

Whenever I sketch out this approach, for example in public lectures, it is always met with some sympathy. Perhaps a kind of weariness towards seemingly complex or complicated management systems is also noticeable here? The approach sounds slim, simple, cheap, relies on personal responsibility and interpersonal interaction.

With increasing company size and the associated complexity and lack of clarity, companies with "Hire & Pay" feel increasingly uncomfortable. At the latest when a key position becomes vacant without notice due to illness, death or voluntary turnover, the CEO calls his or her HR executive and asks to him or her who the suitable successor might be. "The cream always comes to the top" would be a bad answer though. In the future, you want to be better prepared. A new management system could then be the consequence.

Institutionalization and the HR Amplitude

Now, in the course of their development, many companies are moving from the left edge of the game (hire & pay) to the right and intensifying the extent of their institutionalization, more rules, structures, processes, systems, key figures, etc., more HR. This degree of institutionalization can also be called *HR amplitude*. However, there are two directions in which a company can basically go. A company that wants to strengthen its top management will march into the upper right corner (central planning and control). Companies, however, that also rely on personal responsibility, agility and networks, despite increasing complexity and growth, will move into the lower right corner (people-centered enablement). The first alternative is explained in the following section.

Central Planning and Control

There is a very widespread understanding in HR of what HR does and what those colleagues who act in an HR function are responsible for. Almost every student who has to or is allowed to deal with HR at some point learns this view: HR ensures that *the right people* are *in the right place at the right time*—an interpretation based on a highly hierarchical, static understanding. According to this, you have to select the right employees, pay them adequately, develop them, transfer them, keep them and motivate them, at least that is the widespread textbook opinion (e.g. Dessler 2018). A central, responsible unit in a company—the HR department—does something with the human resource in order to achieve the performance that one aspires to as a company.

In recent years, an increasing professionalization has been observed in large companies especially at the level of strategic management systems worldwide. Figure 2.4 shows a simplified overview of the essential building blocks and their linkage in a modern HR system based on the principle of central planning and control.

The starting point is an organizational structure with hierarchical superordination and subordination and a horizontal division of labour. This differentiates between

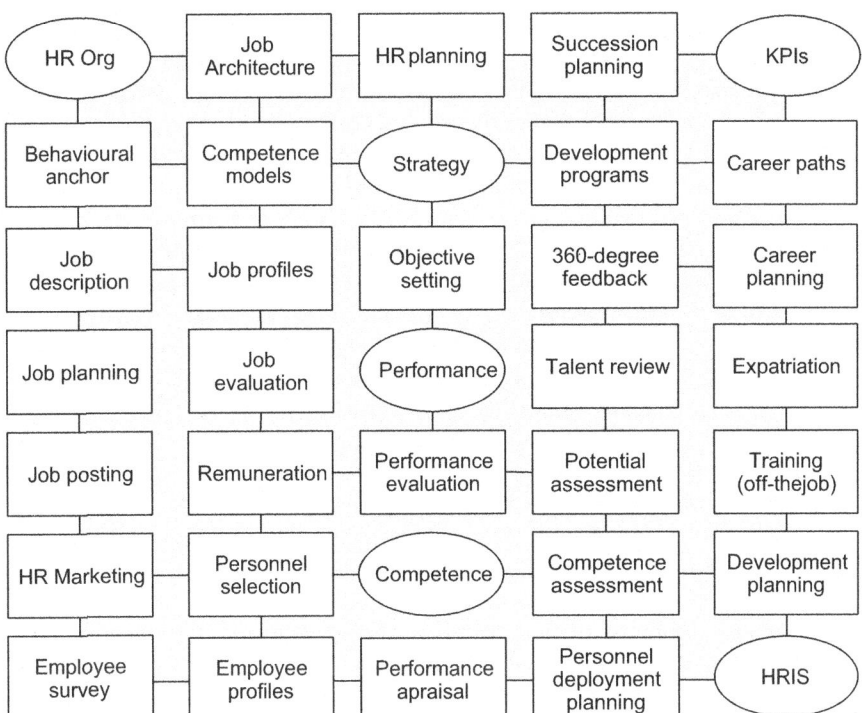

Fig. 2.4 Full-blown central planning and control

different jobs and positions. The jobs themselves are structured within a general *job architecture* sorting all kind of jobs inside the company—Junior Marketing Expert, Buyer, Key Account Manager, Junior Software Developer, Senior Software Developer etc. In parallel, there are *competency models* that describe different sets of skills that may be required for successful task fulfillment (problem solving skills, teamwork skills, communication skills, etc.). In order to interpret the different levels of competencies objectively, there are *behavioural anchors* specified in such a way, that they describe, on the basis of distinct behaviour patterns, what the different levels mean from beginner to expert. If one combines competence models with different jobs and determines the required competence levels, this results in *job profiles* that are ultimately assigned to each position in the company. These job profiles are an essential part of *job descriptions* and an important element for *job evaluation*. Job evaluation itself provides an estimation on how much responsibility is associated with a particular job. It is therefore an important basis for defining *remuneration* in accordance with a general salary structure that shows which salary band corresponds with which job evaluation (job grade). The job description is also a relevant basis for *job planning*: when do we need how many full-time employees in which position? A *job posting* can also be derived from the job description. It is important for *HR marketing* and the subsequent *personnel selection* process, which checks the extent to which an applicant or candidate meets the requirements defined in the job profile. In order to be attractive in HR marketing, the findings of the annual *employee survey* are used in the sense of employer branding. The result of all these efforts in recruiting is the successful filling of positions with employees. The employees themselves have specific, individual *employee profiles*. These are also described along with the competence models already mentioned and should match as closely as possible to the job profiles: the "right" employees with the "right" *competence*. Which competencies are needed, when and in which positions, is ultimately determined by the *strategy*. The (strategic) *HR planning* provides long-term scenarios on future, partly long-term workforce demands: How many employees with which competencies will be needed in the coming years? To ensure that the overarching strategy finds its way from the top to each individual employee, an (annual) *objective setting* is conducted. Objective setting is the transmission belt between the hierarchical levels of the organization. Here you determine which *performance* shall be demonstrated by a team or an employee in a defined period of time. Usually 12 months after the objective setting, the *performance evaluation* then takes place. Both the objective setting and the performance evaluation are part of the (formal) *annual performance appraisal*, a procedure that follows clear rules, forms, cycles and responsibilities. In this context, it is not uncommon for regular *competence assessments* to be carried out on employees. This competence assessment in turn is an essential starting point for *personnel deployment planning*, a mostly operative, short and medium-term procedure that provides information about who should do what, and when, or could do it at some point. This is also about the question of employability. In addition, this regular assessment of competencies helps with personal *development planning*: Through which form of *training* should the

2.2 Types of HR

employee improve which competencies, by when, and to what extent? If the assessment of competencies and employee performance is combined with the *potential assessment*, then the company is in a position to identify so-called high potential employees within the process of a so-called *talent review*. Managers usually do this in a joint, structured, tightly moderated round. Following the identification of the most talented employees, their strengths, weaknesses, professional and personal preferences are taken into account in greater detail, supported by *360-degree feedback*, which then results in long-term *development planning*. Armed with the findings of this intensive process, HR is not only in a position to introduce the talents into a *development program*. Rather, these high potentials can be offered the most concrete *career planning* possible: What do you have to do to move from your current position to your target position? So-called *career paths* help here. They describe very precisely what the individual career steps are, and what requirements these steps are associated with. A distinction is made between management, specialist and project careers. It is not unusual for a junior employee to be assigned to a branch abroad as a special learning opportunity, to what we refer as *expatriation*. If this process of assessment, talent identification and development is operated as closely as possible, the company always has an overview of which employees are ready for which key position and when. The associated consideration, and the drawing of conclusions, are essential parts of the so-called *succession planning*. All this requires the continuous generation of unbelievably extensive information by the most diverse bodies in the company. Their management and intelligent use is simply inconceivable without a corresponding *HR information system (HRIS)*. Once you have this system up and running, you have the chance to pull *KPIs* (Key Performance Indicators) over almost everything in HR at any time. All this requires a sophisticated *HR organization (HR Org)*. It is also the operator of this comprehensive HR machine. It needs the entire range of tools, systems and processes to fulfil its responsibilities: the right employees at the right time in the right place.

Readers who have little to do with HR will ask themselves whether there are actually companies that are really taking this approach in its full-blown version. The answer is, almost all large companies have implemented or at least tried this approach in recent years. Nonetheless, there are at least two groups of people who differ in their view of this approach. Some see it as the ultimate vision of a state-of-the-art HR, professional, integrated, complete. However, the others associate it with adjectives such as "bureaucratic", "technocratic", "Babylonian", "static", "overloaded" or "over-engineered". In their view, increasing complexity is obviously responded to with too much complicatedness.

As already described with regards to the development of companies, we are dealing here with a prototypical example of how a company tries to enable a central unit or the top management to act rationally by means of management systems. The focus here is less on the employee than on requirements on the one hand and HR on the other as a central player who wants to ensure that the right employee is available at the right place at the right time. The following alternative within the HR playing field differs from this.

People-Centered Enablement

People-centered enablement focuses on the question of what employees, teams and networks need in order to master relevant challenges on their own responsibility. Here it makes sense to take a closer look at different challenges and questions along an employee life cycle, starting with the interest of a candidate or an employee, through employment to leaving a company and possibly beyond.

Interested parties, candidates or applicants ask themselves questions such as: "Why should I work in this company? How can I apply? Does the company suit me? What is the current status of my application?" Once a person is actually an employee of the company, the following questions may arise: "What are my strengths, weaknesses, preferences and talents? How can I contribute to the success of my team or company as a whole? How do I share my knowledge, ideas and experiences? From whom can I learn what I need now? How do I find my next challenge in the company? How can I recommend good people for the company? How can I give colleagues feedback? How can I get feedback? How can I get engaged in exciting projects? How can I reward colleagues for good performance? How can I balance my professional and private life? How do we attract and select new employees for our team or project? Who can take my shift today?" At the end of the cycle, employees could raise the following questions: "How do I find my successor, and how can I prepare him or her? How do I ensure a smooth transition when I leave the company?" This list of questions may go on and on and on.

Unlike in the case of Hire & Pay, *not* nothing is done on the HR side. However, what is done is done with the objective of enabling employees and teams to take personal responsibility. This difference is illustrated by a few examples. To this end, one would imagine that company *A* would rely on central planning and control, while company *B* would prefer a form of people-centered enablement.

- Companies A and B both conduct 360-degree feedback. In Company A, HR and senior management receive the results to better assess how to deal with the respective employee in the future. In company B, only the appraised person him- or herself receives the results. Feedback should enable employees to assess their own strengths and weaknesses. He or she may also be supported by a coach when dealing with respective results.
- In company A, the HR department urges that an annual performance appraisal be held to ensure that employees receive structured feedback from their managers at least once a year. In company B, the premise is: Whoever wants feedback is supposed to actively ask for it. In the latter case HR offers tools, platforms, apps or employee training courses on the subject of how to give and obtain feedback effectively.
- In company A, salary is paid as remuneration for work performed. The company buys, so to speak, a service for the price of the salary to be paid. In company B, salary is seen as an enabling prerequisite for work. The employee can only perform because his or her employer takes care of his or her existential security.

- In company A, employees are prescribed specific training measures based on previous competence assessments. In company B, employees are not only responsible for identifying their own learning needs but also for meeting them in a self-directed manner. They have their own budgets or mobile access to virtual or social learning environments at any time.

The approaches of central planning and control are well known within the HR community and have already been described in numerous books. However, in the case of people-centered enablement, there is still a great deal of ignorance and uncertainty. The rest of this book will be about filling that void. In addition, more and more companies are asking themselves how to get from central planning and control to people-centered enablement. Not infrequently this means a painful transformation.

Painful Transformation

There has always been criticism of HR. But at present, concerns about widespread HR practices are reaching a new level. Now at HR congresses or in the relevant blogger scene, there is often talk of "HR as the driver of digital transformation". HR departments that expand HR management systems unhindered in the sense of central planning and control are more obstacles than drivers of any digital transformation. In times of digitization, those companies that recognize this are probably better off. This realization is particularly difficult when considerable energy has been invested in the implementation of traditional systems of planning and control in recent years. You do not even want to think about how much energy, effort and time it takes to introduce a classic performance appraisal system in a company with 10,000 employees and 500 managers. After such a project, how much motivation can an HR manager have to make extensive changes to his or her instrument or even pull the plug completely? At this point, we would like to remind HR professionals that entire industries currently have to realign themselves, in some cases very quickly, radically and comprehensively. Let us just think of the retail or automotive industry. In this light, the pressure to change in HR appears to be more of a light burden.

According to my own observations, doubts in connection with central planning and control are growing in more and more companies. These concerns are fed by numerous impressions but also by factual considerations and arguments:

- Can we really predict what skills our employees will need in 5 or 10 years' time?
- The "babysitting" of our employees leads to a lack of independence and consumes a disproportionate amount of resources.
- Our training department is years behind technical development. We have leading experts in the business line who only need to share their knowledge.
- Our talent management systems always reproduce the same type of executive. Wouldn't we have to open up a lot more here to allow more innovation and diversity?

- Our HR department is hopelessly overwhelmed by the recruitment of rare specialists while our people in the business line know many good people throughout their own professional networks.
- Our incentive systems, which focus on individual performance, primarily lead to demotivation and internal competition. However, in the future, we would need exactly the opposite.
- The multitude of time-consuming management systems not only in HR but also beyond it (budget rounds, audits, etc.) leaves less and less room to take care of customer needs.

The list could be extended over several pages. A more people-centered enablement could be a way out. No matter which company I speak to, they almost always show me the constellation shown in Fig. 2.5.

The current situation is indicated by *position I*. It is not uncommon for reports to be made that companies are in the process of moving in the direction of *position IIa*, but in view of current developments they no longer really want this. This is often justified in connection with the implementation of new HR software. In fact, most HR software vendors sell a more planning and control approach. The near future should be more *position IIb*. From the point of view of many HR managers and managing directors, *position IIb* would be the medium-term goal. Some see the long-term future best represented by *position III*. This transformation is not characterized by a return to hire & pay but by a change in institutionalized, structural framework conditions based on a changing basic attitude and corporate culture.

This indicates a hen-egg-problem. Would it not be necessary to change the corporate culture and the attitude of the company's leaders first, so that changed structural conditions have a chance of success? Remember the almost inflationary

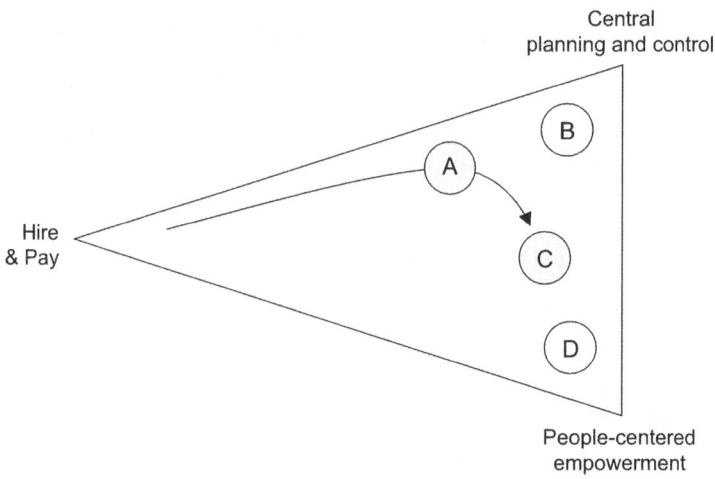

Fig. 2.5 Current and desired HR variety

quote, "Culture eats strategy for breakfast", which these days is mistakenly attributed to Peter Drucker. Conversely, changing cultural values can only be credibly communicated if the structural conditions go hand in hand with them. For a CEO it is not worth preaching trust as long as every imaginable travel expense has to be approved by the next level supervisor. In the end, employees evaluate things not by what is said, but by how concretely decisions are made and actions taken.

In this book I advocate the hypothesis that behaviour in organizations can occur primarily through a change in structural, institutional conditions (see also Chap. 13). If you want personal responsibility, teamwork and diversity, then you should design the structures in the company accordingly. Even if changed structures do not directly result in changed behaviour, it is at least made possible and a corresponding signal is sent to the employees. However, if one starts exclusively or primarily with the cultural conditions, these efforts are already nipped in the bud due to old, non-compatible structural conditions. Social-psychological findings support this view. There has been a debate there for decades as to whether attitudes cause behaviour or vice versa. At the bottom line, empirical findings clearly indicate that behaviour has a greater influence on attitudes than the other way round (Dillard 1993). The ban on smoking in public places has noticeably changed people's attitudes. Would one have changed people's behaviour to the same extent if one had first appealed to their attitude? Probably not.

The Digital Dehumanization of Human Resources Management

What comes after strategic management systems? Currently, in the course of digitization, a further level is emerging in which *artificial intelligence*, machine learning and big data will play a central role. This applies to all core business functions such as logistics, marketing, accounting and HR.

As it will become clear in the further course of this book, scenarios emerge in which talented employees can be identified comparatively, validly using algorithms. For example, the use of large, unstructured amounts of data (big data) will make it increasingly possible to differentiate between suitable and less suitable applicants. Only a few indicators provide good predictive values with regard to the question when and which employee will leave the company voluntarily. The list of possible scenarios could be extended at will. The active and intelligent use of relevant data in the context of HR is intensively being discussed today under the label *people analytics* (see also Sect. 11.3).

So while in the past we tried to use extensive systems, structures, processes and rules to guide cooperation within the company, and the necessary decisions in sensible ways, digitization brings a new level into play. Until now, it was mainly people who were responsible for decisions. In the future this will be taken over more and more by machines. Max Weber would have seen this as a further step towards dehumanization. It is interesting to note that this development does not stop at HR either.

References

Dessler G (2018) Human resources management. Pearson, London
Dillard JP (1993) Persuasion past and present: attitudes aren't what they used to be. Commun Monogr 60:90–97
Morgan G (1997) Images of organization. Sage, London
Parsons T (1951) The social system. Routledge & Kegan Paul, London
Trost A (2017) The end of performance appraisal. A practitioners' guide to alternatives in agile organizations. Springer, Heidelberg

Building an HR Strategy

3

According to my own observations, a growing number companies are facing the practical challenge of rethinking their HR strategy. And, more and more companies are seeking a higher degree of agility. This is accompanied by the question of an alternative type of HR, as outlined in the previous chapter. Now the definition of a desired type of HR may already be a first step in the direction of an HR strategy. Maybe it is already an integral part of it. Nevertheless, an HR strategy requires much more. For example, if you are aiming for further people-centered enablement, you have to put up with the question of what this means in concrete terms with regards to topics such as remuneration, assessment, learning, talent management, etc. This chapter therefore provides a practical guide to developing an HR strategy. This guide does not only present the essential questions that should be asked in the context of strategy development. In addition, possible answers and options are outlined on which to build later.

3.1 HR Strategy: An Overview

In recent years, a certain confusion has been observed with regard to the question of what is meant by "strategic HR". Strategic HR was often seen as a counterpart or even the opposite of administrative HR. Some companies, on the other hand, see in strategic HR all those things that have an international reach, i.e., which affect many or all employees. So while administrative tasks deal with local, everyday, manageable issues, strategic HR deals with large, overarching and fundamental issues. I often encounter an understanding of strategic HR based on the long-term nature of concepts. Accordingly, everything within HR that reaches far into the future is strategic. It is possible that a similar demarcation may be drawn here from mostly short-term topics of administrative HR. Considerations and views of this kind should be treated with caution. They do not really reflect what strategic HR is all about.

HR Strategy

This book takes the view that HR is strategic when it follows a clear HR strategy. In turn, an *HR strategy* describes *what* needs to be focused on, and *how*, in order to be competitive as a company and employer. Accordingly, HR is strategic if it has a suitable answer to this question and acts accordingly. On the one hand, the focus on *what* refers to the strategic challenges of the company from which HR-related challenges derive. On the other hand, the focus is on critical target functions and roles in the company, which are particularly important for the implementation of the business strategy. The *how* is based on the desired understanding of leadership and organization of the company, the structural and cultural context. This is where the type of HR comes into play. This in turn determines how the *strategic challenges* are dealt with. An agile company will respond to the same strategic challenges with completely different solutions and concepts than a traditional, hierarchical company would. This strategic focus on *key HR topics* that are important for overcoming HR-related challenges is also part of the HR strategy.

Building Blocks of an HR Strategy

In the remainder of this chapter, a step-by-step procedure is presented for developing an HR strategy that corresponds to the appropriate type of HR, whichever it may be. First of all, the following steps are to be anticipated in an overview. Figure 3.1 provides a graphical summary.

The starting point for the development of an HR strategy must always be an examination of corporate strategy aspects. Otherwise the development of an HR

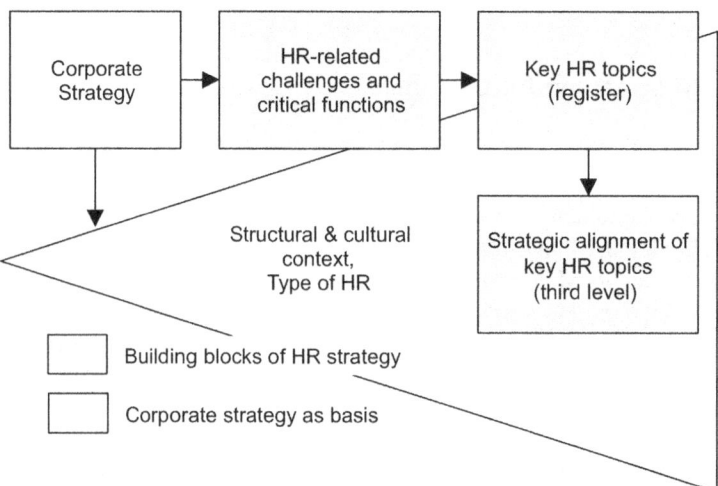

Fig. 3.1 The development of an HR strategy (grey fields) in the overall context

strategy is simply not possible. You have to understand what the ultimate corporate purpose is, and what its raison d'être is. What is the promise to the customer? In addition to this *why*, it should be understood *how* the company strategically differentiates itself from its competitors. Where and how will it be better than its competitors? What is seen as its competitive advantage? This differentiation must be associated with challenges and entrepreneurial opportunities. If this were not the case, competitors could easily copy the core competencies of the company. In this respect, it should be clear what the strategic challenges (and opportunities) of a company are. Taken together, all these aspects form the *corporate strategy as the basis*. No HR manager can act strategically successfully if he or she has not thoroughly understood and internalized this basic situation.

One corporate strategy component refers to the desired understanding of leadership and organization in the company. Do you strive for agility or stability? This book deals with this aspect in relation to the *cultural and structural context*. What is the dominant leadership role? What does cooperation looks like in the company? How self-determined do the teams and employees act, to name just a few facets. Chapter 4 deals comprehensively with relevant criteria that make it possible to understand and assess this cultural and structural context. As already mentioned several times, the appropriate *type of HR* is derived from this understanding. Is central planning and control aimed at, or people-centered enablement? This aspect may already be seen as part of an HR strategy. In this book, we look at the type of HR just as a central guard rail within which the actual HR strategy should be built.

Apart from the question of the appropriate type of HR, all aspects that have been mentioned so far are initially independent of HR. Rather, they take place at a general corporate strategic level. The following building blocks, on the other hand, are central components of what is to be understood here as an HR strategy. The first question that arises here is that of the so-called *critical target functions*. Which functions (or jobs, roles, etc.) are of outstanding importance in view of the company's strategic challenges and competitive advantage? Here we are talking about key functions. Moreover, what other functions are there, whose needs are difficult to meet due to labour market conditions but where there is also a high quantitative need? Here we are talking about bottleneck functions. In contrast, the strategic challenges relevant to human resources are of fundamental importance, as they are usually closely related to the company's strategic challenges. A strategically successful HR manager must be able to express and prioritize which few HR-relevant challenges must be mastered in order to secure the future of the company and its competitiveness.

The answer to these challenges can be seen in the selection of critical HR issues. We are talking here about the *key HR topics*. These are the topics that are finally being worked on. They hold the solution to the challenges they are supposed to address. The picture of the *registers* that are to be drawn, concretely in view of the challenges, is also suitable here. This can involve topics such as employer branding, selection, variable pay for performance, talent identification or other topics. The spectrum of possible topics is wide. While the HR-relevant strategic challenges provide an answer to the *why*, the key HR topics describe the *what*. What needs to be done and what topics need to be worked on in order to successfully master the challenges (the why).

Finally, the HR strategy includes a comprehensive and often difficult to develop answer to the question of *how* these key HR topics should be *strategically aligned*. At the end of the day, this is one of the biggest tasks in the development of an HR strategy. This involves exploring and evaluating possible strategic options. Do we want variable bonuses for individuals or just for teams? Are we putting the employer brand on a broad basis, i.e. with a broad impact on the labour market or more focused (minimally invasive) on specific target groups? Most of this book deals with these kinds of questions.

At this point the circle closes. Because this strategic orientation of the key HR topics must be based on the desired understanding of leadership and organization and thus also on the preferred type of HR of which we spoke at the beginning. Regardless of which key HR topic is seen as part of the HR strategy, its strategic alignment will be different in an agile environment than in a more hierarchical context seeking stability.

Everything that has been described so far relates to the development of the HR strategy itself. The most important determinants and building blocks were briefly outlined. However, it would not be enough for a practice-oriented and modern book if further aspects, which are relevant framework conditions in strategy development, were not briefly examined. This chapter will therefore conclude with an analysis of the interaction between the company headquarters and the decentralized organizational units (branches, divisions, subsidiaries, etc.). This aspect plays an important role in the context of globalization.

All Relevant Questions at a Glance

Finally, all relevant questions are shown in an overview in Fig. 3.2. This overview may also serve as a simple guide. In the right column of this illustration, reference is made to the relevant sections and chapters of this book.

3.2 Corporate Strategy as the Basis

It should be clear to every serious HR manager today that there must be a close relationship between corporate strategy and HR strategy. The latter cannot be defined in isolation from the former. Whether the HR strategy is derived from the corporate strategy, whether the HR strategy is part of the corporate strategy, or even whether the HR strategy should influence the corporate strategy is an interesting topic, but it should not be further deepened at this point. Of course, all variants are conceivable. In the following, however, we will start from the simpler perspective, according to which the HR strategy is derived from the corporate strategy. In this respect, it makes sense to take an initial look at the corporate strategy, at least to some extent. Basically, a lot has already been written on this topic. Outstanding

3.2 Corporate Strategy as the Basis

Question	Chapter/ Section
Structural and cultural framework conditions	
What is the current and aspired understanding of leadership and organization (agility and networks versus stability and hierarchy)?	4
What type of HR (HR triangle) is derived from this understanding of leadership and organization?	2.2
Corporate strategy as a basis	
What is the ultimate purpose or raison d'être of the company?	3.2
How does the company differentiate itself from its competitors in the market (strategic priorities and competitive advantage)?	
What are the critical challenges and entrepreneurial opportunities of the company?	
Building blocks of an HR strategy	
What are the critical target functions in terms of competitive differentiation, needs and labour market situation?	3.3
What are the critical HR-related challenges?	3.4
Which key HR topics (registers) are derived from the critical, HR-relevant challenges?	3.5
How should key HR topics be strategically aligned given the appropriate HR variety?	3.5 5
Relevant conditions for strategy development	
How is the interaction between the corporate headquarters and the decentralized units structured?	3.6

Fig. 3.2 Overview of questions to be answered in the development of an HR strategy

thought leaders, such as Michael Porter, have said elementary things about this. It should therefore be sufficient to focus on three aspects, namely the *purpose of the company*, the *positioning* of the company in the market, and the strategic *challenges and opportunities* of the company. They are enough to be able to build on them and to deal with the development of an HR strategy.

The Ultimate Business Purpose

It is recommended to every employee, every manager and every executive to ask their colleagues the simple but nevertheless difficult question: Why do we actually exist? You will be amazed at the answers you get. "We exist because we exist and that is good because otherwise we wouldn't have any work and we wouldn't earn any money". Some of my business students are surprised when I ask this question about any company. "Companies exist to make a profit. What else?" Employees of a mechanical engineering company could answer the question by pointing out that they build machines. Colleagues in retail might remember that they sell products. Perhaps from time to time we tend to take the existence of "our" company or other companies for granted. "We exist because we've somehow always existed." The daily tasks and the continuity of our daily work offer little room for such simple, difficult questions. But the answer to this question is existential.

Imagine for a moment that you were travelling by car, on your way home from a business meeting. It is 7.00 pm. You are driving on the freeway and you are hungry. You actually want to go home quickly, but you still have 180 miles to go. You have no nerves to worry about what you can or want to eat and where. By any means you do not want to waste time searching for restaurants now. At your business meeting you already had to make numerous decisions. That is why your mind is set now on something familiar.

Whenever I relate this situation, there are about 50% of people in front of me, depending on the age of those present, who are now thinking of McDonald's or Burger King. Why do these companies exist? Among other things, exactly for this.

Do you have a daughter or son of student age? Is your child facing the challenge of furnishing a completely empty one-room apartment in a foreign city in the course of a single weekend in a reasonably stylish, comprehensive but nevertheless inexpensive manner? Which provider are you thinking of? Most people think of IKEA. That is why there is IKEA. Executives at IKEA would never come up with the idea of answering the question why they exist with "we sell furniture and other stuff". They will rather point out that they offer quality of life at good prices.

Does BMW produce and sell motorcycles and cars? No, they offer "sheer driving pleasure." That is their claim at least. Does Apple produce and sell computers and other devices? No, they enable people who stand out from the conformist mass by creating great things ("think different"). Does Puma produce and sell sportswear? No, they give their customers the external impression of a sporty lifestyle. These companies, from McDonald's to Puma, have done an excellent job of using their brand to convey a differentiating and attractive promise to their target groups based on their business purpose.

It should be possible for a company to express its purpose in a few sentences, perhaps even in a single sentence. For some, the question "Why do we exist?" may be easy to answer. But the way to get there is seldom easy. In some situations, companies struggle to find the right answer. After all, it touches on the core of one's self-image and one's own right to exist—a reason not to make it easy to answer this question.

The Positioning of the Company in the Market

While the company's purpose concentrates on the strategic *why*, the strategic positioning of a company is about the *how*. Irrespective of the purpose of the company, it must always be assumed that there are competitors who claim a similar purpose. Entrepreneurs know the principle: where there are no competitors, there is probably no market. So how does a company try to be better than its competitors in what it does (the purpose of the company)? There can be very different answers to this question about their *competitive advantage*. "We will be more successful than our competitors in the coming years because . . .

- we are more innovative
- we are technologically more advanced
- we can offer our products at a lower price
- our products and services are of higher quality
- we communicate our performance promise more effectively (brand)
- our products have a better design
- we have better access to markets
- we have the largest market share in the world".

Very different strategic priorities can play a role here, as the incomplete list of possible responses illustrates. Is it about price leadership, quality leadership, innovation, technology leadership, brand leadership, design, market leadership or customer proximity, growth? A company cannot be superior in all aspects, due to limited resources. It must focus on a few strengths, namely on those priorities that are part of a company's *core competencies* (Hill et al. 2017).

From the outside, companies such as H&M seem to position themselves as price leaders. Gucci, on the other hand, positions itself through quality in the shopping experience. Numerous well-known pharmaceutical giants, such as Roche, Bayer or Boehringer Ingelheim, position themselves through innovation and the development of new, effective drugs, while suppliers of generics, such as Teva (known through the Ratiopharm brand) stand out through price leadership in the market. Lufthansa positions itself through quality and reliability, while the Lufthansa subsidiary Eurowings (like easyJet or Ryanair) differentiates itself through low prices. Some banks position themselves through their local proximity, while ING Diba distinguishes itself through quality in consumer experience.

I am not aware of any company that differentiates itself through price, quality, brand and innovation at the same time. In the end, strategy means concentrating on those few core competencies that are most likely to contribute to a competitive advantage in the market. Every executive or CEO who thinks strategically will have an immediate answer to the question of *how*, i.e. the question of the few competition-relevant priorities. In the course of this book it will become clear how important this point is for the HR strategy. For example, it will be shown that due to these strategic priorities, better employees must be employed in certain functions and roles than in comparable functions and roles on the competitors' side.

Strategic Challenges and Opportunities

Strategic priorities, as just described, are never easy to implement. Otherwise, they would be too easy to copy by competitors. This raises the question of what the critical success challenges of a company are. What hurdles does a company have to overcome in order to either maintain or strengthen its market position in the long term? What threats are on the horizon, or are already there? To put it less academically, you can also ask why the CEO can not sleep at night. In practice, this question often leads directly to the decisive points. Below are a few prominent examples of strategic challenges:

- *Digitization.* Digital technology is developing exponentially. There is therefore a risk of becoming technologically outdone because competitors can produce better products and services much more efficiently through the use of digital technology. However, digitization also offers the opportunity to stand out from the competition.
- *Disruption.* Digitization in particular holds the danger of being slowly threatened by completely new players and their products, and then of being left behind in a short space of time. People are reluctant to cannibalize traditional business with modern, different technologies.
- *Public regulation.* Increasing regulation through public authorities, for example in the financial or energy sectors, reduces entrepreneurial leeway and leads to bureaucratic burdens. In addition, there are dependencies on state institutions, such as the central banks.
- *Changing buyer behaviour.* Customers' preferences with regard to products, services and purchase channels of the relevant target groups in the market are changing. There is a risk that these new preferences will be better served by competitors. At the same time, there is the opportunity to gain advantages in the market by considering new preferences (that are superior?).
- *Political insecurity.* Political conditions at home, in important export countries, or at production sites, are subject to short-term political and social turbulence, which not only make it difficult to plan, but also entail the risk of dramatic losses in some cases. A current example is the Brexit and its unforeseeable consequences.
- *New business models.* Within our own segment, entirely new ways of creating customer benefits, creating value and earning money are emerging. Established business models may be replaced entirely by new ones. This is also a threat and an opportunity at the same time.
- *Scarcity of resources.* Critical, material resources, such as raw materials, are subject to price fluctuations or experience a permanent shortage. The latter drives up prices and reduces the return on sales.

If one asks executives these days the question about the one single reason why he or she cannot sleep they mention digitization in most cases. If this challenge does not reach the top of the list, it is replaced by challenges that are mostly related to digitization, such as disruptive developments, changing customer behaviour or new business models.

As already indicated above, from an entrepreneurial point of view there is also a business opportunity behind every challenge. In this respect, challenges *and* entrepreneurial opportunities should always be mentioned here. For the sake of simplicity, however, we leave it to the former, knowing that the latter can also be meant.

A Different Understanding of Leadership and Organization

All the challenges outlined in the previous section describe external threats coupled with the risk of missing out on opportunities for current developments. However, many CEOs also address internal issues, often with greater emphasis. "The greatest threat comes from within." The list of challenges is usually long. It is about the type of leadership inside the company and the form of cooperation and communication. There is talk of *silo thinking*, of excessively long decision-making paths, of a lack of personal responsibility on the part of employees, of demotivation, of a lack of enthusiasm and optimism. The present fear of making mistakes on all sides dominates over the will to win. This is followed by the martial question, "How do we want to win such a war?" Particularly in the context of the digital transformation, the understanding of leadership and organization obviously developed into a challenge of strategic importance.

For several years now there has been a debate about the necessity of agilization, and there are companies that have made their way in this direction with initial successes. It has been established that no one is more important than the CEO him or herself (see also Chap. 13). This sounds irritating at first, since one often assumes that agile organizations are democratically led and that hierarchies play a lesser role. Then what does the CEO care about what he or she thinks? This is a fallacy. If companies are managed in a highly agile manner, this is primarily due to the CEO, because he or she must not only promote agility, but above all allow it. CEOs who rely on an agile form of leadership and cooperation invest a lot of time and energy in protecting this understanding from hierarchical influences. However, if a company is managed in a traditional, hierarchical manner and silo-thinking, long decision paths, or service according to regulations have been introduced, then the CEO is also responsible for this. One must first assume that the form of leadership and organization is what it is because the CEO wants it that way. In agile organizations, the attitude of the CEO is much more effective than in dehumanized, hierarchical organizations that are structured and managed in the sense of Max Weber.

The understanding of leadership and organization a company is striving for could therefore be a central component of its corporate strategy. It is therefore indispensable for the further development of the HR strategy to have a clear commitment as to what form of leadership and organization will be sought in the future. This will play a central role in particular when it comes to the strategic alignment of key HR topics from Chap. 5 onwards. If, for example, a company relies on network-like cooperation in and between working groups, this has decisive consequences for the design of the incentive systems. If managers are expected to act less as bosses (order and control) and more as coaches, this has direct implications for the question of whether the annual performance appraisal is the appropriate management procedure. In the further course of this book, numerous conclusions of this kind will be comprehensively discussed. At this point, it is sufficient to note that the further development of the HR strategy requires a clear orientation in terms of leadership and organization. In connection with the structural and cultural framework conditions, Chap. 4 deals in detail with relevant dimensions.

Every HR specialist should be able to explain the aspects described in this chapter for their own company in a one-hour presentation. Without comprehensive knowledge of the company's purpose, strategic positioning and challenges, strategic thinking and action in HR is inconceivable. These aspects are the basis for HR-relevant challenges, which ultimately lead to the treatment of selected key HR topics. In addition, the strategic positioning of a company determines which functions and roles in the company have a high strategic relevance and which do not.

3.3 Critical Functions and Roles

As mentioned earlier, you can learn from traditional textbooks that HR is about "the right people, in the right place, at the right time"—the *right* people, not the *best* people. That sounds modest at first. In fact, the question arises as to where in the company "right" or suitable employees are needed, and where the best are needed. You can only afford the best ones in all areas of the organization if you are Google, Netflix or Manchester United, for example. For this reason, a strategic focus is required that is derived directly from the strategic priorities and challenges.

Roles and Functions with High Strategic Relevance

What is the point for a traditional car manufacturer like BMW having the best employees instead of good employees in quality assurance? Probably not much. At best, this requires qualified, reliable employees whose performance corresponds to a previously defined standard. What competitive advantage does the car manufacturer in question achieve when the best possible employees work in the development area of connected cars? Here one must assume that BMW wants to gain a competitive advantage through the rapid and innovative development of connected, autonomous driving. In this respect, we can further assume that this topic is of great strategic importance, which is why investing in the best employees could prove to be particularly worthwhile. Outstanding achievements in this area would be able to take the company a big step forward *overall*.

What competitive advantage would IKEA gain if the world's best cashiers were employed in their stores? Probably none. However, since IKEA appears to have set its strategic priorities on price leadership and attractive product design, it may be worthwhile to employ the best designers and purchasers. Bayer, Roche and Boehringer Ingelheim need the best possible people in the Research & Development function to maintain and increase their competitive advantage, while the generics manufacturer Teva probably needs the best people in marketing and sales.

It is a big step towards an HR strategy to be aware of which functions and which roles are of particular strategic relevance. These are referred to as *key functions* or *key roles*. Identifying them is not always easy in practice. This requires a clear strategic positioning and an understanding of the most important strategic challenges and priorities, as discussed in more detail in the previous section.

Probably the biggest hurdle of this exercise results from the personal sensitivities of relevant decision-makers at top management level. You should avoid throwing the question, "Who represents the most important function in this company?" into the room in front of the assembled executive team, in the presence of the Head of Development, Head of Sales, Head of Production, CHRO, CIO and, or CFO. The following exchange of blows leads to characteristic errors in the argumentation. "What would happen if production didn't exist?", "Who earns the money without sales?", "Who works if HR does not worry about the right people?", "What would happen if IT pulled the plug for a day?". The arguments usually revolve around the question of which function or role one could most likely do without. However, this does not lead to a meaningful result. Rather, the central question must be for each individual function or role: What difference does it make for the company *as a whole* if we not only have suitable but also the best possible employees in this function or role? If no potential for a dramatic difference is discernible, the respective function is *not* a key function. It is important to be aware of the purpose of the company. Which function and, or which role contributes most decisively to both the business purpose and competitive advantage? In practice, it makes sense to first discuss this topic with the HR manager and then personally coordinate the result with the CEO. An objective, algorithmic assessment of strategic relevance is fundamentally difficult. Rather, a holistic assessment is required, which can be helped by the following questions:

- Is the function directly related to competitive differentiation and thus to the competitive advantage of the company (see Sect. 3.2, Corporate strategy as the basis)?
- Does it make a significant difference for the company as a whole to employ the best people in one function instead of just hiring or deploying the most suitable?
- Does a higher performance in this function lead to a clearly disproportionate added value for the company as a whole and to a visible strengthening of its competitive position?
- Is the function the focus of the CEO and the entire Executive Board?
- Do recruiting costs not play a role in the filling of this position because the best employees pay off in many ways?
- Does the search for the best possible employees for this function take place on a global basis?

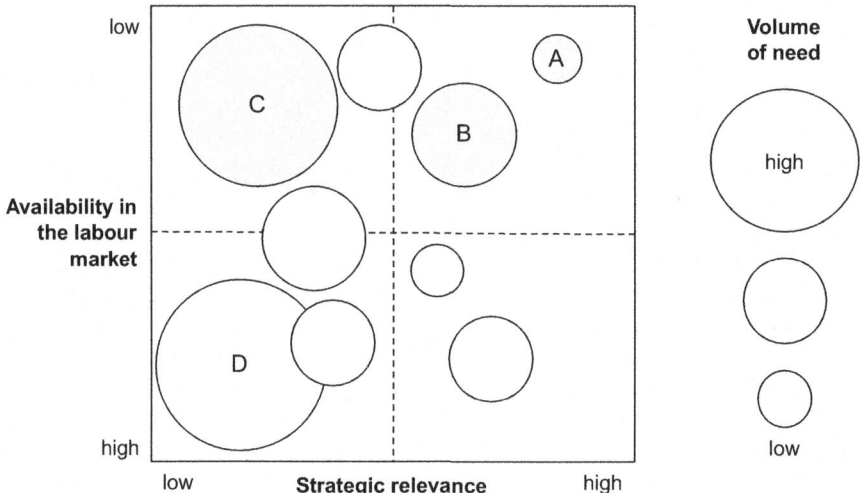

Fig. 3.3 Prioritization of roles and functions

If most of these questions are answered with "Yes", then a corresponding function is probably a key function. The dimension of the strategic functions and roles is represented in the horizontal axis of Fig. 3.3. Those functions that have a high *strategic relevance* (key functions) are therefore located on the right side of this figure.

The circles shown represent different functions and roles in the company. Two further dimensions are shown in this figure, namely the availability of personnel in the labour market, and the volume of needs. These two dimensions are briefly discussed below (Trost 2014; Huselid et al. 2005).

Hard to Fill Functions and Roles

There are functions for which you post a job advertisement, and then you are literally filled up with applications. Filling other positions leads to sleepless nights even for the most experienced executive search consultant. HR professionals involved in the recruitment of employees can usually reliably assess the *availability of personnel* in relation to different functions and roles. We know the number of applications, the search effort and the time to fill open positions from experience. In Fig. 3.3, this dimension is represented by the vertical axis. At the bottom are the functions with high availability (simple hiring). At the top of the chart are those functions that are very difficult to fill due to the limited availability of personnel.

The availability of personnel for different functions and roles is easier to determine than their strategic relevance. There is simply less politics and personal feelings at play here. Nevertheless, in practice there is the danger of classifying too many functions as difficult to fill. In addition to the already mentioned experience of

3.3 Critical Functions and Roles

1 „Piece of cake"	2 "Effort"	3 "Challenge"	4 "Nightmare"
There are many active jobseekers who are interested in this role or function. Post vacancies, collect masses of applications, choose the right ones.	There are few suitable candidates in the labour market who become aware of a role or function on their own initiative. One must actively strive for good candidates.	It is quite difficult to fill a position of this function, but not impossible. Special efforts are required. This requires a broad spectrum of employer branding and sourcing measures.	Trying to fill a position in this function is a task that can hardly be solved because there are almost no suitable candidates and they are neither actively looking for jobs nor are interested in any new opportunity.

Fig. 3.4 Four prototypical situations in assessing the availability of personnel

recruiters, labour market studies, or tools and platforms that analyse demand and supply using Big Data and objectively depict situations in the labour market, can help. However, it can also be more practical to classify the functions into four different prototypical situations, as shown in Fig. 3.4.

The Volume of Needs

Finally, a third dimension, the quantitative need, is shown in Fig. 3.3. This is indicated by the size of the circles. The larger the circle, the greater the volume of new hires needed. The central question is: How many employees are likely to be needed in the coming years within the various roles and functions? Often, a quick glance at the external career page is enough to arrive at a rough, up-to-date assessment. What is meant by "low", "medium", or "high" volume should be defined pragmatically and in line with the size of the company. Experience has shown that this does not require comprehensive, detailed workforce planning. A rough estimation is sufficient.

Key and Bottleneck Functions

The result of this exercise is an image similar to the one in Fig. 3.3. Actually, every HR manager should have an overview of this kind, because strategically important conclusions can be drawn from it. To illustrate this, the functions A, B, C and D in Fig. 3.3 are briefly explained.

A. This is a *key function* with rather low, quantitative volume of needs. For external recruitment, it is a good idea to either engage an executive search agency or initiate your own active sourcing strategies. Alternatively, selected employees from our own ranks can be recruited for this purpose. Voluntary fluctuation in this function can sometimes have dramatic consequences.

B. Function B is also a key function, but with a higher volume of needs. Comprehensive efforts are needed in terms of recruitment and development. The remuneration of employees in this function should be well above the market average.
C. This is a classic *bottleneck function* because demand is high here, but is difficult to meet due to a lack of available personnel. Bottleneck functions can be strategically important, but do not have to be. The main challenge with bottleneck functions lies in talent acquisition. This requires special efforts in terms of talent relationship management.
D. In this function, the approaches described in decades-old textbooks on HR may be applied. Recruitment is passive, e.g., through job advertisements. Selection is more complex than acquisition. You pay tariffs, not more, not less. Training and development is selective and focused. Voluntary fluctuation is a pity but not critical.

As already indicated, strategy always means focusing on what contributes to competitiveness. In this respect, the identification of critical target functions such as key and bottleneck functions is already an important step towards an HR strategy. This exercise makes it clear, which roles and functions the focus should be on. If you have 100 Euro left for personnel recruitment, you should set 90 Euro on critical target functions and 10 Euro on the rest. Anything else would be HR according to the peanut butter principle.

3.4 HR-Relevant Strategic Challenges

Again and again, one encounters companies whose HR strategy is something like this: "Attracting, hiring, developing and retaining the right employees". The problem with this "strategy" is that it is not a strategy but a task description or a poor definition of HR. Everything is in here. And when everything matters, nothing matters. One of the essential components of an HR strategy is to focus on the most important HR-related challenges. This, too, reflects a form of strategic focus because it focuses on what really matters most. Above all, it leaves others out, which is usually far more difficult—Strategy means saying "No". And the more these challenges are related to corporate strategy, the better it is.

Of course, there are also challenges that exist independently of the corporate strategy. An example has already been discussed in the previous section. Key functions have a strategic relevance for the competitiveness of the company. Bottleneck functions, on the other hand, do not have to have this significance, but represent major challenges within HR. If, for example, you have massive difficulties in attracting a large number of trainees every year, this may not be significant in terms of corporate strategy. However, within HR, this problem might be given high priority.

Why Are You Doing This?

HR strategic considerations should always refer to challenges to be overcome. What is the problem? What benefits should be achieved? Not *what* we do is central, but *why* we do something, for *whom*. I suppose most people will agree here. However, practice often looks different. For many years, I have been experiencing that the HR community is essentially concerned with tools, concepts, systems and programs, and that it runs the risk of losing sight of the actual problem or the challenges to be overcome.

This assessment does not come by chance. At congresses of the HR community or at HR training courses conducted by me, or at customers whom I advise, I consistently encounter concepts that are applied in practice. Just think of employee surveys, annual performance appraisal, competence management, expert careers, strategic workforce planning and so on. I have gotten into the habit of asking a mean question in situations like this: "Why are you doing this?" I often have to add, "What problem do you solve with it and who has the problem?" "What would happen to your company if you turned off that concept overnight?" Especially challenging is the question, "What would it mean for your (external) customers if you did not implement this concept?" The surprising thing about the answers is not the answers themselves, but the fact that many people have a hard time finding an answer, especially if you want to know more. Here is an example of a typical conversation:

Since last year we have also been doing employer branding

Why are you doing this?

To better position our company as an attractive employer in the labour market.

And why would you want that?

Because we're having a hard time attracting good people.

And how can employer branding help you?

With an employer brand, we can better attract relevant target groups.

Who is your target group?

For example, process engineers with several years of professional experience in the chemical or pharmaceutical industry.

How large is your relevant target group?

There are very few of them. The labour market is extremely tight.

This means that most of the representatives of your target group are already employed?

Absolutely, at least the ones we want.

Does your target group read job advertisements? Does it visit career fairs or the career pages of companies in your industry?

No, they do not really need that.

Where would you reach your target group?

Very scattered, you can't say for sure.

How many process engineers will you be hiring in the next 12 months?

Just a few, five, maybe seven.

At this point, you can break off the conversation to find out that the solution does not seem to correspond to the problem. An employer branding campaign in the classic sense is unlikely to make much use of this challenge. This is a small, hard-to-fill target function whose relevant target group consists of candidates who are difficult to localize, scattered and passively seeking. In the light of this challenge, it would have been obvious to focus more on active sourcing strategies than on employer branding. However, such relationships can only be identified when the problems and challenges to be solved have been sufficiently understood (cf. also the detailed considerations on the subject of talent acquisition in Chap. 5). Every HR strategy should always begin with the identification of the most important challenges. It should be really clear what these challenges actually consist of. The simple logic, for example, according to which a perceived shortage of skilled workers leads to the development of an employer brand, is definitely not enough. The right solutions and the decisive key issues can only be found when these challenges have been sufficiently understood and extracted.

Stakeholders, Dynamics and Limited Resources

But how do you get to the few selected strategic challenges? On the one hand, there is a complex answer to this question, which attempts to do justice to the complexity and dynamics of interdependent challenges within an even more dynamic context. On the other hand, there is a simple, pragmatic answer. Let us begin with the former.

It is certainly correct to assume that challenges always require people to recognize them as challenges. In practice, we usually speak of *stakeholders*. In the context discussed here, the executives, the employee representatives, the employees or the HR function itself or the external customers may be regarded as potential stakeholders. Different stakeholders will assign different priorities to different challenges. Not just that. They will also interpret the same challenges differently in terms of their significance. Think, for example, of the widespread challenge of employee retention. The loss of a valued employee triggers completely different reactions among different stakeholders, because individual losses have very specific consequences depending on who you are.

3.4 HR-Relevant Strategic Challenges

An additional complexity results from the fact that challenges can hardly be viewed in isolation from each other. Rather, *dynamic relations* and interactions must be assumed. Challenges in talent acquisition might be caused by the lack of attractiveness of the employer, which in turn is due to poor working conditions. This chain of arguments could go on and on and on. In practice, this can lead to endless debates. Rarely does the discussion lead to reasonable results. "Why are we discussing A here? Has it not something to do with B?" The next one says, "But B has something to do with C, right?" Of course, the world is complex. We live in cybernetic systems. Whoever is able to explain these systems in their contexts has good prospects of winning the Nobel Prize.

In the end, you may find that the limitation of available *resources* is the ultimate cause of all problems. If one had all the money in the world and considerably more time, then numerous challenges would either not exist or would appear in a completely different light. However, the simple call for more resources can rarely be a central component of an HR strategy.

Three Times "Why?"

If you want to get to the core of a challenge, then a method that you can easily copy from children can be helpful. You ask the question *why* three times in a row. It seems as if children, when dealing with cause-and-effect relationships, implicitly have a kind of systemic view of the world by suspecting further causes behind the causes initially mentioned. This technique can help to identify causes behind causes and to move from the superficial problem to real challenges. Transferred to the HR context, this could look as follows:

Our executives do not know enough about digitization.

Why?

Because they do not deal with it enough in their everyday lives.

Why?

They do not recognize the relevance of the topic for their area of responsibility.

Why?

Because they are too busy with themselves and their silo and have too little opportunity to perceive the developments around them.

Now it is getting exciting and you could drill even deeper. What looked like a training need at the beginning turns out to be a problem of a completely different nature.

The Pragmatic Approach

The complex approach is now followed by the simple, pragmatic approach. It just consists of asking oneself, together with the CHRO, the question of the greatest challenges relevant to HR at executive level. I have often been able to accompany this exercise and it is always astonishing how quickly an agreement can be reached on this question. Nevertheless, different companies come to different results.

One can assume that senior executives have formed an opinion long before they are asked about strategic challenges. You will never hear sentences like, "True, now that I am thinking about it, I have to say that we're actually having a hard time attracting professionals in the R&D department. Interesting point though". Senior executives normally know less about operations than they think they do. But it would still be amazing if senior executives had no idea of challenges with strategic weight.

Large companies in particular, which have already gone through several phases of institutionalization, rarely find themselves on a completely green field when it comes to HR. Long before one thought about a (new) HR strategy, employees were hired, and positions that were sometimes difficult to fill were filled. Companies often already have a kind of talent management, an annual performance appraisal and training and development. Of course, there has been an at least implicit remuneration strategy since the very beginning. In many cases, dealing with strategic challenges makes it clear that existing approaches reach their limits in the context of changing framework conditions. HR managers, line managers, executives, and frequently also employees, know this and can articulate the problems more or less clearly in the light of many years of experience.

Possible HR-Related Challenges

If one now asks different stakeholders in a company about the strategic, HR-relevant challenges, points are frequently mentioned which are shown in Fig. 3.5.

The points shown in Fig. 3.5 are not exhaustive. The names of the challenges also differ between companies. In fact, as indicated above, it would be important to clearly specify these challenges in their particular quality. Some describe "motivating employees" as a challenge while others would describe a similar challenge as "avoiding demotivation". Nevertheless, the above illustration can serve as a first orientation. Depending on the situation, it might be a good idea to put this list on the executive board's table with the request that he or she marks the three most important points with a cross. That would be an interesting start into a guaranteed to be exciting discussion.

Filling of key positions	Attract employees for bottleneck functions	Selecting the right employees	Offer employees a fair salary	Enabling a balance between work and family
Offering productive working environments	Recognising and exploiting employee potential	Open up long-term development opportunities	Sharing relevant knowledge within the company	Retaining good employees in the company
Secure broad employment opportunities	Building relevant competencies	Securing enthusiasm and a high level of performance	Dealing with different generations	Enabling and promoting diversity

Fig. 3.5 An incomplete selection of possible HR-related challenges

3.5 Key HR Topics and Their Strategic Alignment

On the one hand, an HR strategy consists of the central HR-relevant challenges on which a company wants to focus in the coming years. As described in the previous section, these challenges revolve around the most real HR-related issues of strategic importance. These challenges must on the other hand lead to concrete topics that a company wants to deal with. They address what must be done in the future, which *registers* are to be pulled, just like you would do when selecting certain organ stops. Appropriate resources are required for this. Hardly any company will provide resources for challenges in themselves, unless for those specific things that are at the moment being tackled. We call these topics of strategic importance *key HR topics*. In practice, other designations for this are also encountered. Some speak of cornerstones, the pillars or the building blocks of an HR strategy. In the end, these terms more or less mean the same thing.

From Challenge to Key HR Topics

One challenge may be the recruitment of suitable employees for bottleneck functions. The answer to this challenge could now be the development of an employer brand or the development of a talent community through which promising candidates can be permanently retained. Alternatively, or in addition to this, the company could also concentrate on the development of active sourcing strategies. Passively seeking candidates are actively approached, usually via the networks of the company's own employees. Employer branding, active sourcing, talent communities are potential key HR topics. In the course of this book very different, possible key topics are presented, depending on the challenge. The bandwidth is large.

Once a key topic is considered strategically relevant and adopted as part of the HR strategy, you will do what you have always done. You define those responsible ones who take care of the topic, setup necessary budgets, etc. The topic turns into a project with everything that usually belongs to it.

Often these topics are not completely new for a company. Perhaps for many years there has already been a program to promote young talent, an employee survey, individual, performance-related bonuses or performance evaluation. However, in view of the strategic challenges, one gains the certain impression that the way in which these topics were conceptualized and implemented does not lead, or no longer leads, to the hoped-for results and solutions. In such a situation, an existing theme can also be installed as a key HR topic.

Possible Key HR Topics

Figure 3.6 provides an overview of possible key topics. For better clarity, these topics have been categorized into different clusters with corresponding headings.

The overview in Fig. 3.6 does not claim to be complete. Different companies will also use different terms for the topics mentioned here. Chapters 5–12 deal

Talent acquisition and selection	Learning and knowledge	Engagement and retention
Employer branding Sourcing, approaching and retaining candidates Selection and fit Onboarding	Vocational training Executive development Continuous learning Knowledge management	Working conditions and employer attractiveness Employee survey Employee retention HR Operation
Goals, assessment and feedback	Development and career	Remuneration
Objective settings and performance expectations Feedback Formal judgement	Talent identification Talent development Expert career	Compensation policy Base pay Pay for performance
HR Operation	Managing change and transformation	
HR organization Key figures and control Digital HR and People Analytics	Transformation	

Fig. 3.6 Possible key HR topics

comprehensively with these topics. For this reason, a conscious decision should be made not to go into further detail at this point. Basically, Fig. 3.6 is an excerpt from the table of contents of this book.

The Third Level

Probably all companies deal more or less with *general HR fields of action* (first level). This includes recruitment and selection, as well as the topics of remuneration and training and development. If one were to write an HR textbook, these would be the main headings of the book. Hardly any company will differentiate itself strategically on these topics because they are basically ubiquitous. The statement, "Our human resources strategy is to attract, develop and retain the right people" is completely worthless because it is universal. Every company hires employees, develops and keeps them somehow.

The situation is different with the selection of *key HR topics* (second level). A kind of focusing on the strategically important is already taking place here. Which concrete registers should be drawn up in order to meet the HR-relevant strategic challenges? This is about *what*. What is really important for the future of the company and its competitiveness? The third level now deals with the *strategic alignment* of these key HR topics (see Fig. 3.7).

This third level raises the question of *how* a key HR topic should be designed and implemented. The type of HR (see Sect. 2.2) provides the decisive guard rails. Is central planning and control in the foreground or rather people-centered enablement? Experience has shown that this level presents companies with the greatest challenges, which is why the rest of this book places particular emphasis on this. In fact, the development of an HR strategy takes place primarily at this level.

Once this strategic alignment of a key HR topic has been clarified, the *operative design* can be thought of. What instruments are required? What do they look like in practical terms? Who in the company assumes which role and responsibility? Do we need certain key performance indicators (KPIs) to measure success? What role does technology play here? But now back to the third level.

Level	Content	Meaning
1	General HR **fields** of action	Are largely identical for all companies: sourcing, recruiting, talent development, learning etc.
2	**Key HR topics** ("Register")	Strategic selection (the what) of HR topics that appear to be particularly effective in addressing critical HR-related challenges.
3	**Strategic alignment** of key HR topics	Strategic decisions on how to align key HR topics. This is where the desired type of HR comes into play.
4	Operational **Design**	Operational design of processes, instruments, KPIs, technology and responsibilities.

Fig. 3.7 The third level of an HR strategy in the extended context

Strong Strategic Statements

Strategic decisions are always decisions where the option that seems most conducive to meeting a significant challenge is selected from a set of conceivable options. A situation where there are no alternatives does not require a strategic decision. It is clear what you do anyway. Decisions that suggest certain options also have no strategic weight. No company will ridicule itself with the statement "Success is our strategy" because the alternative (failure) is obviously not a serious option. In principle, the value of a strategic decision is only high if its opposite would also make sense. Only then does strategic differentiation take place.

This thought becomes most obvious when you take a look at the management guidelines of some companies. Then you get to read: "We treat our employees with respect". The opposite would then be: "We treat employees in a disrespectful manner". This could at best be meant seriously on a galley or in a labour camp. Some strategic statements crumble if they are actively questioned in this way. Numerous companies, for example, have made the phrase "Employees are our focus" their motto. Implicitly behind this is the assumption that in the centre there is only room for one. What about the customers? "Yes, the customers are also the focus." And what about the executives? "So are they." This would have completely relegated the first sentence, according to which the focus is on the employees, to strategic insignificance.

Strategic Statements in HR

I get suspicious when a company issues the strategy "We only want the best". Alternatives would be "We want the right ones" or "In research and development we want only the best ones". However, if a company pursues the claim to want "only the best" without restriction, then this has far-reaching implications. Whether one really takes this statement seriously is then determined by the consequences that this statement entails, and by whether these consequences are pursued sustainably, for example in the context of selection or remuneration. That brings us to the third level.

Let us take the topic of talent development as another example. At least two contradictory strategic statements are conceivable here. The first statement could be: Employees are responsible for their own long-term development. A fundamentally sensible alternative could be the following: Managers bear responsibility for the development of their employees. I can imagine entire teams of HR professionals in many companies who would grit their teeth at the decision for one or the other statement. The discussion about this point alone could fill an entire workshop, because one can guess what powerful consequences this decision would have. Who would we need to empower, the employees or the executives? What would be the role of HR? What would this mean for HR tools and processes in the future? This simple example shows how difficult it can be to make strategic statements. They must also be difficult to make or formulate, because otherwise they would have no strategic weight.

In the further course of this book, alternative options and statements on very different, potential key HR topics will be presented. This comprehensive presentation is intended to provide CEOs, HR managers and their teams with valuable orientation.

The Relevance of Stability Versus Agility

Which strategic options a company ultimately chooses depends directly on the current and desired cultural and structural context for numerous topics. At this point we have come full circle. Another example may illustrate this.

In addition to a basic salary, many companies offer their employees performance-related, variable, contingent pay. Offering variable compensation is not in itself a strategic decision, but at best a key HR topic that would now have to be strategically aligned (at the third level). You can make many strategic decisions in one direction or another on this subject. At this point, two opposing options are sufficient to illustrate this. The first option could be: To make individual performance worthwhile, employees who perform outstandingly receive special financial reward. At first glance, that sounds very reasonable. But an alternative statement does not sound bad either: We know that good performance can only be achieved in a team. This should pay off for all team members, which is why outstanding team performance is rewarded financially and consistently. Now you can argue about the right alternative. The decision will not be an easy one, which is one of the ways in which its strategic scope can be seen. Agile organizations, which on the one hand assume a high level of task dynamics, and where employees feel committed first and foremost to their colleagues, will clearly prefer the second alternative. Organizations with a division of labour, on the other hand, will rely on the first statement.

The example presented above, according to which responsibility for long-term development rests either on the shoulders of the managers or on the shoulders of the employees themselves, can also be interpreted accordingly. Agile organizations that rely on self-regulation and self-determination are given responsibility to the employees. This would also correspond to the agile type of HR where the HR function is assigned an enabling role. Organizations striving for stability would interpret this aspect completely differently. Here, responsibility for employee development clearly lies in the hands of managers or in the responsibility of the HR function that plans and controls centrally.

Outlook on the Following Chapters

In later Chaps. (5–12) of this book, very different HR topics common in practice will be discussed in more detail. These topics are structured according to classic fields of action, such as talent acquisition and selection, talent management, remuneration or learning. For each of these topics, it is recalled which HR-related challenges these topics might address and what the content is about. However, the main part of the following remarks will focus on the options available for a strategic alignment. The alternatives presented are largely oriented towards the respective strategic and cultural context of a company. In this respect, the following chapters provide a more concrete definition of how HR topics can be structured in companies with an agile versus traditional hierarchical understanding of leadership and organization.

At the end of each chapter, these strategic dimensions are summarized again for each topic. For executives, HR managers and their teams, these overviews offer a practical basis. Based on these options, whole workshops can be designed in terms of content in order to answer questions about a suitable strategic orientation in a structured way.

3.6 International HR Strategies

Up to now, we have in a way assumed a very simplified, even naive view of companies. Here there is a company with strategic and HR-relevant challenges. We define those challenges, derive key topics, strategically align them and develop appropriate solutions. However, *the* company does not exist in this form, or only rarely, at least not if it is an internationally operating company. Rather, companies consist of company headquarters, of branches, divisions or entire conglomerates of companies or subsidiaries within a group of companies.

If an HR strategy is to be developed and implemented, how does this present itself in a context in which a company actually consists of several parts? In order to answer this question, it is necessary to take a closer look at the company's situation. In the following, in agreement with the valuable considerations of Bartlett and Ghoshal (1998), three particular settings are distinguished. Accordingly, a company is either international, multinational or global. Depending on the situation, this has completely different consequences for the development and implementation of an HR strategy. Section 11.1 takes up this distinction again when it comes to the alignment of the HR organization itself.

Let us start with a simple case. The HR manager and his or her colleagues decide to strengthen executive development. Since the last employee survey and in view of the increasing turnover rates, a key HR topic has been identified in this, which is now to be filled, in terms of content and concept, and brought to life. This makes executive development an integral part of the HR strategy. We could have used any other topic here. The consequences would be quite comparable. In the following, the history of this topic for all three settings—international, multinational and global—will be told from two perspectives, one from the central headquarter perspective, and one from the decentralized perspective, for example from the point of view of a branch HR manager. For illustrative purposes, we will call the global leader for leadership development Jenny. In the French branch (with 2000 employees) we have the local HR Manager Jean. We start with an international company.

Ethnocentric World View in an International Setting

In an international company, the company headquarter sees itself as the centre of the world. The headquarters is, so to speak, the Mecca from which events in all parts of the company are controlled. An ethnocentric view dominates here. Especially in the first years of internationalization, most companies are in this special stage. Products, ideas, knowledge and values are exported from the headquarters to the various locations and decentral organizational units of the company. If the company is a Swedish company, then the key positions "abroad" are often filled with Swedish representatives from the home country to ensure the connection to the head office.

If Jenny, the global leader for leadership development, wants to advance her HR topic globally, she and her project team will consider a corresponding concept. Where appropriate, they will seek feedback from the countries. As soon as the concept is ready, it will be rolled out globally. The thing is exported, so to speak, from the headquarters to the countries. Jean will have to follow the central order. But if Jean in France comes up with the idea of setting up a leadership development program for his country, he will have to ask Jenny for permission. Nothing is done locally without the consent of the headquarter, unless he does not shout it from the rooftops. He just gets started, creates facts and hopes not to be disturbed by the headquarter at some point.

Local Differentiation in a Multinational Setting

In multinational companies, the various units (divisions, branches, subsidiaries, etc.) operate pretty autonomously. There is decentralization and the principle of *local differentiation*. The company headquarter follows the premise to leave the local units alone as far as possible, because one starts from the assumption that they know best what is right given the respective local circumstances. In addition, it is intended to avoid time-consuming and energy-consuming decision-making and coordination processes between local units and the headquarter. The consequence is that each country, each division pursues its own approaches, which ultimately differ from each other in a natural way.

In this case Jenny has a much weaker position than in the case of an international company. In the multinational case, she only has a chance to bring the issue of executive development to the countries if they are convinced of it and agree with it conceptually. If, on the other hand, Jean wants to introduce a program for France, he simply does so, without any coordination with his colleague from the headquarter. As this example shows, HR managers in the headquarter of a multinational company have a much more difficult or weaker position than HR managers who work in internationally managed companies. It seems to me that many Global Heads were not always aware of this before they took on their melodious job.

Global Integration

In a global company, the word "abroad" is simply not used. In a global company, the idea of solving things together is vital, not because the head office wants it that way, but because it is precisely the decentralized units that demand it. Not with all topics, but with many topics it is assumed that not only the company as a whole but also the individual unit benefits from one thing, above all, when it is tackled together. In global organizations, local differentiation is countered by the principle of *global integration*. The headquarter has a facilitating role in the case of global companies. It picks up needs in the different units and leads them to common approaches and solutions.

If Jenny wants to set up a global leadership development program, she will first have to find out whether there is a common need for it in the decentralized units. Either she speaks individually with the representatives of these entities and explores common interests and needs, or she might conduct a joint workshop on the subject to determine whether there is a common basis for a global approach. Should this not be the case, the topic would hardly have a chance of success.

If Jean is interested in an executive development program, he will contact his colleagues in the other units either through Jenny or directly and clarify whether there is a common interest. If this is again not the case, he might develop his own approach. However, addressing a topic in the global community will only take place if the opportunity for synergy is recognized here. The conviction must prevail that as a decentralized unit one will benefit from joint efforts if most other units participate.

Clarify How the Company Operates

The above considerations make it clear that in a company consisting of several parts (divisions, subsidiaries, branches, etc.) it must first be clarified how one actually operates before starting to develop an HR strategy. The scenarios described above are very simplified. In practice, the connections and dynamics usually prove to be much more complex. The three forms of internationality are summarized and graphically illustrated in the Fig. 3.8. Triangles illustrate the headquarter (the roof)

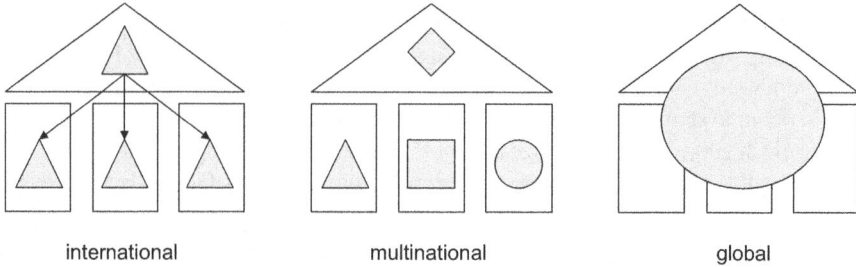

Fig. 3.8 Different forms of internationality

and the rectangles the decentralized organizational units. The grey shaded forms symbolize the respective HR approaches.

I have seen so many freshly appointed HR managers who, from a world dominated by headquarters and ethnocentric thinking, and with a suitcase full of all kinds of favourite concepts, have had the intention of introducing one or the other concept into the new, multinational world. In the first meeting with his or her colleagues from the decentralized units, they signal to him or her: "Very interesting. We should consider it" etc. In fact, they think: "I do not want it, do not need it, and the headquarters have nothing to say to me anyway. I do what my local MD [Managing Director] tells me to do". At that moment the world view of the new "Global Head" implodes. Next, he may run to the CEO, "Can you please tell the local MDs that they . . .", to which the CEO replies, "If you want the decentralized units to do what you want them to do, then you simply have to convince them. If you can do this, you have my blessing. If not, then just not".

In practice, problems often arise from a different perception of corporate reality depending on which authority is looking at it. The classic case is that colleagues in the headquarters assume an international setting, whereas colleagues in the decentralized units see or want to see a multinational reality. Misunderstandings of this kind lead to frustration and conflicts between the headquarters and the decentralized units.

References

Bartlett CA, Ghoshal S (1998) Managing across borders: the transnational solution. Harvard Business Press, Boston, MA

Hill CWL, Schilling MA, Jones GR (2017) Strategic management. Theory & cases. An integrated approach. Cengage, Boston, MA

Huselid MA, Beatty RW, Becker BE (2005) A player or A positions? A strategic logic of workforce management. Harv Bus Rev 83(12):110–117

Trost A (2014) Talent relationship management. Competitive recruiting strategies in times of talent shortage. Springer, Heidelberg

4 The Structural and Cultural Context

In this chapter the structural and cultural peculiarities of hierarchical and agile worlds are compared. Many of the characteristic dimensions described here have existed in leadership and organizational theory for many decades. Douglas McGregor's (1960) description of different images of man or the classification of leadership styles with regard to their employee (consideration) versus factual orientation (initiating structure) as a result of the Ohio State studies of the 1950s are only two examples (cf. Fleishman 1991). Currently, popular scientific, phenomenological attempts to describe agility as an alternative to classical leadership and organization dominate the practical discussion. The internationally acclaimed works of Frederik Laloux (2014) should be mentioned here just as an example.

In contrast to this, this book does not provide a comprehensive, complete description of what makes an agile perspective on leadership and organization different from a hierarchical, traditional one. This book is not a treatise on leadership and organization but a book on HR. Therefore, this chapter describes only those dimensions of agile and traditional worlds that are directly relevant to *what* we do in HR and, above all, *how* we do things.

4.1 The Context and Its Relevance for HR

These dimensions are of central importance for the development of an HR strategy. They provide an orientation framework for the way in which HR, and in particular key HR topics, should be strategically aligned (on a third level). HR in the upper, hierarchical part of the HR playing field (HR triangle) is completely different from an HR in the lower, agile part. There is a close interaction between the way in which HR is strategically aligned in the company and the understanding of leadership and organization (see Fig. 4.1).

If instruments, concepts, systems and programs within HR do not correspond in their strategic alignment to the prevailing or at least desired understanding of

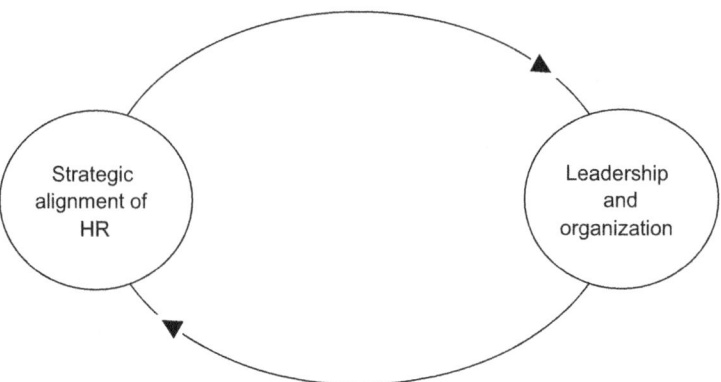

Fig. 4.1 Interrelation between leadership, organization and HR

leadership and organization, then in practice they have no chance of success. They are rejected by the organization. This is the case, for example, when an attempt is made in a conservative, strictly hierarchically managed company to introduce self-organized learning. Bosses will not let that happen. Conversely, hierarchically conceived instruments, such as the individual, annual performance appraisal in an agile company, have little chance of survival. In this respect, leadership and organization enable certain forms of strategic alignment of HR, while those that are not compatible are repelled.

Contrariwise, HR has the chance to either prevent or promote a certain understanding of leadership and organization. In this context there is always talk of "HR as the driver of digital transformation". If a company strives for lateral cooperation within and between teams as part of agile leadership, HR can either promote this or prevent it to some extent, for example through existing performance management systems. As it will still be shown, forced ranking in the top-down performance reviews of employees can downright sabotage lateral cooperation because they turn colleagues and teammates into competitors and obstacles. An HR that adheres to tools of this kind prevents agile leadership and organization.

Structural and Cultural Framework Conditions

An understanding of leadership and organization manifests itself in the cultural and structural framework conditions within a company or a subdivision. A consideration of these rather concrete framework conditions makes the derivation of practice-relevant implications more tangible. What does the statement "Executives must place more trust in their employees" mean for HR? What does this mean for talent management, compensation, assessment and the many other topics we deal with in HR? In the context of digital transformation, there is often talk of the premise that speed is the most important factor. "Only the fast will win. The slow will lose". Who would object to that? But what does this mean for HR? What is the connection between speed and performance appraisal for example? A great one. However, this relation is not always and immediately obvious to everyone. Trust, speed, respect, personal responsibility, overcoming organizational silos are principles of leadership and organization that are difficult to translate into certain forms of institutionalized HR. This is why we can currently observe entire armies of HR managers in many companies, that preach agility but simultaneously carry forward static, hierarchical HR practices. It seems difficult to build the bridge from the abstract world to the real, practical world. It is precisely for this reason that structural and cultural framework conditions are described in the following, which on the one hand are as tangible as possible and from which, on the other hand, very concrete conclusions can be drawn, particularly for HR. When a wide variety of key HR topics are dealt with comprehensively from Chap. 5 onwards, reference is always made to the dimensions of these framework conditions.

Before the selected dimensions are discussed in detail, a brief and summarizing overall impression of the two hemispheres is given. The respective dimensions are briefly addressed. We begin with the traditional, hierarchical world in which stability is sought.

Stability in a Traditional, Hierarchical World

Overall, the company, including its products and services, is developing statically. You do what you do and try to get a little better every year. The employees are basically interchangeable, mainly because the availability of potential employees in the labour market is considered to be very high. In this respect, one can allow oneself to make detailed, static demands on the employees in terms of competencies. All you have to do is pick the right ones. The company clearly determines in a fixed way where and when people work. Employees must therefore adapt their life plans to their professional circumstances. All in all, employees at the lower levels of the organization experience less appreciation than managers. The higher one rises in the hierarchy, the greater the reputation in the company. The tasks of the employees, in turn, are described very clearly. Every employee knows exactly how to get to which results. There are clearly defined standards for the latter. The tasks themselves are as small as possible. Basically, the premise is that you always think first and then act. Even with larger projects you try to think everything through and only then you start with the implementation. The technically superior managers play a decisive role here. They are the masters and act by instruction and control. The rule is, "trust is good, but control is better". You have to guide and motivate employees otherwise you would not get the desired results. That is why employees are told exactly what they need to do, how and when. All things considered, work is carried out in a very subdivided way. Each employee takes care of his or her own area of responsibility. Cooperation and communication is only desired to a very limited extent at employee level and is actually not necessary. Basically, every employee feels committed to his or her direct superior and to no one else.

This simple sketch might sound quite familiar to some readers. Now, in the following paragraph the agile counter-design will be outlined along the same dimensions.

Agility and the Connected World

Existing services and products of your company are continuously questioned. One strives to disruptively displace the existing through one's own new developments. As a company, you are dependent on employees who are difficult to replace. Individuality is valued. It leads to desired diversity, which in turn is seen as the cornerstone of innovation and success. Individual lifestyles are also valued and realized wherever possible. Basically, the employees in the company are the "true heroes". They have more specialist knowledge than their managers. Executives tend to hold back and do not take themselves more seriously than everyone else. You lead as a coach, in partnership, at eye level. The employees themselves are confronted with a high degree of uncertainty on a daily basis. The results of the projects and the ways to achieve them are uncertain. One approaches through iterative steps in which customers are continuously involved. Thinking and acting merge. Employees bear a great deal of responsibility, but also enjoy the necessary trust. You do not have to motivate or direct them. Rather, they act on their own initiative. They decide for themselves when, where and with whom to work. What they do results from the necessities of their responsibility. Almost everything happens in an exchange within and between teams. You are only successful together because there are considerable dynamic interrelations between various tasks and responsibilities. For this reason, our employees and teams are committed to their colleagues and customers, both internally and externally.

In the two sketches above, twelve aspects were indicated which can be divided into four categories: Employees, tasks, leadership and organization. An overview of these categories and their content is shown in Fig. 4.2. The individual categories and dimensions are described in more detail in the following sections.

Employees	Tasks	Leadership	Organization
Individuality	Optimization versus disruption	Professional superiority	Division of labour and task dynamics
Appreciation	Task certainty	Dominant leadership style	Consequences and commitment
Concept of man	Thinking and acting	Autonomy and self-regulation	
Dependency			

Fig. 4.2 Overview of cultural and structural framework conditions

4.2 The Employees

The first category deals with the employees themselves. To what extent is the selection and development of employees oriented to static requirements in terms of competencies? How much individuality is valued? Do the employees enjoy the highest esteem or the managers? What is the dominant concept of man from the point of view of management and executives? Is the company dependent on its employees or vice versa?

Individuality, Diversity and Work-Life Balance

As mentioned earlier, a common and traditional idea of HR is to provide the right employee, at the right time, in the right place. Here the connection between the "right employee" and the "right place" is of central interest. From this traditional point of view, it is about the fit between the requirements of a job on the one hand, and the skills and attitude of an employee on the other. Figure 4.3 shows this idea in a simple way.

The rectangle in Fig. 4.3 shows the requirements related to a job. It symbolizes the proverbial box in which an employee should fit: competencies, a certain degree, a certain form of professional experience, etc. Now, unfortunately, people are rarely the way one imagines them to be in an ideal world, and in view of the increasing shortage of skilled workers, these people may not be sufficiently available in the desired form. They are possibly more like the amoeba-like form in this illustration, very individual. The question now is whether one is happy about the peculiarities of this person. After all, this person has strengths that go beyond what is required. Or does one focus on the deficits hatched in the figure, which may need to be eliminated in the context of targeted training activities so that the employee fulfils the requirements better?

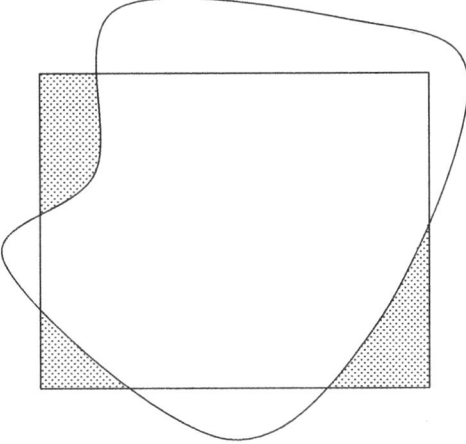

Fig. 4.3 The fit between requirements and the employee

Agile organizations value individuality. In this way, they achieve what is known as *diversity*. The result is a natural range of skills and perspectives that are thought to be particularly conducive to the development of innovation. In fact, it can be seen that complementary strengths amplify each other in various teams and individual weaknesses are compensated by the strengths of others. In diverse teams one appreciates the superiority of others instead of understanding them as a threat to one's own position in the team.

Hierarchically minded companies, on the other hand, interpret diversity much more in the sense of a statistical distribution of employee attributes. CEOs, for example, report that they are making progress on the subject of diversity because they have statistically increased the proportion of women in management positions or because the proportion of foreign members in management is higher than a few years ago. However, diversity should not be confused with statistical variation. Diversity, in the sense of an appreciation of individuality, is rather a question of attitude and openness towards the peculiarities of individuals. This difference can be illustrated by a simple analogy:

> There is a farmer who grows potatoes. During the harvest he selects his potatoes according to certain criteria. They must be round and medium in size. That is what his customer wants. Well, since this year, his buyer's wish is for a greater degree of variety. He also calls it potato diversity. The old criteria remain, but 20% of the potatoes may be smaller, but not too small. The farmer keeps to it. In the end, the desired diversity is achieved. One village further there is another farmer who also grows potatoes. His premise for the harvest is: (almost) every potato is OK, and that is the way it is.

The first farmer seems to be pursuing what can be called diversity management—clear goals, goal-oriented action, metrics, etc. The second farmer may not even know that word. He does not have to know. He would probably fail a diversity audit according to official principles. However, which of the two farmers achieves a higher degree of diversity? This simple analogy makes clear what diversity is about and how diversity is often misunderstood. Diversity is not a question of statistics, but primarily a question of attitude, which in the end leads to natural differences. The result is neither the cause at the same time nor its actual meaning.

One can now go one step further and consider the individuality of entire *life plans* in addition to individual abilities, perspectives and backgrounds of experience. One enjoys his highly flexible single life, while the other sees his main focus of life in the family and his or her three children. One is a single parent, the other wants to take care of his or her sick mother or father. When a company values these individual life plans and actively seeks opportunities to live up to these individual concepts, it achieves what is widely referred to as *work-life balance*. Diversity and work-life balance are very similar concepts in this respect. Companies that think in this direction value the fact that employees have friends, family and a life beyond the corporate world.

Agile companies that keep individuality high align their HR completely differently than companies that do not. This starts with the selection of the employees.

Agile companies communicate significantly more generic requirements—"They must be reasonably intelligent and have a desire for what we do here". Potential and attitude are more important than currently available competencies. They focus much more on their strengths than on their weaknesses in promoting very talented employees.

The Focus Is on the Employee: Really?

Many companies state on their career websites, for example, that their focus is on the employees. Really? What must it feel like for employees to really be the focus of attention in a company? In most hierarchical organizations they definitely are not. The CEO is the focal point there. The CEO not only has the largest and most beautiful office. He or she has the most privileged parking lot, right next to the entrance. Not only the CEO, but also the managers experience a significantly higher esteem than the employees. They do not dine in the canteen next to the "normal" employees, but in a more exclusive executive launch. In many hierarchical companies, the unwritten rule is: the higher you are in the hierarchy or the closer you are to the CEO, the more esteem you enjoy. As already indicated, this form of "absolutist" superordination and subordination is underpinned by visible power symbolism, which unmistakably conveys to the lower caste who has something to say here.

This attitude is rather alien to agile organizations. Anyone who visits such companies as an outsider wonders after a while "who is the boss here?" Then you shouldn't be surprised if you get an answer like the following: "Chelsea is the boss. That was the one with the black T-shirt. She does not usually talk much." Power symbolism, which one knows from hierarchical companies, is completely missing. Managers have no fixed place at the end of the table. You let employees moderate a meeting. Depending on their personal disposition, they hold themselves back or bring themselves in, just like the others do. The parking lot right next to the entrance is ready for the first person to come. If you accompany a CEO who really puts employees at the centre of his or her attention when walking through the company, you are impressed by the closeness to the employees. He or she knows the people by name, remembers a lot from previous conversations. He conveys to every employee: "You are the most important employee for the company at this point, much more important than I am. I am glad you are here."

This form of appreciation can be well illustrated using the *inverted pyramid*. It is shown in a simple way on the right side of Fig. 4.4.

The triangle in this figure shows the classic hierarchy. The left side shows the traditional variant, according to which the CEO, at the top, enjoys the highest esteem. From bottom to top the pyramid becomes narrower and narrower, and at the top there is only room for one. The right side shows the inverted pyramid. It is intended to symbolize that the employees at the grassroots level are the actual stars of the company. The complete structure of the hierarchy is there to enable the

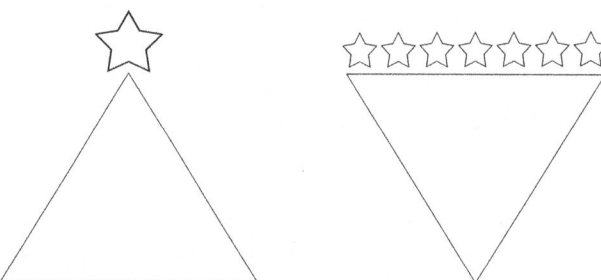

Fig. 4.4 Absolutism or inverted pyramid

employees—they provide the actual performance that matters—for what they do. Managers are servants of their employees.

The Idea of Man: X or Y?

Probably the most important question that an executive, a CEO but also an HR manager or professional should ask him or herself is that of the *idea of man*. In my seminars with HR executives, I discuss the question as intensively as possible. It is an important key for our understanding of leadership and organization and the way we imagine successful HR. The idea of man is the culminated belief we have about the behaviour of people and their motivation. In this respect, this idea is a theory about the human being itself, a set of hypotheses by means of which we predict the behaviour of employees. These hypotheses ultimately determine our own behaviour.

Anyone who thinks of ideas of man in the context of leadership and management cannot ignore the work of the great mastermind Douglas McGregor (1960). Almost 60 years ago he wrote the book "The Human Side of Enterprise", which to this day can rightly be regarded as one of the most important books not only in management theory but above all in HR. In this book McGregor outlined two opposing ideas of man, Theory X and Theory Y. These two theories are already familiar to most readers. I, too, was forced to learn these theories by heart during my studies. But it took me another 20 years to understand their enormous relevance. They are compared in Fig. 4.5.

It will not be discussed at this point, which of the two theories is more true or less true. In the context discussed here, it seems more interesting to shed light on the consequences of whether one believes in one theory or another. Two effects are of particular importance here. Firstly, it can be assumed that managers base their behaviour on their idea of man. Anyone who believes that their employees are lazy by nature will give clearer instructions, will check more frequently and more precisely. Mistrust will dominate. The opposite is true for managers who believe in Theory Y. This first effect is comparatively obvious. However, more exciting is the effect according to which the theories X and Y entail self-fulfilling prophecies. A

Theory X	Theory Y
People have an inherent dislike for work and will avoid it whenever possible.	The expenditure of physical and mental effort in work is as natural as play or rest
People must be coerced, controlled, directed, or threatened with punishment in order to get them to achieve the organizational objectives.	Man will exercise self-direction and self-control in the service of objectives to which he is committed.
People prefer to be directed, do not want responsibility, and have little or no ambition.	The average human being learns not only to accept but to seek responsibility.
People seek security above all else.	The capacity to exercise a relatively high degree of imagination, ingenuity, and creativity in the solution of organizational problems is widely, not narrowly, distributed in the population.

Fig. 4.5 Theory X and Theory Y according to Douglas McGregor (1960)

prophecy is confirmed because you believe in it. Those who believe in Theory X will act accordingly and be confirmed in their point of view. The employees become as described by theory X. The same applies to Theory Y. In the end, the initial idea of man proves to be true. This is the reason why two leaders who follow different ideas of man will never find a common denominator in a discussion on the question of ideal leadership. Both will report opposing experiences, which they each confirm in a contrary way in their personal view.

If you ask managers which idea of man refers to themselves and at the same time ask them to classify other people, you will always come to the finding that managers describe themselves on the basis of Theory Y, but that most others are accurately characterized by Theory X—"All people avoid taking over responsibility, except me". That is pretty bizarre, assuming everyone thinks so. If CEOs or founders are of the opinion that all people—except they themselves—correspond to Theory X, then they will shape their companies culturally and institutionally accordingly. As we have just seen, the likelihood that they will think so is extremely high. It is in the nature of man, so to speak.

If we sum up the central difference between hierarchical companies striving for stability and agile, connected companies as simply as possible, then the two letters X and Y suffice. The former represent the idea of man according to Theory X, while agile organizations tend to feel connected to Theory Y.

Who Dependents on Whom?

If one follows the traditional, bureaucratic understanding of organizations in Max Weber's view, then organizations should be structured in such a way that the employees themselves are interchangeable. You define jobs with specific tasks and responsibilities. These in turn are integrated in hierarchical systems with subordination and superordination. If an employee is absent, whether through voluntary or involuntary turnover, retirement, illness or death, then you just get a new one and the machine continues to run. Behind this dehumanized view is the implicit assumption that employees are not only interchangeable but also available without limits.

An executive who proceeds from these basic conditions will demonstrate a way of thinking and acting that has its roots in a hierarchical, traditional world. Accordingly, the psychological contract is one-sided, "You [employees] get money to do what I tell you, whether you enjoy it or not". If the employee does not accept the deal, there will be someone else who will go into this dependency instead of him or her.

However, there are two important developments to counter this view. First, we are seeing an increasing shortage of talent in certain occupational groups. Think here of software developers, scientists, but also nurses, educators or truck drivers. This increasing scarcity leads to a reversal of dependency relationships. The employee is no longer dependent on the company, but vice versa. The result is a completely new self-confidence on the part of the representatives of these occupational groups. Conversely, employers must adapt their behaviour to these new dependencies, which in turn touches on issues of talent acquisition, retention, appraisal and remuneration.

Secondly, parallel to this first development, it can be observed that the employment relationships themselves are in a process of change towards greater employee independence. Within the framework of HR, we usually assume that employees are exclusively or primarily dependent employees. Nevertheless, reality provides a somewhat different picture (see Fig. 4.6).

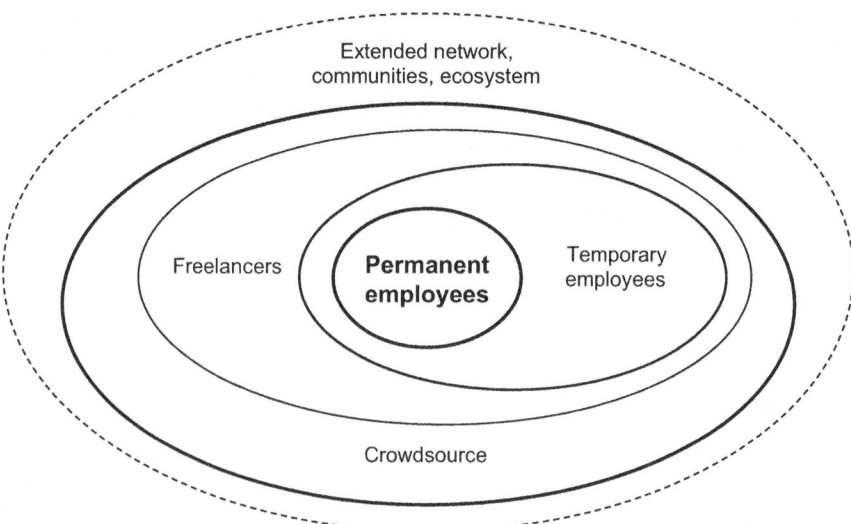

Fig. 4.6 Different forms of employment with varying degrees of dependency

In addition to permanent employees, companies have always had access to *temporary employees*. This type of employment is still likely to involve a certain degree of employee dependency. The situation is completely different for *freelancers*. It seems that more and more qualified people prefer this employment relationship over dependent employment. They decide for themselves which orders they accept. They define their working conditions with a significantly higher degree of autonomy than is normally the case with permanent employees. Freelancers feel above all committed to themselves and their customers rather than to a superior boss.

In recent years, increasing networking and digital, mobile communication have brought to light completely new working conditions to which one should probably become accustomed. A special form describes the phenomenon of *crowdsourcing* (Abrahamson et al. 2013). The company Procter & Gamble, for instance, advertises problems on its "connect and develop" platform, which anyone who wants to contribute to solving can see.[1] Companies that do crowdsourcing accept that the person who is best able to solve a particular problem is probably not employed in their own company. We will probably see a massive increase in this direction in the coming years, as more and more people prefer to work self-determined in self-chosen settings (e.g., in co-working spaces or at home) over institutional dependence. Crowdsourcing allows people to be as good at what they do as they want to be. For those affected, this results in a high degree of experienced self-efficacy.

In addition, numerous people contribute to the value creation of a company, which in various forms can be attributed to the extended network, company-owned communities or an ecosystem surrounding the company. Thus, numerous apps that are used on iPhones, for example, are not developed by Apple itself. The number of independent software developers developing apps within this ecosystem is many times the number of software developers permanently employed by Apple.

In a static, hierarchical world, companies can be compared to a castle. There are the borders to the outside. Either one is within these walls and follows the rules and instructions laid down therein, or one does not belong to the inside. Agile companies, on the other hand, see themselves more as marketplaces or as cities within which there are rules and an enabling infrastructure. The question of the interdependence between employee and employer is likely to lead to entirely new answers in the coming years, which will also require new approaches and ways of thinking with regard to HR.

4.3 The Tasks

Let us now move on to the tasks themselves. Here three aspects are relevant. First are the tasks of the employees to follow up on what has been well established and, where necessary and possible, to optimize it step by step? Or is the challenge to develop

---

[1] https://www.pgconnectdevelop.com/needs/ (last visit on March 31, 2019).

something completely new in order to disruptively replace what may already exist? Second, how clearly is it possible to predict what the desired outcomes of the tasks will be and how they will be achieved? The third aspect examines the question of the relationship between thinking and acting. Is thinking first thought and then implemented or do thinking and acting merge into an iterative process?

David Against Goliath

Most companies probably do exactly what they have been doing for many years. They produce washing machines, cars, books, offer insurance policies or other services. They are good at that. That is what they are familiar with. Every employee makes the proven contribution in his or her position. In order to remain competitive on the market, they try to continuously improve what they do. By doing so, they continuously increase efficiency and quality. As part of continuous improvement processes, employees are encouraged to think every day about how things could be done better. If one follows the argumentation of the great Harvard professor Clayton Christensen (1997), then numerous well-run companies in the history of industry have perished precisely because of this. While they concentrated on their established core competencies, other, mostly unknown and small companies developed solutions that, at first slowly and unnoticed, then faster, brought products and services to the market that at some point were superior to the offerings of previously dominant companies. This is referred to as *disruption* (see Fig. 4.7).

Especially now, in times of digitization, many companies have recognized the threat of disruptive developments. Companies that we find hard to imagine life to be without, such as General Electric, Nokia, Kodak, Siemens, Daimler, Bosch,

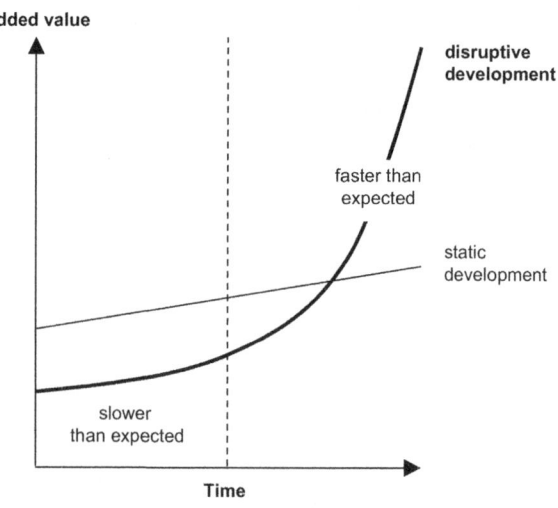

Fig. 4.7 Static versus disruptive development

Deutsche Bank and many others, have developed increasing respect for small, hitherto insignificant, aggressive and highly innovative companies that threaten to displace the large established companies into insignificance with new digital technologies and business models. It is not necessary to mention the numerous examples here. Anyone who is concerned only rudimentarily with digitization and current economic developments knows them.

Companies face a dilemma here. Should they keep what they have under control, where they dominate the market, or attack their existing business with an uncertain new technology? Should they really kill a business with which they are (still) successful and with which they feed the families of the many thousands of employees? Why should Daimler invest in electronic mobility as long as the company is unbeatably successful with combustion engines? Why would Kodak, the inventor of digital photography, have used an uncertain, immature, expensive technology at the time to scratch the business with which they were gigantically successful worldwide? Since the works of Christensen (1997) this dilemma has been called the *Innovator's dilemma*.

This dilemma describes a seemingly insoluble conflict in business strategy. However, what Christensen hardly mentioned, is the accompanying conflict in the way in which numerous companies are managed and organized. Disruptions usually emanate from start-up companies. If you look at the working methods and the culture of these start-ups, you will see that they have completely different rules than, for example, traditional, hierarchically managed companies that focus on stability and long-term planning. Working hours do not play a role. You work in teams and networks, autonomous, self-directed, agile. Rules are broken, not because you want to break them, but because you do not have time to follow them. Decisions are made extremely quickly and close to the customer. The employees are driven and inspired by a feeling to change the world. The vision of making life difficult for the great established ones is an essential part of their motivation. It is a David versus Goliath fight. Referring to the triangle of institutionalization with its two hemispheres depicted in this book, start-ups usually play in the lower left corner, while many of the large established players are located in the upper right corner (see Fig. 4.8).

Companies that are traditional, hierarchical and strive for stability will find it very difficult to create an internal structural and cultural reality that enables or promotes disruptive developments under their own roof. Therefore, one can currently observe a trend in which the large established players invest in start-ups, form venture capital, integrate them into existing corporate structures or develop their own areas in which the company's own Davids should dare to attack. The latter are referred to as "innovation labs" or incubators. The company makes its own "garages" available in which the new start is accommodated in a historical style reminiscent of Apple, Hewlett and Packard or Microsoft. Thus, while the majority of the company continues to pursue optimization in the sense of static developments, disruptive developments are to be advanced in the small cells. John Kotter (2014)

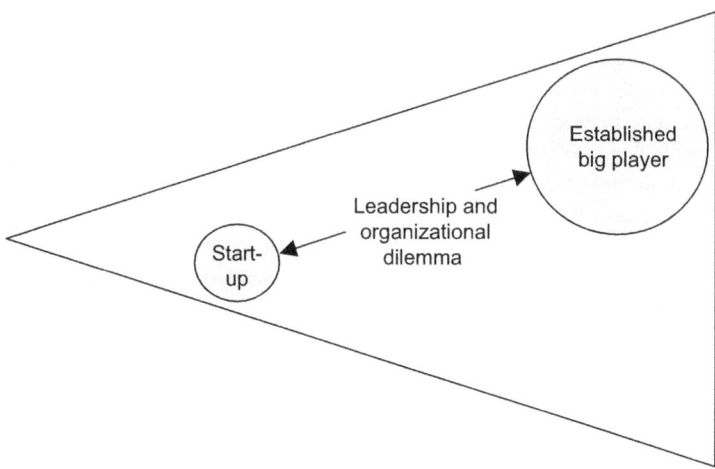

Fig. 4.8 The dilemma of leadership and organization

speaks of the dual operating system. Others speak of hybrid structures or organizational *ambidexterity*.

When it comes to the strategic direction of numerous key HR topics, it will play a major role whether a company or a subdivision sees itself more as a David or as a Goliath. A disruptive David requires in many respects a completely different approach to HR-related issues, compared to a solid Goliath. However, the most difficult question will be what an HR strategy should look like if small, disruptively acting units are to work together under a common roof with traditional, stable remainders.

Certainty of Process and Outcome

In companies, there are tasks in which it is clearly described what the result of the task is and how to arrive at this result. In fact, in the course of industrialization and subsequently in the development of management theory, it was always a central idea to design tasks and working steps in such a way that they could be standardized, with always the same results and always the same processes. In order to keep complexity small, these tasks were divided as much as possible, so that the scope of the individual tasks where as small as possible at the end.

On the other hand, there are also tasks where it is unclear from the outset what the result will look like. There is an idea of the outcome, a vision or priorities, but there is no clear picture of the outcome. In addition to this low *certainty of outcome* there is often a low *certainty of process*. One might know what one will do in the course of a week, but not what the specific actions and work steps will consist of in a month.

4.3 The Tasks

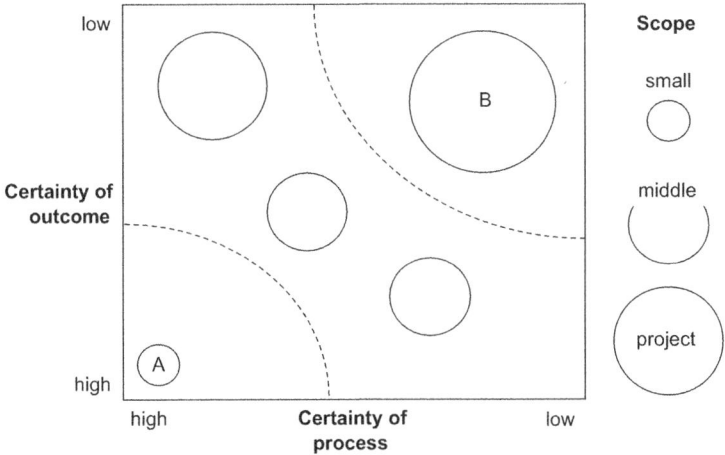

Fig. 4.9 Task certainty and scope (Trost 2017)

Often these tasks are large scale projects. So you do not do these tasks several times a day or even per hour but work on them over a longer period of time.

These three dimensions—certainty of process, certainty of outcome and scope—can be mapped in a corresponding portfolio as shown in Fig. 4.9 (Trost 2017). This then allows the corresponding assignment of different tasks.

The task portfolio in Fig. 4.9 shows the extremes already outlined (A and B). This distinction of tasks is of decisive importance, especially with regard to dealing with HR-relevant topics. Employees who deal with tasks such as A require a different HR than their colleagues who perform B tasks. The relevance is shown on two levels.

On the one hand, we will see that tasks such as A are increasingly taken over by smart technologies such as robots or artificial intelligence. This development has been going on for decades and is currently experiencing a considerable boost as a result of increasing digitization. Not only the very simple tasks, such as the repeated assembly of two components, are affected, but also increasingly higher-value tasks, such as the diagnosis of X-ray images, the determination of the creditworthiness of bank customers or the control of means of transport.

On the other hand, type B tasks must be accompanied by a different understanding of leadership and organization than type A tasks. Instruction and control fail as far as possible. What instruction do you want to give if not even the boss knows the result? Complexity requires a diverse team and connected structures. The annual performance appraisal with its traditional combination of individual target agreement and performance evaluation is not compatible with tasks of this type (cf. Trost 2017). A direct consequence of this distinction arises in relation to the cycles of thought and action, as will be explained in the following section.

Short Cycles, Long Cycles

It is probably one of the German virtues to think things through first and then to start implementing them. First thinking, then acting. Classical *project management*, for example, follows this principle (Project Management Institute 2013). Before you turn the first sod or write the first line of software code, you need to develop project structure plans, specifications and derive network diagrams, Gantt charts, project phases and milestones. One speaks here also of the so-called *waterfall model*. Time schedules, the necessary budgets and responsibilities must be clarified as comprehensively as possible right from the beginning. Planning as an attempt to reduce complexity. However, in extensive projects with low process and outcome certainty this approach can lead to dysfunctional effects that have been known for many years, particularly with regards to the development of software (Weltz and Ortmann 1992). You might work too long on the wrong thing. Uncertainties or discrepancies that occur during the course of the project are ignored with reference to the initial project planning. The product is not accepted by the customer as expected, but this is only realized when this product has already been fully developed. In Fig. 4.10 this approach is graphically symbolized by a large cycle of thinking and acting.

In contrast, an alternative, short-cycle approach has proven to be more successful in software development. In Fig. 4.10 this approach is indicated by the short-cycle iterations. We are talking about *Scrum*, an agile method of project management that seems to be better suited to deal with uncertainty. Here we think in short-cycles, so-called "sprints". Things are planned on a much smaller scale, implemented at short notice and tested close to the customer. The next sprint will follow (Sims and Johnson 2011).

Agile companies think and act short-cyclically, close to their customers. This can be illustrated by various principles that are currently conquering the entire world from Silicon Valley in California. One of these principles is, "fail fast, fail cheap", fail as early as possible and cause as little cost as possible. Whether a product is well

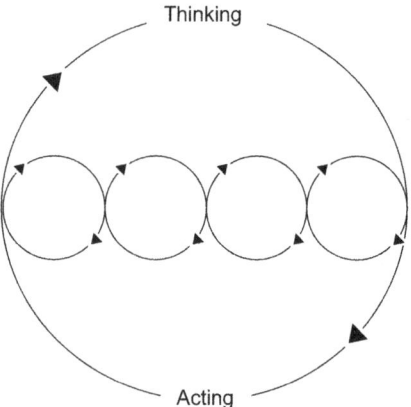

Fig. 4.10 Thinking and acting in extensive and short cycles

accepted by potential customers or not can often be seen at very early stages of product development. Better to do this early, avoid unprofitable further investments and learn from them. This goes hand in hand with the idea of *rapid prototyping*. The success of a product is not only experienced when it has been fully developed and marketing campaigns and production start, but as early as possible on the basis of an early and tangible version of the future product or service. In an environment dominated by software technology, such as Silicon Valley, this attitude was more likely to develop than in German mechanical engineering or the automotive industry. Here you are rightly accustomed to bringing products to market only when their quality is really perfect. Anything else would sometimes result in massive costs, be it in service, in subsequent and costly repairs or in the worst case through necessary recalls. In Silicon Valley, people think in so-called *Minimal Viable Products*, products that are good enough to be delivered quickly, knowing that they are faulty. Subsequent corrections can then be applied by prompt updates over night. This thinking is extremely alien to the good German, reliable engineer. After all, it was clear for decades that as a supplier of a machine, you would lose control of it from the moment it is delivered at the latest. From this moment on, it must function faultlessly and perfectly without any action on your part. In the course of digitization, one will probably be allowed to get used to a different attitude.

4.4 The Dominant Understanding of Leadership

Hardly any other topic is so intensively discussed in the course of digitization and agilization as that of *leadership* and supervision. In fact, it can be assumed that the relationship between employees and managers will change and that this will have immediate implications for the role of managers.

General Knowledge, Expert Knowledge

Traditionally, it was clear that those employees who were the best in terms of their professional skills compared to their colleagues would be promoted. Promotion was not only a question of leadership aptitude but also a sign of recognition of professional strength. Good employees must be offered perspectives and perspectives have always been synonymous of promotion towards the top of the hierarchy. Because this was the case, it was not only the managers who were entitled to receive answers to urgent questions and solutions to acute problems from their managers. In most cases, managers also had this claim against themselves.

In my publications and in numerous lectures I like to use a presentation that illustrates the relationship between managers and employees in a simple and memorable way (see Fig. 4.11).

In the constellations shown in Fig. 4.11 the so-called *T-concept* is used to reflect general knowledge (horizontal bar) and expert knowledge (horizontal bar). Constellation *A* shows a traditional situation. Here the manager (thick bar) has a lot of

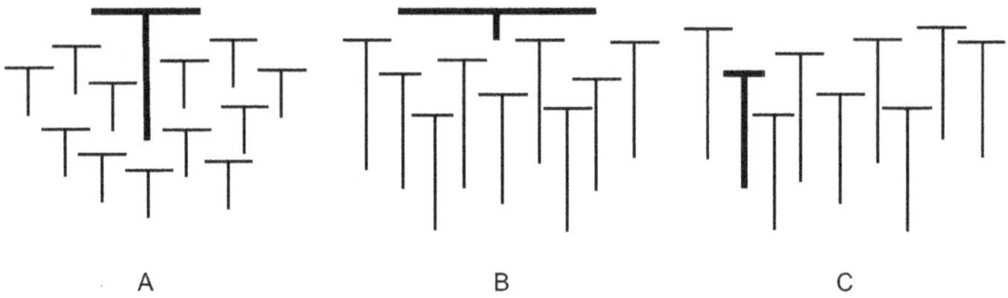

Fig. 4.11 General knowledge and expertise of managers and employees

general knowledge and a lot of expert knowledge. He or she is superior to his or her employees (thin bars) in every respect—the "master". That is why he or she is supposed to be the manager. The employees, on the other hand, are like the manager, just smaller. If an employee has a question or a problem, it is obvious to turn to the (superior) manager. Who else?

Constellation *B* differs from A in that, although the manager has considerably more general knowledge than the employee, he or she is technically inferior. He or she has the overview and sees the big picture, long-term, content wise and strategically. However, every employee has a deeper expert knowledge than the manager. This constellation can be compared to an orchestra in which each musician probably has better skills in playing his or her instrument than the conductor. But the conductor makes sure that the interaction of the experts leads to a great overall masterpiece. If in this constellation the individual employee has a question or a problem, he or she will not only turn to the manager but above all to the others. "Why should I ask my boss if I know someone who knows the answer?" In an ideal setting, the employees complement each other due to a diverse, complementary composition of expert knowledge.

Hierarchical, traditional organizations tend towards constellation *A* while agile organizations tend to identify more with constellation *B*. A major reason for this is the high level of uncertainty in the tasks, as described in the previous section. If something new is to be developed and experience is scarce, then an interdisciplinary team of experts is required. The manager cannot claim to have an answer to everything. This is simply no longer possible. If he or she pursues this claim after all, he or she will work long hours every day, will march into a burnout and in the end will not be a good manager.

In addition, a further variant *C* is conceivable, in which there is no superordinate, permanently installed manager. There are successful orchestras that do entirely without a conductor, such as the Italian orchestra Spira Mirabilis or the wonderful Orpheus Chamber Orchestra (Mukunda 2012), which has won several awards. In such a very democratic setting, depending on the situation, different musicians take the leading role, sometimes only for a few seconds. This case is certainly very rare, but should not go unmentioned, because it is not only theoretically conceivable but also practically possible, as some examples impressively prove.

4.4 The Dominant Understanding of Leadership

Even the simple distinction between constellation A and B has comprehensive implications not only for the adequate understanding of leadership—this will be discussed in the next section—but also for the orientation of HR-relevant topics. Classic top-down performance review or assessment of potential may work in constellation A, but in situation B it definitely only works to a very limited extent. At A, learning is initiated by the manager. The leader may himself act as a teacher (master). At B, employees learn above all from each other. If case C (no manager) prevails in a company or in a sub-area, numerous traditional HR concepts, which obviously provide for decisions and judgements by managers would simply be inconceivable.

Boss, Coach, Partner or Enabler

As already indicated, the constellations just described have a considerable influence on which understanding of leadership may appear to be adequate. Four different *leadership roles* are therefore briefly described below. Behind every role there is a certain understanding of leadership. The traditionally most widespread role might be that of the *boss* or ruler. This term is deliberately chosen here because it describes exactly what it is all about, even in everyday language use. In his or her role as a manager, the boss primarily asks him or herself the question, "How do I get my employees to do what I want them to do?" It is that simple. To achieve this, you have to motivate and control "your" employees, give clear instructions, make decisions and sometimes even punish them. So, or something like that, a boss understands his or her role. It seems as if this understanding of leadership corresponds almost to the stereotypical idea of what constitutes a supervisor. In my lectures, I regularly ask my students to write three things on a piece of paper that a supervisor typically does. The results reflect exactly this picture: making decisions, giving instructions, rewarding, motivating, controlling, giving feedback, etc. In addition to this role of the boss, however, at least three other roles can be distinguished, namely that of the coach, the partner and the enabler (see Fig. 4.12).

The easiest way to understand these roles is to look at a very simple, everyday case. Imagine, an employee needs a decision, A or B. First of all, an employee can of course make the decision him or herself. But if he or she turns to the manager and the manager acts as boss, then he or she will make a decision and inform the employee—"Do B, not A".

If the manager acts as a *coach*, he or she will leave the responsibility with the employee and react with questions, "How would you decide? What would be the advantage of A, and what of B? Who would you have to talk to in order to better assess which alternative is the better one? Is there also a third option C?" Some great leaders use a simple technique to respond to questions asked by employees: When an employee comes to the manager with a question, the employee gets three questions back and one of them really does a lot of work. A coach believes that the employee knows the answer or at least has the potential to find the right answer him or herself.

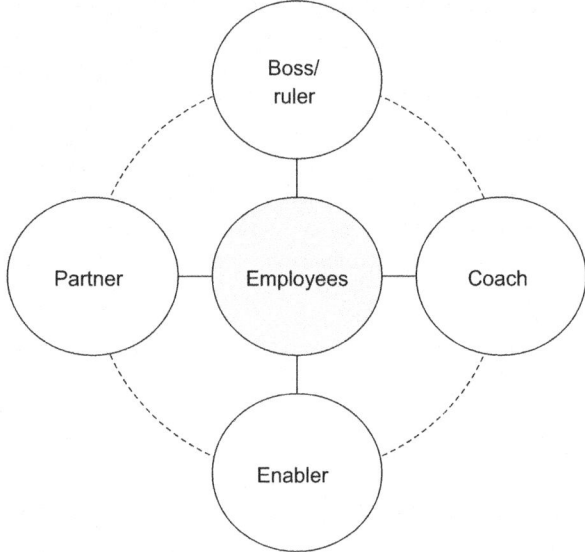

Fig. 4.12 Possible dominant leadership roles (first published in Trost 2017, Unter den Erwartungen. Wiley. p. 83)

This is partly due to the idea that the employees themselves have more expertise than their respective supervisor (constellation B in Fig. 4.11). The coach assumes that whenever he or she makes a decision as a manager or solves a problem, he or she deprives the employee of an important learning opportunity and thus of the important chance to experience self-efficacy. Coaches therefore write short e-mails—"What do you think?". In the long run, coaches receive fewer e-mails from their employees than bosses.

An executive who acts as a *partner* sees him or herself in a certain way as a normal, equal member of his team. You act at eye level. If a decision is needed, the partner will look for a solution together with his or her colleagues. "What do *we* want to do?" "Let's think *together* about what is the right decision for *us*". One can understand a leader who acts as a partner rather than a kind of speaker, similar to the dean of a faculty or the class representative. He or she represents the team to higher levels. These managers are often elected by their colleagues for a certain period of time. A habitus of power, subordination and superiority is completely alien to these managers and would not be accepted by the team members anyway.

Some say, that good leadership is about making sure all employees have the framework conditions they need to do a good job and develop their potential. Leaders who think this way see themselves as *enablers*. In the sense of the inverted pyramid already described, they interpret their role as that of a service provider towards their employees. In some industries there has never been a different understanding of leadership. Think, for example, of sport, art or literature. Athletes, musicians and some authors also have managers. However, their task is not to tell the guided ones what he or she has to do in a particular situation, but to ensure that the guided ones can do what he or she does best. The manager merely takes care of the necessary framework conditions.

Strictly speaking, and for the sake of completeness, the four roles just described would have to be supplemented by a fifth one. It is indicated in Fig. 4.12 by the middle circle, the "employees" themselves and describes a form of leadership without really leading. Here the responsibility is completely transferred to the employee or the employees of a team. Here the manager signals that he or she does not want to have anything to do with certain issues—"Please take care of it. I do not want to have anything to do with it and do me the favour of not asking my opinion, advice or permission here".

Good managers know their dominant role, which they normally play. They communicate this to their employees and colleagues in a very clear way. But good managers also know when and to whom they should slip into other roles. Depending on the situation, the partner also acts as the boss and then returns to the partner role. When I coach executives, I regularly ask my coachees to weight the different roles with points, "If you had to describe your leadership role, how would you distribute ten points among the different roles?" The discussion is also exciting when I ask my coachees to make this assessment for their own leaders on the one hand and on the other to describe what expectations their employees might address to them. The results usually provide an astonishingly valuable basis for further discussion of the question of how a manager is effective or wants to be effective.

If you are looking for bosses, you will find them above all in traditional, hierarchical organizations. Hardly any other characteristic is so closely connected with hierarchical understanding as this special leadership role. It is compatible with the Theory X previously described. In agile organizations the coach, the partner or the enabler are more at home.

As we will see in chapters to follow, the understanding of leadership also has a considerable influence on almost all HR-relevant issues. Douglas McGregor has already pointed out that a coach never judges. Anyone who has the future and salary of an employee at their disposal by means of a performance evaluation can never act as a coach or partner towards this employee. This aspect alone indicates how comprehensive the HR-related implications of the understanding of leadership are.

Autonomy and Trust

The leadership roles described above are closely linked to *trust*. Now one may object that trust is something that has its place among friends, in the family or in the support group, but not in the hard business. Presumably, no student of business management has so far taken a class in the subject of trust. Trust appears to many to be a soft, irrational construct. Anyone who thinks in this way misjudges the great significance of this important social phenomenon. It is about the assumption of being able to predict the behaviour of others without knowing for certain that this behaviour will actually happen. In this respect, trust can to some extent replace formal rules, formal agreements, but also institutional constraints and control.

Life and living together would not be possible without trust. The great German sociologist Niklas Luhmann (2000) has dealt comprehensively and scientifically with this phenomenon. If one were to try to summarize his findings in a single sentence, one would come to the conclusion that *trust reduces social complexity*. That is a wonderful sentence. Customer-supplier relationships become easier when they are based to some extent on trust. The same applies to the relationship between managers and employees or the relationship between employees and teams.

Trust manifests itself institutionally in the freedom of choice and personal responsibility of employees and teams. In addition, trust affects working conditions, *autonomy* and employees' scope of action. In classic industrial and organizational psychology, this scope of action describes a space consisting of three independent dimensions, as shown graphically in Fig. 4.13.

Big scope for action stands for flexible working conditions. Employees decide for themselves *where* they work (flexible workplace), *when* they work (flexible working hours) and with *whom* they work (flexible organization). All this presupposes a high degree of trust, which is why, for example, in the case of the highest form of working time autonomy, we also speak of trust-based working hours (cf. also Sect. 10.1).

Especially those companies and divisions that rely on new ideas and innovation are well advised to offer their employees a high degree of autonomy. We know, partly from scientific studies, but also from personal experience, that people often have the best ideas when they are not in their regular work setting: on holiday, on the way home, on weekends while exercising, while showering, sometimes even sleeping. We even know that boring meetings and congresses are more conducive to creativity than those events that demand concentration and constant engagement. If one takes these considerations seriously, one comes to the conclusion that traditional, fixed working environments are obviously not conducive to what many employees are paid for. In some ways, traditional, fixed working conditions can discourage employees from doing their jobs being creative.

Fig. 4.13 Scope for action

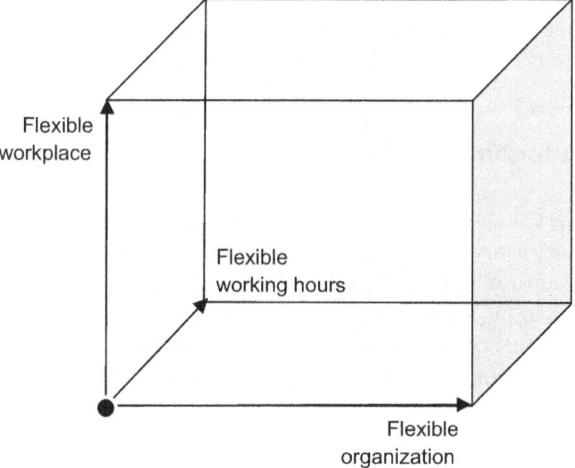

While traditional, hierarchical companies tend to rely on their employees being at their workplace at specific and controlled times, agile companies rather rely on personal responsibility, trust and self-control. Agile companies are confronted with a significantly higher complexity than hierarchical, static companies. In this respect, it makes sense to reduce complexity through trust in order to be able to concentrate on the essentials. Agile organizations try to keep the probability of accidental, informal encounters between employees with different roles and functions as high as possible. As we will see, these considerations have implications not only for key HR topics, such as working time or forms of collaboration, but even for issues of architecture and the physical working environment.

4.5 Organization, Dynamics and Commitment

The fourth category of relevant framework conditions deals with the question of organization and thus with the cooperation and mutual commitment of managers, employees, teams and customers. How high is the degree of division of labour and what is the relationship between the tasks? A central aspect will be the commitment and dedication of employees and teams. Are employees committed to higher authorities or to their colleagues and customers, internally as well as externally?

Division of Labour and Task Dynamics

The division of labour and the division of entire organizations into so-called *departments* has led to an enormous increase in efficiency in numerous organizations over decades. Each employee, each team concentrated solely on their respective task. These individual tasks were then integrated at a higher level. It was right for an employee to concentrate solely on assembling a single component, for example, as long as someone knew how this isolated task could be integrated into the manufacture of a complete product or service. This total output was nothing other than the sum of isolated individual outputs (see Fig. 4.14).

In agile organizations, on the other hand, a dynamic of interdependent tasks is assumed—connected products require connected organizations. In contrast to what is shown in Fig. 4.14 tasks are in a cybernetic interrelation with each other, as graphically outlined in Fig. 4.15. These multiple interrelations might be extremely complex.

The different circles in Fig. 4.15 stand for individual tasks. The arrows in turn symbolize internal customer-supplier relationships. The output of one task is at the same time the input for another task. In addition, there are critical relations (solid

$$\bigcirc + \bigcirc + \bigcirc + \bigcirc + \bigcirc + \bigcirc$$

Fig. 4.14 The total output as the sum of isolated individual contributions

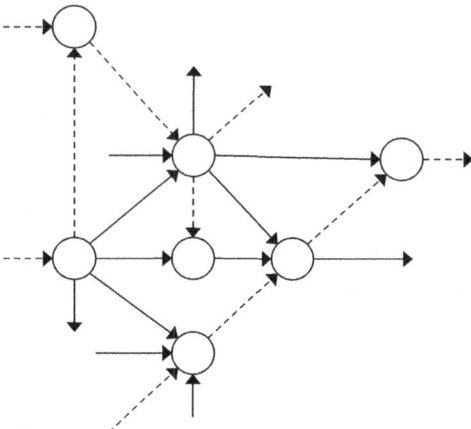

Fig. 4.15 Cybernetic interrelation of interdependent tasks (Trost 2017)

arrows) and those that are rather uncritical (dashed arrows). The special thing about this constellation of high *task dynamics,* is among other things, that the individual employee can only be successful if the interaction functions well overall. In my lectures I like explaining the division of labour constellation with a galley, in which the overall performance of the ship results from the sum of the coordinated individual efforts. The constellation with high task dynamics can rather be compared to a football team. Here, the individual player can only win if the system of the team as a whole works better than the opponent's system.

In a setting of divided labour it is easier to assess the individual performance of employees on the basis of the results than in the case of high task dynamics. Incentivising individual performance in the context of high task dynamics can even be dysfunctional and foment competition among employees where cooperation and exchange would be critical to success. These two examples show the great importance of the task context with regard to HR-relevant topics.

Consequences and Commitment

If you ask an employee the simple question of what he or she is doing to determine whether he or she has done a good job, you can expect one of two opposing answers. Answer *A* could be, "I have done a good job when my manager is satisfied with the results of my work". Presumably, especially in hierarchically managed companies, a large number of employees thinks so, even if they would not admit it on the spot. While they are working on something, a presentation, a report, a concept, they ask themselves tacitly: "Will my boss like that? What if she is not happy with it?" In this case, employees are primarily committed to their managers. The consequences of one's own work result from the reactions of the direct manager. Once you have done things to the satisfaction of the manager, you experience praise, recognition,

4.5 Organization, Dynamics and Commitment

possibly a bonus and, at the end of the year, a positive evaluation in the annual performance appraisal. If the manager is not satisfied, then criticism, possibly punishment or a bad, formal evaluation is to be counted on. This is how it works in hierarchically managed companies. The customer does not play a role in this thinking in the first place. However, if a customer should suddenly speak critically to the employee, he usually receives the answer, "I can't do anything about it. It comes from above". This constellation can hardly be better summed up. It is shown as constellation A in Fig. 4.16.

The agile counter-project is shown on the right side of Fig. 4.16. In this constellation (B), employees or teams are primarily committed to their customers, both internally and externally. "I have done a good job when my customer is happy" corresponds to answer B of the question formulated at the beginning. The order comes from the customer. Therefore, the consequences come from the customer in the form of praise, criticism or feedback, which one actively catches up with. In this setting, the manager only has the task of moderating this relationship between employee, team and customer, "You do not have to ask me [the manager] whether I think this idea is good. Who is the customer of your idea? Have you talked to the customers yet? What does the customer say about this?"

What appears to be a comparatively simple consideration here essentially concerns a fundamental problem of organization. Albert Bandura, one of the world's leading psychologists in the field of motivation and learning, emphasized the importance of self-efficacy like no other. Bandura (1997) explains the conviction of being able to do something meaningful for others on one's own free will as one of the most important sources not only of motivation and fulfilment but also of learning itself. Particularly in organizations with a high division of labour and a commitment upwards, employees are deprived of precisely this basis. It simply does not matter. The employee does what he or she is told, and he or she gets paid for it. The explicit and psychological contract is only based on this. However, self-efficacy and the associated motivation, fulfilment, meaningfulness and learning opportunities require

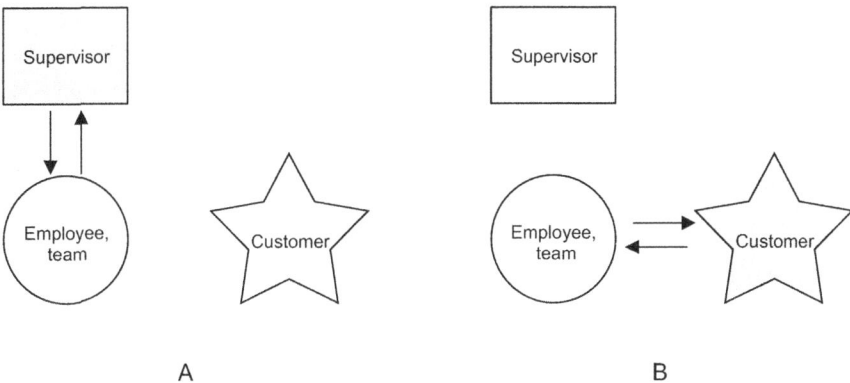

Fig. 4.16 The commitment of employees and teams

that employees add value for others. Nothing else means "work." Employees have to do this with a sense of personal responsibility. But above all, they must experience the consequences of their thoughts and actions.

All companies thinking about agility will agree that they want less silos but more lateral collaboration and networks. They do this for the sole reason mentioned above: teams and employees should experience the consequences of their decisions and activities directly. Engineers should experience directly how their planning is received in production. Marketing people should see whether and how their material works in sales. Colleagues from the headquarters should be able to feel for themselves what their central policies are doing in the branch offices. Everything can be traced back to the simple formula, according to which networks enable and promote the experience of consequences.

Now HR looks different in a connected organization, in which employees and teams experience the consequences of their actions, than in a hierarchical organization with a division of labour and sheltered silos. Assessment, feedback, potential recognition, learning, incentives and many other topics have at least the chance to be thought horizontally, to the left and to the right in network-like organizations. Agile organizations explicitly strive for it. Therefore, a talented employee in these companies is only accepted as a talent if the others on the same level see him or her the same way and not just the management team one or more levels above. Job rotation, mixed project teams, informal working groups, so-called "communities of practice" or Working Out Loud. These are all concepts that have the primary purpose of promoting lateral networks. Learning is understood as an activity of self-directed exchange between colleagues. It is called social learning. These few examples should suffice at this point.

4.6 Current and Future Status

In the previous sections, twelve dimensions of cultural and structural framework conditions, divided into four categories, were described. It would go too far to consider these dimensions as equal or even independent from each other. Obviously, they are not. Some dimensions, such as the image of man or lateral versus horizontal commitment, are very generic and of overriding importance, while others are more specific. It is also obvious that some dimensions co-vary, even one dimension might be seen as the cause of another dimension. In this respect, this list should not be considered as too scientific overall. In any case, they have proved to be very helpful in practice.

Based on these dimensions, executives can assess where their company currently stands, and where they want to go in the future. It can also be helpful here to involve managers and employees, at least when it comes to assessing the current situation. In Fig. 4.17 once more all dimensions are shown at a glance. For example, a simple presentation of this kind, in which all relevant dimensions are strikingly compared, can help in the context of a workshop to make a joint classification of the current situation and to develop an idea of the future.

4.6 Current and Future Status

	Hierarchical world	Agile World	
	Orientation towards statically described employee requirements	Individuality and individual life plans are appreciated	
	Internal esteem rises with the hierarchy level	Employees are the "true heroes" (inverted pyramid)	
	Tendency towards a culture of control and mistrust.	Tendency to have a culture of openness and trust	
	Employees (highly available) depend on their employer	The company is dependent on its (hard-to-replace) employees	
	As a company you try to get better every year in what you do (static)	You try to destroy what already exists by new (disruptive) products and services	
	Outcomes and processes of small task are certain and clearly described	Outcomes and processes of projects are uncertain and need to be developed iteratively	
	Things are thought (planned) through to the end before action is taken	Things are developed iteratively in short cycles.	
	Leaders are the ultimate experts	Employees are the real experts	
	Managers act primarily as "bosses" - "Employees do what I want"	Managers act primarily as coaches, partners or enablers	
	Employees act according to standards and instructions	Employees decide on their own responsibility (much scope of action)	
	Tasks are performed independently of each other within a divided labour	The tasks and employees/teams are highly interdependent (dynamic)	
	Employees are primarily committed to their managers	Above all, teams are committed to their colleagues and customers.	

Fig. 4.17 Overview of all dimensions of structural and cultural framework conditions

References

Abrahamson S, Ryder P, Unterberg B (2013) Crowdstorm. The future of innovation, ideas and problem solving. Wiley, Hoboken
Bandura A (1997) Self-efficacy. The exercise of control. Freeman, New York
Christensen CM (1997) The innovator's dilemma. Harvard Business School Press, Boston
Fleishman EA (1991) Taxonomic efforts in the description of leader behavior: a synthesis and functional interpretation. Leadersh Q 2:245–278
Kotter JP (2014) Accelerate. Harvard Business Press, Boston
Laloux F (2014) Reinventing organizations: a guide to creating organizations inspired by the next stage in human consciousness. Nelson Parker, Brussels
Luhmann N (2000) Vertrauen. Ein Mechanismus der Reduktion sozialer Komplexität. UTB, Stuttgart
McGregor D (1960) The human side of enterprise. McGraw-Hill, New York
Mukunda G (2012) Leaders do not matter (most of the time). Harv Bus Rev Blogs. https://hbr.org/2012/08/leaders-dont-matter-most-of-th.html
Project Management Institute (2013) A guide to the Project Management Body of Knowledge (PMBOK® Guide). Project Management Institute, Inc, Newtown Square
Sims C, Johnson HL (2011) The elements of scrum. DyMaxicon, Foster City
Trost A (2017) The end of performance appraisal. A practitioners' guide to alternatives in agile organizations. Springer, Heidelberg
Weltz F, Ortmann RG (1992) Das Softwareprojekt: Projektmanagement in der Praxis. Campus, Frankfurt/M

Talent Acquisition and Selection

5

Even at the end of the last century, the topic of *talent acquisition* was still based on completely different workforce demands in the light of a very different labour market situation. Recruitment primarily meant the placement of job advertisements paired with a few advertising measures. Personnel selection as part of recruitment was primarily concerned with the valid, reliable and objective prediction of future performance. All this has changed completely. When recruitment is considered today, concepts such as employer branding, active sourcing, talent relationship management, candidate experience etc. appear on the radar. And even the selection of personnel no longer deals with the one-sided selection decision of the company. Candidates also make decisions for or against an employer. And when it comes to hard-to-fill positions, the candidate's decision is particularly important. All this puts a new, sometimes unusual light on the topics of talent acquisition and selection. In the end, this also applies to the introduction or integration of new employees in the context of onboarding. For a long time now this is seen as much more than just a quick technical introduction.

In contrast to most of the topics discussed below, the topics of talent acquisition and selection are not directly related to the cultural and structural framework conditions. This means that the strategic dimensions presented here can be considered regardless of whether a company is striving for stability or agility. An increasing importance of these topics results with certainty from digitization. More and more companies are recognizing dramatically growing needs, for example in the area of software development, for which there are not enough people available in the labour market.

5.1 Employer Branding

In most companies, the development of an *employer brand* is an answer to the increasing shortage of skilled workers. We call all measures to develop an employer brand *employer branding* (Trost 2014).

Focus on Candidate or on Requirements

Employer branding is based on the idea that employers must convince potential candidates in tight labour markets. In the past one was used to the opposite. Applicants had to convince employers to be accepted by the employer in the end. In this respect, the development of an employer brand always requires a high degree of appreciation towards potential candidates. This, in turn, goes hand in hand with appreciation of one's own employees, as described in Sect. 4.2. Whether this esteem is already a lived reality can be seen immediately by looking at the *job advertisements* of a company. Do the demands or requirements on the applicant dominate? Do you put your own expectations as an employer in the foreground? Or do you primarily find arguments for why a potential applicant should be interested in a job or an employer? The latter signals appreciation at least at this point. The starting point for this relationship between "what do we want" and "what do we offer" has its practical origin already in the briefing interview with the business line when it comes to preparing the advertisement. How much time is spent on the first question and how much time on the second?

If you take a look at most *job advertisements*, for example on job boards or on the career pages of most companies, you will immediately notice that two topics still dominate job advertisements, namely the responsibilities associated with the job and the requirements that a suitable candidate should meet. The strategic direction in these cases is clear:

> In our job advertisements, we primarily communicate the responsibilities and requirements associated with the position in question. (1-1)

This approach is somewhat arrogant. Imagine a candidate presenting himself in this way and first articulating his expectations in his cover letter, and finally mentioning in a casual sentence why he thinks he is the right candidate. One would reject this applicant instantly due to arrogant behaviour. Most companies, on the other hand, act in exactly the same way. They put their own wish list in the foreground.

Employers who choose to focus on the candidate's perspective act in a completely different way. In their advertisements, they convey a short version of what we call an *employee value proposition*, a convincing answer to the question of why a motivated, talented and qualified candidate should be interested in this particular job.

> In our job advertisements, we primarily provide reasons why a suitable candidate should be interested in the job. (1-2)

Of course, this strategy will also convey requirements and responsibilities, but with more restraint and a reference to further information, which will be made available to the interested candidate in a second step.

Fig. 5.1 The simplified logic of an Employee Value Proposition (EVP)

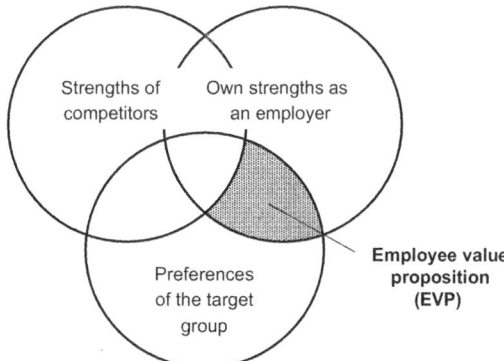

The Employee Value Proposition as the Core of any Employer Brand

A core element of employer branding is to develop a promise, which appears attractive in the eyes of the relevant target groups and communicates the strengths of the employer in an authentic way. In addition, this promise should differentiate itself from the strengths of other competitors in the labour market. This is also referred to as *employer positioning*. Basically, the employer's promise is nothing more than a convincing answer to the question of a suitable, motivated candidate, "Why should I work in your company?" In practice, the term *employee value proposition (EVP)* has also established itself for this purpose, a terminology first brought to consciousness by the authors of the legendary book "The War for Talent" by Michaels et al. (2001). The development of this EVP is usually preceded by a comprehensive reflection of one's own strengths as an employer, the preferences of relevant target groups and the peculiarities of competitors (see Fig. 5.1).

Interviews and focus groups are conducted with current, new and former employees, managers, executives and applicants. Employer studies are used or career pages of other companies are studied in detail. Then assessments of the strengths of the competitors, their own strengths as employers and the preferences of the target group are systematically compared. In the end, the EVP reflects those aspects that one can offer as an employer, which at the same time addresses the preferences of the target groups and where competition has less to offer. The EVP is then effectively communicated within the framework of suitable campaigns via target group-relevant channels such as the career website, image ads and videos or via social media channels.

Reach

Recently I had an interesting conversation with the CEO of a leading automotive supplier. He presented me with the results of a study in which a large number of companies in the automotive industry were shown in a two-dimensional diagram with regard to their level of both awareness and popularity. The study was based on a survey of students from a wide variety of disciplines from all over Germany. At the top right were the usual, known and popular brands: Bosch, Porsche, BMW, etc. His company was in the more lower left bottom corner. He then reached for a thick pencil and showed where he would like to see "his" company in 3 years: somewhere in the upper right corner. That was a strategic announcement. The face colour of the HR director next to us turned increasingly more pale from minute to minute at that moment. Now the question is, do you really want to do this? Does that even make any sense? The underlying strategic statement in this case is as follows:

> We want to be known and liked as an attractive employer in the labour market as a whole. Basically, everyone should want to work for us. (2-1)

This strategic alignment of an employer brand requires an enormous HR marketing budget, especially in this case. Is this budget even available? This budget must be particularly high if the company itself does not have a strong brand, which could be the case with many hidden champions, for example. There is also the risk of significantly increasing the number of applications. One might be happy about that at first. Each further application also requires administrative effort and increases the probability of unsuitable applicants. The latter is accompanied by cancellations, which could be a problem if you do not want to lose these people as customers.

An alternative could be to focus on bottleneck functions when developing an employer brand. As already explained in Sect. 3.3 these are critical target functions with a high workforce demand on the one hand, but on the other hand difficult to meet due to current and future labour market conditions. Let us think, for example, of truck drivers in the logistics industry, or the nursing sector in senior citizens' facilities or software developers in those companies that dare to make a move towards digitization.

If you build an employer brand that only concentrates on those relevant target groups that are suitable for bottleneck functions, you will arrive at a completely different, strategic statement:

> We do not want to be attractive to everyone at all. Only with certain selected target groups do we want to appear on the radar as an attractive employer. (2-2)

The concept of the so-called *persona* is receiving increasing attention here (Dion and Arnould 2016). Instead of describing a target group on the basis of technical requirements, one sketches their employer and media preferences, life ideas, attitudes, preferences, habits, social contexts in the most concise way possible. Finally, if one tries to bring all these aspects comprehensibly to the point, one ends up with a persona, a prototypical description of a candidate that one wants to reach at the end. From this, measures are derived as to how one wants to reach one's target group. Approaches that actually originate from police investigation, *profiling*, go in a similar direction. Transferred to talent acquisition, the question here is how the target persons you want to reach and attract in the end really are, what moves them or where they are.

Choosing one or the other strategic direction with regard to the reach of an employer brand sometimes has massive implications with regard to the effort required and its impact. One should be aware of that.

The Degree of Differentiation

When more and more companies discovered the topic of employer branding at the beginning of this century, the development of a *general* employer brand was usually the focus of interest. In addition to the corporate brand, a promise should also be developed and conveyed that communicates the special attributes of the company as an employer as a whole. Adidas has developed *one* employer brand. Audi has built *one* employer brand. The same applies to numerous other companies (see Trost 2013). It was tacitly assumed that the underlying EVP should represent an employer in its entirety.

> Our employee value proposition represents us as one employer to all relevant target groups. We have only one core proposition to which we are fully committed. (3-1)

The advantage of this strategic priority is certainly that at the end one appears with uniform visual and textual elements and the same claim or slogan, regardless of which function or which job is to be marketed. The difficulty of this approach, on the other hand, is to find a common denominator where there is ultimately a risk of a lack of differentiation from other employers, which is often expressed in a certain arbitrariness. In the marketing language, this can also be referred to as a minor brand differentiation or a *branded house* (see Fig. 5.2).

In the case of a branded house, one pursues the establishment of a dominating brand core (this is indicated by the grey circle in Fig. 5.2). When marketing individual functions or jobs, adjustments are made that are as marginal as possible—a certain image motif, an additional argument in addition to the overarching promise.

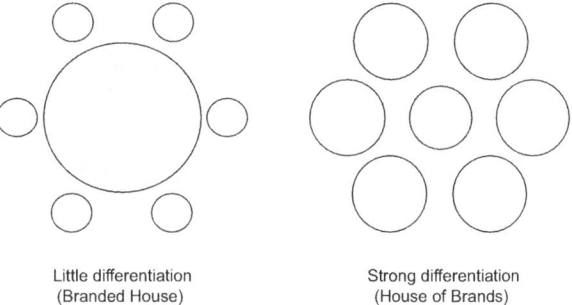

Fig. 5.2 Low versus strong differentiation of the employer brand

Little differentiation (Branded House)

Strong differentiation (House of Brands)

The strategic orientation is different when a kind of *house of brands* is pursued. Here a strong differentiation is aimed at in the development of the various EVPs, while reference is made to a rather small, common brand core.

> We have developed a separate employee value proposition for each critical target function because we have to reach heterogeneous target groups. A single proposition would not do justice to diversity. (3-2)

The advantages and disadvantages of the strategy of strong differentiation is complementary to the strategy of low differentiation. The outstanding argument for strong differentiation can be seen in the fact that the special features of individual jobs and functions can be developed and transported in a much more accentuated way. The bottom line, when deciding for or against strong differentiation, is always whether target groups can be reached and convinced primarily through the employer itself or through the respective jobs.

The Right Amplitude

As part of an own employer branding project for a large, yet surprisingly unknown company, the head of the communications department confessed the following to me, "I get paid for *not* appearing in the public media. That is what our CEO wants. Every time the name of our company appears in any local newspaper, I immediately get into trouble with the CEO". Over the years I have learned that this is not an isolated case. Often, it is the public restraint, modesty and discretion that are enormously important for family-run companies. They want to avoid public debates about what they are doing, because it distracts from value-adding work. Some founders can not forget the German RAF terror of the seventies and therefore do not want to draw attention to themselves, their company or their family. How is employer branding possible given such way of thinking? In this case, the strategic orientation of the employer brand might be as follows:

> We appear rather as quiet and discreet and are convincing, above all, in personal communication. We do not push but offer good reasons to everyone who might be interested. (4-2)

Of course, these companies need a convincing EVP. Only the way it is communicated has a special character. You act in a personal way, focused and in direct exchange. These companies like the adjective "minimally invasive" in this context. It is obvious that this approach works best when companies are looking for a small reach.

Other companies operate completely differently. They want to cause a sensation, increase their popularity and this in a spectacular and unforgettable way. The strategic statement then sounds more like this:

> In order to be perceived as an attractive employer, we display the fireworks. We appear as a whole, very self-confident, and visible from afar. (4-1)

At the beginning of an employer branding project, this should also be considered carefully and with the necessary empathy. The plan to display the fireworks visible from afar will not find favour, whether one likes it or not, in those companies that prefer modesty and restraint.

Pure Advertising?

Employer branding takes place in numerous companies as follows. You deal in some way with your relevant target groups, reflect on internal strengths and research what your competitors have to offer. After a few workshops, a somehow formulated EVP is on the table, which is finally approved by the management and then put into the hands of a creative agency. The agency in turn develops creative elements with uniform text and image language in various formats—advertisements, banners, booth stands, maps, brochures, trade fair material, etc. The agency also develops creative elements for the advertising industry. All this aims at presenting the employer in a uniform and attractive way in different communication channels and situations. There is nothing wrong with that at first. For most companies, it has already been a great step forward in recent years to present themselves more professionally and attractively as employers. In a way, this exercise is an important basis that companies can hardly do without in the face of competitive labour markets. Those who confine themselves to this basis implicitly or explicitly follow the strategic premise:

> In employer branding, we focus on the external presentation of our company as an attractive employer. (5-1)

But what happens if a potential applicant or candidate actually starts to take an interest in an employer and dives deeper into the reality of that company? This person may apply via the online application portal set up for this purpose. The person comes into direct contact with employees, managers and HR professionals. He or she sees and experiences the company from the inside, for example during an interview. Whenever a person comes into personal contact with the employer in any way, we refer to these situations as *touchpoints*. These situations always transported something about the company. If these touchpoints are taken into consideration, the employer brand strategy goes well beyond the mere external appearance.

> We convey a continuous candidate experience in all touchpoints in which candidates come into contact with us. (5-2)

The best examples of integrated brand strategies do not come from the field of employer branding. Apple is one of the world's most expensive brands. Hardly any other company has mastered the art of conveying a consistent customer experience as perfectly as this company. All touchpoints with Apple share the same experience, whether you are dealing with Apple stores, product packaging, the products themselves, or Apple's presence on the Internet.

Employer Branding from the Inside

For the sake of continuity, I will also begin this section with a short anecdote. The managing director of a leading sportswear manufacturer explained to me in a very lively conversation: "I do not need such nonsense [original sound] as 'employer branding' or as you call it here. I treat the staff neatly. And with my help, word gets around". Referring to the classical logic of marketing and the well-known four Ps, this entrepreneur concentrates less on the promotion P but rather on the product P, in this particular case paired with an effective measure on public relation (employer PR), the attempt to spread one's own employer attractiveness via public media. His strategic statement could be formulated as follows:

> We do not give serious thought to systematic employer positioning. We try to be an attractive employer. The rest will come by itself. (6-2)

This, too, is at least a strategic option that is more reminiscent of the Hire & Pay variant than of employer branding in the context of institutionalized HR. In the latter case, the following alternative is sought, as explained at the beginning:

> We have a strategically developed, well-formulated employer positioning based on comprehensive analyses, which is specifically communicated to relevant target groups. (6-1)

The question of whether an employer follows an elaborate employer positioning based on analyses or not is of particular relevance when it comes to external communication. To what extent should anything that will be transported into the labour market follow a uniform and controlled language and how does this translate in the use of social media? With this particular topic this subchapter closes.

The Role of Social Media

For several years now, it has been observed that employees operate their own profiles on the widespread social media. They move to platforms such as *Facebook*, *Twitter* or *Instagram*. In addition, many maintain their presence on career networks such as *LinkedIn*. Depending on the platform, the content posted by employees is either more private or professional. While on platforms such as Facebook or Instagram private content is usually shared, content on LinkedIn is supposed to be professional content. Whenever employees communicate something, they also provide more or less insights into their professional environment, which offers a kind of reflection of their respective employer. As a company, this may be seen as an opportunity or a threat. The opportunity, of course, lies in seeing employees as *brand ambassadors*. They represent your company and convey authentic insights to the outside world. At the same time, many companies do not want their employees to disseminate content, which, from the company's point of view, should not reach the outside world. The range of sensitive content is very broad. Think here of confidential information (e.g., new product developments, financial matters) or interpersonal matters, which should better be dealt with in a personal exchange (e.g., differences of opinion). Finally, this issue also touches on data protection issues. Some colleagues do not want to see their behaviour at the company Christmas party publicly documented. Companies that on the one hand use social media as a communication channel but at the same time want to keep the aforementioned threats to a minimum tend towards the following strategic premise:

> The use of social media is always carried out by a central authority (e.g., communications department). In this way, we ensure that the published content is adequate. (7-1)

However, in pursuing this strategic direction, companies pay the price of limited authenticity. In my lecture, I show students from time to time different presences of employers for example on Facebook paired with the question, "Who might post the contents in the respective company". Whether the students are right or wrong, at the end I can't judge. However, it is noticeable that all those present very quickly agree on whether the content comes from a central instance or from the employees themselves. Apparently they have a very fine instinct for this. Content that is posted by the communication department or by the HR marketing team obviously feels embellished, smoothed, polished, artificial or somehow even fake. This does not invite users to post comments, to like the content or even share it. And, this form of central communication also poses considerable challenges for internal social media managers. Their everyday life is characterized by not only running after possible content, but also gathering answers from the respective company divisions to incoming user questions. On the one hand, this is associated with a high coordinative effort and, on the other hand, it costs time that one does not have in the context of social media. Users today expect answers in real time—not within a few hours but minutes.

It is therefore not surprising that precisely those companies that trust their employees pursue the opposite strategy. In the sense of less controlled or trusted communication, they encourage their employees to use social media on their own responsibility and to share those contents that they themselves consider adequate.

> We want our employees to be able to communicate independently about their employer via social media. This is how we achieve authenticity. (7-2)

Both strategic options, central and trusted communication, are graphically illustrated in Fig. 5.3. The large grey circle stands for the outside world (e.g., the external labour market) the internal circle stands for the company and their employees (black dots). There is a white dot in the centre. It symbolizes a central instance. The arrows stand for communication.

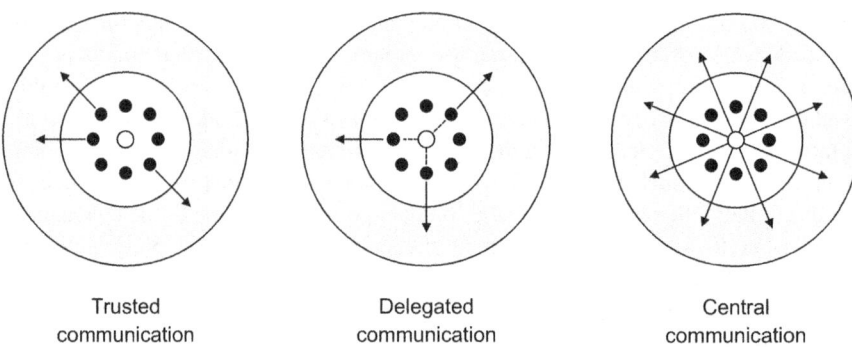

| Trusted communication | Delegated communication | Central communication |

Fig. 5.3 Possibilities of an internal division of roles in the use of social media

In addition to the already presented strategic possibilities of trusted and central communication, a third option is indicated in Fig. 5.3, namely that of delegated communication. This option represents for many companies a viable balance between control and authenticity. Selected employees post content on their own responsibility. Their activities are moderated by a central instance. Typical examples can be found in connection with the recruitment of trainees. Here, companies select a small group of trainees, arm them with smartphones and support them in maintaining the appropriate channels.

Employer Branding Strategy

The dimensions of a strategic orientation described in this subchapter (see Fig. 5.4) result in what can be described as an *employer branding strategy*. In any case, it is essential to be clear about this at the very beginning, before starting any analyses, activities, campaigns or the like. I have been practically involved with this topic for many years and got the impression that the awareness of how to strategically align the employer brand issue is seldom sufficiently present. In the following subchapter on the subject of candidate search, approach and retention, these considerations are taken up and deepened. In the end, these lead to what can be described as a *talent acquisition strategy*.

5.2 Sourcing, Approaching and Retaining Candidates

While employer branding is about convincingly attracting attention to yourself as an employer, sourcing for, approaching and retaining candidates focuses on how to find potential candidates and applicants, approach them and, if necessary, remain in long-term contact with them (Trost 2014). For this purpose, two extreme scenarios are presented first, namely the passive, vacancy-focused scenario and the active, candidate-focused scenario.

Focus in job advertisements	1-1 Requirements In our job advertisements, we primarily communicate the responsibilities and requirements associated with the position in question.	1-2 Employee value proposition In our job advertisements, we primarily provide reasons why a suitable candidate should be interested in the job.
Reach in the labour market	2-1 Large range We want to be known and liked as an attractive employer in the labour market as a whole. Basically, everyone should want to work for us.	2-2 Focused target groups We do not want to be attractive to everyone at all. Only with certain selected target groups do we want to appear on the radar as an attractive employer.
Differentiation of the employer value proposition	3-1 General Our employee value proposition represents us as one employer to all relevant target groups. We have only one core proposition to which we are fully committed.	3-2 Differentiated We have developed a separate employee value proposition for each critical target function because we have to reach heterogeneous target groups. A single proposition would not do justice to diversity.
Visibility of communication	4-1 Loud and dominant In order to be perceived as an attractive employer, we display the fireworks. We appear as a whole, very self-confident, and visible from afar.	4-2 Quiet and personal We appear as rather quiet and discreet and convince above all in personal communication. We do not urge but offer good reasons to everyone who might be interested.
Mediation of the employee value proposition	5-1 In the public image In employer branding, we focus on the external presentation of our company as an attractive employer.	5-2 Continuous experience We convey a continuous candidate experience in all touchpoints in which candidates come into contact with us.
Elaboration of the employee value proposition	6-1 Analysed and defined We have a strategically developed, well-formulated employer positioning based on comprehensive analyses, which is specifically communicated to relevant target groups.	6-2 Naturally from the inside We do not give serious thought to systematic employer positioning. We try to be an attractive employer. The rest will come by itself.
Use of social media	7-1 Central communication The use of social media is always carried out by a central authority (e.g. communications department). In this way, we ensure that the published content is adequate.	7-2 Trusted communication We want our employees to be able to communicate independently about their employer via social media. This is how we achieve authenticity.

Fig. 5.4 Overview of all strategic dimensions of employer branding

The Passive, Vacancy-Focused Scenario

Basically, this scenario describes a widespread approach as described in classical textbooks on human resources management under the traditional term "recruitment" (e.g., Dessler 2018). The starting point of the effort is an open *vacancy* that needs to be filled. The requirements are defined and translated into a job advertisement, which is then published in the relevant media and platforms. Then you wait for the incoming applications, which are then reviewed, evaluated and processed accordingly. Where the classic job advertisement fails, you engage an executive search consultancy. As soon as the position is successfully filled, the process is completed. One says goodbye to the unsuitable candidates. That is it, more or less. This approach is also referred to as *vacancy-focused* because vacancy is the centre of all activities here. The vacancy triggers the process, it represents the problem and if the vacancy is filled, the problem is solved.

> We search for candidates once we face an acute need. As soon as a vacancy is filled, the process is completed. (1-1)

This approach can be described as passive because one leans back to wait for things to happen after the job advertisement is published or the recruiter has started his or her work. Especially when using passive media, such as job advertisements, one relies on the existence of so-called actively seeking candidates, on people who are not only suitable but also actively looking for a new opportunity.

In fact, there are many companies and HR professionals who feel most comfortable with this approach. Behind this is often a form of modesty and restraint. To entice employees away from other employers through active poaching is a far cry from these companies. They consider this to be potentially unethical or even damaging to their business. After all, you do not want to make enemies of suppliers and customers. Therefore one prefers to rely on the initiative of the applicant "who wants to come to us of his own free will".

> In sourcing candidates we are above all cautious. We do not impose ourselves and rely on the initiative of interested applicants. Any form of aggressiveness would not correspond to our values. (2-1)

It is no coincidence that this approach is to be found above all in the centrally planning and controlling type of HR. There, the HR department is responsible for filling vacant positions, usually in conjunction with a recruiting department and the HR business partners with decentralized responsibility. It is not uncommon for colleagues in the HR organization to have an administrative view of things, manage incoming applications, organize job interviews, draft employment contracts, etc. This is often expected to be the case in the line of business. According to a division of labour, each division expects the other to fulfil its assigned tasks and responsibilities.

> Searching for and approaching candidates is primarily the task of the HR department. The departments take care of their own businesses. (3-1)

Before evaluating this approach, the alternative scenario should be outlined and the associated strategic statements should be presented. Subsequently, the two strategic orientations are compared and placed in the context of HR-relevant challenges.

The Active, Candidate Focused Scenario

When I took responsibility for global recruiting at SAP AG several years ago, I visited the talent acquisition team at the North American headquarter near Philadelphia. When I arrived one time for my first meeting with the local team, I met a group of real warriors, all extremely well trained, respectable men. "Alright Armin, you wanna talk about our recruiting strategy? So, here we go ...". Then it really took off and I found myself in a different world. We were talking about "massive targets, fast and aggressive attacks, kill the competitor, stretching KPIs", etc. Somewhat longingly I remembered my colleagues in the HR department in Germany and how nice they all where there. Above all, however, it was at this key moment, finally, that it became clear to me what the phrase "War for Talent" is all about. These guys were at war with Oracle or Microsoft. That was not HR, as I was used to, but a tough form of sales.

This notion of recruitment or *talent acquisition is* based on an understanding that potential candidates must be actively and directly approached. The assumption is consistently made that the suitable candidates are at best passive seekers, already have a job, but may be open to something new.

> We're heading straight for candidates. We take the "war for talent" literally. Our search strategies are cheeky, courageous, and sometimes at the limit of what is ethically and legally justifiable. (2-2)

Meanwhile the term *active sourcing* has become established for this approach. Common active sourcing approaches include *employee referral programs* (employees recruit employees) or searching for and contacting seemingly suitable candidates on career networks like LinkedIn. In addition, there are approaches that latently reach legal or ethical limits or even exceed the limits of good taste. These approaches are also called forms of *guerrilla recruiting*—somewhat evil, but comparatively effective on a small budget.

Active sourcing is hardly conceivable without the active participation of management. Indeed, in practice, the initiative for such pathways often comes from the departments rather than from colleagues in the HR department. For example, employee referral programs make explicit use of colleagues' networks. My own research has shown that this approach is extremely powerful. We were able to show that on average seven recommendations lead to three placements, a ratio that can rarely be achieved with any other instrument (Berberich and Trost 2012). Addressing candidates via LinkedIn is more likely to be successful if it is done by representatives from management than by a colleague from HR or a executive search consultant. The latter in turn depends on the reputation of the consultancy. A Siemens manager recently got to the point when he proclaimed for his company that Siemens had 350,000 recruiters.

> With us every employee is a recruiter at the same time. When looking for and approaching candidates, we consistently rely on the networks and commitment of all our colleagues. (3-2)

Active sourcing with active involvement of the business line is conceivable above all in the case of an HR type that relies on the power of the line. Here, employees and managers take over responsibility for recruiting new colleagues. They are enabled and accompanied by the HR function. Especially in agile organizations it is important that employees, teams and executives experience the consequences of their actions (see Sect. 4.5). When departments themselves are responsible for recruiting new colleagues, they immediately experience the consequences of their efforts, but also the consequences of their possible passivity.

The active, *candidate-focused* approach not only searches for candidates for vacancies but also vice versa—vacancies for candidates. Basically, we are constantly sourcing suitable candidates, especially for bottleneck functions, regardless of the acute demand. Whenever you meet people or get to know them better during internships, for example, you look at the situation as a kind of job interview and assessment situation. Numerous companies have therefore set up *talent communities* in recent years. Good, promising people, who you get to know wherever and whenever, you integrate them into a pool of candidates, stay in permanent contact with them and hope in the end to be able to hire one or the other candidate for the company (Trost 2014).

> We are constantly sourcing candidates independent of acute needs. Whenever we have found good candidates, we maintain long-term contact with them (candidate focus). (1-2)

As already indicated, this approach is particularly worthwhile when it comes to filling bottleneck functions. There is a permanent high demand here, which is difficult to meet. Here, it is not uncommon to strive to bind representatives of the same target group. So it is not surprising that, for example, the so-called "Big Four" of financial auditing Deloitte, KPMG, EY and PWC have been successfully relying on talent communities for a long time. They are looking on a large scale and continuously for university graduates, especially in business administration.

Fun or Networking?

There are two opposing ways of the strategic alignment of talent communities. The classic one operates in such a way that, for example, interns are evaluated at the end of their internship and are included in a pool after a simple assessment. From there, these candidates receive interesting offers. It is about joint events, support during studies, fireside chats, greeting cards and gifts for Christmas or birthdays. In the end, one hopes to be able to hire as many candidates as possible for a job from the pool. All this is coordinated and controlled by a team responsible for this in the HR function. The business line has very little to do with it. Or they are involved here and there for one or the other action at the friendly request of their HR colleagues.

> We (HR) built pools of promising candidates, which we "keep warm" in the long term to cover needs in the line. (4-1)

To candidates, this approach implies a kind of promise of future career prospects in the company, sooner or later. At least they are told that they have a good chance of doing so. The retention activities themselves embody the company's active commitment to the candidates, who in a way are taken by the hand.

A strategically opposing orientation of talent communities, on the other hand, conveys a slightly different message to a promising candidate:

> You have attracted our attention and we are convinced that our company could offer you attractive opportunities for employment in the long term. We can neither tell you nor promise you where the journey will take you, but we offer you the exclusive opportunity to actively network with colleagues from areas of the company that are of interest to you and to work together on manageable tasks. Whether you will be successful with us and start a successful career is primarily up to you. We open doors. It is up to you to go through this door and convince our colleagues of your cooperativeness.

As you can see, this approach is less about communities of candidates (talents) than about communities of candidates *and* current employees. In the past, networking among candidates has hardly really worked, because candidates hardly see any benefit in it. Networking with interesting people from the business line is much more attractive.

> We offer promising candidates exclusive opportunities to network independently with the specialist departments. (4-2)

In the end, the natural consequence of successful and active networking is that vacancies are filled. At best, the HR department plays a coordinating role here.

Current and Possible Sourcing Strategies

Many companies have aligned their strategies, processes and responsibilities in relation to HR marketing and recruiting in times when the shortage of skilled personnel was even less noticeable and the HR function saw itself primarily responsible for administrative tasks. In this respect, it is not surprising that even today the sourcing strategies of numerous HR departments tend to have a passive approach and that responsibility lies primarily with the HR function. This *current* sourcing strategy is indicated in the lower left in Fig. 5.5.

This raises the question for companies to what extent they could expand their strategy or the playing field in the portfolio shown in Fig. 5.5. Two questions need to be answered in this context. Firstly, is it possible, given the company's *culture, to be* more direct, more active towards candidates and more aggressive or competitive towards competitors in the labour market? Secondly, how strong is the *readiness* on the part of managers and employees within the business line to participate actively in the search for and approach of candidates? Depending on how the answers to these two questions turn out, the playing field of a *possible* sourcing strategy can be

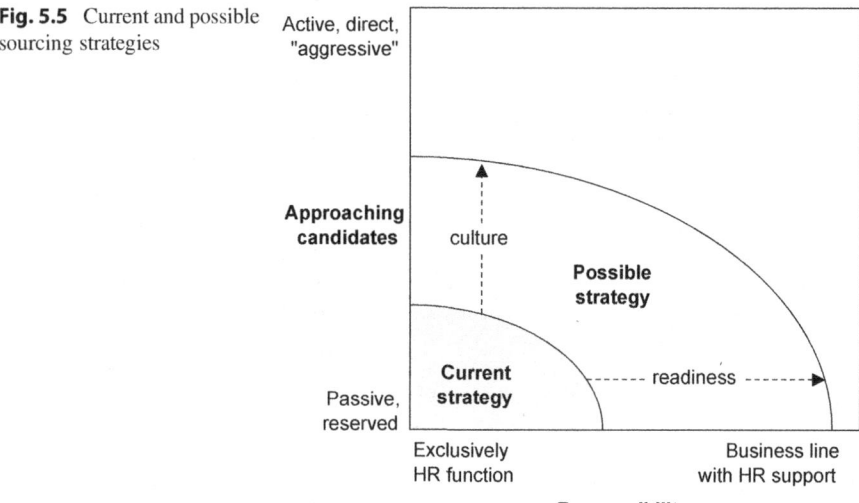

Fig. 5.5 Current and possible sourcing strategies

expanded and more active sourcing strategies can be applied as shown graphically in Fig. 5.5.

The Right Strategy Depending on the Target Function

When choosing the search strategy, companies should always pursue a mixed strategy according to their needs and target functions. Section 3.3 already dealt in detail with the importance of critical target functions and the definition of key and bottleneck functions. Four different scenarios are distinguished below (see Fig. 5.6). Depending on the scenario, it may be appropriate to focus on certain strategies.

The *simple (operational) hiring* scenario is used when it is relatively easy to fill vacant positions because there is a high availability of suitable candidates in the labour market, most of whom are actively searching for jobs. This case is independent of the quantitative needs. *Difficult mass hiring* refers to so-called bottleneck functions. As mentioned already, the aim here is to recruit a large number of new employees with comparable profiles, although recruitment itself is proving very difficult due to external labour market conditions. Difficult *specialist hiring* involves filling singular positions. In this context, it is less the volume in terms of personnel requirements that plays a decisive role, but rather the fact that you are looking for an individual, hard-to-find expert. The situation is similar when it comes to *strategic search*. However, the special feature here is that, due to strategic challenges, one is not only looking for a suitable candidate, but also for the best one. In contrast to specialist hiring, recruiting costs play a very subordinate role here.

These four scenarios are described in detail below. A summary overview of the special features and strategies in relation to the respective scenarios can be found in Fig. 5.7.

5.2 Sourcing, Approaching and Retaining Candidates

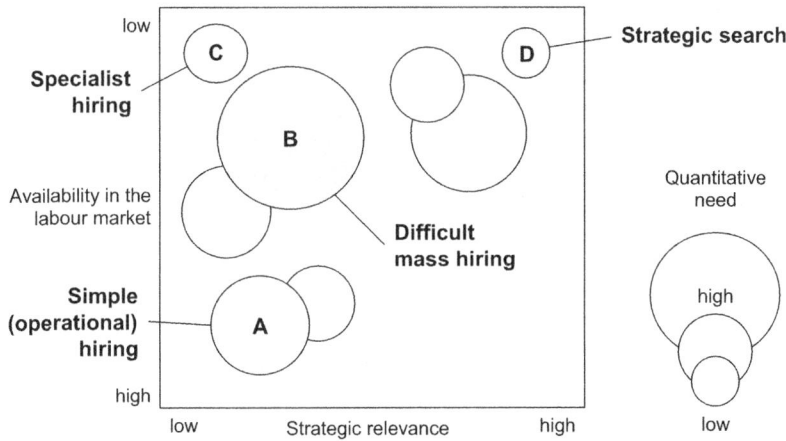

Fig. 5.6 Four different scenarios in talent acquisition

Scenario		Description	Strategies
Simple (operational) hiring		High availability of personnel in the labour market. Usually no high strategic relevance	Passive approach to candidates, e.g., by means of job advertisements, cooperation with recruiting agencies
Difficult mass hiring		Low availability of personnel in the labour market and quantitatively high demand (bottleneck function)	Employer brand, talent communities, broad involvement of business line in the search and approach of candidates
Specialist hiring		Low availability of personnel in the labour market and singular, specific needs	Specific employee value proposition, active sourcing, intensive involvement of the business line
Strategic search		Difficult to meet demand and high strategic relevance of the position (key position)	Executive search. Determination of activities and responsibilities on a case-by-case basis

Fig. 5.7 Strategies for talent acquisition depending on the needs (scenario)

Simple (Operational) Hiring

This case describes a situation that many companies have considered to be normal for many decades. It is assumed that there is more demand on the labour market than there are vacancies to offer. These people actively seek employment opportunities, apply and the employer's task is simply to select the appropriate ones. The company

Infineon therefore aptly refers to this scenario as "Post and Select". Recruitment here works exactly as it has always been described in classic HR textbooks. You place an ad, collect applications, and select. No more, no less. Every company can report on jobs, roles or functions to which this case still applies. In this respect, traditional, rather passive recruitment practices can rightly be used here. Anything else would be a waste of money and effort. Neither an employer brand, nor a talent community or even active sourcing is required here.

Difficult Mass Hiring

This case presents companies with very special challenges and is in no way comparable with the scenario described above. One might be faced with the almost impossible task of hiring 100 software developers within a few months. A medium-sized company is desperately looking for opportunities to fill 20 trainee positions. A nursing facility hires 30 new nursing staff every year. A financial auditing company addresses the needs of several hundred university graduates for a specific business area. In this case, an employer cannot avoid pulling a whole series of registers:

- A convincing employee value proposition, communicated via a large number of target group-relevant channels (see Sect. 5.1). In particular, arguments for the corresponding bottleneck function should be conveyed.
- A broad involvement of the business line in the search for and approach of suitable candidates. Just think of employee referral programs, target-group-focused university marketing, presence at certain events and trade fairs.
- Building a talent community for long-term retention of potentially suitable candidates. Only in this scenario does this concept really make sense, because the implementation and operation of talent communities is only worthwhile when starting from a certain quantitative need.
- Simple forms of active sourcing, for example through targeted search and approach of candidates on platforms such as LinkedIn.
- Structural measures to optimize the candidate experience. This includes simple application modalities and selection processes that focus more on speed, transparency and appreciation than just a valid selection procedure.

As this simple list already shows, the difficult coverage of large requirements requires a comprehensive recruitment system in the sense of talent relationship management (Trost 2014). It is not unusual for a carefully assembled team consisting of HR professionals and representatives from the target function to take care of a particular bottleneck function, moderated and led by a so-called Talent Relationship Manager.

Specialist Hiring

Every company knows the special case in which the filling of a single position turns out to be an incredibly hard nut to be cracked. The demand is singular, but qualitatively specific. Because comparable positions are rarely filled, companies have only limited experience. Even the HR Business Partner, who is rather unfamiliar with the subject, finds it difficult to understand and classify the special feature of this vacancy, "And what exactly does a Big Data Analyst do?" In this scenario, the call for an executive search consultant quickly is made in practice, which leads to high costs in the long term. The difficult search for experts is only about filling singular positions in individual cases. On the other hand, this case occurs very frequently, so that the multitude of different expert positions to be filled can lead to extremely high costs if executive search agencies are involved right away.

A generic employer brand does not help here either. Rather, it requires an employee value proposition that conveys the specificity of a particular expert position. A talent community is not worthwhile either. The quantitative demand is too low for this. The search for suitable candidates must definitely be carried out actively, because at best one can find and attract passive candidates. The difficult search for experts requires the active assumption of responsibility by the demanding department. A case like this can hardly be solved successfully by a central HR function. At the very least, considerable opportunities are wasted if the department in need stays out of the business here.

If, for example, a hiring manager notifies the HR department of a personnel requirement with a request for an appropriate candidate search and it turns out after an initial interview that this is a case for specialist hiring, then the reaction of HR could sound as follows:

> All right, all right. This seems to be a case requiring *specialist hiring*. That means the following: We set up a small team consisting of one HR professional and two representatives from your area. These colleagues will devote 10–20% of their time to this search over the next four weeks. We then develop a powerful employee value proposition rapidly and cooperatively. At the same time, we set up a meeting in which we systematically check our networks and draw up lists of potential target candidates. We then fire from all cylinders in the sense of active sourcing. Colleagues of your department will approach targeted candidates. They are already reserving time for talks in the near future. Until we can agree on that, we won't get started. This is a challenging issue, which requires special efforts. This place is on fire. That is why we can't avoid taking a rapid reaction force approach. Are we clear?

Most companies react differently today. They erroneously treat a specialist hiring case as if it were a simple (operational) hiring one, which will certainly lead to frustration, waste of time and failure.

Strategic Search

If a personnel requirement is classified as a strategic search, this should in turn trigger a completely different process than that described in the scenarios outlined above. In the case of a strategic search, the costs for filling the vacancy usually play a subordinate role. The CEO has the search on his radar and conveys the necessary interest, urgency and strategic scope. Not infrequently he or she is the client. In addition, the search is often global.

In this case, there are perfect reasons for engaging an executive search consultancy that, especially in the case of an international search, also operates internationally and has corresponding access to the respective local markets and industries. A central HR function or representatives from the business line can rarely succeed.

While in the scenarios described above it is advisable to establish structures, processes and instruments before the need arises, in a strategic search it is quite conceivable and also professional to act on a case-by-case basis. Relevant questions are discussed: Who or what are we looking for, why? Who or what are we *not* looking for? Who can support us externally and who are the internal contacts? What do we offer or what do we want to offer—also in the sense of an employee value proposition?

Talent Acquisition Strategy

In this and in the previous subchapter, strategic dimensions in the context of talent acquisition were shown (see Fig. 5.8). It became clear that there is no one way to develop and deliver an employee value proposition. Rather, it was shown that there

Reason for candidate search	1-1 Vacancy focus	1-2 Candidate focus
	We search for candidates once we face an acute need. As soon as a vacancy is filled, the process is completed.	We are constantly sourcing candidates independently of acute needs. Whenever we have found good candidates, we maintain long-term contact with them.
Activity of search and address	2-1 Restrained	2-2 *Active, cheeky and courageous*
	In sourcing candidates we are above all cautious. We do not impose ourselves and rely on the initiative of interested applicants. Any form of aggressiveness would not correspond to our values.	We're heading straight for candidates. We take the "war for talent" literally. Our search strategies are cheeky, courageous, and sometimes at the limit of what is ethically and legally justifiable.
Responsibility for candidate search	3-1 Personnel department	3-2 Department
	Searching for and approaching candidates is primarily the task of the HR department. The departments take care of their own business.	With us every employee is a recruiter at the same time. When looking for and approaching candidates, we consistently rely on the networks and commitment of all our colleagues.
Management of candidate pools	4-1 Entertain	4-2 Networking
	We (HR) built pools of promising candidates, which we "keep warm" in the long term to cover needs in the line.	We offer promising candidates exclusive opportunities to network independently with the specialist departments.

Fig. 5.8 Overview of all strategic dimensions of candidate search, approach and retention

are different types of employer branding. Active sourcing was compared with passive sourcing, with or without the involvement of the business departments. You can act with a focus on vacancies or candidates. However, it became clear on the last pages that the strategic alignment should also be oriented to the respective problems, needs and scenarios, which in the end always leads to mixed strategies. The development of a *talent acquisition strategy* involves a rigorous definition of what one wants to do in concrete terms in relation to the last scenarios presented.

5.3 Selection and Fit

Personnel selection in most textbooks is explained like this: If you have several applicants for a job to choose from, the question arises as to which applicant is the right one (e.g. Dessler 2018). The solution lies on the one hand in the clear definition of what is theoretically meant by "right" (the requirements of the job) and on the other hand in the application of valid diagnostic selection tools in the assessment of applicants. It is that simple. Also the problem is rarely as easy to understand as in this case. On the one hand, one wants to avoid hiring unsuitable candidates. This is also called the *alpha error* or "false positive". On the other hand, one does not want to reject suitable candidates. This in turn is called the *beta error* or "false negative" (see Fig. 5.9).

It appears that the selection of personnel is merely a matter of forecasting future performance. In the end, the validity of the selection process determines whether an employee's actual performance is in line with the forecasted performance. However, this would be far too simple. The following considerations show a number of strategic options, which can be very differently aligned. We start at the beginning, i.e., with the determination of the requirements.

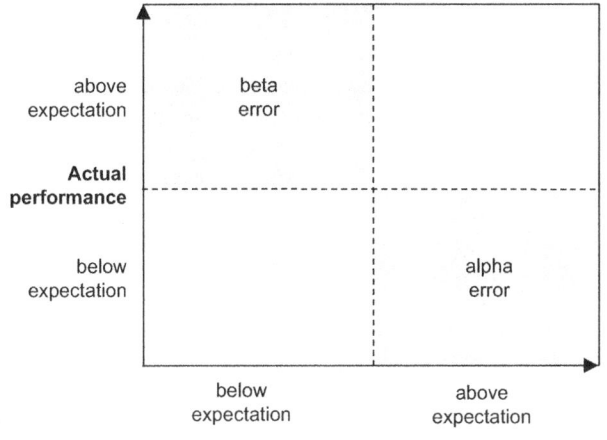

Fig. 5.9 Alpha and beta errors in personnel selection

Short-Term and Long-Term Fit

In his book "Why good people can't get jobs", Peter Cappelli (2012), leading professor for HR at the Wharton School, cynically called it the "Home Depot Syndrome". If there is a vacancy to be filled in a company, you simply go to the warehouse and get the new employee who fits exactly into the gap that has arisen within the organization. Behind this is quite obviously the view of an organization as a static machine. One also speaks here of the *machine metaphor* (Morgan 1997). From the moment the new employee is fitted into the machine, it continues to run perfectly. However, this presupposes that the missing component (the employee) has been understood exactly beforehand.

This view reflects the common textbook view. In fact, the description of relevant requirements is almost always the starting point for all recruitment measures. The so-called HR Business Partner meets with the hiring line manager and discusses the necessary requirements that the future employee has to meet as precisely as possible. This is done in the hope of finding an employee who will be able to fulfil his or her responsibilities from the very first day or at least after the shortest possible introduction phase.

> We fill vacancies. The starting point for this is always the most detailed possible description of job-specific requirements. Finding requires knowing what you are looking for. (1-1)

I suspect that the hierarchical, static nature of an organization can already be recognized by the differentiation of the requirements set out in job advertisements. The more comprehensive and detailed they are, the more the organization strives for stability and predictability. Agile organizations think differently. From the very beginning, they follow a principle that is in harmony with a very widespread phenomenon. Randomly pick any employee from your organization and ask them how many of their current tasks still have to do with what they were originally hired for. Ask an employee who has been with the company for five or more years. In many companies the answer will be "little" to "nothing at all". Employees develop in their respective contexts, change functions, divisions, spend time in other countries and branches, which is highly desirable in organizations that rely on lateral networks. If you think this principle through to its end, you arrive at a strategic alignment, like the following one:

> We occupy careers whose developments are always uncertain. Therefore, our requirement profiles are always as generic as possible. Above all, candidates must fit the company. (1-2)

Agile organizations are primarily concerned with the question of whether an employee fits the company as a whole. They do this by never leaving a selection decision solely to the hiring manager in need, but by actively involving representatives from other areas in the decision-making process. The leading question is always, "Could you also imagine working with this person?" The natural consequence of this is that social factors, motivation, aspects of personality and cognitive disposition (e.g., intelligence) become more important. The well-known Stanford professor Robert Sutton (2007) put it in a nutshell in his book "The No Asshole Rule". He was motivated to write his book in the context of a new appointment of a professor, whereby the colleagues agreed on the principle not to hire an "asshole",[1] even if his or her professional, scientific qualifications were outstanding. This was certainly not mentioned in the job advertisement.

Potential for Future Development or Current Suitability?

However, another reason why companies feel compelled to keep their requirements more generic is the increasing talent shortage. The job market is simply no longer able to pre-select rare talents with a sophisticated, extensive wish list of requirements. This applies in particular to bottleneck functions and partly to key functions (see Sect. 3.3). As a result, companies are increasingly being forced to move away from the priority of finding and selecting exactly those employees who can successfully fill their positions from day one. In summary, this approach can be summed up as follows:

> We hire employees so that they can perform their assigned tasks well in their respective positions within the shortest possible time. Anything else would be a waste of resources. (2-1)

Does an employee really need to have a certain level of a specific language skill or can he or she develop it? How good must his or her skills be in using office applications the day he or she really starts employment? In view of the increasing talent shortage, it is worth asking two questions when reviewing job profiles and job advertisements:

– What skills does an employee *definitely* need to have on the first day of employment?
– What skills can an employee *learn* in a reasonable amount of time, provided his or her potential is recognized?

The consideration of *potential* compared to current competence does not have to be an emergency but can be recognized as an opportunity. This consideration is graphically illustrated in Fig. 5.10.

Imagine, for the filling of a position, the highest possible level of competence in relation to any skill that is desired. At a certain point in time (indicated by the vertical dashed line) the choice is between candidate A or B. Considering the left side in the above figure, one would definitely choose candidate A. He or she has a higher level

---

[1] The reader may be irritated by the use of this ordinary terminology. Robert Sutton himself searched in vain for an alternative. Obviously and interestingly, for what this word describes, no other, more civilized term seems to exist.

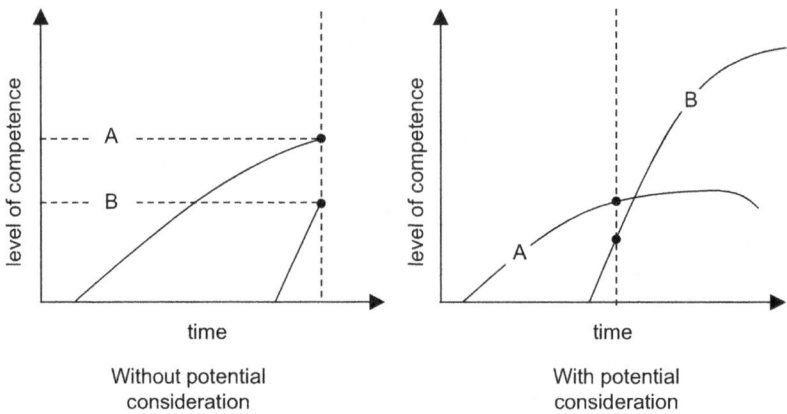

Fig. 5.10 Comparison of two candidates with and without potential consideration

of competence. However, what can already be seen is the faster learning curve of candidate B. Extrapolating the progressions of the two learning curves, a long-term development could result, as indicated on the right side of the figure. According to this, B would certainly be the better choice in the long term.

> Potential is more important in personnel selection than current competence. This enlarges the relevant target group and is more promising in the long term. (2-2)

The problem, of course, is that at the time of the decision it is not known how a person's learning curve will develop. Potential is basically a hypothetical factor. In connection with the topic of talent identification (Sect. 8.1), the question of how to recognize potential will be dealt with more intensity in the further course of this book.

Efficiency Versus Effectiveness

There is a rule of thumb in recruiting that is not scientifically proven, according to which a company should receive approximately as many applications per year as there are employees currently employed. It is not easy to define exactly what is meant by an application. However, if one assumes that applications include the usual contents, such as motivation letter, curriculum vitae, certificates, etc., then this already means a considerable flood of data for medium-sized and large companies. This is the essential reason, why enterprises went over since the late nineties to map recruiting processes electronically. At that time we still spoke of "e-Recruiting". The introduction of these applicant tracking systems was primarily aimed at making the lives of HR employees and recruiters in particular easier. Companies thus pursued what can be described as an *efficiency strategy*. The aim was to keep the workload per application (cost-per-hire) as low as possible, which in turn opened up the opportunity to reduce the overall processing times and time-to-fill.

> The processing of many applications requires above all efficiency. It is the basis for a competitive time-to-fill and a reasonable cost-per-hire. (3-1)

Technology has made it easier to collect, compare and semi-automatically assess applicant data. Furthermore, these recruiting systems could be used to forward applications from one point in the organization to the next, for example from HR Business Partner to hiring manager. In all phases, this technology resulted in more efficiency. Further efficiency gains were achieved through the partial relocation of selection processes to shared service organizations and the increasing use of artificial intelligence.

Now cost-per-hire is not everything. In fact, costs play a subordinate role, especially in key positions. This raises the question for employers as to whether they want to make their selection process as efficient as possible or as effective. Effectiveness, as opposed to the pure reduction of costs, aims at making the right decisions on the one hand—on the part of all parties involved, including the applicant. Among other things, this is a question of validity and elaboration. On the other hand, the selection process should already be designed in such a way that suitable candidates are not only not alienated, but convinced and attracted.

> Hiring new employees is always a big investment. In the end, it is therefore a matter of making the right decisions and attracting suitable candidates. (3-2)

While an *effectiveness strategy* should definitely be pursued for key and bottleneck functions, employers may allow themselves an efficiency strategy for the other non-critical functions (see Sect. 3.3). In the course of presenting further dimensions of strategic alignment, the significance of the effectiveness strategy will be dealt with at a later point of this chapter.

Who Is Supposed to Benefit from Aptitude Testing?

Every action in HR has a customer. The corresponding activities should serve to solve a problem of this very customer. This fundamental thinking has already been comprehensively discussed in the first half of this book. If this is or should be the case, who is the customer of personnel selection and whose problem is supposed to be solved with it? When I ask this question to my students during my lecture, I almost always get this answer: "HR or the hiring manager are the customers. You have the problem to minimize the alpha and beta error. The solution to this problem can be seen in the application of aptitude-testing procedures". Probably also many HR professionals would agree instantly with this answer. The underlying strategic premise is therefore:

> Hiring managers and recruiters are the customers of aptitude testing procedures. These procedures help to select the right candidates. (4-1)

Even today, this way of thinking is deeply anchored in the practice of personnel selection. This is done precisely by those companies that act quite self-confidently, even arrogantly in the labour market, and that make no secret of "torturing" their applicants as hard as possible. They want to see if the applicant demonstrates enough strength to survive this. The decisive question then is: who gets the results of the aptitude diagnostic procedures used. Who receives the report from the assessment centre or the score from the intelligence test? According to the above strategy, the managers and recruiters. Who else, one is inclined to ask in many companies?

In fact, this perspective only reaches half of reality. In the end two instances always make a decision, the potential employer *and* the potential employee, i.e., the candidate—unless we are dealing with slave trade. There is also a risk of alpha and beta errors for the applicant or candidate. He or she can refuse the right job or take the wrong job. His or her decision is also highly relevant and at the same time subject to considerable uncertainty. This is all the more true the more options the candidate might be able to choose from. This risk also has relevant consequences for the potential employer since hardly any company will have a serious interest in employing people who end up regretting their commitment. Why should employers not therefore strive to empower the candidate in his or her decision?

> Candidates are the customers of the aptitude testing procedures. They are intended to help the candidate decide whether the company/job is right for them. (4-2)

If this strategic priority is taken seriously, candidates are offered to disclose results of aptitude testing procedures and discuss them with them. If an assessment centre is conducted, the candidate should always be expected to learn at least as much about him- or herself, and about the company in question, as the employer does. It is also possible that the candidates will be offered measures from which only or primarily they themselves will benefit. Simple variants of this measure are non-binding open house opportunities or discussions with current employees coupled with a clear message: "We do not evaluate you. Experience us and get an idea". Some companies offer online tests that are designed solely to enable potential applicants to self-assess whether a job is right for them.

Whether managers and recruiters on the one hand or the applicants on the other hand are customers of the selection process is of course not an either-or decision. Companies will always reserve the right to be customers themselves. The only question is to what extent one actively supports the decision-making process of the applicants.

The Positive Candidate Experience

How does a recruiter know that he or she has done a good job in the selection process? First of all, he or she certainly recognizes this by the fact that a position was

5.3 Selection and Fit

filled within a reasonable time with a sufficiently suitable candidate. That is for sure. But who has to be satisfied with the selection process in the end? Here there is one obvious answer and an underestimated one. The obvious answer refers to the hiring manager and his or her team. They finally also experience hardship and through a successful selection process their hardships are rewarded. If they are happy, everything is fine.

> Managers and their teams are the customers of personnel selection. We make every effort to ensure that they are satisfied with the process, methods and decisions as a whole. (5-1)

The underestimated answer, on the other hand, focuses on the candidate him- or herself. How does the candidate report on the selection process—even if he or she has received a rejection? This question is now regarded as a key question when it comes to the positive experience of applicants and candidates. In the HR community, the concept of the *Candidate Experience* has certainly spread. This is about three criteria from the applicant's point of view: speed, transparency and appreciation (see Trost 2014).

- *Speed.* Reactions to applications or decisions in the course of the application and selection process are faster than those of the competitors in the labour market.
- *Transparency.* The applicant is always aware of the current status of his or her application and knows the next steps. He or she knows why and which testing procedure is used and when, and receives appropriate feedback.
- *Appreciation.* The applicant will be treated with full respect in a personal manner. Good applicants are clearly told that they are interested in them personally.

I have already discussed their selection processes with countless companies and have always asked the question how one or more criteria of a positive applicant's life could be optimized at which step. The results were always illuminating and amazingly varied. The principle is:

> We treat applicants as customers and do everything in our power to be faster, more transparent and more appreciative than our competitors in the selection process. (5-2)

It seems to me that most companies here have considerable potential for optimization. Many optimizations do not even lead to higher costs. For illustration purposes, a small selection of simple practical examples is shown in Fig. 5.11.

As always when it comes to the design of the customer experience, the active involvement of the customer—in this case the candidate—also helps here. In practice, it is advisable to go through the entire so-called *candidate journey* together with newly hired employees. One considers the complete communication and interaction with applicants and candidates from the first moment of the meeting (e.g., the announcement) up to the first day at work. It may be possible to print out all relevant materials—typical job advertisements, screenshots of career and application

Speed	Transparency	Appreciation
It will take no longer than ten minutes to submit an application.	Before applying, the applicant will be taught how the selection process works in concrete terms.	Introduction of all interview participants being communicated along with the invitation to the interview appointment.
An interview appointment within a few days after the application. Corresponding time slots are provided at an early stage.	Participants after an assessment centre receive personal feedback and a written report.	The applicant will be greeted by the receptionist with his name and accompanied (with a golf cart) to the interview location.
A personal appointment (with the applicant) is arranged for the signing of the employment contract.	Via an app, applicants are informed about the status of their application on a real-time basis.	A personal contact during the entire process.

Fig. 5.11 Practical examples for shaping a positive candidate experience

pages, mail communication, brochures, photos of premises encountered by applicants during interviews, typical employment contracts, etc.—and display them on several pin boards. It is illuminating to get a closed picture of how a company presents itself to a candidate along all touchpoints. Above all, such an exercise provides valuable hints for improvement potential relatively quickly.

Who Is Supposed to Convince Whom?

There is a widespread unwritten law that requires the applicant to convince the potential employer and hiring manager in particular. The applicant competes for a rare, coveted position and in the end the employer decides who gets the offer. It is always been that way. Therefore, it has always been the applicant who was nervous before the interview and rarely the interviewer.

> It is in the nature of personnel selection that candidates need to convince their potential future employer. It is always been that way. (6-1)

However, the tide is turning on bottleneck functions in particular. Companies recognize this in an almost intuitive way. As soon as you realize that a position is difficult to fill, you will start to try to convince a candidate who seems suitable. If this idea is taken seriously, it is only one step towards a strategic alignment of personnel selection:

> In the direct interaction with applicants we recognize the special chance to convince as an employer. (6-2)

From this moment on, the selection process and the associated interaction with candidates become a vehicle for the employee value proposition and the employer brand (see Sect. 5.1).

Artificially Intelligent Selection Procedures

Where there are large amounts of data (big data) and feedback loops, the use of *artificial intelligence* is not far away. It is already possible today to use available data such as résumés, job profiles, LinkedIn presences and intelligent algorithms to make a sufficiently valid prediction of how professional recruiters would make a selection decision. Through machine learning, these algorithms become better and better in a short time. The only thing they need is constant feedback.

This works according to a principle that has been called empirical test construction in psychological diagnostics for decades (Joseph et al. 2001). For example, employees or applicants are divided into two groups, suitable and unsuitable, successful and less successful, people who have achieved a leadership position and those who have not. Then one considers infinitely many characteristics and looks for possible statistical covariation. The result are algorithms that say, for example, that people who have studied in these universities for so many years, have worked in this role, have at least this grade in sports, more than 1000 followers on Twitter, have been most successful. Why that is the case does not matter at all. Artificial intelligence does not really understand. It does not even care about theoretical explanation. Artificial intelligence simply searches for statistical relations and optimizes them by machine learning. In the context of HR, we now call this *people analytics* or *predictive analytics* (see also Sect. 11.3).

In the future, more and more companies will move towards making selection decisions on the basis of such statistical judgements. They assume increased efficiency and rely on the superiority of artificial intelligence over biased social judgement.

> We strive to make personnel selection decisions based as far as possible on artificial intelligence, appropriate algorithms, and big data. This enables us to achieve greater efficiency and objectivity. (7-1)

Those who follow this premise sooner or later find themselves in the situation of having to explain to an interested applicant that an algorithm has made or at least prepared the decision. Cynical thinkers also talk about "hiding behind a black box". It is probably a question of attitude whether a company wants this or not. This is contrasted with the striving to always let people make decisions about people and their future. In the end, someone (a human being) should always have the responsibility over a decision.

> Decisions about people and their future are always made by people. Such decisions require the assumption of personal, interpersonal responsibility. (7-2)

In psychological diagnostics, decisions made on the basis of experience, personal judgement, or intuition are called *clinical judgements*—even if they have no pathological significance. From a scientific point of view, these judgements are not always superior in terms of their validity. Often the opposite is even true (Meehl 2013).

Bear the Consequences of the Selection Decision

Before a candidate is appointed as professor at a German university, he or she undergoes an extensive selection procedure. Part of this procedure is always a trial lecture in which the students who are present can verify or assess his or her pedagogical abilities. Unofficially, this trial lecture is also affectionately called "audition". After a candidate has finished his or her "audition" at my faculty and left the classroom, for example, the students who are still present, are asked who could imagine this candidate as a professor at our faculty and who can't. If the majority votes against the candidate, the procedure for the candidate is basically over. So here it is more or less the customers who decide who gets a chance as a candidate and who does not.

To what extent is it conceivable in public services that citizens are involved in the selection decision? Should a bank, for example, attach importance to the judgements of its customers when hiring private or corporate financial advisors? Depending on the industry, the type of products or services and the type of customer relationship, this possibility will vary. Basically, it might be worthwhile at least to think about it.

As already mentioned in Sect. 4.5 agile companies in particular attach great importance to the fact that a decision should always be taken by the authority that has to live with the consequences of the respective decision. The prospect of having to bear the consequences of one's own decision increases motivation to critically deal with the respective decision, which in the end may lead to more intelligent decisions. If wrong decisions are made, this enables experience and learning for the future. In the practice of recruiting, the relevant instances are either the customers or the colleagues.

> Selection decisions are made by those who bear the consequences in the long run: future colleagues and customers. This increases motivation, the quality of the decision and enables learning. (8-2)

In hierarchical and static organizations this thought seems rather strange. Decisions here are generally made by managers. This is simply due to their formal role and position. They also make other decisions, such as about investments, because they ultimately bear overall responsibility. This principle applies here:

> Selection decisions are always made by the respective managers in coordination with the responsible HR professionals. They are responsible for this and have been trained accordingly. (8-1)

In a world where there is division of labour, the HR department plays an active role. Either it accompanies the selection process or in the end it even makes the selection decision. It is argued that HR professionals with years of experience in this field are needed to make selection decisions. In fact, it is usually the case that HR professionals rarely experience the consequences of their actions for themselves. Once an employee has been hired, the HR department has little chance of knowing whether its actions were successful or not. The missing feedback is of structural nature. Section 11.1 further deals with this consideration when it comes to HR organization.

Long-Term Candidate and Team Orientation

Traditional recruiting focuses primarily on the acute, static requirements in a position, articulated by the hiring manager. The applicant has to convince him or herself that he or she will be able to call up the necessary skills from day one, if possible. This has always been the case and is more than understandable from a practical point of view. In this subchapter, alternative strategic options were compared with this view (see Fig. 5.12). Here a completely different orientation was added. Career orientation instead of job orientation, candidate orientation, putting the candidate at the centre, employers (not applicants) who have to convince, orientation towards long-term potential and less towards acute skills, teams, colleagues who not only have to be happy with a selection decision but also have to bear its consequences. Of course, validity, reliability and objectivity still play a role in predicting performance and behaviour. In the course of agilization and, above all, in view of the talent shortage, these classic themes are increasingly moving to the background.

5.4 Onboarding

No matter how you do it, the first few days of work present each new employee with a special challenge. It is always like that. There are simply too many unanswered questions that concerns people in relation to almost everything. This does not require any further explanation at this point, since probably every reader of this book has already gone through such a challenge.

But this situation can be critical not only for new employees, but also for the company. This raises the question for companies of how to bring new employees to an appropriate level of productivity as quickly as possible. The first days and weeks in particular will probably decide whether the new employee will stay with the company. Last but not least, we know that new employees share their experiences made during the first few days with friends and acquaintances. In this respect, there is even a connection between the employer image and the design of the first days and weeks of new employees. All targeted activities aimed at introducing and integrating new employees are referred to as *onboarding*.

Two Opposing Testimonials

When new employees talk about their experiences after a few days in their new job, their stories can sound very different. In the following, two fictitious experience

Specificity of requirements	**1-1 Specific and job-related** We fill vacancies. The starting point for this is always the most detailed possible description of job-specific requirements. Finding requires knowing what you are looking for.	**1-2 Careers and companies** We enable careers the developments of which are always uncertain. Therefore, our requirement profiles are always as generic as possible. Above all, candidates must fit the company.
Requirements to be met by the candidate	**2-1 Current competencies** We hire employees so that they can perform their assigned tasks well in their respective positions within the shortest possible time. Anything else would be a waste of resources.	**2-2 Future potential** Potential is more important in personnel selection than current competence. This enlarges the relevant target group and is more promising in the long term.
Priority in applicant selection	**3-1 Efficiency** The processing of many applications requires above all efficiency. It is the basis for a competitive time-to-fill and a reasonable cost-per-hire	**3-2 Quality and effectiveness** Hiring new employees is always a big investment. In the end, it is therefore a matter of making the right decisions and attracting suitable candidates.
Customers of aptitude diagnostics	**4-1 Managers and recruiters** Hiring managers and recruiters are the customers of aptitude testing procedures. These procedures help to select the right candidates.	**4-2 Candidates** Candidates are the customers of the aptitude testing procedures. They are intended to help the candidate decide whether the company/job is right for them.
Clients of the selection procedure	**5-1 Department** Managers and their teams are the customers of personnel selection. We make every effort to ensure that they are satisfied with the process, methods and decisions as a whole.	**5-2 Applicants** We treat applicants as customers and do everything in our power to be faster, more transparent and more appreciative than our competitors in the selection process.
Instance to be convinced	**6-1 Applicant convinces employer** It is in the nature of personnel selection that candidates need to convince their potential future employer. It has always been that way.	**6-2 Employers convince applicants** In the direct interaction with applicants we recognize the special opportunities of convincing these as an employer.
Use of artificial intelligence	**7-1 Maximum usage** We strive to make personnel selection decisions based as far as possible on artificial intelligence, appropriate algorithms and big data. This enables us to achieve greater efficiency and objectivity.	**7-2 People over Systems** Decisions about people and their future are always made by people. Such decisions require the assumption of personal, interpersonal responsibility.
Decision maker	**8-1 HR managers and HR** Selection decisions are always made by the respective managers in coordination with the responsible HR professionals. They are responsible for this and have been trained accordingly.	**8-2 Colleagues and clients** Selection decisions are made by those who bear the consequences on the long run: future colleagues and customers. This increases motivation, the quality of the decision and enables learning.

Fig. 5.12 Overview of all strategic dimensions for selection and fit

reports will be presented. It becomes apparent that behind these reports there are opposing, strategic alignments of onboarding. Here is the first story:

> The first working day was pretty exciting, because I didn't know anybody except my future boss and some colleagues from HR. I knew where to go and was led into a room with twelve other new hires. There we were first welcomed by the managing director and then by the HR director. Then we got an introduction to technical and organizational matters—software, data protection, privacy, security, employee ID, etc. Then my boss introduced me to the team. In the following days, I took part in an extensive introductory program, which probably every new employee has to complete. This took place in the training building. At the end of the program my boss discussed the first weeks with me, so that it became clear to me what I have to do first. The plan was for me to familiarize myself step by step with my new job and the environment. As far as possible, my boss always took half an hour or more of this time for me in the first few days, which I found quite useful.

That is the first story. Here is the second one:

> The good thing was that I got to know many of my future colleagues long before my first day at work. With one of these colleagues I had arranged a time and meeting place on the first day. She then took me straight to my future team. In between I had to make a short detour on the first day in order to clarify a few formal things. All other organizational and technical things I was able to clarify in advance via the intranet. There was basically no grace period for me. I was thrown straight into the deep end and was fully involved in a project. Having two buddies taking care of me was extremely helpful. The two had also only been with the company for half a year. Apart from a kind of accompanying program, there was hardly any real introduction. The only exception was a one-day training session on networking, teamwork and conflict management. Otherwise, my buddies gave me a list of names. They said it would be good if I met these people sometime in the course of the next four weeks. They said I would never drink as much coffee again in my life as I in the next four weeks. They were absolutely right.

Obviously, these two experience reports differ in key aspects. Behind both stories there is an implicit or explicit strategy, the special features of which are resolved and explained in the following.

When Does Onboarding Start?

There are activities in the business context that involve hardly any significant effort, but that nevertheless have a lasting effect. One of these activities is to send a message as a manager or as a team to a future, new employee a few days before his or her first day at work with the simple sentence "We look forward to working with you"—an SMS or e-mail is all it takes. For the new employee, this one sentence already represents an important step towards social integration.

The range of possible activities long before the first day at work can of course be extended at will to meet the needs of the employees. Just think of an invitation to the company party, contact persons who are available and keep in touch, training materials on products or simple podcasts, access to the intranet, networking with future colleagues via social media, etc. These considerations touch the question of when onboarding begins. As described above, a premise can be as follows:

> We regard onboarding as a comprehensive, social and professional process that begins long before the first day of work. (1-2)

Or you can consider onboarding as a comparatively short activity in the context of the first working day—a kind of check-in—just like in a hotel or an airplane. Then the premise is more like this:

> We see onboarding more as a kind of check-in that starts when the employee has actually arrived. (1-1)

As with other issues, most companies will tend to make the strategic alignment of onboarding in relation to this aspect dependent on the respective target function. Onboarding for the future CEO will certainly be different from onboarding for the future holiday cover, to name just two extremes.

The Hard and Soft Side of Onboarding

Imagine a simple, generic case. A new employee is insecure in a particular situation, acts in the way that seems right to him and thereby demonstrably commits a fatal error. This case is conceivable in many variations and in a wide variety of settings. The forklift driver has engaged reverse gear instead of forward gear. When using a computer program, the save button was confused with the delete button etc. Now to the actual question: Where did the company make an error?

There are two possible answers to this question, but there is no contradiction between them. Nevertheless, it seems that companies have a tendency to think either one way or the other. The first possible answer is: "You should have shown the employee how to do it right". Companies that respond in this way probably tend towards the following strategic premise:

> Above all, we teach new employees the basic, technical, methodical and professional things. The rest comes from actual practical experience. (2-1)

The alternative answer could have been: "The employee should have been told from the outset that he or she should ask a colleague for advice in case of any uncertainty, no matter what it is or how insignificant the matter seems at first". This answer addresses the social side of the problem rather than the technical side.

> We see onboarding primarily as a social process. That is why at the beginning we mainly convey aspects of interpersonal relationships. (2-2)

Agile companies tend to be more strategic in the latter direction. If employees learn at an early stage to whom they can turn in the event of uncertainties, if they lose their shyness to articulate their uncertainties to others, if they learn to master conflicts, if they learn to actively seek feedback, if they learn that asking questions is always better than not to do it, then employees have the necessary social "operating system" that best helps them in the acquisition of all remaining things, including technical, professional concerns. The first answer is static: Learn *this* and you can *that*. The second answer is agile: Learn *this* and you learn *everything*.

Babysitting or Cold Water

Instantly, one could be inclined to describe onboarding activities as good and professional when new employees receive extensive and systematic instructions at the beginning of their employment relationship. But this can also be seen differently. Werner von Siemens, for example, is credited with the following statement: "It is not our custom to give special instructions to every new entrant. Those who want to work will find enough work here" (Kocka 1969, p. 297, translated by the author). This quotation is usually used as an example of an inadequate view. But perhaps this legendary German entrepreneur was not so wrong. Two strategies face each other here. The strategy outlined here is based on the assumption that employees become productive most quickly when they are "thrown in the deep end".

> So that our new employees learn quickly, we encourage them to jump into the cold water or throw them into it. Anyway, we are at their side. (3-2)

The professionalism of this approach ultimately consists of standing by and intervening when the new employee reaches his or her limits. This strategy always requires individual support, coupled with the ability to balance trust and support according to the situation.

The strategic antithesis of the cold water strategy is characterized by the fact that new employees are instructed and systematically introduced regardless of their abilities, maturity or courage. They are "wrapped in cotton wool", "taken by the hand", "babysitting" is carried out.

> We take new employees by the hand for the first few days and weeks. This helps them to reduce feelings of insecurity. (3-1)

Also with regard to this dimension, companies will always opt for a mixed strategy. In pure form one will find in practice neither the one nor the other variant. The bottom line is the question in which direction a company is in principle moving. Do you want as much "cold water" or as much "babysitting" as possible?

Responsibility for Onboarding

Let us put ourselves for a moment in a situation, which may be familiar to every reader in some way. One morning the class teacher enters the classroom. She is being accompanied by a shy looking pupil, the new guy. His family just recently moved to town. In this very moment he is confronted for the first time with his new class,

Fig. 5.13 Who is responsible for the integration of a new hire?

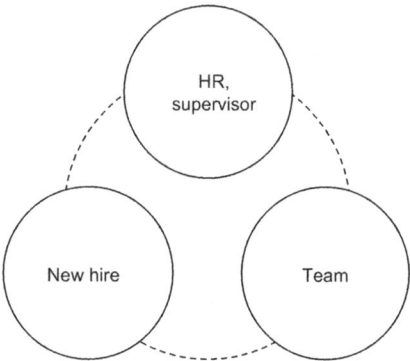

whose pupils have been familiar with each other for a long time. From now on the phase of integration begins, for everyone.

This situation can be compared to that of a new employee who is now to become part of a well established and developed team. In the class there is the teacher, the new pupil and the class. Who is responsible for successful integration? And who would this be in the case of the introduction of a new employee (see Fig. 5.13)? Is it he himself (the new one), or the team (the class), or the boss, or HR (the teacher or the school)?

The strategically undifferentiated answer to the above question could be: "All are responsible, somehow". Rather exaggerated would be the reference to only one of these three roles, such as the explicit expectation that it is the task of the new person to actively integrate do everything alone. If this does not succeed, he or she has failed. The constellation would be completely different if one were to refer solely to the integrating team and to the need for a kind of welcome culture paired with visible measures to be taken by the team.

What happens or can happen in such a process is quite complex from a socio-psychological, group-dynamic point of view. Each role has its own perspectives, combined with its own abilities, fears and dynamics of mutual attributions of characteristics and behavioural expectations. In this respect, it seems rather difficult to derive a general, meaningful strategy from psychological points of view. However, from an HR strategy point of view it would be helpful to formulate at least one tendency explicitly. What would this look like in a more hierarchically managed company? What would be the tendency within a more agile organization? According to these contrasts two alignments can be distinguished. We can assume that the following premise is obvious in a hierarchical company:

> The responsibility for the introduction of new employees lies with the manager and HR. They take care of necessary activities, programs, processes, etc. (4-1)

Companies that think this way will sooner or later end up with standardized introductory programs or training courses, guidelines and checklists for hiring managers. In a way, this orientation would be prototypical for the HR variety of central planning and control. On the other hand, people-centered enablement would lead to different conclusions. Here the following principle would rather dominate:

> New employees and host teams share responsibility for the integration of new colleagues. In return, they receive support from a central source. (4-2)

This principle follows the basic idea of agile organizations explained in Sect. 4.5 according to which those actors should always be responsible for a cause who ultimately have to live with the consequences. In the case of onboarding, this is the new employee and the welcoming team. If the integration of the new employee does not succeed, it is they who have a problem. In this respect, it might be logical to see responsibility in their hands.

Compatibility and Implementation

Summarizing the strategic dimensions of this topic (see Fig. 5.14), it becomes clear that they do not necessarily contradict each other. Instead of an either-or-approach an as-well-as-approach is also conceivable. The only question here is how much of which option should apply. This topic also appears to be relatively simple in terms of its implementation. The basic remuneration is difficult to change. The same applies to topics such as objective setting or talent identification. However, if a company wants to tackle the issue of onboarding in order to change it institutionally, the time and political effort seems comparatively low.

Time frame	1-1 Short-term	1-2 Long-term
	We see onboarding more as a kind of check-in that starts when the employee has actually arrived.	We regard onboarding as a comprehensive, social and professional process that begins long before the first day of work.
Content focus	2-2 Technical	2-2 Interpersonal relations
	Above all, we teach new employees the basic, technical, methodical and professional things. The rest results from actual practice.	We see onboarding primarily as a social process. That is why at the beginning we mainly convey aspects of interpersonal relationships.
Training mode	3-1 Babysitting	3-2 Cold water
	We take new employees by the hand for the first few days and weeks. This helps them to reduce their insecurity.	So that our new employees learn quickly, we encourage them to leap into cold water or throw them into it. Anyway, we are at their side.
Responsibility	4-1 Parent instance	4-2 New employees and team
	The responsibility for the introduction of new employees lies with the manager and HR. They take care of necessary activities, programs, processes, etc.	New employees and host teams share responsibility for the integration of new colleagues. In return, they receive support from a central source.

Fig. 5.14 All strategic dimensions of onboarding at a glance

References

Berberich M, Trost A (2012) Employee referral programs. Books on Demand, Norderstedt
Cappelli P (2012) Why good people can't get jobs. Wharton, Philadelphia, PA
Dessler G (2018) Human resources management. Pearson, London
Dion D, Arnould E (2016) Persona-fied brands: managing branded persons through persona. J Mark Manag 32(1–2):121–148
Joseph R, Lopez S, Sumerall S (2001) In: Dorfman W, Hersen M (eds) Understanding psychological assessment: perspective on individual differences, 1st edn. Springer, New York, pp 1–15
Kocka J (1969) Unternehmensverwaltung und Angestelltenschaft am Beispiel Siemens 1847–1914: Zum Verhältnis von Kapitalismus und Bürokratie in der deutschen Industrialisierung. Klett, Stuttgart
Meehl PE (2013) Clinical versus statistical prediction. A theoretical analysis and a review of evidence. Echo Point Books & Media, Brattleboro, VT
Michaels E, Handfield-Jones H, Axelrod B (2001) The war for talent. Harvard Business School Press, Boston, MA
Morgan G (1997) Images of organization. Sage, London
Sutton R (2007) The no asshole rule: building a civilised workplace and surviving one that isn't. Sphere, London
Trost A (2013) Employer branding. In: Trost A (ed) Employer branding. Arbeitgeber positionieren und präsentieren. Wolters Kluwer, Köln, S 13–75
Trost A (2014) Talent relationship management. Competitive recruiting strategies in times of talent shortage. Springer, Heidelberg

Goals, Assessment and Feedback 6

One might think that *performance management* is a matter of course in any reasonably managed company. Once a year, individual performance and development targets are agreed upon with every employee. In addition to this forward-looking view, the performance of the past months is reviewed in retrospect. In the event, the employee receives structured feedback from his or her direct supervisor. All of this takes place within the annual *performance appraisal*. In recent years and in the course of growing digitization and agilization, hardly any other concept has come under as much criticism as this classic one. As early as 2017, in my book "The End of Performance Appraisal", I put forward the thesis that classical performance appraisal could work in strictly hierarchical worlds, but that it fails completely in an agile context (Trost 2017). In view of this insight, more and more companies are asking themselves: What now?

6.1 Objective Settings and Performance Expectations

Objective setting is certainly among the most widespread leadership or management procedures worldwide. The idea behind it is very simple. Performance expectations are discussed and defined with employees at regular intervals. This usually takes place within the framework of annual performance appraisals (DeNisi and Pritchard 2006). A whole range of expectations is addressed by means of goal setting. For example, some companies expect the agreement upon goals to have a motivating effect on their employees. In addition, goals are used to synchronize the performance of individual employees and entire teams with overarching goals. Finally, it is assumed that a reflection or even an evaluation of performance is possible above all if performance expectations have been determined in advance.

There is a classical approach to objective setting, which is described below. As will become clear later, its strategic orientation is based on a traditional, hierarchical understanding of leadership and organization. Only with this understanding is target agreement in its widespread form sufficiently compatible (see also Trost 2017).

The Classic, Strategic Alignment

Traditional, hierarchically managed companies think in terms of divided labour. Tasks are designed in such a way that each employee devotes him or herself individually to his or her special responsibilities. The aim is to achieve a high level of process and result certainty. You know what to do and how to do it. This was discussed in detail in Sect. 4.3 in relation to the task environment. Since a rather static development is assumed, it seems sufficient to take a look at the targets once a year, in a long cycle. As stated in Sect. 4.5, employees in hierarchical work environments are primarily committed to their managers, which is why performance expectations are agreed upon with the direct manager. The manager, in turn, acts as what has already been identified as the "boss" in this book. Targets are not set somehow. Rather, there are company-wide rules that determine when, who and how goals are to be agreed and documented. There are forms and above all the widely known *SMART rule* that is supposed to be applied. Accordingly, goals must be formulated in such a way that they are *s*pecific, *m*easurable, *a*ttractive, *r*ealistic and *t*ime-bound. The results often end up in the HR department or in the HR information system. If all the points just mentioned are translated into strategic statements, the classic approach can be summarized as follows:

> Objectives are agreed upon individually with each employee. This ensures personal commitment and clear responsibility. (1-1)

> The agreement on objectives always takes place with the next higher manager. He or she has the overview and bears the overall responsibility. (2-1)

> Objectives are agreed on regularly (annually). This allows synchronization with other internal processes, which also follow a regular cycle. (3-1)

> Objectives are set top-down. In this way, we ensure that the sum achieved is what is important for the company. (4-1)

> It is expected that goal settings will be handled similarly for all employees. There are clear, formal and binding rules for this. (5-1)

> Individual objectives are treated confidentially. They are a matter between the employee and his direct superior. (6-1)

In the further course of this section, a corresponding counter-draft for companies with a more agile understanding of leadership and organization is presented. Before doing so, the possible limitations of this approach will first be discussed.

The General Problem with "Smart" Objectives

Regardless of whether a company is managed hierarchically, traditionally or in a more agile manner, there are fundamental problems about the understanding of goals. Especially companies with a hierarchical background report on problems regularly. If you take a closer look at the goals agreed in numerous areas of the company, you will immediately see that most of them have very little to do with the SMART rule. Production employees agree about "cleanliness", bus drivers agree about "punctuality", salesmen agree in matters of "friendliness". The "objectives" between different employees with similar roles hardly differ at all.

In fact, in tasks with high results and process certainty, it is very difficult to agree on smart objectives with each individual employee every year anew. In such a task environment the agreement of objectives cannot make any sense. After all, a whole group of employees is expected to meet common and stable *performance standards* in the long run. All bus drivers should be on time. All people in sales should be friendly. All teachers should communicate their teaching material clearly. All hotel housekeeping staff should leave rooms in perfect condition. These standards have always applied and will continue to apply. Should there be any changes, this will be discussed by all parties concerned when the new standards become relevant. So what is the point of talking once a year with each individual bus driver, salesperson, etc., about what the individual objectives are? Practically, this makes no sense at all to many managers and employees.

Similarly problematic is the demand for a smart target setting for tasks with low process and result certainty and big scope (projects). Tasks of this kind are defined in such a way that results are not clear from the outset and cannot be clarified either, making the formulation of smart objectives simply impossible. This is one of the reasons why scientists will tend to avoid a "smart" target agreement, for example. Nevertheless, it goes without saying that one also pursues a direction with tasks that are fraught with uncertainty. However, this direction can rather be described in terms of common *priorities*. What are the focal points? What is the vision? What is the most important aspect of what is to be achieved? What are *key results* that we want to ensure in all cases? In the following, we will therefore talk less about a target agreement and more about a definition of *performance expectations*, regardless of whether this definition is made with the direct supervisor, with internal or external customers, with colleagues or with oneself.

Under certain conditions, the agreement of "smart" objectives only works with medium result and process certainty and with medium scope. At first this has nothing to do with agility or hierarchy but is a general context factor. However, if we take a closer look at agile companies, we will inevitably come to the conclusion that the definition of performance expectations in this context must work differently than in traditional, hierarchical contexts.

Toxic Effects of Individual Goals in Connected Organizations

In a divided working environment, individual goals are fundamentally conceivable. However, in a connected one with a high degree of task dynamics (cf. Sect. 4.5) individual goals can be toxic. The reasons for this are obvious. In connected working contexts, it is assumed that the individual can never be successful alone, but only the entire system. This is due to the interdependence of tasks, employees and teams.

> Performance is only achieved by whole teams. This is why performance expectations are only defined with teams as a whole. (1-2)

No expedition team climbing on the Nanga Parbat would ever come up with the idea of defining individual goals. If, for example, a single mountaineer were to orient himself towards his personal goal of climbing the summit as quickly as possible, this could jeopardize the success of the entire team and ultimately his own safety. In this respect, in agile companies with dynamic task contexts, only team goals but never individual goals are conceivable.

What Do You Do for Whom and Why?

Every employee, every team should be able to answer the following question: What do you do for whom and why? Here it is expressly not a question of what one *is*—sales representative, accountant, marketing specialist—but who profits from one's own work and how. Work basically means generating added value for someone else. Who is this *someone else*? Who is the customer of your work? Only in the rarest cases can the answer be "my boss". This is only the case if, for example, you are an assistant to an executive. Otherwise, there must be internal or external instances that are recipients of work results.

If this is the case, then the question arises as to why, especially in hierarchically managed companies, employees agree goals with their direct superiors. Would it not be more obvious to commit oneself to one's own customer and to make agreements with this instance either internally or externally?

> Teams are primarily committed to their (internal and external) customers. They are therefore also used to define performance expectations. (2-2)

As explained in detail in Sect. 4.5, customer engagement is a key feature of agile organizations. The hierarchically minded manager might feel irritated by this thought. He or she tends to ask what else he or she is good for. The answer is simple. He or she is there to make exactly that happen. For example, in the role of a coach, he or she challenges employees to answer questions such as: "Who are we doing this for? What does the customer think about this proposal? What do our customers expect concretely?"

On the left side (A) in Fig. 6.1 this logic is shown graphically. The solid arrow indicates the employee's commitment and dedication to his or her manager.

At first glance, the commitment and dedication of an individual employee in an agile setting appears more complex than it might appear from the left side of Fig. 6.1. Employees in an agile world are committed not only to their leaders, but also to their

6.1 Objective Settings and Performance Expectations

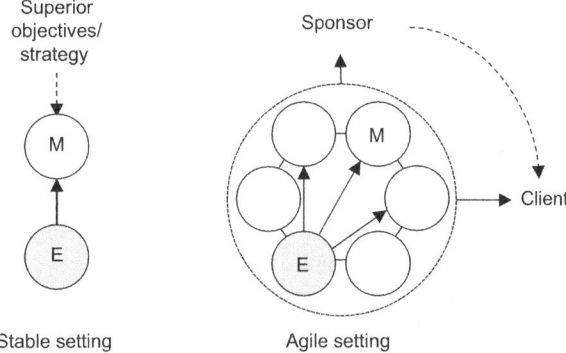

Fig. 6.1 Commitment and dedication of an employee in a stable, hierarchical setting and in an agile setting (E: employee, M: manager, first published in Trost 2017, Unter den Erwartungen. Wiley. p. 159)

team colleagues. In this setting, it is usually difficult to distinguish between individual and collective performance. The manager in the role of a coach or partner is always part of the entire team. There is a *common* commitment in this respect. The team as a whole is not committed to a superior manager but on the one hand it is committed to the client and on the other hand to an internal sponsor—if the latter exists. As indicated in the figure above, it is assumed here that the internal sponsor is also indirectly committed to the customer.

Goal Agreement Versus Goal Setting

Related to the agreement about goals, it is repeatedly pointed out that goals are motivating for those who have them. This hypothesis is based on extensive research of the psychologists Locke and Latham (1984). In the *Goal Setting Theory* postulated by them, they justify the assumption that people who have previously set themselves a corresponding goal perform better under the same conditions. However, for the sake of completeness, it should be added that this effect only occurs if the person who has the goal feels fully committed to his or her goal. Locke and Latham refer to this as target commitment, which is achieved above all when targets are not just set by an authority but performance expectations are mutually agreed upon.

> Performance expectations are mutually agreed on. This is the only way to ensure that those affected are committed to fulfil these expectations. (4-2)

If goals are mutually agreed on between a manager and an employee, this presupposes a partnership approach. Any form of superiority and subordination, like when the manager acts as a boss, can destroy the motivational effect of objectives because a genuine form of agreement (at eye level) is not fully compatible with the hierarchical system.

Personal Responsibility and Openness

The traditional idea of objective setting is that goals are a matter between an employee and his or her manager. However, the responsibility for ensuring that goals are defined at all lies mostly with the manager. After all, it is him or her who conducts the annual performance appraisal and is trained for it. Target agreement is seen as a (pure) management task. The documented results the manager is credited with, or the company as a whole. This view is obvious if one assumes that goals are necessary to control an entire organization.

In an agile context you see things a little different. Whether you agree on smart goals, priorities, performance standards or key results, they are needed by the people and teams concerned because they provide guidance and create the necessary commitments—between team members, colleagues, internal customers and suppliers, connected project groups, etc.—and they are the key to the success of your business. But if teams, employees, project groups themselves are the main beneficiaries of a somehow structured agreement of goals, expectations, priorities, etc., then it is logical or consistent to leave the responsibility for this to them. Then the partners themselves decide when they consider such an agreement of performance expectations to be reasonable and when they carry it out. In an agile working world characterized by personal responsibility and networks, it simply makes no sense to link agreements of performance expectations to the rotation of the sun around the earth, as the father of *Management by Objectives*, George Odiorne (1965), put it so well.

> Performance expectations can always be defined if it appears to be appropriate for the respective partners. (3-2)

If one takes the idea of individual responsibility seriously, the question arises as to whether the agreement of goals should or may be made into an obligation. At this point, at the latest, hierarchically thinking managers and HR professionals have serious doubts. Where do you get when you do not have to do anything anymore? Is that not naïve and unrealistic? That is what one might think. In fact, from an agile perspective, it seems naïve and unrealistic to believe in the benefits of a measure if those who act on it do not see the benefits. Rather, it is based on the assumption—not entirely far from reality—that things can only be done with the necessary reliability and commitment if the relevant people understand why they are doing something and how they could benefit from it.

> Performance expectations can be defined, but people do not have to. This is the responsibility of employees and teams. There are no binding rules or formats for this either. (5-2)

If you want to empower employees and teams instead of patronizing them, you will give them help—guides, checklists, templates, webinars, (peer) coaching, an app, workshop formats and related tools. Mandatory, standardized forms and preconfigured fields in any HR systems, on the other hand, are far removed from agile organizations. Rules and standards are dispensed with as far as possible and established at best when they are actively demanded and desired by the people as a common basis.

Target Transparency Versus Drawer

In hierarchically managed companies with a division of labour, individual goals are usually treated confidentially. As indicated above, they are regarded as a matter between the employee and his or her manager. The practical probability is high that they will disappear in the much-cited drawer or in a corresponding system for a year. In connected working environments, on the other hand, where lateral cooperation and coordination across departmental borders are important, this idea is rather distant.

> Performance expectations are communicated internally. This form of transparency strengthens commitment and facilitates lateral communication and collaboration. (6-2)

I have got to know companies that have very successfully switched over to publishing agreed performance expectations on the intranet or in an internal wiki. The public creates commitment and transparency. Why make performance expectations a secret? Even for hierarchical companies with division of labour, this idea is not entirely foreign. After all, there have always been job descriptions which make it clear to everyone in the company who is responsible for which tasks.

Target Agreement in Agile Working Environments

In the following, a simple, practical scenario will be used to illustrate how a definition of performance expectations in a more agile way can take place, irrespective of the industry or size of an enterprise.

The members of a team, or employees with comparable roles in the company, meet and look for an answer to the question: "What does good work mean for us?" They do this from the perspective of their customers, which is why they start with answering questions like "Who are our customers?" or "For whom do we do what we do?" Neither the presence of a manager nor any official form is required in the first step. An empty sheet of flipchart paper is enough. If deemed necessary, facilitation could be useful. The employees carry out this exercise because they consider it important either on their own initiative or because it was directly asked of them by a manager. When and how often it is carried out is essentially determined by the team itself. The results of this discussion also belong to the team and its members. They decide what happens to it. Some teams keep the documentation in a virtual drawer. Some communicate these in the company's own intranet. Some in turn print out the results in the form of posters and attach them to their office walls, visible to everyone. Whether the performance expectations developed here are "smart" targets is completely irrelevant. In most cases this results in common performance standards, quality criteria, benchmarks for good work, success indicators. The format is irrelevant. No official and structured form is needed. The employees formulate things in the way that makes the most sense to them, without having to work through a fixed format or even let it distract them.

Up to this point, performance standards are being developed. However, a comprehensive, binding agreement is not yet in place. For this it needs another instance. At best, the employees concerned reached an agreement among themselves. On a progressive, particularly consistent level, the employees present their results to their customers and ask whether they agree with the points outlined. Is that what you expect from us? Subsequently, appropriate changes are made. Of course, it would also be conceivable to actively involve customers in the process as early as possible.

Now one wonders what a manager's role might be in this scenario. Hierarchically thinking readers are probably tormented by this question during the entire reading of this scenario while their agile thinking colleagues do not even think about this question. In organizations with a more agile understanding of leadership, leaders act as coaches, partners or enablers (see Sect. 4.4). As coaches, they initially hold back in the development of performance standards and let the employees do the work. Then they listen to the results, demand more clarity, higher or lower standards, challenge or level the standards in order for them to be more realistic. From a hierarchical standpoint one has to assume that employees tend to set their performance standards low. But, experience has shown, that exactly the opposite is the case and the manager must intervene in favour of lower standards. Of course, this effect can only be observed if the remuneration systems are geared accordingly. This is referred to in more detail in Chap. 9 about remuneration. Managers who act as partners are equally involved right from the start. They regard performance standards as common standards to which they also commit themselves. They avoid sitting at the end of the table and having the last word on everything while the employees concentrate on the common cause. Enablers also address the question of what employees need to meet their performance needs. They do this together with the employees.

This scenario described above is not intended to be an ideal agile approach, but merely to illustrate that there is a more agile, simple and practicable alternative to the classical one described at the beginning. The difference between hierarchy and stability, on the one hand, and agility and networks, on the other, becomes particularly clear when it comes to goal setting and performance expectations and the associated strategic dimensions (see Fig. 6.2). If a single question had to be used to determine which side a company is on, then the question about how employees know what they are supposed to achieve in their work might be the one.

Relevant unit	1-1 *Individual employees*	1-2 *Teams*
	Objectives are agreed individually with each employee. This ensures personal commitment and clear responsibility.	Performance is only achieved by whole teams. This is why performance expectations are only defined with teams as a whole.
Partner of the agreement	2-1 *Next level manager*	2-2 *Internal and external customers*
	The agreement of objectives always takes place with the next higher manager. He or she has the overview and bears the overall responsibility.	Teams are primarily committed to their (internal and external) customers. They are therefore also used to define performance expectations.
Time	3-1 *Regular cycle*	3-2 *Demand-oriented*
	Objectives are agreed regularly (annually). This allows synchronization with other internal processes, which also follow a regular cycle.	Performance expectations can always be defined if it appears to be appropriate for the respective partners
Direction of power	4-1 *Superordination and subordination*	4-2 *Eye level*
	Objectives are set top-down. In this way, we ensure that the sum achieved is what is important for the company.	Performance expectations are mutually agreed upon. This is the only way to ensure that those affected are committed to fulfil these expectations.
Regulation	5-1 *Commitments and Standards*	5-2 *Voluntariness without standards*
	It is expected that objective settings will be handled similarly across all employees. There are clear, formal and binding rules for this.	Performance expectations can be defined, but people do not have to. This is the responsibility of employees and teams. There are no binding rules or formats for this either.
Communication	6-1 Confidentiality	6-2 Transparency
	Individual objectives are treated confidentially. They are a matter between the employee and his direct superior.	Performance expectations are communicated internally. This form of transparency strengthens commitment and facilitates lateral communication and collaboration.

Fig. 6.2 Overview of all strategic dimensions of objective setting and performance expectations

6.2 Feedback

To become really good at something, people need feedback about what they are doing or achieving. This probably also applies to all the skills that people acquire over time, be it at work, in sports, in the arts or at most other fields where competence matters. If we raise children well, we will give them feedback. Most children demand this as well. When young people are trained in companies, they receive as much feedback as possible from their teachers and colleagues. Good teachers give feedback. Good students ask for feedback. The relevance of feedback hardly needs to be discussed. Nobody would seriously denigrate the importance of this subject. It is therefore not surprising that most companies have made attempts in recent decades to institutionalize feedback in some way. The subject seems too important to be left to chance or the good will of individuals.

Feedback Rules and Processes

It is hard to find a training course on leadership that does not explicitly address the topic of *feedback rules*. Firstly, there is the assumption about providing feedback being one of the core management tasks, an assumption that will be put to the test later in this chapter. Secondly, when conveying feedback rules one follows the assumption that feedback is successful above all when feedback is given "correctly". For example, it is taught that feedback should always be descriptive and not evaluative. Not: "that wasn't good", but: "that is how you did it and that led to ...". Feedback should be factual and not personal. Feedback should be clear, understandable, correct and so on. When companies go even further, they not only convey the rules of giving feedback but also the rules of taking feedback. "Listen carefully", "be open-minded", "avoid a defensive response" or the like. However, it can be assumed, that the mere communication of feedback rules is only partly sufficient to give and receive feedback effectively. As will be shown later, the setting plays a role within which feedback is given and received. Who gives whom why feedback and what happens with it?

Even more problematic are the very widespread approaches to anchoring *feedback processes* institutionally. Probably the most prominent approach is to make feedback a central component of an annual performance appraisal. Here, managers are asked or even obliged to give their employees individual feedback on their behaviour, performance and skills once a year in retrospect. It is assumed that employees only receive feedback from their managers, or above all, when they exert the famous "gentle pressure" on managers. As will still become apparent, under certain circumstances this attempt also really falls short.

Before we go into alternative perspectives, we first want to clarify what it is that constitutes good feedback, and under which conditions the desired improvements might be acknowledged.

Openness to Feedback

Feedback does not always have to be social. Often, technologies or simply the results of work processes provide feedback. However, in the context discussed here, only *social feedback* should be considered, in which one person gives feedback to another person. This form of feedback is usually used in the context of HR strategies and leadership.

By feedback itself we mean the reflection of the behaviour of the one receiving feedback in order to improve his or her behaviour accordingly. Whether feedback is good or effective is therefore always and exclusively dependent on the feedback recipient, the actual and only customer of the feedback. A feedback provider can adhere to all feedback rules and put all his personal motivation and passion into it. If feedback is not appropriately received by the recipient, the feedback is simply worthless. It may happen in everyday life when giving feedback lets the feedback provider loosen up mentally, and emotionally—"I had to get rid of that. I feel better now". Actually, this has nothing to do with effective feedback. A prerequisite for feedback to reach its recipient is his or her *openness towards feedback.*

Of course, the openness of a feedback recipient towards feedback is greatest when the feedback recipient actively asks the feedback provider for feedback. Openness also depends on other factors. In the context discussed here, it seems useful to focus on those factors from which conclusions can be drawn for the strategic alignment of institutionalized feedback. Therefore, a simple theory of openness is presented below. A graphical representation of this theory is shown in Fig. 6.3.

Whether or not an employee is open to feedback depends first and foremost on the expected *consequences* of the feedback. Is the feedback still a feedback or already a judgement or even a formal judgement? If an employee experiences feedback as negative, does he or she have to fear that this may have extrinsic consequences for his or her performance evaluation and thus for his or her salary and future career development? Formally and temporally, feedback and formal judgements can be separated. But whether this separation is perceived by the employee is another matter. Should the employee fear consequences from his subjective perception due to negative feedback, he or she will adopt a defensive attitude and start negotiating, the opposite of showing openness.

Feedback is only accepted if the feedback recipient perceives a positive intention on the part of the feedback provider. Does the feedback provider really want to help? Does he or she have good intentions? Or does the feedback provider want to harm the feedback recipient? The bottom line is that appreciation is a prerequisite for effective feedback. This appreciation in turn depends on the motivation that the feedback recipient attributes to the feedback provider. As an employee, you may ask yourself implicitly or explicitly why a feedback provider gives feedback. What is the *motivation* of the feedback provider? Is he or she doing this on his or her own

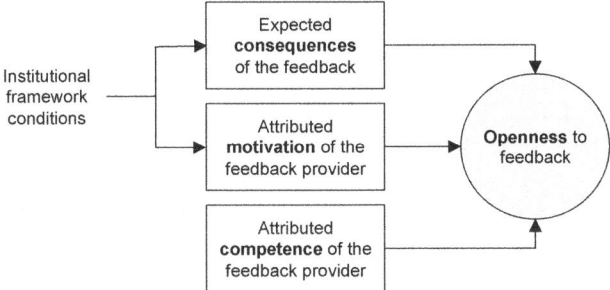

Fig. 6.3 Factors of openness to feedback

initiative because he or she wants to? In this case one also speaks of *intrinsic* attribution of motivation. Or does the feedback provider only give feedback because a third party (HR, a higher level of authority) expects this from him or her? This would correspond to an *extrinsic* attribution of motivation. A feedback recipient will place less value on feedback if he or she extrinsically attributes the motivation of the feedback provider to it. For example, if a child apologizes to another child after the father has "ordered" that child to apologize, this reduces the perceived value of signalling remorse. As shown in the next section, the expected consequences and the attribution of motivation will depend directly on the institutional framework conditions in the company.

Finally, openness towards feedback received depends on the attributed *competence* of the feedback provider. This aspect is obvious and requires little further explanation. Of course, people accept the feedback of another person above all when they can be confident that the other person is able to give them constructive feedback. Conversely, the unsolicited giving of feedback holds the latent, implicit message of superiority over the feedback recipient.

Situational and Institutional Framework Conditions

Let us imagine the following simple situation for a moment: After a meeting, a feedback provider, Anne, says to employee Ben (the feedback recipient) the following, "You rarely get involved in the discussion. But I am sure the team could really benefit from your expertise". What is interesting now is the dynamics of this feedback, which depends on the situational and institutional framework conditions. Different framework conditions are outlined in Fig. 6.4 in a simple way. The instance shaded in grey indicates who triggers feedback in the given situation, i.e., who takes the initiative.

Below is a brief explanation of the different situations in Fig. 6.4. Conclusions are then drawn on the effectiveness of the feedback.

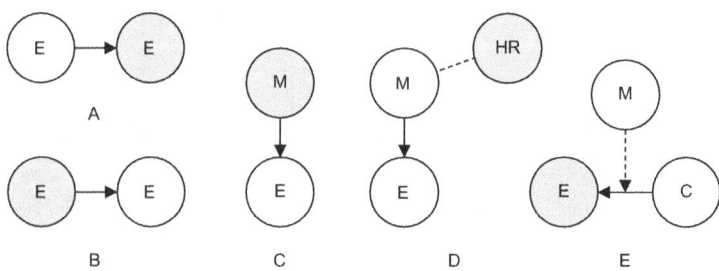

Fig. 6.4 Situational framework conditions of the feedback. Grey shaded circles indicate who triggers feedback (E: employee, M: manager, C: customer)

A. The employee (trigger) actively asked his or her colleague for feedback after the meeting. "Anne, how do you see my role in the group? From your point of view, is there anything I could do better?" One can hardly assume a greater openness on the part of the feedback recipient than in this situation.
B. One colleague Anne (Trigger) gives the employee an unsolicited feedback. "Ben, by the way, what I've always wanted to tell you..." This situation is risky for feedback provider Anne, as long as she is not certain whether feedback recipient Ben shows the necessary openness. In some cultures, unsolicited, negative feedback is one of the things you should better never do.
C. Anne as feedback provider is the boss of the feedback receiver Ben. The initiative comes from her. She (trigger) does not know at this moment whether Ben shows the necessary openness. In addition, the matter now becomes threatening for the feedback recipient Ben. Possibly already at this moment a later, negative evaluation announces itself, which could tempt Ben to defend himself.
D. Anne gives Ben a feedback, because HR as third party (trigger) wants it that way. Ben knows this, which causes an extrinsic attribution of motivation. As Ben's boss, Anne may even be asked to formally document her feedback. Now the matter is not only threatening for Ben. He also wonders whether Anne gives him feedback because she has to (extrinsic) or whether she wants to (intrinsic).
E. Ben actively asks Anne for feedback, Anne is Ben's customer. Both meet at eye level. In his or her role as a coach, Ben's direct manager encourages actively asking for feedback directly from the customer. As will be shown in detail below, this situation is the ideal setting especially in agile organizations.

The comparison of these different framework conditions shows quite well that the question of when feedback is effective is less about adhering to any feedback rules than about the dynamics triggered by the framework conditions, which in itself can be conducive or even less conducive. In particular, the institutional framework conditions are the subject of an HR strategy when it comes to feedback. In the following, strategic dimensions around this topic will be pointed out and discussed, building on the previous considerations.

Responsibility for Feedback

Numerous companies conduct regular employee surveys. Employees are often asked to give their consent to a statement such as the following: "My direct manager regularly gives me feedback on my work performance". Usually the results of this statement are devastating. As a result, managers are asked even more intensely and emphatically to fulfil their leadership duties. If, in view of these results, an annual performance appraisal has not yet been implemented, consideration will certainly now be given to introducing such a tool. As a manager, you have to conduct a mandatory meeting in which giving feedback is an integral part. That is how it is argued in numerous companies.

Behind the above-mentioned statement of the employee survey and the subsequent considerations and consequences there is an unspoken strategic attitude according to which managers and ultimately the company are responsible for ensuring that employees receive regular feedback.

> As a company, we are responsible for ensuring that our employees receive regular feedback. (1-1)

This basic strategic attitude is understandable but at the same time dangerous. The above theoretical considerations lead to the conclusion that good feedback can be thwarted by turning it into an obligation for line managers. Prescribed (extrinsically motivated) feedback is less appreciated by employees than voluntary, intrinsically motivated feedback. In addition, feedback actively collected by employees is associated with greater openness on the part of the feedback recipients. An alternative strategic statement on the responsibility for feedback could be as follows:

> The employees themselves are responsible for obtaining feedback. (1-2)

In companies that commit themselves to this strategy, the CEO clearly communicates: "Feedback is important. If you want feedback, get it. Good employees do this very often".

Relevant Feedback Providers

At the same time, the traditional view outlined above assumes that feedback must happen top-down, which corresponds to a classical understanding of leadership. The manager gives instructions on how to achieve what. Later he or she then tells the employee whether he or she has acted in the expected way.

> Employees receive feedback primarily from their direct manager. Giving feedback is one of the most important management tasks. (2-1)

This principle may not fully work in work settings in which employees have a higher level of expertise in their respective field than their managers. Section 4.4 has dealt with this using the so-called T-concept. Furthermore, especially in agile working environments, employees and teams are not committed to their managers but primarily to their respective (internal or external) customers. From them—not from the direct manager—one gets feedback instead of passively receiving it from the direct superior. Accordingly, the strategic statement is as follows:

> Employees primarily ask for feedback from their (internal/external) customers or colleagues. (2-2)

Managers who have internalized this thinking will always challenge their team with questions such as: "Who are you doing this for? Who should benefit from it?" and finally ask the question about what the customers think of the proposal. These managers secretly convey the attitude that they do not have to be satisfied with a work result themselves, but that always those who are to benefit from it should.

In a company I recently advised, we developed a simple method to institutionalize this idea. Instead of an annual, individual object setting, teams (not individuals) are encouraged to think systematically about who their customers are and what performance expectations they have (see previous Sect. 6.1). And, consideration is already being given to who should be actively asked for feedback and to when this should happen. This is about answering simple questions together, such as:

- What went well and should we continue for the future?
- What didn't go so well and what should we improve in the future?

This form of conscious reflection can and should be carried out at any time if the participants consider it useful. Executives only have a facilitating role according to their role as coaches. At least in this company, this approach works excellently and far better than the annual performance appraisal that has been practised to date.

The Right Time for Feedback

Suppose an employee tries to sell a car to a potential customer and an experienced colleague accompanies him passively. Following the sales talk, the car salesperson can receive or experience four levels of feedback.

- *Result.* The customer buys the car. In the long term, the employee receives feedback on the sales achieved in the course of a year. If the turnover is high, the seller has done a good job. This form of feedback is not social in nature but more factual and related to tangible outcome.
- *Process.* A colleague gives the car salesman feedback on the form of the conversation immediately after the conversation. He or she shows how the salesperson behaved and in what way this may have affected the customer's choice. In addition, he or she may outline in which situation the car salesman could have acted differently or better.
- *Person.* The colleague tells the car salesman that he is a particularly talented, skilful, empathetic, result-oriented salesman. Everything he or she says does not refer to the behaviour of the car salesman but to him as a person. "Wow, you really are a good salesman."
- *Self-regulation.* The colleague's feedback refers to the way in which the car salesman reflects on his behaviour and deals with successes or failures, for example. "Don't take the rejection personally," or "You should question your sales strategy more often."

Previous findings in feedback research indicate that different levels of feedback also lead to different degrees of feedback success (Hattie and Timperley 2007). Accordingly, people are most likely to learn when they receive feedback at the *process* level. In sports, this has always been a matter of course, for example in golf. Trainers almost exclusively give feedback on the swing, while the result is rather irrelevant, at least in the training situation. They give this feedback immediately. The annual appraisal interview, on the other hand, and the feedback it contains, usually relate to results to and the person. It is usually too late to provide feedback on an employee's concrete behaviour (process). In this respect, it is not surprising that more and more companies are realizing that it is not enough to give feedback once a year. However, it is surprising, that many companies have taken years to arrive at this simple insight. Feedback within the framework of an annual performance appraisal is based on the following strategic orientation:

> Employees receive regular feedback. There is a fixed (annual) cycle for this. (3-1)

Companies that adopt the process concept and rely on direct feedback increasingly tend towards this strategic alignment:

> Employees always ask for feedback when they think it makes sense. Good employees do this promptly and frequently. (3-2)

This latter premise can hardly be institutionalized by rules and processes. Still, it is possible to create framework conditions that promote, simplify and enable frequent and immediate feedback. Those who are active in social media, for example, experience the daily, rapid giving and accepting of feedback in an almost natural way. A new, widespread approach that takes up these considerations is the implementation of so-called check-ins or feedback apps.

Check-in and Feedback Apps

More and more companies are recognizing the limits of classic, long-cyclical, regulated feedback processes that take place top-down. In response, a recent international trend has been to establish so-called check-ins and feedback apps. *Check-ins* probably go back to the company Adobe in 2012.[1] Once every 3 months (not annually), an employee and his or her manager meet, give each other feedback and talk about mutual expectations. The process does not affect salary adjustments and is essentially informal—no forms, ratings, rankings, etc.—and not linked to other HR processes. In principle, check-ins are voluntary and can be initiated by the employees themselves. This process is often enriched by a *feedback app* that enables employees to give and receive feedback on whatever concerns them at any time,

---

[1] http://www.adobe.com/check-in.html (last seen on April 1st, 2019).

cross-functionally and independently of the hierarchy level of the feedback providers and recipients. Since then, companies such as SAP, Accenture, General Electric and Deutsche Telekom have followed suit, to name just a few.

This approach points in an agile direction. Feedback should be more frequent. Employees bear more responsibility in obtaining and, above all, giving feedback. Feedback is understood not only as a top-down phenomenon, but as something that can and should take place laterally, from left to right. However, this well intended approach leaves the unanswered question of why employees need a formal event, such as check-in, to talk to their manager. And what empowering contribution does an app make when it comes to giving unsolicited feedback to colleagues? A tool of this kind is certainly nice. It addresses behavioural preferences that users are used to from other platforms. Nevertheless, it seems to be largely unclear what should ultimately provide the expected added value. If you talk to companies that have embarked on this path, you quickly get the impression that the main thing since then has been to offer an alternative to the classic annual performance appraisal (which you no longer want). There was possibly a lack of courage for a total abolishment or for the introduction of radically different approaches.

Whose Feedback Is This?

Employees probably give and take feedback infinitely over the course of a working day. One expresses an opinion over some work result, comments on a decision or says something about some form of behaviour by someone else. We can not help ourselves. Giving and taking social feedback is a natural part of any form of collaboration and communication, in which you cannot *not* give feedback. Even if you do not say anything about something, it can already be a form of feedback. But when we talk about feedback in the HR context, we rarely think about *informal feedback* that takes place at almost every moment at work. Rather, we have processes in mind that regulate feedback in some form. We assume that at certain times or on selected occasions, certain people would need to give feedback to others in a predefined form on a platform provided for that particular purpose. In HR, we tend to think technically and formally.

Data is generated once we do this and encourage employees to give feedback in this way. An employee gives another employee five stars for special help via a feedback app. The manager spontaneously gives an employee an appreciative comment for a special performance—"Thank you Ben, well done. Keep it up." Now a question arises about who owns this feedback. Who can see who has received which feedback from whom? Who can draw what conclusions from this? In a hierarchical context, one will tend to answer that feedback is in the interest of the company, which is why feedback can be centrally documented and, if necessary, viewed by hierarchically superior instances.

> As a company, we have an interest in the feedback that our employees receive. This is why we document feedback in a centralized way. (4-1)

The reasons are obvious. Finally, the feedback that an individual employee receives can be used to draw conclusions about his or her activities and impact within the company. Insights of this kind could at some point be considered in the context of a formal evaluation, an aspect that is more fully addressed in Sect. 6.3.

Agile thinking companies, on the other hand, would generally assume that feedback belongs to whoever receives it. The feedback recipient decides what happens to the feedback. It is in his or her hands whether he or she (intrinsically) accepts a feedback or not, whether he or she shares the feedback or keeps it for him or herself etc.

> Feedback belongs exclusively to the feedback recipient (employees, teams). He or she is the primary customer of the feedback. Therefore, central documentation is out of the question. (4-2)

For many of the strategic options discussed in this book, it depends on the context which option is more appropriate. While one option may well work in a hierarchical and static environment, the other option primarily leads to potential success in agile organizations. It is not so much a question of evaluating the options generally, but rather of which one fits within which context. This is only partly the case for the two options on who owns feedback that have just been described. Although hierarchical companies would like to see feedback as not only belonging to the feedback recipient, holding this view is not advisable. Once feedback recipients know that feedback can be "used against them" in some way, this has a dysfunctional impact not only on the feedback recipient and his way of dealing with feedback, but also on feedback providers. The boundary between feedback and formal judgment is a thin line. However, the associated social dynamics are completely different. Companies that translate feedback into judgement destroy feedback. They fall, so to speak, into the evaluation trap. This is one of the topics covered in the following subchapter.

A Matter for the Company or the Feedback Recipient

On the previous pages, a total of four strategic dimensions related to feedback have been addressed (see Fig. 6.5). Who ensures feedback? Who receives feedback from whom? Whose feedback is this? What is caused by the feedback? All in all, there is a core idea here in which all these dimensions can be unified. Is feedback a matter for the company or a matter for the feedback recipient? Large parts of the previous discussion can more or less be reduced to this question.

Responsibility for feedback	*1-1 Company* As a company, we are responsible for ensuring that our employees receive regular feedback.	*1-2 Employees* The employees themselves are responsible for obtaining feedback.
Primary feedback provider	*2-1 Direct manager* Employees receive feedback primarily from their direct manager. Giving feedback is one of the most important management tasks.	*2-2 Internal and external customers* Employees primarily ask for feedback from their (internal/external) customers or colleagues.
Trigger for feedback	*3-1 Cyclical and passive* Employees receive regular feedback. There is a fixed (annual) cycle for this purpose	*3-2 On demand and active* Employees always ask for feedback when they think it makes sense. Good employees do this frequently and promptly and frequently.
Ownership and documentation	*4-1 Company* As a company, we have an interest in the feedback that our employees receive. This is why we document feedback in a central instance.	*4-2 Feedback receiver* Feedback belongs exclusively to the feedback recipient (employees, teams). He or she is the primary customer of the feedback. Therefore, central documentation is out of the question.

Fig. 6.5 Overview of all strategic dimensions related to feedback

6.3 Formal Judgement

Whenever people meet, what in social psychology is called *social judgment* takes place. Usually in fractions of a second, the counterpart is assessed as a whole. Is this person more or less sympathetic to me? Is the person dangerous or not? Do I like this person or not? Does this person tend to be stronger or weaker than me? It is good that people have this instinctive ability. It is indispensable in the coexistence of people in social systems and is absolutely necessary for survival (Fiske and Taylor 1991). In addition, social judgement formation is always relevant for people in guiding their actions. How one thinks about another person determines in a certain way one's own behaviour towards that person.

The Special Nature of Formal Appraisals

Since this is also the case in the relationship between a manager and an employee or even between employees at the same level, it is sometimes argued that it would be a matter of fairness and transparency to make these judgements known and to articulate them. However, it does not always correspond to the common value attitudes to say what one thinks about another person. Also, from the point of view of HR policy, there is hardly any compelling necessity to do so. When we think of judgement in the context of HR, then it concerns rather *formal* judgement, which stand in direct relation to HR-relevant decisions.

This is exactly the difference to the already discussed concept of feedback. In the case of feedback, it is always the (intrinsic) responsibility of the feedback recipient to reflect on the feedback, to derive conclusions and, at best, to optimise their own behaviour. From a formal evaluation, however, (extrinsic) consequences are derived *over the* judged one. A practical situation may illustrate this. If an employee is told by his or her manager that he or she would do well to be more actively involved in team meetings, this is first and foremost feedback. If, in addition to this notion, the manager pulls out his smartphone, opens the employee appraisal app and places a check mark in the "Team Capability" field, this information is passed on to the HR department, it is then included in the employee's overall assessment and finally, if this has consequences for the employee's future development and payment, then this is no longer just feedback but a formal judgement. Formal judgments have formal, clearly regulated and extrinsic consequences for the person being judged. Otherwise they are seen as basically irrelevant. There are a number of common fields of application:

- Employees whose performance is evaluated as positive receive appropriate variable pay, a salary increase, promotion or talent nominations. The latter usually takes place if their potential is also judged to be high.
- Employees whose performance is judged negative are transferred internally, receive targeted development measures or are laid off.
- The competencies of the employees are assessed in order to determine their development needs and their internal deployment possibilities.

In most cases, formal judgements of this kind take place within the event of the so-called *annual performance appraisal*. They belong to the standard repertoire of HR. The extent to which they make sense, on the other hand, depends on the structural and cultural framework conditions of a company. While classical, formal judgements can work well in the context of hierarchically managed companies, they completely fail in agile and connected working environments (cf. Trost 2017). In the further course of this section, individual aspects of this topic will be further examined. The later chapters of this book deal in more detail with those issues that have to do with the consequences of formal assessments. These include continuous learning (Sect. 7.3), talent identification (Sect. 8.1), base pay (Sect. 9.2) and variable pay (Sect. 9.3). Therefore, the following section focuses exclusively on the formal judgement process itself.

The Boss as Judge

When companies, consultants, HR software manufacturers and other players in the HR community think about formal judgement, most of them assume that the employee will be evaluated by the immediate supervisor. Deviations from this practice are rare, though increasingly frequent. The strategic premise is accordingly:

> One of the central tasks of a manager is to formally evaluate employees at regular intervals. (1-1)

However, this approach is not without problems, especially if a company strives for a more agile understanding of leadership and organization. The dominant view on leadership is of particular relevant in this context. As already explained in Sect. 4.4 different leadership roles can be distinguished: the boss, the partner, the coach and the enabler. A manager who takes on the role of the boss has no problem at all with the formal judgement of employees. Moreover, formal assessments underpin his leadership position.

Managers, on the other hand, who act in the role of a coach, partner or enabler, perceive the obligation to have to formally assess their employees as completely incompatible with the relationship they maintain or strive for with their employees. The great Douglas McGregor expressed it as follows: "The role of judge and the role of counsellor are incompatible" (McGregor 1960, p. 117). What McGregor calls a "counsellor" largely refers to the role of the coach as described in this book. And whoever makes formal judgements acts as a kind of judge. Partnership leadership or leadership as a coach requires eye level, while formal assessment goes hand in hand with superiority and subordination. Mick Jagger acts as band leader of the Rolling Stones out of the role of partner. It would be hard to imagine that Mick Jagger would ever have been willing to formally assess Keith Richards—Hey Keith, it is January and time for the performance evaluation. In the same way, for example, the dean of a faculty would never do this to his fellow professors, whom he or she leads in a certain way. However, it is safe to assume that Mick Jagger will give his band mates countless feedback during a band rehearsal.

> Leadership is at eye level. That is why our managers do not judge their employees, but encourage critical self-reflection. (1-2)

Having fear of being judged by his or her manager might result in fear or anxiety. The employee hardly acts towards his or her manager in an authentic but rather in a tactical manner. It is about appearing in a positive light to the manager. Feedback turns into negotiation—"I do not think I did that badly at all, considering ...". Shortly before the annual appraisal interview, you really speed up and present yourself in the best possible manner. One speaks here also of the so-called Santa-Claus-effect. Companies that treat their employees as responsible people tend not to want all this.

Forced Distribution

A common form of formal evaluation is to divide employees into different performance categories: A, B and C players. A-players are high performers who demonstrate outstanding performance. B-players belong to the wide majority in the middle. They do their job according to expectations. C-players, on the other hand, are poorly performing employees who are supported and carried along by others.

If managers are given a free choice as to how they classify their employees, at least some managers will assign all employees to category B. Others do employees

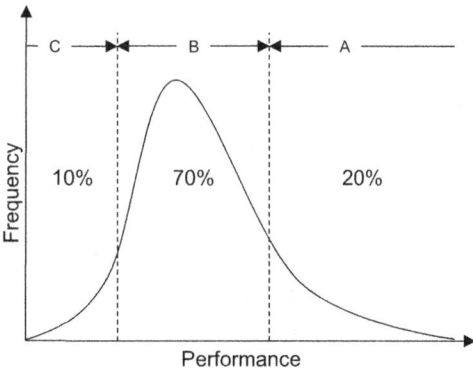

Fig. 6.6 Forced distribution (Since employees are not selected randomly during recruiting, it is more likely to assume a distribution skewed to the right than a normal distribution) (first published in Trost 2017, Unter den Erwartungen. Wiley. p. 112)

the favour of classifying them as A-players all around (Murphy and Cleveland 1995). This is especially the case when managers act as coaches or partners. What is often lacking is a balanced differentiation. Rather, a form of avoidance behaviour becomes evident. Positive evaluations avoid complex discussions with the judged ones. The motivational backgrounds of these assessment strategies are manifold.

In order to counteract such tendencies, some companies use so-called *forced rankings* or *forced distributions*. They determine centrally that a certain percentage of employees must always be assigned to one of the respective categories (Grote 2005). An example of this is illustrated graphically in Fig. 6.6.

This approach became known above all through its consistent application at General Electric under the leadership of the legendary CEO Jack Welch (cf. Bartlett and McLean 2006). A-players were consistently promoted. C-players were consequently laid off. To this day, many companies see it as a role model for consequence performance orientation.

> The consistent handling of employee evaluation procedures requires clear distribution policies. Anything else leads to arbitrariness and evasive behaviour. (2-1)

There are good reasons in favour of forced distribution. However, the major disadvantage of this strategy, is that it does harm any form of collaboration, mutual support, sharing of knowledge, experience and ideas. Forced distribution policies turn colleagues into competitors, hurdles on the way to personal success. If, as a professor, I were to use forced distribution when grading exams, this would mean the end of learning groups on the part of students. This raises the question for companies as to whether they are prepared to pay this price. Agile companies that rely on lateral collaboration, communication, teamwork and alignment with overarching goals will certainly not do so.

> We consider forced distribution to be toxic. It jeopardizes everything that we attach particular importance to in a connected, collaborative world of work. (2-2)

Internal competitive situations can never be completely ruled out. Some things remain competitive in companies because they seem particularly attractive and are

6.3 Formal Judgement

rare at the same time. Salary increases are subject to limited resources and require prioritization. Not everyone can become CEO. To that extent, a dilemma is opening up here in a certain ways. Agile companies avoid differentiating individual performers for the reasons mentioned above. At the same time, selected treatment of individual A-players is often unavoidable.

Performance or Performer?

It has already been pointed out in connection with the topic of feedback that the content of feedback can be located at different levels, namely at the level of the person, the process, the result and self-regulation. The same applies to the formal assessment. In the following, a distinction is to be made between two main levels: that of the person on the one hand and that of the process and result on the other. Is the *performance* assessed or the *performer*? This distinction is illustrated by a practical example (see Fig. 6.7).

Let us assume that an employee has fulfilled the agreed performance expectations for several years. He is even a little above it. At some point, his performance seems to collapse. The colleagues and the manager note this with concern. Usually, what is referred to as a *situational performance dialogue* then takes place. If the matter is handled professionally, the dimensions of ability, motivation and conditions are discussed. Can the employee currently not perform, does he not want to or do external conditions prevent him from doing so? Measures to restore the accustomed level of performance are discussed together. Let us continue with the assumption that the employee's performance recovers for a short time, but then slumps even further.

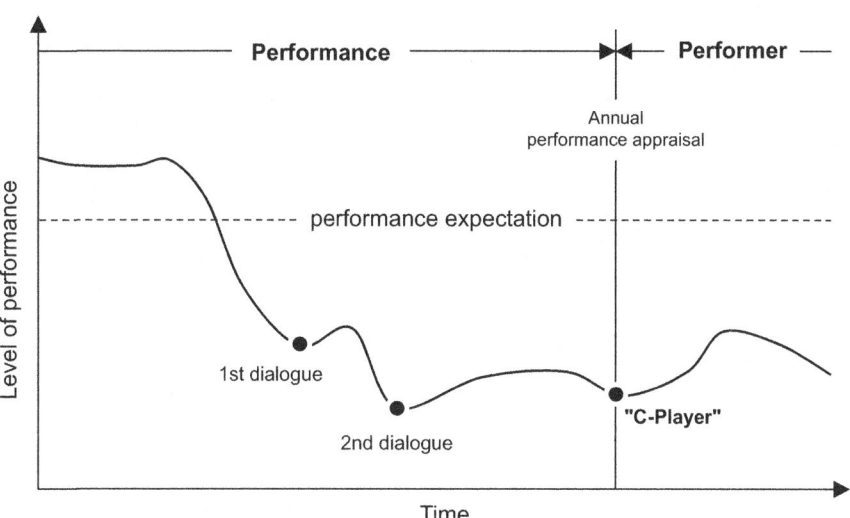

Fig. 6.7 Assessment of performance and performer (Trost 2017, p. 112)

This is followed by a second dialogue. But even after that the employee does not find his way back to his original level.

A few weeks later, the annual performance appraisal takes place, which is accompanied by a formal performance review. The employee is now classified as a C-Player. There is now a change in the content level of the assessment. Up to the formal performance review, the focus was primarily on *performance* and the related factors. The performance appraisal is used to evaluate the person. Now the focus is on the *performer*.

Of course, performance and performer are connected. The person, the performer, is inferred from the performance. Whoever performs poorly is a C-Player. Anyone who shows above-average performance is an A-player. Conversely, performance is explained by the characteristics of the acting person (the performer). An employee achieves above-average performance because he or she is an A-player, has special skills and is permanently motivated.

However, it plays a decisive role in practice on which level one moves and which contents one focuses on. This difference has already been highlighted in the context of the levels of feedback outlined in the previous Sect. 6.2. So there is a difference if you say: "You always use a lot of full-packed slides at presentations and talk very fast. I regularly have problems following you" (performance). Or if they say, "You are a bad speaker" (performer). The former considers the process, the behaviour. The latter considers the person. This results in two opposing strategies. The first strategy can be summarized by the following premise:

> We formally evaluate performance and behaviour. Not people, but the work is our priority. People are only assessed when their future is at stake inside or outside of the company. (3-2)

This is based on the fundamental assumption that the behaviour and performance of employees and teams can be adapted and changed. Especially in agile companies, the review of performance, behaviour and results is a continuous team process. Performance thinking requires a focus on performance.

The assessment of *persons*, on the other hand, has the consequence that decisions are made about those *persons*. And, only when it comes to consequences about the person, an assessment of the person can make sense. The focus is not on behaviour or performance, but on the question of how to deal with an employee (the performer) in the future. Possible consequences are promotion, transfer, termination but also salary increases, individual bonuses, etc.

> We rely on the formal evaluation of persons. This enables us to make meaningful decisions about the people being assessed with regard to their professional future and their remuneration. (3-1)

In contrast to the assessment of performance and behaviour, the formal assessment of individuals usually takes place only once a year. Anything else would hardly be practicable for the majority of companies. This is also due to the fact that the consequences associated with the formal assessment of individuals hardly appear feasible in a continuous process.

In the end, there will always be mixed strategies arising from the formal assessment of performance and performers, both in hierarchical and agile companies. But here, too, the question is ultimately which dominant tendency is aimed for.

The Right Time to Deal with Weak Performance

It is cynical to report an employee's situations of poor performance in the course of the annual performance appraisal in January that go back several weeks or even months and have never been discussed since. As a manager, it is just as cynical to tell an employee in such an institutionalized moment that he or she has actually been dissatisfied with his performance for a long time. Managers who do so obviously demonstrate a weak performance at that very moment.

This statement is made this clearly because it cannot be the subject of a strategic alignment anyway. By any means one must right away address weak performance of an employee or a phase of weak performance. There is simply no rationally justifiable alternative here. One might argue that strong performance is not directly addressed either. This in turn can be illustrated by an analogy. We do not always and directly talk about our health. But a disease should be given immediate attention.

Continuous and Qualitative Review of Performance and Behaviour in the Team

The classical approach of formal *performance evaluation* follows an annual cycle. Once a year, the employee and his or her supervisor meet and discuss the employee's performance over the past 12 months (DeNisi and Pritchard 2006). This discussion finally leads to an overall assessment along given scales. It is not uncommon for only one scale of measurement to be used, on the basis of which an overall grade of some kind is awarded. It ranges from "entirely below expectations" to "far above expectations".

> The performance of our employees is formally assessed once a year by their direct superiors on the basis of structured guidelines. (4-1)

It is often argued that this approach corresponds to a consistent performance orientation. "Those who expect performance from their employees must also regularly assess their performance and derive consequences from it". That is only partly true. You can also argue differently. Like this:

> We are an extremely performance-oriented company. Therefore, we cannot and will not afford to discuss performance and behaviour of each individual only once a year. We do this continuously. We are aware of the fact that performance is only ever achieved in teams. There the conscious reflection on performance must also take place actively. The last thing we want is to banish this topic to the seclusion of an annual performance appraisal meeting. A formal assessment based on standardized, uniform scales does not help us. We talk about performance in terms of content. This is the only way to make sense of each individual and the team as a whole.

This is a fictitious statement by an HR manager, presumably from an agile company. It shows an entirely different form of formal assessment of the formats used. Readers who are used to agile work will feel reminded of the agile method of product development called *Scrum*. In a team setting, employees take on certain tasks in short cycles, which they report on regularly within the team. This example shows very nicely that even in agile working environments formal assessments—of performance not of performers—take place, but within a significantly shorter cycle and more intensity than is the case with hierarchically managed companies. Qualitative formats are often given preference over quantitative formats (rankings, scales, etc.).

> We assess (joint) performance continuously and within teams. We primarily use qualitative formats. (4-2)

This should not give the impression that agile companies avoid personal consequences with regard to individual employees. In most cases, the opposite is the case, especially with regard to underperforming employees. This is particularly impressive at Netflix, a company that is known for its agile management and organizational understanding. Netflix consistently separates itself from those colleagues who no longer meet performance expectations (cf. McCord 2014).

All strategic dimensions and statements presented in this subchapter are summarized in Fig. 6.8.

Role of the manager	1-1 Formal assessment	1-2 Coaching and Reflection
	One of the central tasks of a manager is to formally evaluate employees at regular intervals.	Leadership is at eye level. That is why our managers do not judge their employees, but encourage critical self-reflection.
Distribution policies	2-1 Clear distribution targets	2-2 No forced distribution
	The consistent handling of employee evaluation procedures requires clear distribution policies. Anything else leads to arbitrariness and evasive behaviour.	We consider forced distribution to be toxic. It jeopardizes everything that we attach particular importance to in a connected, collaborative world of work.
Subject of the assessment	3-1 Persons (Performer)	3-2 Performance and behaviour
	We rely on the formal assessment of persons. This enables us to make meaningful decisions about the people being assessed with regard to their professional future and their remuneration.	We formally evaluate performance and behaviour. Not people, but the work is our priority. Persons are only assessed when their future is at stake inside or outside the company.
Assessors and formats	4-1 Structured and top-down	4-2 Lateral and qualitative
	The performance of our employees is formally assessed once a year by their direct superiors on the basis of structured guidelines.	We assess (joint) performance continuously and within teams. We primarily use qualitative formats.

Fig. 6.8 Overview of all strategic dimensions for formal judgement

References

Bartlett C, McLean AN (2006) GE's talent machine: the making of a CEO. Harv Bus Sch Case 2003:304–349

DeNisi A, Pritchard R (2006) Performance appraisal, performance management, and improving individual performance: a motivational framework. Manag Organ Rev 2(2):253–277

Fiske ST, Taylor SE (1991) Social cognition. McGraw-Hill, New York

Grote RC (2005) Forced ranking: making performance management work. Harvard Business School Press, Boston, MA

Hattie J, Timperley H (2007) The power of feedback. Rev Educ Res 77(1):81–112

Locke EA, Latham GP (1984) Goal setting: a motivational technique that works! Prentice Hall, Englewood Cliffs, NJ

McCord P (2014) How Netflix reinvented HR. Harv Bus Rev (January/February), 60–77

McGregor D (1960) The human side of enterprise. McGraw-Hill, New York

Murphy KR, Cleveland J (1995) Understanding performance appraisal: social, organizational, and goal-based perspectives. Sage, London

Odiorne GS (1965) Management by objectives. A system of managerial leadership. Pitman, New York

Trost A (2017) The end of performance appraisal. A practitioners' guide to alternatives in agile organizations. Springer, Heidelberg

7 Learning and Knowledge

This chapter deals with the short to medium-term acquisition of knowledge and skills. In textbooks, it is usually referred to as "training and development" (e.g. Jackson and Schuler 2012). Training in the broadest sense describes what is equated here with learning. However, we meanwhile recognize that learning is far more than the use of formal training, seminars or courses. Learning also takes place within the framework of possible programs, both formal and planned. Rather, the rapid acquisition of knowledge and skills is informal, continuous, demand-driven, social and mobile.

The chapter begins with vocational training, which is certainly mid-term or long-term, although it does not extend over the long cycle of a lifelong career. The special topic of management development is similar. This will take place either as part of a temporary measure or on a continuous basis. A central theme within this chapter is continuous learning. This chapter closes with another special topic, namely knowledge management. Of course, this is not only about the acquisition and exchange of knowledge, but also about questions of knowledge identification and retention.

The other part of training and development is long-term and deals with the development and the careers of people or employees across whole life-cycles. It will be discussed in Chap. 8.

7.1 Vocational Training

In connection with my consulting activities for the German company Diehl AG, I studied their company biography. There is a picture of the impressive apprentice workshop from the thirties on which the prominent lettering can be seen on the back wall: "Only those who learn to obey can later command!" (Schöllgen 2002, p. 73, translated by the author). At a company visit I realized that this lettering had been painted over in the meantime. This saying is indicative of an attitude that shaped vocational training many years ago. Obedience, discipline, order, diligence were dominating values, which were decisive for the strategic alignment of vocational training at that time. Today things are different, even though traces of this attitude can still be seen in some companies. In the following, different dimensions of a strategic alignment in relation to vocational training are proposed and described.

Cool and Not So Cool Training

The extent to which training companies have detached themselves from these historical principles in the design of their training system can be seen when one talks to current or former trainees and lets them report on their training. In a "cool" case, it sounds like this:

> As an apprentice I had a lot of responsibility right from the start. I was often trusted with tasks that were actually too big for me. But the trust and help of older apprentices really helped. It was always very important to our trainers that we dealt with our customers as often as possible. This provided me with a lot of insight. My instructors were super relaxed about it and also really asked a lot of us. They always wanted you to come up with ideas yourself. Actually, everybody was really nice. You were never alone and we could work together on projects that we could even define by ourselves. Later I also helped the younger apprentices. I have to say, that is when I learned the most.

It is obvious that this report reflects a very modern, mature understanding of education. Students in my lecture who speak in this way about their previous education are regularly envied by those fellow students who talk about their rather "uncool" experiences. Their reports tend to sound something like this:

> In my training I was allowed to do more and more difficult tasks step by step. There was also a clear plan, which had been communicated to us at the beginning of an apprenticeship year. The trainers explained to you very precisely how to complete the tasks and you were only allowed to do something for customers if you were really good at it. And most of them were pretty strict. Once a year we also had to do a project with others that our instructors had defined. They always had an eye on how we ran the project. Sometimes we were even allowed to present the result to a member of the executive board. That was actually pretty cool but also really stressful. It was often like a competition with the other trainees. You somehow always tried to be better than the others. Of course you put a lot of effort into it but I think the atmosphere wasn't always that good.

What seems somewhat anecdotal here on the basis of fictitious reports basically describes two possible, contradictory strategic alignments with regard to vocational training. On closer listening one recognizes dimensions, which are briefly discussed in the following. Among other things, it is about learning opportunities, diversity and the level of cooperation and belonging.

Learning Opportunities, Trust and Cold Water

Several years ago I held an open space event for a large bank. Together with 120 pupils and apprentices, we spent a day at the local bank academy developing ideas on how to attract trainees in the twenty-first century. The idea was to work directly with the target group on this issue. Completely enthusiastic and impressed by the variety of ideas, the CEO asked me afterwards whether I would be prepared to present the results of this event at the next, big HR Manager Conference. I decidedly refused because I thought that trainees should do this themselves. I insisted. Finally, we held a one-hour presentation at the conference, during which four trainees presented their thoughts and ideas, moderated by me. The uncertainty before the event was massive. The trainees were really nervous. In the end, it was a complete success. The trainees were incredibly proud. Their HR managers and trainers were just as proud and impressed. It could not have been better.

Of course I could have presented the results of the open space event, and certainly I would have been able to do that due to my experience. But: whenever an experienced person does something, less experienced people loose the chance to learn. Companies that recognize this act according to the following strategic premise:

> We offer our students every learning opportunity imaginable and encourage them to take on challenges that they currently consider as being too big. (1-2)

Other companies, on the other hand, think differently. This is less a question of capabilities or motivation. This is primarily about being allowed. They are afraid and doubt the abilities of their apprentices. At the very least, they want to be on the safe side and avoid risks:

> We can only assign a task to trainees when we can rely on their abilities. Anything else would be too risky. (1-1)

Companies that want to open up every conceivable learning opportunity for their trainees recognize unlimited possibilities for this. To give just one example: Newcomers are welcomed every year in numerous companies—a group of quiet, shy, insecure and expectant young people. Who performs the welcoming? Does the HR director do this or is this task taken over by trainees from the second year of vocational training? If the training manager does this, he or she takes away a learning opportunity—even if he or she had good intentions.

Diversity and Co-design Versus Conformity and Standards

I know an extremely innovative training manager from a large German mechanical engineering company. He told me about a very well functioning "Best Practice". Groups of trainees from different educational backgrounds receive a large block of ST37 steel. The block has a length, width and height of 30 cm each. The simple task is: Think about what you can do with it and generate as much revenue as possible by the end of this year. This exercise provides a variety of learning content. It is all about technology, production, product design, innovation, marketing, sales, cost accounting, project management, group dynamics and much more. All it takes is a block of steel, trust, time and support where it is demanded. These things can hardly be described in a standardized curriculum. Perhaps this idea even came from trainees themselves. Of course, it is conceivable that at some point they might come up with the idea of replacing the steel block with something more digital.

In many companies, on the other hand, training is highly pre-structured. There are clear curricula. It is determined who has to learn what, when and how. Some even speak of an industrialization of education. To a large extent, these contents are also prescribed by the respective chambers or by other central bodies. It is often argued that trainees actively want this and see this as a sign of professionalism. These companies follow the strategic premise:

> We adhere to clearly structured training plans that determine what needs to be learned when and how. Our trainees also ask for this clarity and structure. (2-1)

However, numerous examples from companies show that despite overriding requirements and the necessary synchronization of training with the static plans of vocational schools, freedom can be created. These in turn offer space for the preferences, inclinations, talents and interests of those affected:

> The timing and content of the training, as far as possible, lies in the hands of the trainees themselves. (2-2)

In the end, it will always be a question of finding the right balance between these two ends of the continuum. The decisive factors are the determining tendency and the question of how far one wants to go in one direction or the other.

As a university professor I can, on the one hand, give my students projects and centrally define who has to take care of which project. When I do that, the students always ask me what concrete expectations I have, so that in the end they might get the best possible grade for what they deliver. The guidelines and standardizations lead directly to a focus of the learners on what is relevant for the final evaluation at the end. The motivation to learn tends to be of extrinsic nature.

> First and foremost, trainees learn content material relevant to the examination. All else would be unrealistic. A certain amount of pressure makes sense here. (3-1)

Things are completely different when I give my students a framework, but they define their own projects within this framework and decide for themselves who wants to work with whom. With this approach I hardly have to worry about the motivation of the students. They do their projects on their own, so they are more intrinsically motivated, even though I am formally forced to give marks at the end.

Every pupil, every trainee, hears the advice several times in his life that one learns for life and not for school. Some of those affected are irritated by this, since it is common knowledge that personal consequences can follow from the grades alone. So you learn to finally get good ones. The relevance of the content to be learned is directly linked to the exams. Pupils, students and trainees who experience proximity to customers at an early stage at least have the chance to see learning content in a different light. They learn that they need learning content to solve the problems of others (the customers).

> Curiosity and experienced relevance are the best teachers. This is why we link our trainees with customers and their problems. (3-2)

In this respect, it can be a good idea to lead trainees from the protected areas of a training workshop into real life. Good companies that educate trainees do this as intensively as possible. Trainers, on the other hand, who accept a focus of trainees on examination-relevant subjects and grades, have presumably capitulated. They have accepted that their students adhere to the Theory X in the sense of McGregor's (1960) and not to the Theory Y.

Learning by Teaching

Teaching is a wonderful way to learn. Good teachers know this, which is why they see themselves not only as providers of knowledge but also as moderators of learning. In this respect, it is to be welcomed that pupils in schools are already being asked to convey something to others, for example in the form of short presentations. Here it is not so much the listening students who benefit, but above all the presenting students themselves. Communicating something to others creates commitment. Pupils, trainees or students experience this directly in their informal learning groups. There is a difference between learning by heart in a socially isolated setting or being motivated by the mere presence of others to explain something in one's own words.

> Trainees are pupils and teachers at the same time. They learn by sharing their knowledge and experiences with others. (4-2)

The traditional, conservative understanding of teaching and learning is based on other assumptions. Here there is the professionally superior and experienced master. He, and only he, has the assigned task of imparting knowledge and skills to inexperienced young people. The application of the T-concept in the context of professional superiority of managers in Sect. 4.4 is recalled here.

> Trainees (little knowledge) learn from their trainers, teachers, foremen and managers (much knowledge). It has always been that way. (4-1)

In Germany master craftsmen are highly respected personalities in numerous companies. This is not to be questioned in any way here either. As a professor, I find myself in a similar position and naturally enjoy the social esteem I sometimes encounter. However, it would be too brief if masters and professors were to see each other in a learning context as the sole resources of learning. This would hide the social possibilities of learning from and with each other.

Buddies and Reversed Mentoring

In modern companies that educate apprentices, trainees help other trainees. Partly this is supported by mentoring programs—in the language of future generations here one also speaks about Buddies and *Buddy programs*. Trainees do not only learn with each other but also from each other. In this way, the weaknesses of some are compensated or supplemented by the strengths of others. Joint projects play a decisive role here. Some companies even go one step further and use trainees as a learning resource for experienced and superordinate employees and even executives—trainees as mentors for managers. The latter is also referred to as *reversed mentoring*. Trainees train managers in the use of social media or convey the preferences, interests and life perspectives of younger generations. Here, too, the teachers themselves learn first and foremost.

In many industries, trainees are a wonderful resource because they represent current and future target groups in the markets. Just think of industries such as retail, fashion, gastronomy or financial services. If the fashion company H&M wants to understand the preferences of young target groups, it should learn from its trainees. If banks want to understand how future generations want to make financial transactions, they should listen to their trainees. Retailers can learn from their apprentices which products have a chance of success and how to position them. The list could be extended at will. If a company wants to learn from young target groups, it asks them to contradict and question existing things.

> We encourage our trainees to objectively and constructively challenge their trainers, teachers and managers. (5-2)

This attitude is diametrically opposed to the attitude of the company Diehl from the 1930s presented at the beginning of this subchapter. And more and more instructors are facing a dilemma at this point. At least in a number of areas, companies complain about a decline in *training maturity*. This concerns primarily aspects such as discipline, resilience and compliance with basic interpersonal manners (Dobischat et al. 2012).

> It has always been one of the virtues of a good trainee to be obedient to trainers and managers. (5-1)

Therefore, it is understandable that trainers should again focus on traditional values such as obedience and punctuality. Often they see the necessity of having to catch up on a lacking education at home.

Treating Trainees as Adults

In addition to the development of training maturity described above, another important trend can be observed in vocational training. In its annual report, the German Federal Institute for Vocational Education and Training (Bundesinstitut für

Delegation of tasks	*1-1 Avoiding risks* We can only assign a task to trainees when we can rely on their abilities. Anything else would be too risky.	*1-2 Opening up learning opportunities* We offer our students every learning opportunity imaginable and encourage them to take on challenges that they currently consider too big.
Structuring the training	*2-1 Fixed training plans* We adhere to clearly structured training plans that determine what needs to be learned when and how. Our trainees also demand this clarity and structure.	*2-2 Self-controlled training* The timing and content of the training is as far as possible in the hands of the trainees themselves.
Motivation to learn	*3-1 Relevant examination contents* Trainees learn above all those contents, which are relevant for the examination. Anything else would be unrealistic. A certain amount of pressure makes sense here.	*3-2 Curiosity and relevance* Curiosity and experienced relevance are the best teachers. This is why we link our trainees with customers and their problems.
Main instructors	*4-1 Teachers, masters, instructors* Trainees (little knowledge) learn from their trainers, teachers, foremen and managers (much knowledge). It has always been that way.	*4-2 Trainees* Trainees are pupils and teachers at the same time. They learn by sharing their knowledge and experiences with others.
Subordination	*5-1 Obedience* It has always been one of the virtues of a good trainee to be obedient to trainers and managers.	*5-2 Critical Reflection* We encourage our trainees to objectively and constructively challenge their trainers, teachers and managers.

Fig. 7.1 An overview of all strategic dimensions of vocational training

Berufsbildung 2017) reports a continuous increase in the starting age of trainees in Germany. In 2017 this was almost 20 years. And yet there has been a clear increase in the number of over 20-year-olds for many years. Should trainees now be treated like big children or like young adults? Summarizing the dimensions presented in this subchapter (see Fig. 7.1), these two perspectives are more or less reflected by the contrasting strategic options.

7.2 Executive Development

In order to understand *executive development* in its current, widespread form, one has to take a look into the past of training & development (T&D). Companies that begin to institutionalize T&D usually do so by offering training modules and modules that are in demand in the company. Three days project management, business English I, II, III, presentation, moderation, two days introduction to accounting and finally: Good leadership, two days, twelve participants, conducted by an external management trainer. After some time, these training modules often develop into comprehensive executive development programs, longer-lasting measures consisting of several training modules, coaching, projects, etc. In the following, the basic logic and strategic alignment of these programs in their traditional form are presented. Subsequently, an alternative way of aligning is outlined.

The Separation of Strategy, Business Context and Learning Context

If you look around in large or medium-sized enterprises for their executive development practices, then it is highly probable that you will find programs, which are based on a logic shown in Fig. 7.2.

The starting point for the design and implementation of a development program are the requirements in the *business context*. What are the current and future tasks of executives in the company? What particular challenges will they face in the light of future strategic challenges and therefore what requirements must they meet? In the latter case, it is not uncommon to think in terms of competencies, which in turn result from an overarching corporate strategy. From this business context, *learning objectives* are derived in line with the target group of managers. These learning objectives are then translated into a suitable qualification program, the *learning context*: Which content should be taught by which trainer? In addition, the appropriate teaching and learning formats will be considered: Presentation, group work, case studies, projects. With regard to the latter, strategic questions are often included into the program in order to encourage the participants to deal with overarching questions of business competitiveness. Finally, it can be about the type of assessment or the determination of the learning success.

> The content of executive development is derived from the overarching corporate strategy. (1-1)

In the end one hopes for the so-called *learning transfer*. How much of what the participating executives have learned can and will they apply in their respective business context? The basic assumption of this logic is that the clearer one sees the

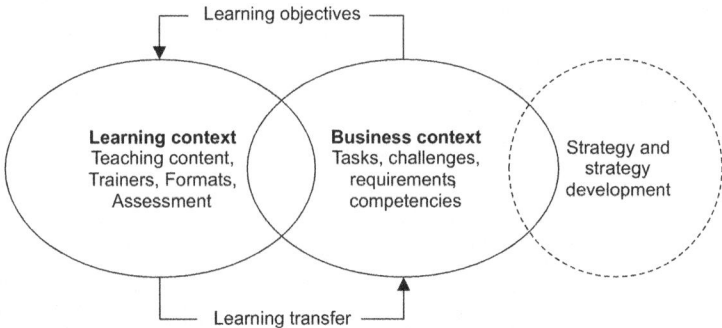

Fig. 7.2 The connection between strategy, learning and business context

business context, the better the needs derived from it, and the better they are then translated into the learning context, the more successful the learning transfer will be (cf. Baldwin and Ford 1988).

Traditional leadership development programs are inspired by corporate strategy. However, the development of the corporate strategy takes place elsewhere and is not part of the development program itself. Basically, this follows a sequential thinking. First comes the corporate strategy and then, building on this, the development program is designed.

MBA Light

In this context, a separate consideration should be given to learning content, which is of a very fundamental nature. In most cases, managers cannot look back on any basic education in business administration. They are often engineers, lawyers, computer scientists or graduates of various scientific disciplines. Others, for example, have undergone technical vocational training. In view of this, many companies feel compelled to provide their managers with basic business management training. It deals with accounting, legal aspects, strategic management or other basic disciplines of business administration. Often participants in these programs are either assigned to so-called Executive MBA programs at regional universities, or smaller versions of MBA programs that are offered "in-house"—these are then called "Mini MBA" or "MBA Light" sometimes. These programs usually have little to do with leadership and do not fall within the context of the discussion taking place in this chapter. Basically, the benefits and design of these programs seem to be independent of the structural and cultural framework conditions of a company.

Strategically Derived Leadership Competencies at Different Levels

Almost all large companies have *competence models* for leaders. They describe nothing more than a set of skills that are considered necessary to be successful as a manager or executive in the respective company. Despite all the differences in respective industries, markets, strategic challenges and positioning, these hardly differ from company to company: strategic thinking, result orientation, customer and market orientation, ability to work in a team, building and maintaining networks, employee development, leading through transformations, international mobility and sensitivity, digital competence. They are usually created top-down and iteratively. At the end of the day, the executive board decides on future competencies based on their strategic relevance.

> Leadership competencies are defined top-down. They are part of the strategic priorities of the company as a whole and describe how leaders should be. (2-1)

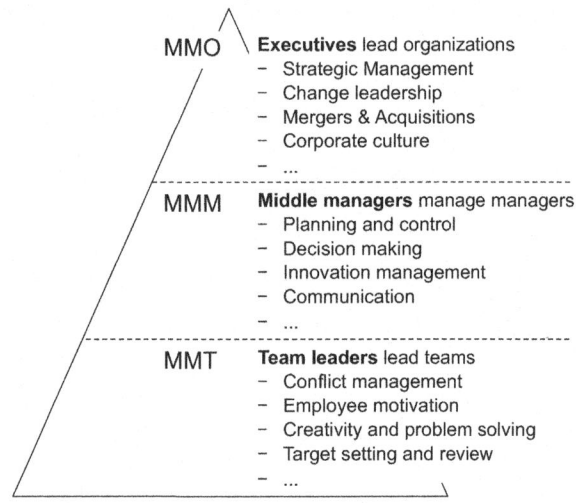

Fig. 7.3 Leadership competencies and challenges at different levels

Competence models have the significance of relevant learning objectives in the context of leadership development, at least on a generic level. In this regard, it is common to distinguish between leading leagues. A very widespread differentiation is known firstly to top management, executives or C-level (manager managing organizations, MMO), secondly to middle management, managers who manage managers (MMM) and thirdly to the level of group or team leaders (managers managing teams, MMT). Within these levels, special challenges and required leadership competencies are described. Therefore the learning content on these levels is different (see Fig. 7.3).

Executives at C-Level lead not only executives but entire organizations (MMO). They are responsible for strategy (why), systems and corporate culture (how). In this respect, this mostly global target group deals with different issues than its colleagues on the level below. On this particular level you will find division managers, middle managers (MMM) who, from their sandwich position between strategy and bottom-line operation, deal with topics of planning, control, communication etc. In team leader training, on the other hand, the curriculum reads completely differently again. This is where contents come into play that are directly oriented to employee issues (e.g. conflict management, objective setting and performance review) as well as topics relating to day-to-day operations (creativity, problem solving, etc.).

> We design training programs for our managers based on strategic considerations. This enables us to ensure that our managers learn what the company needs. (3-1)

As explained in relation with the separation of strategy, business and learning context, the translation of strategy into requirements, of requirements into competences, of competences into training content, of training content into training programs, of training programs into learning, of learning into application (learning transfer) is seen as the central value chain of leadership development. The benefit at the end depends on the quality of the translation from one step to the next.

Strategic Tasks

It does not take much imagination to see that this value chain can lead to losses. The entire program may fail due to the weakest step of translation. What is really left of the initial strategic considerations in the concrete application in the business context? In the light of this uncertainty, it was obvious for many companies to embed strategic issues more directly in their management development programs. From then on, the idea of *action learning*—learning from and with each other on the basis of real challenges—was used here (Marquardt et al. 2009). Participants in leadership development programs are assigned questions of strategic importance. These topics are usually defined centrally by top-management. These questions are dealt with in various teams consisting of participants from different functions, divisions or regions. Analyses, conclusions and options are then ceremoniously presented to top management at the end of the program. All this adds to the already high workload of the managers selected for the program. This concept is described in detail in the context of talent development (Sect. 8.2). As will still be shown, there are different strategic options for alignment here as well. Are topics chosen by the participants themselves or defined top-down? Are topics dealt with on-the-job or on-top-of-the-job?

Teachers and Learners

External trainers, so-called management trainers, are usually mandated in management training courses. Depending on the management league, there are not only considerable differences in quality but also in the fee that these trainers subsequently charge. While for executives well-known professors from still more prestigious business schools are flown in, on the level of the team leaders not infrequently one might accept regional freelancers, which one can get engaged for 500 Euro per day. An experienced trainer with professional superiority conveys content to participants with appropriate learning needs. We have probably known this principle for centuries. The knowledgeable imparts his knowledge to the ignorant. It was like that at school already.

> Managers (learners) learn from professional management trainers and mentors (teachers) who have professional superiority. (4-1)

Management trainers themselves are of course aware that this claim to superiority is not altogether justified. The managers present are of course more familiar with their respective business context. They know their employees and the wider environment much better than the trainer. So how can a management trainer successfully conduct an executive training if the learners know their business context much better than the trainer? The simple solution is to convey leadership as a kind of craft: That is how you give feedback. That is how you set goals. This is how you deal with underperforming employees. Concrete instructions for action, techniques, checklists, questionnaires, orientation frameworks etc., are offered. These techniques are framed by much-quoted *leadership theories* that are considered universally valid: the Maslow pyramid, the four levels of communication, leadership roles, leadership styles, Blake and Mouton, Blanchard, Herzberg, Vroom and Yetten (Robbins and Judge 2016).

Hotels, Business Schools, Corporate Universities and Academies

Management training usually takes place off-the-job, in seminar and conference hotels, at renowned business schools, in corporate universities and academies far away from the company campuses, if possible in inspiring surroundings. This is expected to have a number of advantages. A physical distance between the learning context and the business context makes it psychologically easier for learners to reflect on their leadership behaviour. You enjoy the benefits of professional learning and reflection environments. In addition, distant learning contexts offer the possibility of informal evening networking—the so-called "get-together". In these gatherings, there is often room for work-related communication on a technical as well as interpersonal level.

The physical and thus also psychological separation of learning and business contexts requires a transfer of learned content into the real context following the management training. An essential factor for learning transfer is the experienced relevance of conveyed contents for coping with personal challenges (Baldwin and Ford 1988). For this reason, participants in management training courses are repeatedly asked to reflect on the content they have just presented in the light of their respective practical management realities and to derive conclusions.

The Responsibility Lies with the HR Department

The previous presentation conveys a certain idea of the complexity of such executive development programs, which should not be underestimated. This involves strategic considerations, questions relating to the program design and its operation. Many factors need to be coordinated: Participants, dates, contents, materials, locations, external trainers, etc. All this takes place within a given time and cost framework. In most companies above a certain size, a team within the HR department takes care of all these things.

> As a company, we bear responsibility for the development of our leaders. (5-1)

The head of this team reports to the head of T&D, who in turn reports to the Head of HR. The Head of HR then reports directly to the CEO or to a member of the executive board. In addition to the already discussed separation of strategy, business and learning context, the physical separation of learning and application environment, the outsourcing of trainer responsibility, another form of separation in the sense of division of labour can be seen in this organizational anchoring of the topic. While executives take care of their respective business, their development, on the other hand, is the responsibility of a separate and at the same time central department somewhere within the HR department. Section 11.1 further elaborates on key considerations regarding the organization and positioning of the HR function.

Everything that has so far been presented in this subchapter on the subject of leadership development sounds largely reasonable. In fact, what has been outlined so far reflects current practice in most large and medium-sized enterprises. However, as in the entire book, an agile counter-draft will be presented on this topic, which may be more compatible with self-determined and networked leadership and organization.

Strategy Development = Executive Development

When executives get together, lock themselves up for several days to think about the future of the company, or when many executives perhaps get together with leaders and customers in open-space events to discuss future issues, they learn, get inspired and network. Strategy development always means dealing with ambiguity and uncertainty in a dynamic environment. External keynote speakers and lateral thinkers are often invited for this purpose. When, finally, a form of certainty or orientation emerges from an uncertainty experienced together, the participants have obviously learnt.

> The development and implementation of corporate strategy is part of executive development. (1-2)

Traditionally, those responsible for executive development in the HR department also see themselves responsible for the development of a corporate strategy. The latter is seen as a management task, while the HR function is more likely to see its challenge in creating appropriate development programs based on the corporate strategy. This does not have to be that way.

One of the better-known examples of this form of leadership development is provided by General Electric. There, management development is closely linked to the location Crotonville north of New York, where the General Electric Management Development Institute is located. Already in the time of Jack Welsh, this institute, this location developed into a place for mental openness, inspiration and international networking with other executives but also with customers. Jack Welsh once said he spent two thirds of his time there (Ben-Hur et al. 2012).

Leadership Role, Leadership Expectations, Leadership Effectiveness

Behind the self-determined way of leadership development there is less the conviction that one can convey "good leadership" to many managers at the same time in a uniform manner using common leadership theories and leadership tools. Rather, it is about the responsibility and special nature of the manager him or herself. Here, leadership development rather means offering a framework for reflection within which a manager learns to understand his or her own leadership behaviour in leadership situations, to classify its impact, to recognize behavioural options and to evaluate them for him or herself.

> Responsibility for the development of our managers lies within the managers themselves (5-2).

This may sound a bit abstract. A concrete, simple example may help at this point. Imagine a situation that every manager experiences almost daily.

> You receive a mail with an attachment from your team. May it be a concept, a presentation draft, a contract, an offer or just any kind of work result. The team writes: "Hello John [the manager], enclosed you find the draft etc. Is that okay with you?"

When I am with executives, I like to present this simple case. Then comes the question, "What will you do?" The answers are usually as follows: "I look at it and if I notice something that could perhaps be done better, I send it back accordingly amended". In the eyes of managers, I sometimes read the slightly irritated question: "What else?" But then I react with the actual question: "Why are you doing this?" The most common answer: "Because I am the boss and because bosses are supposed to do that". I am not letting that count. Again, "Why are you doing this?" I have to put it in concrete terms: "What do you think your employees expect from you?" Finally the different leadership roles come into play, as they were described in Sect. 4.4 of this book.

- If the employees expect the reaction of a *boss*, then they want an approval, a "green light" from their manager. They are dumping the responsibility on their boss. If he or she thinks it is good, then it is good and the team is relieved of the later consequences of their work. That is the easiest way for the team.
- Would the employees like a further perspective or feedback? Then they see their leader as a *partner*. The responsibility remains with the team (including the manager). They only enrich themselves with the added perspective of others.
- Do the employees want to be challenged, for example by difficult questions? Then they expect a *coach*. Even then, they retain the responsibility themselves and simply face the hard questions of their managers.
- Or do the employees simply seek support from their boss through further clarification, information, time, budget, etc.? In this case, they expect a leader who acts as an *enabler*.

Many managers implicitly assume the role of the boss, but have neither reflected this nor ever clarified it with their employees. Often they do not even see the alternative behavioural options. If, however, the expectations of the employees and the role understanding of the manager do not match, sometimes situations arise, which might be kind of bizarre. Even this simple, everyday case shows the great potential for friction losses due to leadership. What about more complex situations?

A good friend of mine was a newly appointed HR director in a large corporation. He sees himself primarily as a coach. One day he received an interesting offer from a supplier, which he passed on to his team. His accompanying question: "Can we do that?" For a few weeks he went back to his team and asked for their opinion. To his astonishment, he received the answer: "Yes, we did that". This is another small case, which nicely shows how a lack of clarification of roles can lead to absurd situations. He saw himself as a coach and expected the expert opinion of his employees in order to make joint decisions. But they interpreted his role as boss and his question accordingly as an instruction.

Learning to lead means finding one's role as a manager, recognizing appropriate options for action, evaluating them and understanding the personal impact on employees. I am convinced that no leader has yet been able to improve his or her leadership strength because he or she uses leadership tools consistently or has understood the Maslow pyramid. The development of one's own leadership strength requires active engagement with oneself in leadership situations as outlined in this section.

Critical Leadership Situations

Together with 30 executives from a division of a large financial services company, I once held a two-day event with the aim of developing a common understanding of leadership. In the course of this event, I asked the managers to describe critical leadership situations on prepared templates. Two questions: What was this leadership situation? What was the challenge in this situation?

A central challenge of leadership is dealing with *ambiguity*. In many situations there is not one solution. Rather, it must be recognized that different options lead to disadvantages in each case. If, for example, I involve employees in decision-making processes at an early stage, this creates uncertainty and opens the door to rumours and fears. If I inform employees at a later point in time, when things are clearer, they feel ignored and confronted with a fait accompli. The damage can be substantial in both cases. Leadership situations with a high degree of ambiguity coupled with the probability of causing great damage are called *critical leadership situations*. These are the situations that have the potential to rob managers of sleep.

In the event mentioned above, we collected the descriptions of critical leadership situations and then had them evaluated with regard to their common relevance. We wanted to select the twelve situations that would give as many managers as possible a stomach ache. The managers were then asked to deal with these situations in groups, to develop options for action and to evaluate them.

What was originally planned as a workshop to develop common leadership principles evolved over the course of this event into probably the most effective leadership development measure anyone present—including myself—had ever experienced. The fact that we could actually close the event at the end with a common understanding was only regarded as a valuable accompanying benefit.

Peer Counselling

Once 10, 20 or even 30 managers from different functions, from different generations, with different backgrounds of experience, are together in one room, there is an incredible amount of leadership intelligence present. Confucius is credited with the following quote: "Whenever I walk with two people, one of them will be my teacher". Every manager brings something with him or her from which every other manager can learn something. Leadership development can mean actively using and moderating this potential. The event described above provides only one example of how this can be done in practice. We also refer to this as *peer counselling*.

> Leaders learn from and with others in the course of joint reflection. They are teachers and learners at the same time. (4-2).

According to my own observations, many companies have already given this approach a try. Not everyone was successful doing it. One reason why this approach sometimes fails is that the active use of this opportunity may signal to others that you are not a good leader. "I've been a successful executive for many years and do not need that." In the end, it is often only the reflected and self-critical executives who make use of the offer. But those who need support the most tend to stay away. The following factors, among others, seem to be critical for success:

- The CEO should act as a role model and take part in peer counselling. His or her message should be: "Anyone who is not prepared to play an active role in dealing with leadership challenges is not a good leader in this company".
- It requires targeted irritation, for example through feedback to the manager (see the example of Google in the following section). Managers must become aware that they experience a situation as challenging and that they are reaching their personal limits. The following Sect. 7.3 (Continuous learning) deals with this in more detail.
- Of course, peer counselling requires a culture of trust. The articulation of one's own challenge must be understood as a strength and not as a weakness. Contents and contributions from peer counselling must never be the subject of decisions on promotions or salary.

The role of external management trainers is not to impart knowledge about "good leadership" but to moderate learning processes. They structure processes and their results. They give impulses and ask simple questions that are often difficult to answer with precision because they seem so simple: "Why would you do this? What would this behaviour lead to? What do your employees expect? Why do you consider the situation critical?" etc.

Who Are You? How Do You Want to Be? What Do You Stand for?

What would happen if Richard Branson, founder and long-term CEO of Virgin were described by centrally defined leadership competencies and how would Jack Welsh, the former and legendary CEO of General Electric, be judged along these competencies? Would it be possible to evaluate Mahatma Gandhi on the basis of Sir Winston Churchill's leadership skills? These considerations seem absurd. After all, these leaders were unique individuals who were faced with their respective challenges.

Some extraordinarily ambitious graduates of my faculty sometimes confess to me in personal conversations that they are striving for an upper management position in their career. I respect that. Then they want me to tell them what it takes. I always meet this question with the counter question: "How do you want to be?" This counter-question always causes irritation, because they are used to set themselves up to pre-formulated answers to the question "How do you have to be?" Great leaders have never asked themselves what they have to be like. They became more of what they always have been and so they were just right, authentic and effective in the face of their respective challenges.

For managers, their development therefore raises the question of who they really are, how they want to and can be and what opportunities they see for themselves to have an effect on others. Bob Goffee and Gareth Jones put it wonderfully in a nutshell with their 2006 book and its title "Why should anyone be led by you?" They conclude:

> Discovering who we are is likely a lifetime process involving continual testing and learning, trial and error, and many twists and turns along the way. Every twist results in learning, and learning is always done in conjunction with others (Goffee and Jones 2006, p. 33).

The focus is not on uniformly defined competencies but on diversity and individuality, as described in detail in Sect. 4.2. This promotes responsible management development.

> Managers define their required competencies independently. They should reflect who they are, how they want to be and how they could be effective in the company. (2-2).

In addition, a decisive part of this self-discovery deals with the question of what a manager stands for. Having an answer to this question as a manager is of fundamental importance. At the same time, it seems like many managers have never given serious thought to this issue. A good manager stands for something, for an idea, a vision, for certain values. He or she has an idea of togetherness and how work should be done in the future. Weak managers only react to acute, manageable challenges with short-term decisions and actions. Strong managers, on the other hand, think fundamentally, strategically and visionary. An effective but disturbing exercise of reflection that encourages thinking in this direction is the so-called grave eulogy. Executives are asked to write their own eulogies. There is only room here for fundamental things. Content that descendants will always remember. Whoever can write this eulogy knows what he or she stands for.

Leadership Feedback or Assessment

As part of an amazingly extensive project called Oxygen, Google identified a model within its own organization that describes what successful executives do differently from their less successful colleagues (Garvin et al. 2013). The result is reflected in eight different behaviours. Summarizing these behaviors, the simple conclusion is that successful, good leaders are coaches, partners, and enablers, just as described in Sect. 4.4 in this book, no more, no less. This project was originally driven by the question of what leadership really is good for. In the end, this resulted in a framework that helps managers understand their own leadership successes, reflect on and optimize behavioural options (Garvin 2013).

This idea is not new in itself—at least from a methodological perspective. 360-degree feedback or upward appraisals have existed for several decades and are established in numerous companies (Atkins and Wood 2002). Methodically, things are always the same. Managers are evaluated by their employees along certain dimensions of leadership quality. With 360-degree feedback, there are four additional assessment perspectives, namely the superior manager, colleagues on the same level, internal and, or external customers and the manager him or herself. There's a report at the end.

Nevertheless, there are two varieties of these systems, which differ fundamentally in their dynamics, a distinction which some companies do not seem to be aware of. The first type of practice falls into the category of central planning and control. It follows the premise:

> Through regular, structured management evaluation and feedback, we (HR) identify the development needs of our managers. (6-1)

The customer of this variant is a central figure, for example the HR department or even the executive board. First and foremost, this instance receives the report and not the manager or focus person him or herself. As soon as control comes into play and the managers concerned have to assume possible consequences depending on their assessment, there is the potential for a dysfunctional dynamic due to formal judgement (see Sect. 6.3). Of course, given such a situation, a manager has reasonable interests in looking good in the end. This has only little to do with feedback. Rather, leaders will develop and use tactics to influence the results in their own favour. Experienced managers certainly can do that.

The alternative way relies less on central planning and control than on enabling managers through feedback. It follows the strategic orientation:

> Structured management feedback offers our managers the opportunity to identify their own development potential. (6-2)

The difference between the first and the second variant is surprisingly simple. Firstly, this variant is based on voluntariness and the conviction that feedback has a positive effect above all when it is actively demanded by the feedback recipient (cf. Sect. 6.2). Secondly, only the manager receives the report. He or she is the customer of the system. Google practices exactly this type of manager feedback. Afterwards, managers have the opportunity—not the obligation—to use development modules depending on their individual result.

> Managers develop and use development opportunities independently. They themselves know best what helps them. Above all, they receive appropriate support (e.g., coaching, budget). (3-2)

If, for example, a manager receives the clear feedback that he or she has too little regard for the development opportunities of his or her employees, then he or she can discuss this very topic with other managers and reflect on how something like this could actually work or be improved.

A Matter of Responsibility

All strategic statements dealt with in this subchapter are compared in an overview-like manner in Fig. 7.4. If one summarize these opposing options of strategic alignment, then the concept of *responsibility* would be appropriate. In hierarchical organizations striving for stability, the responsibility for the development of their executives lies in the system that follows certain guidelines, rules, processes, judgements, etc. The individual manager subordinates himself to this system and if everything goes according to plan, he or she experiences an appropriate development for the organization. In agile and networked worlds, the responsibility lies with the manager him or herself. It is their task, among other things, to reflect on development needs, to experience and develop their own identity and form of action, to be teachers and learners at the same time.

Relation to corporate strategy	1-1 Strategy determines content	1-2 Strategy as part of development
	The content of executive development is derived from the overarching corporate strategy.	The development and implementation of corporate strategy is part of executive development.
Managerial skills	2-1 Strategic Default	2-2 Self defined and reflected
	Leadership competencies are defined top-down. They are part of the strategic priorities of the company as a whole and describe how leaders should be.	Managers define their required competencies independently. They should reflect who they are, how they want to be and how they could be effective in the company.
Program development	3-1 Strategically aligned	3-2 Self-controlled
	We design training programs for our managers based on strategic considerations. This enables us to ensure that our managers learn what the company needs.	Managers develop and use development opportunities independently. They themselves know best what helps them. Above all, they receive appropriate support (e.g. coaching, budget).
Instructors	4-1 Teachers, (external) trainers	4-2 Other executives
	Managers (learner) learn from professional management trainers and mentors (teacher) who have professional superiority.	Leaders learn from and with others in the course of joint reflection. They are teachers and learners at the same time.
Accountability	5-1 Companies, HR	5-2 Executives
	As a company, we bear responsibility for the development of our managers.	The responsibility for the development of our managers lies within the managers themselves.
Management evaluation	6-1 Formal, centralized assessment	6-2 Feedback
	Through regular, structured management evaluation and feedback, we (HR) identify the development needs of our managers.	Structured management feedback offers our managers the opportunity to identify their own development potential.

Fig. 7.4 All strategic dimensions of executive development at a glance

7.3 Continuous Learning

Hardly any CEO wanting to be taken seriously will not agree with the statement that employees should learn continuously, preferably lifelong. A kind of joke has gotten passed around in the HR community recently. The CFO says to the CEO: "What if we invest in our employees and they leave us?" The CEO responds, "What if we do not invest in our employees and they decide to stay?"

When it comes to continuous learning, task certainty is the central factor that decides how learning should function in practice. Section 4.3 dealt with process and result certainty in quite a detailed way. It became clear that in some, mostly hierarchical working environments there is clarity about what employees should achieve in the context of their work. There are clear standards regarding the expected

7.3 Continuous Learning

work results. At the same time, in such working environments, the paths, the processes and the results are very clearly defined and described. On the other hand, there are working worlds in which exactly the opposite is the case. Teams work on projects in which it is not clear at the beginning where the journey will end and not even the way is visible. Whenever it comes to innovations, new product developments, etc., you are more likely to be dealing with such worlds.

This distinction should therefore be recalled because it is particularly relevant in relation to continuous learning. In the following, learning in these two worlds is presented separately. Figure 7.5 shows a summarizing comparison of the dimensions discussed below.

It should be noted that in agile companies the what is listed on the left side also takes place. However, those on the right side are added, which is indicated by the plus signs in the Fig. 7.5. Hierarchical companies, on the other hand, are predominantly located on the left-hand side. We start with this side. It needs less explanation because, firstly, it is more widespread in practice. Secondly, it is precisely this side that is sufficiently described in every current HR textbook (Jackson and Schuler 2012). The following presentation will deliberately turn out to be emphasized and kind of extreme. Just as how extreme it is perceived probably depends on the experience of the observer.

Continuous Learning in a Hierarchical and Stable Setting

Employees in a hierarchical world striving for stability fulfil their assigned tasks in the course of their daily professional lives. Then, once a year, they are invited by their direct supervisor to do a performance appraisal or *development dialogue*, during which they receive an assessment of their performance and competencies. The competences to be assessed correspond to a previously defined competence

Task certainty & stability		Uncertainty & agility
Prescribed learning needs	+	Reflected learning needs
Requirements as a driver for learning	+	Relevance as a driver for learning
Learning as an individual process	+	Learning as a social process
Planned learning	+	Incidental learning
Learning takes place off the job	+	Learning = Work, Work = Learning
Learning on stock (just in case)	+	Learning on demand
Formal learning	+	Informal learning
Learning from teachers	+	Learning from others
Learning by instruction	+	Learning by trial and error

Fig. 7.5 Learning in stable and agile working environments

framework or job profile. They are part of the job description and indicate the levels of competence required to successfully complete the assigned tasks. Learning requirements always arise when employees deviate from the respective target job profile.

> Employees are given (on the basis of formal assessments) the fields of competence in which they have learning needs. (1-1)

The reasons for learning in a particular field therefore always arise from the requirements associated with the respective job. If, for example, an employee is faced with the requirement to demonstrate English language skills at a certain level in daily conversations with customers and suppliers and the employee cannot demonstrate this to a sufficient degree, then this is a reason for initiating necessary learning activities.

> The most important drivers for learning are the given work-related requirements, which are documented in the job description. (2-1)

When we talk about employees here, we always mean individuals. Everything that is done or considered in connection with learning—assessment, job profiles, competence profiles, learning needs, learning activities, etc.—always refers to individual employees. From a technical point of view, the individual employee is the object. This is even reflected in current digital learning systems.

> Learning activities are always focused on the individual. In the end, it is the employee who learns. (3-1)

Overall, learning is a planned process. As already indicated, the annual competence or development review, for example, clarifies why and, above all, how an employee should develop further. This is why *development planning* is also referred to in this context (Trost 2017). Finally, the HR department learns about the cumulated learning needs of the various departments and can initiate and offer appropriate learning measures like courses, seminars, webinars etc. The employee can also prepare for this and knows what learning measures will be required in the course of a year.

> Professional learning requires planning. At certain times of the year, employees should know what they are supposed to learn, when and how. (4-1)

Learning itself takes place mainly off-the-job, in the form of seminars and courses. The company may have its own training facility for this purpose. They are also called "Academy", "Corporate University" or simply "Training Center".

> Learning requires a protected area outside the daily work environment. Then we hope for the transfer of learning. (5-1)

7.3 Continuous Learning

It is believed that learning requires protected areas outside the daily work environment. This allows people to focus on learning and to enjoy a professional and inspiring learning environment and infrastructure.

Ideally, employees acquire learning content at a time when they do not yet need it in their work context, but might need it at some point. They are thus prepared for any case of need or "emergency". Fire-fighters should also have learned to extinguish fires before these fires burn anywhere. In this respect, employees learn to stock up in a certain way.

> Our employees learn in advance so that they have relevant knowledge available when they need it. (6-1)

We certainly are aware that employees may be learning every day, regardless of the learning events they attend. Learning is, so to speak, a welcome side-effect of the daily confrontation with the given challenges. However, this form of informal learning is not part of the company's internal learning strategy because it is difficult to be managed.

> Learning takes place primarily within the framework of formal measures. This enables professional planning, control and operation. (7-1)

For the operation of the learning events professional trainers from internal or external are engaged. From time to time, internal experts are also used as trainers, but this is more the exception. Professional trainers are characterised by the fact that they have a technical superiority over learners. In addition, they bring along didactic experience needed to make the learning process effective.

> Employees learn from professional trainers who have professional superiority and didactic experience. (8-1)

In the end, trainers teach knowledge and skills in a way that has always been successful, even though teaching methods and learning media have become more modern and adapted to the target group. Regardless of whether a seminar is about language skills, dealing with office solutions, project management methods, work techniques, communication, conflict management or whatever, the employees benefit from the fact that the respective trainers instruct them, in addition to the theoretical basics, how to do something right.

> Employees learn by trainers instructing them and teaching them how to do things right. (9-1)

When employees have completed a learning activity, the challenge is to transfer what they have learned into practice. This learning transfer is ensured above all by adapting the learning content in advance to the future needs of the employees and their work context.

Most of the aspects of traditional learning that have just been presented in a brief manner show a certain similarity to the considerations of the previous subchapter on executive development. Of course, this is no coincidence. Finally, learning should also take place within the framework of executive development. The following comparison of continuous learning in agile contexts will also show parallels to what has already been said. But because this is also about learning from non-executives and whole teams, the following considerations are more general. We therefore begin with an overall model of learning.

A Simple Model of Agile Learning

In order to understand how continuous learning works in agile work environments, a simple model, graphically depicted in Fig. 7.6, helps. In the following, the principles of agile learning are explained using this model and compared with the hierarchical viewpoint.

We start in the lower left area of this model. *Ignorance* describes a condition in which employees are not aware of their incompetence or lack of knowledge. You may be comfortable with your inability to do anything. One may at first look patronizingly at this state. In fact, this is the normal state for everyone. We are aware of our lack of knowledge only minimally. This is also good in a way. Because, if you knew what you do not know, you probably would fall into a deep depression right away. Almost everything you could know about the world, you do not know. We cannot and do not have to be aware of everything.

Irritation and Relevant Uncertainty

However, learning first requires *irritation*, the awareness that one can no longer progress in a situation with current knowledge or with current behavioural patterns.

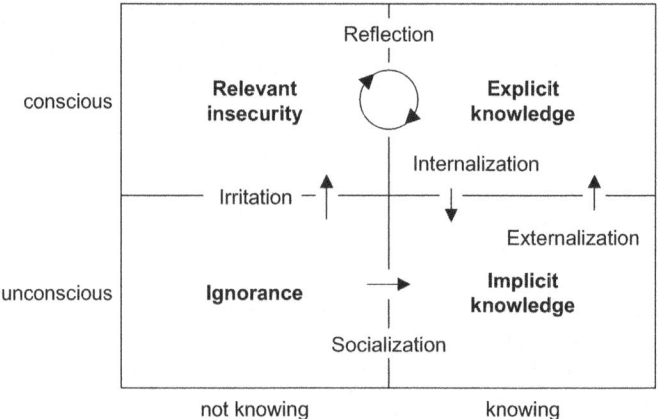

Fig. 7.6 A simple model of agile learning

7.3 Continuous Learning

It leads to a consciously experienced *insecurity*. One recognizes or feels that there are or could be better strategies for solving a problem, which one does not currently know or master. When HR managers and executives attend my seminars, they almost always bring this uncertainty with them. They are familiar with their current HR practice and at the same time know that there are better strategies that they cannot initially grasp. If this uncertainty does not exist I, as a trainer, do everything I can to irritate the participants.

Uncertainty can only lead to learning success if it is experienced as *relevant* for those affected. Imagine two employees who both attend a project management seminar, employee A and employee B. A was sent there by his boss. She neither suffers from insecurity nor is she aware of what she is actually supposed to do at the seminar. But she is open and perhaps the course is worth it against all initial expectations—"Let's have a look. At least the hotel is beautiful". What this employee takes away from the seminar is a seminar folder and possibly a hangover from the "Get Together" the evening before. Employee B was recently promoted to being a project manager. His uncertainty consists in the fact that he is aware of his lack of knowledge in leading complex projects. For him, this is a problem of high professional relevance. Given that this seminar is good, this colleague will not only take a folder home with him, but a solution. The decisive difference between employees A and B is the relevance they experience. You learn something best when you really want to learn it from an intrinsic drive (cf. Baldwin and Ford 1988).

As long as employees do a job that has been assigned to them and that they fully master, there is little chance of irritation. For some this might even be a comfortable condition. In a static world, this is also an advantage from an entrepreneurial point of view. You have the employees who have their craft under control and on whom you can rely at all times. Employees in a disruptive environment, on the other hand, rarely feel this kind of situation. They are in a persistent state of conscious uncertainty because every day they solve problems that they have never solved before and thus reach the limits of their competence. Section 4.3 already dealt in detail with the process and result certainty of tasks. It became clear that especially in agile worlds, employees are faced with tasks that entail that it is not clear from the beginning what the result might be (uncertainty of results) and how to get there (process uncertainty). If one pairs ignorance with the unconditional will to solve the relevant problems, then the best breeding ground for learning is created. In this respect, in agile worlds it is not so much the long previously defined competencies that are the drivers for continuous learning as the continuing relevant uncertainty and curiosity.

> The most important drivers for learning are relevant uncertainty coupled with curiosity. (2-2)

Hierarchical companies that are on the way to becoming more agile deliberately focus on irritation, for example, by giving their employees and managers insights into contexts that are foreign or even strange to them. Companies, for example, conduct *learning journeys* where participants are given the opportunity to gain personal insights into environments that are unfamiliar to them. Executives from hierarchical companies visit co-working spaces of agile start-up companies or go on a pilgrimage to Silicon Valley. An essential motivation for making these journeys is to irritate but at the same time to create trust in alternative worlds of work and solutions. These trips provide fewer answers, but above all arouse questions and curiosity.

I am often asked by CEOs to do keynotes on leadership and organization in front of their assembled management team. The task is usually to "turn the world view of these managers upside down". This also represents a possibility to induce irritations "from the outside" into the company.

But also on an individual level employees can be stimulated to a kind of self-irritation. It is a central feature of agile organizations that employees and teams bear a considerable degree of personal responsibility. This applies to their daily work and also to continuous learning. In the sense of the HR type, which focuses on enablement, the role of the company is to empower employees to learn independently. This also means that employees reflect and recognize their own learning needs. The irritation and awareness of uncertainty described above must take place in the employees themselves and be less driven and articulated by the direct manager.

> Employees must develop, reflect and recognize their own learning needs. This is the only way to assume a necessary motivation to learn. (1-2)

Here, for example, coaching can help, which can be provided by the respective manager or another trusted person. Simple, guiding coaching questions can be:

- What do you see as the greatest challenges in your work in the future?
- What should you improve in the future and why?
- What could help you to become better in these areas?

Instead of matching employees from a superior perspective with predefined competencies, competence catalogues can help employees to locate themselves and articulate corresponding needs. This makes competences less normative and more empowering, possibly making it easier for employees to accept them.

Learning = Work, Work = Learning, Learning = Conscious Reflection

Scientists at a research institute are working on an open, scientific question. They deal controversially with their object of research, carry out studies and at the end a scientific finding or insight is available. Obviously, the scientists have learned. A team of software developers is faced with the challenge of developing a solution for a specific problem that does not currently exist and which nobody knows about before the start of the project. The team takes the matter up and in the end there is the solution. In this case, too, the team has learned something. A sales team tries to gain a foothold in a foreign country with a foreign culture. In the beginning, deliberate, relevant uncertainty dominated. The team gets involved and after several months of hard work the sales development in the country picks up speed. The sales team has learned. Employees and teams who tackle a new challenge learn—always. This is

7.3 Continuous Learning

also—or especially—the case when they fail. Therefore, especially in agile worlds, no difference is made between learning and work.

> Learning is best done in a real work context. We see no difference between learning and work. Work = learning, learning = work. (5-2)

The central engine driving learning and working is conscious *reflection*. Based on relevant uncertainty, hypotheses are formulated, things tried out, ideas generated, prototypes developed. You actively seek feedback from customers at an early stage. All these are part of an overall learning process.

It is therefore not surprising that methods such as Scrum play such a major role in agile worlds. *Scrum* is a method of agile product development (Sims and Johnson 2011). It provides for fast planning, reflection and feedback loops, so-called sprints. One deliberately does not assume classical project management, according to which one already knows at the beginning what is to be done in the course of a project. Rather, decisions and actions are taken up in a short-cycle, iterative steps, as already described in Sect. 4.3. In this respect, Scrum is not only an alternative, agile method of managing projects, but also a format of conscious reflection and thus learning, which explicitly provides for failure as well as experimentation.

> Employees learn by taking the opportunity to experiment and fail. (9-2)

The same applies to the increasingly widespread method of *design thinking*. People who devote their time to this method are called upon to develop ideas and present them using the familiar and popular LEGO bricks. That sounds absurd at first, because how do you want to represent an alternative business model in the insurance industry with LEGO building blocks? However, this forces people to deliberately reflect. They should not only articulate their implicit ideas in spoken but also make them physically tangible. If you stroll through Potsdam (Germany) today, then you should not be surprised if an executive suddenly presents his LEGO to you and asks for feedback. At the School of Design Thinking at the Hasso Plattner Institute in Potsdam, for example, managers are deliberately asked to carry their ideas out into the real world and obtain feedback from ordinary people—not from colleagues, analysts, consultants, investors. Some participants of these events still talk about their enlightenment for years. What takes place here is learning directly on the product, close to the customer, consciously and in the form of cyclical reflection.

Informal Learning

Above all, this learning takes place without specific planning. Learning is somewhat a natural consequence or a positive side effect of work. This is also referred to as *informal learning*. One of the best known thought leaders in this field is Jay Cross, who has impressively drawn attention to the fact that 80% of learning in organizations is informal (Cross 2006) and only 20% is formal, i.e. within the framework of formal learning events and training measures. At the same time, Cross pointed out that common T&D departments concentrate their budgets primarily (up to 80%) on formal measures. His conclusion was accordingly obvious. Should not much more be invested in informal learning, i.e. in frameworks that promote learning as a natural by-product or part of work? Agile companies focus primarily on this.

> We focus above all on informal learning. To this end, we create appropriate framework conditions that make this possible and promote it. (7-2)

Almost all aspects explained or touched upon in the following sections fall into this category: connectivity, open learning environment, new challenges, new projects, spontaneous encounters, customer proximity, etc.

Social Learning

Because dealing with complex issues usually requires the involvement of entire teams and networks, reflection and the associated learning processes in agile worlds are usually social processes, which are all the more lively, inspiring and controversial the more diverse the social constellations are.

> Learning is also a social process. This is why learning and reflection processes usually take place in groups and networks. (3-2)

Even in more hierarchically managed companies, social learning processes can be implemented with manageable effort. Employees develop individually by learning individually, each for him or herself. But it does not always have to be about the question of the individual "Where and how can *I* get better?" but about: "Where and how can *we* get better?" You can appoint an individual colleague to a project management seminar or an entire project group to optimize their own project work. As soon as learning processes are socially applied, the social dynamics come into play, which in turn can be an essential factor for successful learning.

Everyone is familiar with the disillusionment of individual employees who have spent several days at a seminar off-the-job and who realize shortly after their return to the work context that they can only apply what they have learned if the social environment is suitable. You certainly cannot improve teamwork by sending a single team member to a group dynamic seminar.

I am therefore seeing more and more companies that are thinking about replacing individual development dialogues (as part of the annual performance appraisal) with appropriate group procedures. These are simple workshops in which, in addition to one's own performance expectations, the question is also raised as to what the team needs in order to be able to meet these expectations. Often it is not about development measures but about procedural, organizational or financial aspects. But the desire for joint development can also arise. In this context, it is not uncommon to speak of *organizational development* in which the conditions and cooperation of entire units are the common focus. Managers who fulfil their role as enablers are particularly open to formats such as these.

Internalization: From Explicit to Implicit

The result of the active and conscious reflection process described above is *explicit knowledge*, knowledge that is conscious and can therefore be articulated. Very often we practice things on a conscious level in order to become familiar with them. It is like learning to drive a car. This is also the case when learning to play an instrument or when acquiring professionally relevant skills. We carry out actions and thoughts consciously and in a controlled manner. It is called practising. Academically speaking, the process of *internalization* takes place here. As soon as one is sufficiently familiar with something, products, solutions, processes then knowledge, experience and maturity become normal. Consciousness saves its limited resources for other things and moves what is learned into the subconscious long-term memory. Explicit knowledge then turns into *implicit knowledge*.

Externalization: From Implicit to Explicit

But also the opposite way is not only possible but especially important in practice: the transfer from implicit to explicit knowledge. This is also referred to as *externalization*. Externalization occurs, for example, when an experienced, knowledgeable employee shares knowledge with less experienced colleagues. This sounds easier than it often is, because experienced employees often find it difficult to articulate their knowledge in such a way that the others understand it.

However, in a corporate context it is not so much the question of articulating implicit knowledge that is decisive as the question of relevant access. Employees always want access to knowledge and to those who have it when they need it immediately, because relevant uncertainties are usually experienced situationally. These uncertainties can have a different flight altitude or range of magnitude. A simple, spontaneous uncertainty could be, for example, that when you work with Excel, you suspect that something must somehow be simpler, but you do not have the solution ready. "Isn't there this function called vertical lookup? How'd you do that again?" In connection with a foreign-language conversation, you lack the right word. Or you do not know how to deal with an employee's behaviour in an acute social situation. But there are also uncertainties at high altitudes with great implications, "digitization is coming and we have to deal with it. But to be honest, we do not have a plan yet". Spontaneous uncertainties cannot be planned. They are part of everyday working life and the greater an employee's personal responsibility is, the more often these uncertainties fill the hours and the day.

> Learning must always take place when it is necessary. We cannot and we do not want to plan this. (4-2)

When employees spontaneously acquire knowledge and skills, this is also called *incidental* learning, situational learning without a planned intention. In practice, this spontaneous learning process is also referred to as *micro-learning* when short,

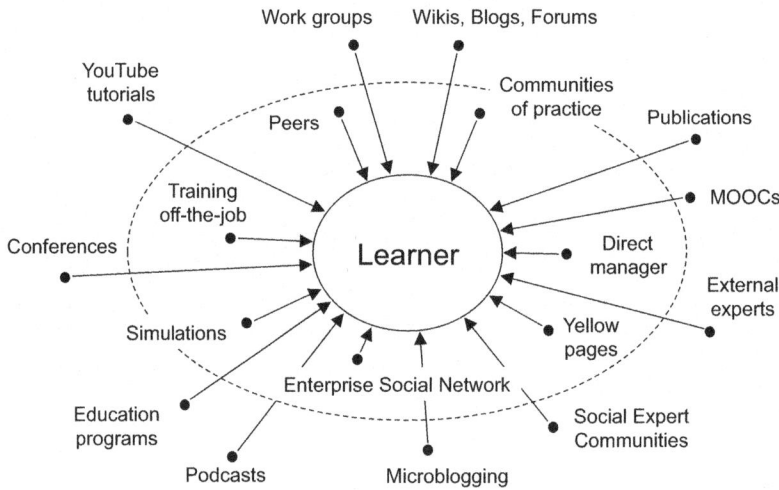

Fig. 7.7 Access to learning resources in a modern learning environment (Trost 2011)

manageable units used. These learning units (video tutorials, podcasts, etc.) usually take only a few minutes. The challenge here is to create short-term access to relevant knowledge. The company can have an enabling effect in this respect. An obvious step is to open up access to relevant *learning resources* or at least not to deny it. Figure 7.7 shows a modern learning environment with internal and external learning resources that can be suitable for incidental learning (see Trost 2011).

Just imagine that an employee experiences acute irritation, i.e., has a relevant question or problem for which he or she is looking for an answer or solution at short notice. What options are available to him or her? In a modern working environment, the employee concerned is surrounded by numerous learning resources. Within the company he or she can ask colleagues or his or her direct manager. There are Yellow Pages through which he or she can find experts in the company. Perhaps off-the-job training will be offered in the near future. *Communities of Practice* are informal groups within a company that share related interests and exchange information on a regular basis (McDermott et al. 2002). So-called *enterprise social networks* are becoming increasingly widespread (Wehner et al. 2017). Essentially, these are internal social media platforms that enable cross-functional and cross-hierarchical communication, collaboration, networking and thus learning.

Outside the company, employees have access to YouTube tutorials, external work groups, expert communities and communities on various social media platforms, training opportunities and, of course, publications, conferences, wikis (e.g., Wikipedia), blogs and Internet forums. Another interesting development can be seen in the so-called *MOOCs* (Massive Open Online Courses)[1]. Here Internet

---

[1] An example of this is my own introductory lecture "Human Resources Management", which is available on YouTube in 20 sessions with a total duration of 24 h.

users are offered complete lectures and course programs via the Internet (Castillo et al. 2015).

Until a few years ago, many hierarchically managed companies still had the hurdle of limited Internet access. Incidental learning on the Internet was equated with private surfing on the Internet at the expense of business. In the meantime, this problem has largely been solved since employees have been carrying their own Internet access around in their trouser pockets. When employees learn on their mobile devices whenever and wherever, we refer to this as *mobile learning*.

This development illustrates another trend towards continuous learning. In the past, learning was primarily for stock, that is, in the event that one could use what one had learned at some point. For whole armies of students this is the normal case. You learn "just in case" during your studies. Modern learning environments, on the other hand, allow *learning on demand* i.e., when the irritation is acute.

> Learning takes place on demand and at short notice, when employees and teams recognize their learning needs. (6-2)

It could be worthwhile for a company to carry out relevant needs on the part of employees with regard to their daily learning environment, for example within the framework of a workshop. The focus is on the question of how employees could be better empowered for incidental learning on demand. What formats, platforms, networks, apps, or whatever would be helpful from the employee's point of view?

Be Careful About Filter Bubble

Several years ago, the Internet, especially Web 2.0 and social media were regarded as a saviour for modern learning. We talked of learning 2.0. Many trusted in Google's vision of making the knowledge of the world available to all people. Today we are a little smarter. While the Internet is an important, external access to learning resources, current platforms are increasingly failing in their ability to irritate Internet users. They tend to do the opposite. In my lectures I ask students to perform a Google search for a specific search term (e.g., "fitness"). I do, too, and all students can see my search results. Then I ask who sees the same results on their smartphone. Nobody. We then jointly determine that the closer two students are to each other, the more similar are their search results. For most students, this is a shocking insight. Search results, posts shown on Facebook, etc., are censored and selected according to personal preferences. If one represents a certain point of view, then one will find in the Internet above all what fits one's own point of view. Anything that does not fit in with one's own position is consistently ignored by the operators of the largest platforms. This phenomenon is known as a *filter bubble* or echo chamber (Pariser 2012). Possible irritations are systematically avoided by algorithms.

Socialization

If one learns a foreign language at school, one first learns vocabulary, words, the material of a language, so to speak. In addition, one learns grammatical rules that explain how words are to be used and linked. All this takes place as a conscious process. Children learn a language in a completely different way. In particular, they apply the rules of grammar at some point without ever having consciously reflected on them. This process of unconscious appropriation of knowledge is also called *socialization*. You learn by unconscious imitation. In Fig. 7.6 above, this step is found in the lower half.

Socialization also plays an important role in the corporate context. This is the case, for example, with regards to onboarding (see Sect. 5.4). New employees acquire values and culturally desirable behavioural patterns primarily by working together with established employees and unconsciously adopting behavioural patterns. "Why are you doing this?" "Because that is what we're doing here. I never really thought about it."

> Employees learn from and with others. They are teachers and learners at the same time. (8-2)

Socialization can be used strategically in companies by linking employees with those people from whom employees can and should learn consciously or unconsciously. If employees who are involved in marketing tasks spend some time with their colleagues in sales, they will automatically absorb the requirements, needs, mechanisms, etc., of their sales colleagues, which could be a success factor for further cooperation. If employees are specifically guided through different areas, we refer to this as *job rotation*, a measure that has always been successfully implemented, especially in the context of trainee programs. Interdisciplinary, diverse teams are another approach. Here, employees benefit from the complementary skills of their colleagues simply by working together. This idea can even be extended to customers. The great founder and long-time CEO of SAP Dietmar Hopp once said, "If you want to learn something, just spent time with the customer". The idea behind all this is simple and reflects the thought that has just been outlined. By working together and spending time together with colleagues or clients, you learn their needs and the way they work. This happens in large parts even without conscious reflection.

What Has Always Existed

As described at the beginning of this subchapter, in a hierarchical, static world we find a different understanding of learning than is the case in an agile, connected world. It was pointed out that even in an agile world there will be much of what has always existed in a hierarchical world. However, this understanding is complemented by agile elements. In addition, the focus is shifting from one side to the other. The right side in Fig. 7.8 shows the strategic statements in line with the agile view. If you have a closer look at these statements on the agile side, you will

7.3 Continuous Learning

Identification of learning needs	*1-1 Default* Employees are given (on the basis of formal assessments) the fields of competence in which they have learning needs.	*1-2 Reflected* Employees must develop, reflect and recognize their own learning needs. This is the only way to assume a necessary motivation to learn.
Driver for learning	*2-1 Formal requirements* The most important drivers for learning are the given work-related requirements, which are documented in the job description.	*2-2 Relevance* The most important drivers for learning are relevant uncertainty coupled with curiosity.
Learner	*3-1 Individual employees* Learning activities are always focused on the individual. In the end, it is the employee who learns.	*3-2 Learning as a social process* Learning is also a social process. This is why learning and reflection processes usually take place in groups and networks.
Time	*4-1 Learning according to plan* Professional learning requires planning. At certain times of the year, employees should know what they are supposed to learn, when and how.	*4-2 Situational, spontaneous learning* Learning must always take place when it is necessary. We cannot and we do not want to plan this.
Relation to work	*5-1 Off-the-job and transfer* Learning requires a protected area outside the daily work environment. Then we hope for the transfer of learning.	*5-2 Real working context (on-the-job)* Learning is best done in a real working context. We see no difference between learning and work. Work = learning, learning = work.
Occasion	*6-1 Learning on stock* Our employees learn in advance so that they have relevant knowledge available when they need it.	*6-2 Learning on demand* Learning takes place on demand and at short notice, when employees and teams recognize their learning needs.
Planning and control	*7-1 Formal learning* Learning takes place primarily within the framework of formal measures. This enables professional planning, control and operation.	*7-2 Informal learning* We focus above all on informal learning. To this end, we create appropriate framework conditions that make this possible and promote it.
Instructors	*8-1 Teachers, trainers* Employees learn from professional trainers who have professional superiority and didactic experience.	*8-2 Others* Employees learn from and with others. They are teachers and learners at the same time.
Learning method	*9-1 Instruction, Teaching* Employees learn by instructing them and teaching them how to do things right.	*9-2 Try it out* Employees learn by taking the opportunity to experiment and fail.

Fig. 7.8 Overview of all strategic dimensions for continuous learning

notice that all this has always existed in hierarchical contexts. But still, the institutional foundations have rarely been taken care of. Learning needs have always been reflected. Relevance has always been the best teacher. Learning has also always taken place in groups, as a social process. In an agile world, these things are actively supported, while in a hierarchical context all of this happens rather randomly. This is exactly the practical difference between the two sides.

7.4 Knowledge Management

Probably everyone has heard the statements many companies constantly share about people being their most important asset. This refers to the extensive experience of the employees, their skills, abilities, motivation, health and also their knowledge. The special thing about knowledge is that knowledge is more than mere information (Nonaka 1994). Knowledge is information paired with the ability to use this information creatively in the context of a problem, an ability that is primarily attributed to humans and, more recently, to artificial intelligence. In the following, we stick with the human being as the central owner of knowledge—"knowledge needs a knower".

Retaining, Identification and Transferring Knowledge

People are naturally mobile and transient. They leave companies. Some die or get sick. In this respect, the first question that arises is how companies can *retain* knowledge of their employees. For many employers, this question arises in the context of demographic changes, for example. How do we ensure that the knowledge of experienced employees remains within the company when entire generations retire in the short or medium term?

A second challenge is the *identification of* knowledge. Who in the company has what knowledge? Are there colleagues in the company who have exactly the knowledge that I need now when dealing with my current problem? How do I find these colleagues? Knowledge about the knowledge of others can be a valuable basis for not committing mistakes that have already been made again or for not reinventing the much quoted wheel.

If it is the case that there are colleagues with relevant knowledge in the company, then the challenge is to *transfer* this knowledge. So how does the knowledge from Simon, who has relevant knowledge, get to Susan, who could benefit from Simon's knowledge?

These three challenges of knowledge management are dealt with in the remaining parts of this section: retention, identifying and transferring knowledge. Above all, it will be discussed how these challenges can be mastered institutionally and which options of strategic alignment are conceivable.

Knowledge Management, for Whom?

Let us first consider a typical case. Based on an age structure analysis, a company in the sensor and automation technology sector finds that it will lose a considerable number of experienced engineers and scientists due to their retirement in the coming years, particularly in the area of research and development (R&D). The company clearly regards R&D as its key function. A young generation of engineers is available. Now the company is asking itself how it can secure the knowledge of its experienced colleagues and transfer it to its young colleagues. It concentrates exclusively on the R&D area. It has been decided to focus on this particular *scope* of managing knowledge.

Now, let's turn to the second case. In the course of its internationalization strategy, a globally operating management consultancy decides to establish its so-called practices globally. While consulting was previously organized on a regional basis, international teams are now taking care of clients from specific industries. For example, there is an IT practice for companies in the IT sector or a unit that focuses on customers in the financial and insurance sectors. As a consequence, the company strives for a better exchange of knowledge between consultants at the international level across borders. This, in turn, applies equally to the employees of all practices.

These two examples already show two possible strategic alignments of knowledge management with regard to their scope. The first company would probably support the following strategic statement:

> Knowledge management concentrates on as few strategically important key areas or functions as possible. It is the only place that is worth the effort. (1-1)

The company in the second example would completely reorient the scope of its desired knowledge management:

> We regard knowledge management as a comprehensive initiative, which is more or less relevant for all employees of the company. (1-2)

Whether a company decides on one or the other variant obviously has to do with the relevance of the topic for possible target functions. The comprehensive option is certainly more complex than the focused one.

Humans Versus Database

When the topic of knowledge management presumably received more and more attention in the 1990s, the trend was to solve the challenges of knowledge management primarily in technical terms (cf. Milton and Lambe 2016). The idea itself was very simple and based on a centuries-old practice from science. People who have special knowledge document this in a *knowledge database*. Knowledge thus

Fig. 7.9 The collect approach of knowledge management

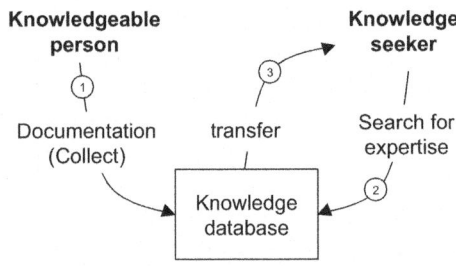

Fig. 7.10 The connect approach to knowledge management

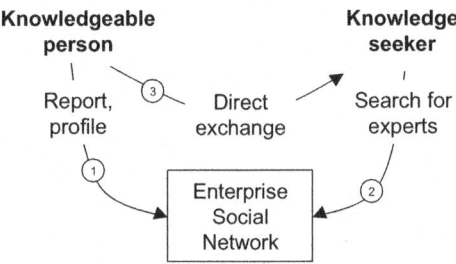

becomes directly accessible to other people. This decouples the (transient) knowledgeable from his or her knowledge, in which knowledge is transferred to an enduring medium. The latter can not only be reproduced but also made accessible to a broad target group via appropriate systems. The knowledge seeker can now search for relevant knowledge in the knowledge database and by reading the knowledge content this knowledge is transferred to the knowledge seeker (see Fig. 7.9).

This approach is also referred to as the *collect approach*. Knowledge is collected centrally and made available to others.

> In order to make knowledge permanently available to others and to become independent of individuals, knowledge must be documented centrally (collect approach). (2-1)

This is contrasted by the so-called *connect approach*. This is not so much a technical solution based on a database of documents as an interpersonal approach that aims to connect those who have knowledge with those who seek for knowledge. Practically this can work as shown in Fig. 7.10.

Employees with knowledge draw attention to their knowledge on an internal platform. They do not document their knowledge, but present the areas in which they have knowledge or experience. They develop a personal expert profile and report on their experiences, based on previous projects for instance. The easiest way to do this is to use so-called *Yellow Pages*. Increasingly, companies are using enterprise social networks. Here, expertise is only indicated in keywords, in a directory on the intranet, in a physical book or in an app.

7.4 Knowledge Management

The approach of the international strategy consultancy McKinsey & Co. is somewhat more complex. (cf. Bartlett 1996). Whenever a consulting project has been successfully completed, the respective consultants are asked to outline their findings and experiences in a comparatively short document. The primary aim is to make it visible to other consultants which challenges they have faced and how they have dealt with them. This enables knowledge seekers to become aware of those colleagues who possess relevant knowledge. Therefore, the actual transfer of knowledge does not take place via reading static documents, but via direct, interpersonal exchange. People talk to each other in the context of a given problem situation.

> The transfer of knowledge takes place through social, personal and problem-related exchange (connect approach). (2-2)

The consulting firm McKinsey & Co. originally tried the collect approach, but failed. It seems that numerous companies that have dealt with this issue in the past have had similar experiences. Overall, one can rightly state that the collect approach has little chance of success compared to the connect approach. Employees simply do not have the time to document their knowledge. This applies especially to the best and most committed employees. Above all, most employees are simply not aware of their knowledge. Their knowledge is implicit and not directly accessible through their consciousness. As already described in the previous Sect. 7.3 in the context of continuous learning, this step requires the difficult process of externalization. If you ask an experienced employee the question "What do you know?" he or she will find it difficult to narrow down relevant knowledge. Where to start and where to end? He or she will eventually fail when being asked to articulate his or her knowledge explicitly: "Can you describe the content of your knowledge?"

Obligation or Incentive

A colleague recently told me about his interesting experiences with the introduction of knowledge management in a military unit. A platform was set up for sharing knowledge. All soldiers (mainly jet pilots) were sufficiently informed and the whole thing could start. Unfortunately, nothing happened at all. On closer inspection, it quickly became clear that soldiers could not be motivated by simply offering them a platform and providing the necessary information. It took an order. So an order was given by an authority and the thing took off.

This story may sound a little strange at first. In fact, many originally hierarchically managed companies report similar circumstances. Employees are afraid to share knowledge or to comment on the knowledge of other colleagues because their superiors are breathing down their necks: "Have you gotten so far with your work that you still have time to share knowledge?" Employees want to avoid the impression of being underutilized or of not concentrating entirely on their "actual" task.

In such situations, a clear request from the CEO can be very helpful. He or she can and may emphasize in his announcement that only those managers are good managers whose employees share their knowledge. It can be communicated to employees that those employees who do not share their knowledge will never have a chance to benefit from promotion. Sharing knowledge is not something you do when you have nothing else to do, but is an essential part of the job. Anyone who assumes responsibility in their job naturally shares their knowledge. An extreme, binding strategy in the context of knowledge management may therefore be:

> Employees have a duty to share knowledge and to take care of relevant knowledge. This is monitored and controlled from a central location. (3-1)

Possibly companies with hierarchical origins should start with this strategy and keep it going until knowledge sharing becomes normal and becomes part of the corporate culture.

An opposing strategy is to make knowledge sharing as simple and attractive as possible for employees in order to pave the way for voluntary work. Depending on how knowledge management is designed operationally, interpersonal incentives can also be created, as is the case with well-known social media. Good contributions will be rewarded by likes, comments or other forms of social recognition.

> Employees are empowered to share knowledge and take care of relevant knowledge. There are interpersonal incentives for this. (3-2)

Even elements of *gamification* are conceivable here. Motivating, playful elements are applied in areas that initially appear boring by nature, but which generate positive, emotional feedback through incentives and amplifiers during corresponding activities. By sharing attractive knowledge content, employees can collect points or so-called "badges", reach higher levels, compete for better positions in internal ranking lists, etc.

A summarizing overview of the three dimensions presented around the topic of knowledge management can be found in the following Fig. 7.11.

Scope	*1-1 Focus on key areas*	*1-2 Focus on relevance*
	Knowledge management concentrates on as few strategically important key areas or functions as possible. It is the only place that is worth the effort.	We regard knowledge management as a comprehensive initiative, which is more or less relevant for all employees of the company.
General approach	*2-1 Collect Approach*	*2-2 Connect approach*
	In order to make knowledge permanently available to others and to become independent of individuals, knowledge must be documented centrally.	The transfer of knowledge takes place through interpersonal, personal and problem-related exchange.
Motivation	*3-1 Commitment*	*3-2 Empowerment and incentives*
	Employees have a duty to share knowledge and to take care of relevant knowledge. This is monitored and controlled from a central location.	Employees are empowered to share knowledge and take care of relevant knowledge. There are interpersonal incentives for this.

Fig. 7.11 All strategic dimensions of knowledge management at a glance

References

Atkins P, Wood R (2002) Self-versus others' ratings as predictors of assessment center ratings: validation evidence for 360-degree feedback programs. Pers Psychol 55(4):871–904

Baldwin TT, Ford KJ (1988) Transfer of training: a review and directions for future research. Pers Psychol 41:63–105

Bartlett CA (1996) McKinsey & co.: managing knowledge and learning. Harvard Business School, Boston, MA. Case 1996(June):396–357

Ben-Hur S, Jaworski BJ, Gray D (2012) Re-imagining Crotonville: epicenter of GE's leadership culture. Harv Bus Rev 2:74–82

Bundesinstitut für Berufsbildung (2017) Datenreport zum Berufsbildungsbericht 2017. Informationen und Analysen zur Entwicklung der beruflichen Bildung. Bundesministerium für Bildung und Forschung, Bonn

Castillo NM, Lee J, Zahra FT, Wagner DA (2015) MOOCS for development: trends, challenges, and opportunities. Inf Technol Int Dev 11(2):35–42

Cross J (2006) Informal learning: rediscovering the natural pathways that inspire innovation and performance. John Wiley, San Francisco

Dobischat R, Kühnlein G, Schurgatz R (2012) Ausbildungsreife. Ein umstrittener Begriff beim Übergang Jugendlicher in eine Berufsausbildung. Arbeitspapier 189. Hans-Böckler-Stiftung, Düsseldorf

Garvin DA, Wagonfeld A, Kind L (2013) Google's project oxygen: do managers matter? Harvard Business School, Boston, MA. Case 313–110, April 2013

Goffee R, Jones G (2006) Why should anyone be led by you? What takes to be an authentic leader. Harvard Business School Press, Boston

Jackson EJ, Schuler RS (2012) Strategic human resource management. Blackwell, Malden

Marquardt MJ, Leonard HS, Freedman AM, Hill CC (2009) Action learning for developing leaders and organizations. American Psychological Association, Washington, DC

McDermott R, Snyder W, Wenger E (2002) Cultivating communities of practice: a guide to managing knowledge. McGraw-Hill, Berkshire

McGregor D (1960) The human side of enterprise. McGraw-Hill, New York

Milton N, Lambe P (2016) The knowledge manager's handbook: a step-by-step guide to embedding effective knowledge management in your organization. Kogan Page, London

Nonaka I (1994) A dynamic theory of organizational knowledge creation. Organ Sci 5:18–19

Pariser E (2012) The filter bubble: what the Internet is hiding from you. Penguin Books, London

Robbins SP, Judge TA (2016) Organizational behavior. Pearson, New York

Schöllgen G (2002) Diehl. Ein Familienunternehmen in Deutschland 1902–2002. Propyläen, Berlin

Sims C, Johnson HL (2011) The elements of scrum. DyMaxicon, Foster City

Trost A (2011) Personalentwicklung 2.0. In: Trost A, Jenewein T (eds) Personalentwicklung 2.0. Wolters Kluwer, Köln, S 11–28

Trost A (2017) The end of performance appraisal. A practitioners' guide to alternatives in agile organizations. Springer, Heidelberg

Wehner B, Ritter C, Leist S (2017) Enterprise social networks: a literature review and research agenda. Comput Netw 114:125–142, 26 February

Development and Career 8

This chapter deals with the long-term side of training and development. The focus is not on learning as quick acquisition of knowledge and skills, but on the long-term development of individual potentials and talent in the context of long-term life and career plans. Of course, development and career have a high personal significance for employees not only with regard to their personal growth and life satisfaction but also with regard to their existential conditions. On the part of companies, on the other hand, the desire to either develop their own employees into positions and levels of greater responsibility or to create framework conditions that promote and allow precisely this has always been in the foreground. If you think about measures, instruments, processes or systems to this end, you will come directly to the topic of *talent management*. Even if the term talent management describes both from an academic point of view, namely talent acquisition (Talent Acquisition, see Chap. 5) and talent development, in practice it is rather the latter that is meant. These include the two main disciplines of talent identification (Sect. 8.1) on the one hand and talent development (Sect. 8.2) on the other.

Traditionally, careers and development have usually been thought of vertically. Accordingly, a person's career was successful when he or she climbed several management levels within the hierarchy in a short period of time. Today, we look at careers in a more differentiated way and also recognize the long-term development of expertise as a possible path. We are talking about the so-called expert career. This is also discussed in more detail in this chapter (Sect. 8.3).

8.1 Talent Identification

There is the widespread idea that talent finds its way in a natural manner. "The cream always comes to the top." The history of mankind provides several biographical examples. Just think of Albert Einstein, for example, who, after completing his studies, did not find a professorial mentor (supervisor for a doctoral thesis) and therefore accepted a position at the Bern Patent Office, not least to feed his young family. In his spare time he then studied theoretical physics and in 1905 wrote four historically important publications. One of them was finally accepted by the University of Zurich as a doctoral thesis. Einstein was awarded the Nobel Prize in 1921 for another work (Fölsing 1995). There's no stopping talent. At least, this is what one might deduce from Einstein's biography.

In the terminology differentiating various types of HR, this philosophy refers to the "Hire & Pay" approach: you do not have to worry about the talent of the employees. It unfolds on its own. One could even go further and postulate that talent that does not find its way in a natural way is not a real talent. However, very few companies are comfortable with this way of handling it. In professional sport, too, this restraint and belief in the natural course of events would not be enough (cf. Berger and Berger 2005). Rather, the focus is on identifying talent within the framework of institutionalized activities, processes and instruments, finding it and then systematically promoting it. This subchapter deals with the first part, talent identification.

Finding the Personal Vocation

In individual development, people go through a series of characteristic life phases that can be distinguished from each other. Developmental psychological findings in relation to what is called human ontogeny suggest this idea. Several psychologists describe these developments in the form of *life tasks*, such as the famous Erikson (1959) or later Kegan (1983). At an early stage in life, children must acquire values and social norms, learn language and later develop an identity. This goes hand in hand with the task of occupying an independent place in the family and in society.

Probably one of the most important and life-shaping tasks is to recognize one's own vocation or profession. It is about a destiny in the working world, something for which one was born—your own *talent*. What can or could one really do well in life, better than most other people? In which activity do you feel "in your element" (cf. Robinson 2009)? What are the tasks which, when performed with effort, become joy and fulfilment, regardless of the objective burden? We can assume that people who have found their real profession tend not only to be more successful but are also happier and healthier.

In my lectures, I regularly advise my students of business administration to look for a different perspective if they experience no interest, no joy, no inner drive in dealing with business issues: "Do me a favour and stay in my lecture until it is over. But then at the latest you should quit your studies and do something else". I am well aware of the implications of what I am saying here. In principle, every human being should take responsibility for finding his calling, his talent, his destiny and for acting accordingly in adequate consideration of existential conditions.

The Responsibility of the Company

In the context discussed here, however, the question now arises as to what responsibility employers should assume. A simple point of view based on a dehumanizing perspective in the sense of Max Weber could be to take no responsibility at all for this. You have jobs to fill. For this purpose, employees are hired who appear to be sufficiently qualified for the associated tasks. For the fulfilment of the tasks the employees receive an appropriate salary and thus the matter is settled. For companies that think like this, talent identification is definitely not a key issue.

The situation may be different for those companies that have an interest in exploiting the development potential of their employees in a targeted manner. They have this interest because they expect a higher performance, want to keep good and ambitious employees or because they find it difficult to recruit suitable candidates from outside and therefore want to develop employees with corresponding potential internally. Therefore, the following strategic orientation of talent development is obvious to many companies:

> We regard it as a central leadership task to recognize talent within the company. We have the appropriate procedures for this. (1-1)

Most large companies use the so-called *performance potential matrix* for this purpose. Due to their characteristic subdivision, they are often referred to as "9-block" in practice (see Fig. 8.1, cf. Michaels et al. 2001).

Managers at higher levels meet once a year for a so called *talent review* and classify their subordinate employees according to the dimensions of performance and potential. Those employees who not only demonstrate outstanding performance, but who are also attributed a great deal of potential are referred to as *high potentials*. In practice, other terms such as "talents", "stars" or even "heroes" also circulate. These high potentials will then be supported with development programs.

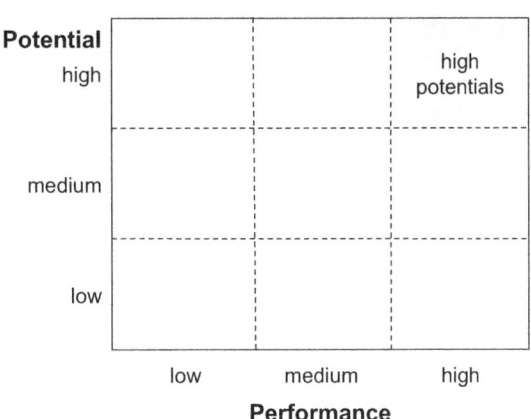

Fig. 8.1 The performance potential matrix (9-block)

This classification of individual employees as high potentials is usually preceded by a corresponding nomination by the respective direct supervisor. Conversely, this means that employees who are not recognized as particularly talented by their direct managers have no chance of joining the circle of colleagues worthy of development and promotion—the direct manager is therefore a kind of bottleneck for career development. At this point, at the latest, the responsibility of managers becomes visible in all its implications.

Employee Responsibility

While the responsibility of the company and its managers leads to a form of institutionalized dependence of employees on their direct superiors, other companies pursue an approach that presents the company as a universe of opportunities—internally as well as externally. "So many challenges. So little time" is what these companies and their employees say. This is an appeal to employees to actively recognize and seize this richness of opportunities. The strategic alignment of talent identification then presents itself as different in this respect:

> Employees should recognize their special talent themselves and bring themselves into play on their own responsibility. We in turn actively promote this. (1-2)

Employers who commit themselves to this alignment do *not* do nothing. They do not leave the employees alone, as would be the case with the HR type of "Hire & Pay". Rather, they undertake numerous institutionalized activities to empower employees through their personal talent reflection. First and foremost you offer coaching measures, whereby in the rarest cases the direct supervisor takes on the role of coach—rightly so. Alternatively, in more and more companies we find so-called *talent managers* who assume such a role. The best way to describe these talent managers is to see them as kind of internal executive search consultants and executive coaches. They not only know the internal needs and developments in the company but also actively deal with their clientele, the employees themselves. The talent managers themselves are outside the reporting line, but enjoy unrestricted trust right up to the top floors. They often report directly to the CEO.

To Have Talent or to Be Talent

It may seem like conceptual subtlety to distinguish whether an employee *has* talent or *is* a talent. In fact, however, there is a significant connotation behind this. If one assumes that an employee is a talent, then this assumption may also imply that other employees are not, otherwise the statement that an employee is a talent would not have any differentiating significance. In most cases, being a talent is assumed to be part of a selected elite in the company:

8.1 Talent Identification

> For us, a talent is someone belonging to a selected elite: employees to whom we attribute the long-term potential to master challenges of strategic importance. (2-1)

According to my own observations most large companies prefer this strategic alignment in terms of their understanding of talent. The use of the performance potential grid shown above already suggests this point of view. After all, hardly any company that follows this methodology will accept to find all its employees in the high potential category.

On the other hand, there will be considerably fewer problems with the assumption that everyone *has* talent, some talent, in something at least. The question then again is to what extent the particular talent of an employee may be relevant in the company.

> Every employee has a special talent. In the end, it is all about discovering this talent, developing it and using it within the company, wherever it may be. (2-2)

I have never encountered a company that follows this view 100%. But I have seen many companies discussing this approach again and again. "Does not every employee have some talent?" "Why do we think in such an elitist way?" "Can we afford to concentrate on just on a small group of choice candidates?" "And what about all the others?" That is what the concerns sound like. In this respect, it is strategically important to define the orientation relatively early in one or the other direction in order to avoid an eternally recurring rolling up of the same questions and concerns.

High Potentials: Right Potentials

Whenever there is a debate about talent management in companies, there is a high probability that at some point the following question will be articulated: "Do we really want high potentials or are we not looking for the *right potentials*? Experience has shown that this question affects nods of approval. There it is again, the old idea of the right employee in the right place at the right time. What moves the questioner is obvious. You have employees in front of you who are somehow good, or even particularly talented, but who in the end do not seem suitable for certain key positions. If those are identified and encouraged accordingly, this leads to unfulfilled expectations, disappointments and, above all, misguided investments on the part of all those involved. In fact, this aspect touches on a central dimension of strategic alignment in relation to talent identification. A classic expression of this dimension could be formulated as follows:

> We're betting on right potentials: Employees who have the potential to meet specific long-term, success-critical requirements. (3-1)

This approach is clearly very demand-driven. It focuses on specific target positions, target functions or target levels and the specific requirements associated with them. Companies that only want to develop future leaders as part of their talent management follow this approach. The same applies to companies that want to focus their talent management on specific key functions, such as key account management, design or research and development. Or talent management is about covering bottleneck functions internally, because it is particularly difficult to recruit personnel from the outside. In connection with this alignment, it is not surprising if the question of the relevant requirements follows in the next step. Then it is only a small step towards the development of corresponding *competence models*.

Section 7.2 addressed the particularities, advantages and disadvantages of competency models in the context of leadership development. It became clear that the alternative to static, sometimes very narrow requirements is to open up the content (see also the considerations on diversity in Sect. 4.2). One outlines necessary strengths, but does this in a more generic way. Studies show that, in practice, three characteristics are widespread in identifying *potential* (Silzer and Church 2009): performance development, motivation and personality.

- Has an employee shown an outstanding, above-average development of his or her performance in what he or she has been doing over the past few years? This aspect primarily reflects his or her predisposition and ability to learn, which is closely related to his or her level of intelligence. Past development seems to be the best predictor of future development.
- Does an employee show outstanding motivation for what the company does or intends to do, but also for how the company acts in relation to its corporate culture? Actually, it is about more than just motivation. It is about enthusiasm, passion, hunger for new challenges, burning, the famous sparkle in the eyes.
- Is an employee a natural role model for others or does he or she obviously have the potential? Is the employee more stable in his or her personality, attitude, values or at least more mature than most others? Does he or she have the natural gift to lead others?

Companies with a more generic understanding of talent will probably prefer the following strategic statement, although the generic dimension may vary from case to case:

> Regardless of long-term needs and specific requirements, we rely on personalities with outstanding learning abilities and enthusiasm for what we do as a company. (3-2)

Who Needs to Be Convinced?

Regardless of how an employee sees him- or herself, what strengths, talent and ambitions he or she recognizes, it is relevant in the entrepreneurial context how others see the employee. On the one hand, talent identification is a personal process that has to do with self-reflection and self-perception. On the other hand, it is also about a process of social judgment. For example, an employee only receives targeted support within the framework of a classically designed talent management system if superordinate managers recognize his or her talent. How the affected employee assesses himself remains unaffected by this for the time being. In this respect, the relevance for action often only arises from the fact that others classify an employee as particularly talented in one way or another.

This aspect touches a strategic dimension in the context of talent identification: Who needs to be convinced of talent regardless of how an employee views him- or herself? A more modern strategic alignment could be formulated as follows:

A talent is only a talent if others (colleagues at the same level, internal and external customers) see it the same way. (4-2)

In practical implementation, this is usually referred to as *peer nomination* (of high potentials). Colleagues at the same level explicitly advocate promoting a specific colleague, a process that is systematically managed. Some companies demand references from different departments from their talent candidates. Even obtaining external references, such as from customers, is conceivable in some cases. Sometimes a look at internal platforms, such as *enterprise social networks,* on which employees exchange ideas and experiences or build internal networks with followers, similar to Twitter, can also help. In such cases, it might make sense to recognize only those colleagues as talents who take part in internal exchanges but who are above all capable of generating a natural resonance internally.

This strategic alignment can hardly be found in practice in its pure form, but at best in addition to the hierarchical end of the dimension discussed here. This other end represents the classical, vertical, approach of talent identification, as it has already been hinted at here several times.

A talent is only a talent if superiors see it that way. (4-1)

Both ends of this dimension are not mutually exclusive. Rather, the question is what weight is attached to the two sides. In a traditional, hierarchical world, the only thing that matters is how superiors judge an employee. It can be assumed that managers will continue to play a central role in talent identification in the future. However, the increasing horizontal commitment of employees and teams to their customers, but also the changing role of executives towards more coaching and leadership in partnership, will give the approach of peer nomination greater weight in the long run.

Transparency Versus Discretion

For many years it was quite common, according to my own observations, not to disclose their nominations to the junior people who had been identified as talent.

And even if one did, one did not shout this from the roof. There were understandable reasons for that. The aim was not to create expectations on the part of these candidates themselves that might not be fulfilled in the end, which would ultimately lead to a certain disappointment on the part of those affected. And the last ones to be disappointed were those chosen. In addition, they wanted to avoid other employees developing feelings of envy or even an internal struggle for the favour of superior executives—"Why them and not me?" They also wanted to protect talents from intrinsic and extrinsic pressure.

> We treat the nomination of a talent very discreetly. In this way we avoid exaggerated expectations and resentment on the part of others. (5-1)

This strategic alignment functions as long as no direct relevance for the candidate him or herself or for others is derived from a talent nomination. In fact, the practice in many companies is that selected junior candidates are on the radar of higher management levels and are concentrated on these people in the assignment of certain tasks or possible promotions. And because there are no acute plans for these candidates, that is enough for now. So better do not panic, one tends to say.

However, as soon as selected high potentials are earmarked for specific and sometimes challenging development programs, they will have to be notified. Finally, it cannot be ruled out that a development program for a candidate is not currently an option, for example for personal or private reasons. You are currently building a house, the third child is on the way, time is very precious at the moment and a development program or even expatriation is simply unthinkable at the moment.

It is not uncommon for companies to advertise their talent management programs. Not only employees, but also external candidates and applicants should know that they exist. Under these conditions, it is also obvious that one makes no secret of the talent nomination of a colleague and the process of targeted talent identification, even if this does not necessarily have to be communicated in the employee magazine. Accordingly, the alternative draft of the strategic alignment is roughly as follows:

> We are very open about the nomination of talent. This is in the interest of the people and the company as a whole. (5-2)

Of course, there is no need to discuss which alternative is the better one, especially when a talent is nominated by its peers.

Digital Talent Identification

My first contact with *people analytics* was probably at an international HR conference in Zurich in 2012, where Prasad Setty, Vice President People Analytics at Google, was a guest speaker. At that time he announced his vision full of hope and conviction: "All people decisions at Google are based on data and analytics". What

8.1 Talent Identification

other company than Google could have formulated such a vision back then? Meanwhile, he never misses an opportunity to share the experiences he has gained since then.[1] Its history is remarkable and reflects a development that will certainly be followed by thousands of other companies.

Once a year hundreds of Google's executives, managers and talented nominees meet in San Jose, California to make decisions about who will be promoted in the coming months. These were gigantic events, which were connected with an enormous organizational, logistic and technical expenditure. Prasad Setty, for his part, and his team developed an algorithm based purely on available data that could predict with astonishing precision and validity the decisions that were elaborately generated during these events. He concluded, that Google could replace the whole act. Through machine learning his algorithm will learn to generate decisions of equal or even better prognostic validity with minimal effort. The strategic premise behind it will sound like music to the ears of numerous people analytics protagonists of today:

> As far as possible, talent nominations are based on data, algorithms and artificial intelligence and machine learning. (6-1)

The implementation of this strategy is already very much possible today, provided that companies have a reasonably solid data basis. In most cases, just a few indicators, which only need to be weighted and combined accordingly, are sufficient. With increasing technical infrastructure and access to big data, the development of valid algorithms can be developed in the context of a simple bachelor thesis. That is all it is.

The story of Prasad Setty continues. He suggested to the executive board that they should rely on his algorithm in the future. This proposal was completely rejected, which finally led to a changed vision of people analytics at Google: "All people make decisions based on data & analytics", which could make absolute sense. Imagine an employee receiving an automatically generated message telling him or her that he or she has been nominated and identified as high potential. He or she gets the explanation: "We cannot really justify this decision. It is based on an algorithm". Of course, this algorithm must remain secret in order to avoid a dysfunctional, distorting form of response. After all, you want your employees to meet their challenges and not just fit an algorithm. Google came to the conclusion that decisions about people must always be made by people. In the end, it always takes someone to stand behind a decision. Anything else would be "Hiding behind Black Boxes".

It is hard to explain the poles of this strategic dimension better than on the basis of this story. In the end, the question is whether employee-related decisions are made by machines or only supported by them. Correspondingly, the opposing premise is with regard to digitized talent identification:

---

[1] He gave one of his wonderful presentations at the 2014 Google conference re:work. It can be seen on Youtube (https://youtu.be/KY8v-O5Buyc, last seen on April 31, 2018).

> Talent nominations are social processes that are supported by data. All people-related decisions are made by people. (6-2)

Anyone who took a closer look at Google's changed vision will have noticed that a major change from the original version is not just to support decisions. What is especially emphasized is the sequence "All people make decisions". This statement addresses the question for whom people analytics can be intended. The current debate on this topic clearly shows that people analytics is an instrument for decision-makers on the upper floors. Google anticipated the development and showed that artificial intelligence should empower *all* employees. Unfortunately, this point of view is frighteningly underexposed today. Subchapter 11.3 (Digital HR and People Analytics) takes up this idea again and deals with it in greater depth.

External and Personal Understanding of Talent

To sum it up, we can say that the traditional understanding of talent in hierarchical organizations striving for stability has a certain extrinsic character. It is defined from the outside what a talent is. It is above all the institution that decides who has sufficient talent or is a talent. The criteria are defined explicitly and independently of the internal candidates to be identified. If an employee is identified as having high potential, this nomination passively happens to him or her. As the overview-like juxtaposition of strategic options in Fig. 8.2 shows, the right-hand side reflects a personal and social understanding of talent. It depends on the employee him or herself and his or her effect on others. Even the decisions and judgements of others about a talent are predominantly personal and social.

8.2 Talent Development

It is one of the most uplifting experiences for a person in his or her life not only to recognize his or her talent but also to develop it. If one wants to understand the process of how talent develops in principle, then there are different ways to do so. One of my personal approaches to this topic is the study of biographies of successful people from the history of mankind. No matter whose life you are contemplating, be it the biographies of Albert Einstein, Angela Merkel, Paul McCartney, Richard Branson, Tiger Woods, Steve Jobs, Mahatma Gandhi or Leonard Bernstein, sooner or later you will recognize certain similarities and basic patterns from which a talented person him or herself but also companies as a whole can learn. These people knew their individual talent, they were worried about but not afraid of great challenges, they had an unlimited will to succeed, they met outstanding personalities and mentors, they had the chance to do what complemented their talent, they were disciplined and enjoyed what they did. Even though each life story is unique, they are similar in many fundamental aspects. Nevertheless, there are three very different variants of these parallel stories.

Responsibility	**1-1 Executives** We regard it as a central leadership task to recognize talent within the company. We have the appropriate procedures for this.	**1-2 employees themselves** Employees should recognize their special talents themselves and bring themselves into play on their own responsibility. We in turn actively promote this.
Having or being a talent	**2-1 A talents is part of an elite** For us, a talent is someone belonging to a selected elite: employees to whom we attribute the long-term potential to master challenges of strategic importance.	**2-2 Everyone has talent** Every employee has a special talent. In the end, it is all about discovering this talent, developing it and using it within the company, wherever it may be.
Criteria	**3-1 Critical success requirements** We're betting on right potentials: Employees who have the potential to meet specific long-term, success-critical requirements.	**3-2 Personalities** Regardless of long-term needs and specific requirements, we rely on personalities with outstanding learning abilities and enthusiasm for what we do as a company.
Judgement	**4-1 Senior executives** A talent is only a talent if superiors see it that way.	**4-2 Colleagues and clients** A talent is only a talent if others (colleagues at the same level, internal and external customers) see it the same way.
Communication	**5-1 Discretion and restraint** We treat the nomination of a talent very discreetly. In this way we avoid exaggerated expectations and resentment on the part of others.	**5-2 Transparency** We are very open about the nomination of talent. This is in the interest of the talents and the company as a whole.
Role of Analytics	**6-1 Basis** As far as possible, talent nominations are based on data, algorithms and artificial intelligence and machine learning.	**6-2 Support** Talent nominations are social processes that are supported by data. All people-related decisions are made by people.

Fig. 8.2 All strategic dimensions of talent identification at a glance

Three Variants of Talent Development

There are personalities who have had to fight for almost everything in their lives themselves. Steve Jobs is a good example of this. As the son of a Syrian refugee, he built up almost everything he had achieved by his own efforts, sometimes even against massive resistance from the company he founded. For example, he assumed responsibility for visionary challenges or developed partnerships with other key personalities. Think of the technical genius Steve Wozniak, the technical father of the Macintosh or John Lasseter, the visionary head behind Pixar who created such wonderful movies as "Finding Nemo" or "Toy Story". Some people apparently do not mind being on their own. It may make them strong, and they may find their way. Albert Einstein's example mentioned earlier also falls into this category.

In an entrepreneurial context, this is reflected in the words of a former CEO of SAP, who said: "You do not have to actively promote talent, otherwise they're not talent". With reference to the HR triangle discussed in this book with the different types of HR, this perspective refers to what we named *Hire & Pay*. Companies that think like this do not have any institutionalized talent management. They leave the employees to themselves and not infrequently even with great success. "The cream always comes to the top."

In professional sport, on the other hand, there are currently practices that deviate significantly from this. In the context of the possible HR type *central planning and control* usually takes place here, the second variant of talent development. As soon as a talent—usually already in childhood—is found and identified, the talent undergoes a targeted path or plan of development. Individualized but also standardized training programs are developed and consistently operated in accordance with innumerable performance parameters. Numerous measures and concepts are available for this in the entrepreneurial context. Think here of pre-designed, detailed career paths, comprehensive potential assessments, 360-degree assessments, regular performance appraisals and reviews, targeted job assignments at home and abroad. You do something with the most talented people. The strategic alignment can be summarized in the following statement:

> As a company, we have a responsibility to develop our most talented people. (1-1)

With all the professionalism that is characteristic of this variant, some may cynically consider this procedure as a form of babysitting—"Do as you are told. Stay involved but do not think. Just give everything and someday you will become a big one". The trainer, HR or the company as a whole bear the responsibility.

In the third variant of talent development, people receive a high degree of support, but are responsible for their own development. These people have parents who stand behind the preferences of their children, even if these seem kind of absurd from the parents' point of view. People who have access to valuable networks because of their origin, their social environment or for other reasons, but who have to make something of them themselves in the end. People who have the unbelievable luck to grow up in a state that not only allows them a free choice of occupation but also provides them with the necessary qualification opportunities. They must walk the path themselves and ultimately bear the responsibility for what has been achieved. Some people grow up in a labour market that opens up a universe of opportunities and perspectives, for example due to economic conditions. They only have to orient themselves in this way on their own. In the entrepreneurial context, this is about the HR type of personal responsibility and *people-centered enablement*. The company conveys the unambiguous message:

> We offer more exciting opportunities and challenges than you have time to explore. Here you can develop according to your preferences and inclinations. We support you in finding your own way and assure you of a framework conducive to development. However, the responsibility for your development lies in your own hands.

8.2 Talent Development

Summarized in a statement, the strategic alignment is as follows:

> The responsibility for the development of our employees lies with the employees themselves. We enable them for this where necessary and where desired. (1-2)

In the following sections, the two extremes of central planning and control on the one hand and people-centered enablement on the other are discussed along essential dimensions of talent development. We start with the concept of career paths.

Normative and Descriptive Career Paths

Some HR managers tell me about the increasing number of requests by young employees in particular to have a clear outlook at the beginning of their career, a plan for their future. This touches on the concept of *normative career paths* that has existed in numerous companies for many years. It describes in detail how long an employee is supposed to hold which position at which level in which function and for how long. It describes what the responsibility is and what you have to be capable of. These plans include prescriptive phases, which extend over several years. This goes hand in hand with the message that this is the only way for a career to proceed. In this respect, the nature of these career paths is normative, i.e. prescriptive and binding.

> Employees expect clear perspectives and (normative) career paths. That is why we describe and prescribe precisely as possible how one could achieve a target position in the long term. (2-1)

This form of normative career paths can be found primarily in traditional, hierarchically managed companies that assume the best possible stability and predictability. They expect employees to be subordinated to the existing structures, which are mainly static in nature. Individuality and personal responsibility both are rather alien to this concept. In this respect, this approach is primarily compatible with the HR type of central planning and control.

In agile organizations such a view seems rather strange to employees and executives, or at least seems incompatible. An HR manager in a company with 2000 employees will probably react as follows when an employee asks about career paths: "Yes, we have 2000 different career paths. I cannot tell you what your personal career path will look like. That is up to you. Ask me again in ten years, then we'll both know better".

However, instead of leaving employees completely alone—which would be the "Hire & Pay" type—employees are offered transparency about previous experience, so-called *descriptive career paths*. The example of a large retail company can illustrate this idea. In this company there are today about 120 store managers. In a simple investigation, they were asked what they had done before. In a further step, the holders of these leading positions were confronted with the same question. These steps were repeated over and over again. In the end, the investigation resulted in a vivid tree or a network of countless career paths with numerous cross struts. If you want to know how to become a store manager, this simple, descriptive analysis will tell you. The basic idea is reminiscent of Amazon: "Employees who do X today in most cases have done Y before". These career paths are more comparable to beaten paths. They do not proceed in the way that a central authority has defined it, but in the way that people have moved and developed in the past.

> There are as many career paths with us as there are employees. We offer our employees transparency and orientation about previous experiences and careers of others. (2-2)

Of course, this can also be done in a less time-consuming way, which seems necessary especially when positions cannot be clearly distinguished from each other. This is often the case in agile organizations. Here the stories of individuals presented in internal forums, workshops, career conferences and in personal conversations help.

However, when it comes to the question of how employees develop in the long term, regardless of whether they follow normative or descriptive career paths, reference is usually made in practice to the so-called *70-20-10 rule* of talent development. Although this rule has never been empirically proven, it provides an initial, pragmatic classification of possible starting points (cf. McCall 1998; Michaels et al. 2001).

The 70-20-10 Rule of Talent Development

There is a simple exercise that I like to do with my MBA students. I ask them to first write something on a piece of paper that they think they can do very well, better than most other people. Then I ask the students where or how they learned this. I then collect their thoughts on the blackboard. Surprisingly, the result is always the same, more or less. 70% was learned through experience. You became really good at something because you could or had to do it, so you practised it often enough. 20% was learned from and with others. You had colleagues, supervisors, role models, a mentor from and with whom you learned something. 10% was learned through formal training, in the context of a formal education or training program.

Many companies make active use of this rule, which seems to make sense. In essence, this rule appeals on the one hand to a balance and blend of different learning opportunities. On the other hand, it stresses the importance of practical experience. In the following, these three components and their possible strategic alignment will be examined in more detail. We start with practical experience.

Cold Water

If you ask a person who has really come a long way in his or her life what was most influential for his or her development, then you often get an answer like this: "There was this moment when I was faced with a huge challenge and someone gave me the

8.2 Talent Development

confidence to master this challenge". Sometimes the simple phrase "you can do it" changes your whole life. There are situations where people have no choice but to accept being faced with an overwhelming challenge. People probably learn the most from such situations.

Within the framework of talent management, it is therefore a matter of giving access to situations of this kind in a targeted manner. One speaks here also of so-called *stretch roles* or *stretch jobs*. Classic challenges of this kind are the position as assistant to a top executive, assuming the role of project manager for a difficult project, expatriation or a deputy position. In many cases, these challenges can also be found on a smaller scale, for example when trainees at McDonalds are given responsibility for managing a restaurant for a day or a week. McCall (1998) also speaks of internal schools here. Accordingly, every company has schools in different areas and roles in which one can learn something new in a practical way. One only needs to know what could be learned in which school. Now you can send employees or high potentials to specific schools. In everyday language, this is also referred to as "cold waters", into which employees are deliberately thrown (see also Sect. 5.4 about Onboarding). "John, what you lack is experience abroad. That is why we're sending you to our Singapore branch for two years". In this case, the company assumes responsibility for the development of its employees, an approach that is particularly conceivable in traditional, hierarchically managed companies:

> To ensure that our high potentials learn as quickly as possible, we throw them in at the deep end when and where it makes sense from the company's point of view. (3-1)

Even if an ambitious, talented employee wishes to jump into certain cold waters, he or she will not be allowed to do so in a traditionally hierarchical context. Rather, he or she is dependent on receiving the corresponding chance or permission from the top.

In a more agile context, on the other hand, finding cold waters works primarily via lateral networks within the company. It is expected that employees will seek challenges themselves and bring themselves into play accordingly. This can even go so far that employees create new challenges for themselves together with their colleagues because they recognize the opportunities and needs associated with them on their own initiative.

Companies can make a lot of institutional contributions here. A simple concept that has gained increasing attention in recent years is the so-called *internal talent market*. In essence, this is nothing more than an internal project exchange or employee exchange, comparable to well-known job boards on the Internet. On the one hand, employees present themselves with their personal profiles and outline their experiences, knowledge, internal contacts and preferences for upcoming projects and the like. On the other hand, projects or project ideas will be communicated on this platform. In the end, the aim is to create internal transparency about people and challenges in order to bring people and projects together in a self-directed way. Increasingly, internal platforms in the sense of an enterprise social network are assuming this function. But it can also be done with less technical means. Think of internal events at which projects and project ideas are presented and discussed across departments and roles, forums, conferences, project fairs, and internal networking events.

Companies can also try to lower barriers to *internal mobility* or actively support it. This is about seemingly simple things. How easy or how difficult is it for an employee to change departments, take on a new role in the company or work in another country? What formal approvals, for example from HR or a supervisor, are required? What support does the employee receive if he or she wishes to go abroad for a longer period of time? Depending on a company's attitude towards this, the corresponding interests of its employees are welcomed and promoted or made more difficult. Overall, agile companies will tend to sign the following strategic alignment:

> Talents search for cold water on their own and jump in by themselves. We create transparency, trust and reduce obstacles. (3-2)

The bottom line is that the topic of leadership plays a decisive role in this strategic orientation. For this reason trust is explicitly mentioned in the statement above.

Mentors and Mentoring

There is an internationally very successful talent show, which is known under the name "The Voice". In the initial phase of this show, during the so-called "blind auditions", selected candidates have the opportunity to be convincing in front of a number of potential mentors. They've got 90 seconds to do that. Interestingly, the mentors, who are very prominent artists, cannot see the candidate. If a mentor is convinced of the candidate's potential during this 90-second performance, he or she activates a buzzer. If no mentor presses the buzzer, the show for the candidate is over. If, however, several mentors decide in favour of the talent, then the talent ultimately has the opportunity to decide with whom he or she wants to work with. There is hardly a better way to link mentors and mentees.

There are a number of key principles behind this. Both the mentor and the mentee want to win in the end. The mentor needs the mentee and vice versa. This requires unrestricted, mutual commitment and trust. Mentoring programs can only function if these principles are adhered to.

In business practice, these principles can be easily replicated. Imagine a situation in which selected high potentials have the opportunity to present any topic to the assembled executive board. The members of the board then signal their preferences. In the end, the talent decides whom he or she wants as a mentor. If no board member is interested in promoting a particular talent, the apparent talent can leave the program. The principle here is: if you do not convince now, you won't convince in the future.

Talents must win their mentors' approval themselves. If they can't, they will have little chance to succeed in the long run. (4-2)

There are also less extreme approaches, such as that of a division of a large German automotive supplier. There, for example, photo albums of potential mentors and mentees created by them are used as a basis for personal and mutual identification. Mentors choose mentees whose albums they find appealing and vice versa.

Having a strong mentor can be invaluable to corporate talent. Mentors are usually representatives from senior management, strong personalities with influence and networks. Their role is to support their mentees emotionally and motivational—"You can do it". They bring talented people into contact with people who can be of great importance for the further development of a talent—"May I introduce our CFO to you?" "Talk to Dr Meyer first!" "Keep your hands off this project". "Now you must act. Do not lose any time". But mentors also benefit from their mentees. They have to. Otherwise they do not take the relationship and their role seriously. By strengthening their mentees, mentors can strengthen their own position, build lasting supporters and establish connections in different business areas. In addition, mentors can learn from their mentees in the sense of what is referred to as *reversed mentoring*.

In contrast to the "The Voice", the assignment of mentors to mentees in most companies is more externally determined and works according to formal rules. "The talents starting with A to F in the last name will be taken over by the CFO. The talents from G to L please go to the CMO etc.". A somewhat more intelligent approach is to use matching methods to make allocations either on the basis of information already available (same university, home region, professional focus, etc.) or on the basis of criteria used specifically for this purpose.

We assign a mentor from senior management to each talent. In doing so, we systematically pay attention to the correct fit. (4-1)

The probability of a functioning, trusting mentor-mentee relationship is rather low with this approach. Although the approach here is very systematic, in the end it is mainly chance that decides the outcome. Then the relation does not work because of the matching but despite of it.

Career Coaching

Another development measure that has always existed in both hierarchical and agile companies is *career coaching*. However, at its core, it addresses an understanding that can primarily be reconciled with an agile point of view. A coach always leaves the responsibility for the development of an individual career plan to the coachee him or herself. The coach asks good questions only. A typical question could be: "What is really important to you in your personal development?" Answering a question like this in the solitude of the quiet closet certainly leads to a less reflected answer than in the presence of a person you respect. This is precisely the power of coaching. The task of the coach is not only to ask the right questions at the right time, but also to create an environment in which the coachee can articulate himself without fear. The coach never derives consequences from what his coachee says that go beyond the coaching situation. It is the sole task of the coachee to come to his or her own conclusions for him or herself and his or her future. Once this particular dynamic of coaching has been understood, it becomes immediately clear why this role can never be assumed by the direct superior.

Action Learning

A process typical of talent management involves the so-called *action learning*. In essence, action learning describes learning from and with others through real challenges (Marquardt et al. 2009). In practice, this is usually as follows. Let us assume that one company has identified 15 high potentials and is now conducting an action learning program (see Fig. 8.3).

The starting step would be a kickoff-event, in which all 15 participants are present and a top executive explains and assigns three topics of strategic relevance for the company. We are also talking here about *learning projects*. They comprise real problems, which the participants in mixed groups should from now on deal with in order to finally point out and evaluate concrete options for action. Topics could be: Digitization, the Chinese market, shortage of talent, sustainability, etc.

> Our high potentials learn from and with each other on the basis of strategic tasks or learning projects that are assigned to them in addition to their regular work (on-top-of-the-job). (5-1)

From now on, phases of project work, joint training events and workshops will alternate. The final stage is a presentation of the results, usually to a high-ranking committee. This program is enriched by active support from senior management (sponsoring and mentoring). These programs usually take place in addition to the regular work of the high potentials—learning on-top-of-the-job.

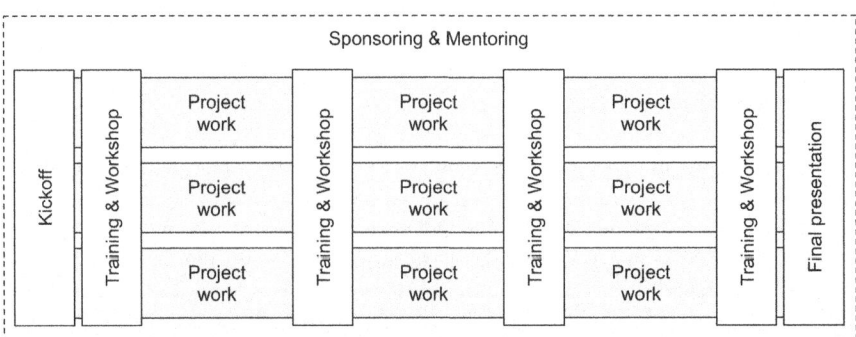

Fig. 8.3 Action learning

8.2 Talent Development

Programs of this kind tend to work quite well because their format reflects several principles of learning. Participants can actively present themselves, come together with talented colleagues, mostly from other areas and countries, form long-lasting networks, experience a dynamic mix of cooperation and competition, have access to senior management, learn to deal with strategic issues, exchange ideas in workshops and receive professional input in well-prepared training events. However, practice has shown time and again that the participants in these programs are *not* promised in advance that the proposals developed will be implemented afterwards. If you do this, you end up creating groups of frustrated high potentials who do not really feel taken seriously.

Where Do Strategic Challenges and Learning Projects Come from?

For the Head of Talent Management, the classic action learning approach described above usually begins by asking senior management for suitable learning projects and at the same time by wanting to have responsible sponsors and mentors named for them. In real-life practice, the Head of Talent Management often chases after the topics and people and experiences reactions such as: "You asked me to do this only recently. Has it really been another year since then?" The program concludes with perfectly staged presentations, choreographed down to the last detail, in which the high potentials try to make the best possible impression. On the one hand this is understandable, on the other hand these appearances rarely provide authentic impressions of how the presenters deal with strategic challenges in everyday life.

This raises the fundamental question of where the strategic tasks or learning projects that are ultimately dealt with by the participants come from. The widespread scenario described above assumes that these topics are picked up at the top and assigned to the candidates. This does not have to be this way. This scenario is only *one* of several possible ways to go. Figure 8.4 shows the variation of possible options systematically.

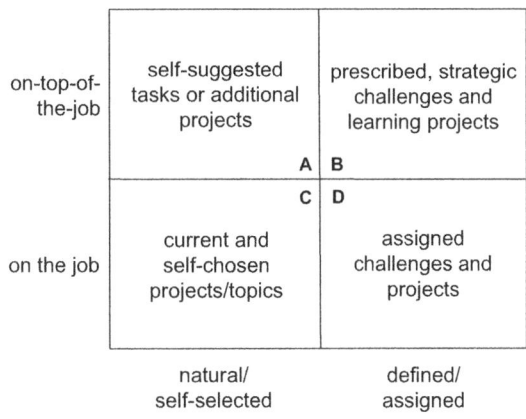

Fig. 8.4 The origin of learning projects and strategic challenges

On the one hand, a distinction is made between challenges that are either naturally *chosen* or proposed by the high potentials themselves or are *prescribed*. On the other hand, a distinction is made between tasks, topics and projects that are either part of the already existing range of responsibilities of those affected *on the job* or are dealt with *on top of the job in* addition to their daily work.

Case *B* describes the classical approach. Learning projects are handed down from the top and the high potentials are allowed to work on them together with others in addition to their actual work. That this means an additional burden is desired in a certain way, after all the high potentials are supposed to demonstrate a particular level of resilience. What is decisive in this case is that these are often learning projects that explicitly allow failure. It is left completely open here whether anything will happen with the results afterwards. Rather, the focus is on throwing a kind of puzzle at the people that they can work their way through. The advantage of this approach is that groups of participants can each be assigned a topic.

This is not always the case in the other scenarios, such as case *D*. This case describes a situation that has already been explained in connection with "cold waters". Within the scope of the regular area of responsibility of a high potential, he or she is assigned a special, stretching challenge. The associated problem is real. The leap into the cold water, however, is done in the sense of an instruction—"Susan, we [HR, superior management] want you to take responsibility for this project. It may be too big for you, but it is a good thing. You will learn a lot". These are typical stretch jobs.

Case *C* describes a scenario that differs in every respect from the classical on-top-of-the-job approach to prescribed challenges. Here, high potentials choose their own cold water. It is assumed that talented employees can do this. You have to be able to see for yourself what is strategically important for the company. Above all, however, these problems are real challenges from the natural area of responsibility of the respective high potential.

> For our high potentials, learning from and with each other on the basis of strategic problems is a natural part of their daily work (on-the-job). (5-2)

In practice, the concept of *Working Out Loud* is increasingly gaining ground (cf. Stepper 2015). In this process, employees network with other employees in so-called circles and work on topics from their regular work that they have brought in themselves. In this respect, this concept is fully compatible with this scenario and can be an essential component of talent management. Because in this case each high potential brings in its own topic, it is difficult to work on tasks together in groups. Rather, the employees benefit from the mutual, constructive exchange, an approach that is certainly comparable to peer counselling.

That leaves case *A*. In addition to their actual work (on-top-of-the-job), high potentials are asked to propose strategic topics, tasks or learning projects. Already this process of searching for topics is a learning process for the high potentials itself, because already here it shows, who can recognize and articulate topics, which can have a strategic relevance, on their own initiative. In most cases, an announcement is made here by top management in the form of content guidelines: "As you all know, the increasing digitization represents a challenge and an opportunity of strategic proportions for us. Please bring in topics or challenges alone or in groups that may be relevant in this context". At the end, for example, a committee decides on the acceptance and allocation of the topics proposed.

Formal and Interpersonal Approaches

You can regard talent management very objectively and data driven. In a somewhat extreme stage, a talent is regarded as an objects with certain attributes. These include characteristics along specific competences, personality traits, proven successes, a development history and other factors that appear relevant, such as mobility, professional preferences, etc. Where possible, the HR function, and in particular the talent management team, has an IT system that shows exactly where a talent is in relation to the variety of characteristics. In Sect. 2.2 this comprehensive approach has already been presented as an HR type of central planning and control. This approach makes it possible to plan and control the development of people very objectively. At least that is the claim. And because one assumes that one can only manage what one measures, as much as possible is measured (see also Sect. 11.2, Key figures and control). People analytics may be seeing a Renaissance of this path.

If you want to understand more about how this approach works, you have to look into the field of competitive sports. Here in particular, not only the measurement of athletes, but also the precise assignment of training measures has long been a matter of course (Berger and Berger 2005). In addition, data is decisive in determining when which athlete is used where and in which constellation. The book "Moneyball" by Michael Lewis has brought this philosophy to public attention.[2] The story told shows how an initially hopeless team becomes a winning team through the smart usage of data.

Even though *people analytics* increasingly refers to this story, it seems rather hopeless to create a direct transfer into the corporate context. There is a difference between a runner, a golfer, a weightlifter or a prospective manager. This is simply due to the fact that in the business context the challenges and the respective environment can hardly be predicted. Nevertheless, a certain ambition in this direction can be seen in many companies, which is often highlighted by software vendors. Companies that think this way rely on objective procedures, processes, systems and formal assessment methods when developing their high potentials. Behind this attitude is the explicit claim of being able to eliminate the human factor with all its weaknesses and biases. Neither sympathy nor empathy, neither subjective assessments nor social judgement tendencies should play a role.

---

[2]The book "Moneyball: The Art of Winning an Unfair Game" by Michael Lewis (2004, published by Norton) was 2012 put on screen with Brad Pitt in the leading role.

> In developing our most talented people, we rely primarily on objective processes, data, systems and formal assessment methods. (6-1)

For some companies, this objective, formal approach is synonymous with professionalism and control. In the past 20 years, I have experienced more than one HR manager or managing director who, after presenting a deeply objective, formal—not to say "technocratic"—approach, clearly signalled: "That is exactly what I want". This is opposed by companies and their representatives who would never come close to the idea of taking this path. This attitude was impressively expressed in a statement by a person responsible for talent management at an international logistics company, whom I once met:

> The last thing we want is technocratic talent management, in which employees are measured and treated from the distance. We talk to our people. We currently have 200 young and very talented people in the group. We have a team of three talent managers who do nothing else but travel around the world to talk to these wonderful people. We all know them personally, their status, history, ambitions, strengths and even their family context. We try to discuss development opportunities in each individual case. We keep an eye on internal needs and developments within the company. We are directly attached to the executive board and whenever personnel decisions of strategic importance are made, we come into play. We are somehow internal executive search consultants and internal development consultants in one. This works precisely because we cultivate and enjoy trusting relationships in all directions.

With this special approach, the agile principle of *People over Processes* becomes apparent. One relies on the continuous, interpersonal exchange. Understanding talent means dealing with it personally, which of course requires a personal encounter, trust and intensive dialogue.

> When accompanying our most talented people, we focus primarily on personal support and interpersonal exchange. (6-2)

What is stored in extensive systems in the first scenario is represented in the minds of talent managers in the latter approach. Of course, this involves a risk. The dependence on talent managers but also their influence on the development of talents and the filling of key positions is certainly enormous.

Formal Fit and Trust

In industrial and organizational psychology, a distinction is made between so-called statistical and clinical judgment formation (cf. Meehl 2013). A *statistical judgement* is formed according to clear rules, algorithms and on the basis of relevant information. This is the case, for example, when clear requirement profiles are compared with the profiles of possible candidates when filling a position. This is also referred to as matching. *Clinical judgment*, on the other hand, is based on trust, elaboration and even intuition, which at the same time does not rule out the possibility that these judgments are well-founded and made after intensive consideration. Scientifically

8.2 Talent Development

socialized practitioners prefer statistical judgements over clinical judgements. The latter tend to be associated with gut feeling and a lack of rationality.

In talent management, this distinction is of paramount importance. After all, talent management eventually leads to the internal filling of key positions, i.e. positions with high strategic relevance for the company as a whole. It is therefore not surprising that in recent years an attempt has been made to make decisions in this respect as rationally, i.e. statistically, as possible. Whenever internal candidates are evaluated and assessed according to predefined competency models, this consideration is followed. This means that an internal candidate is suitable for a key position if it matches the predefined requirement criteria as closely as possible.

> The placement and promotion of a talent is based on the formal match between his or her suitability and a requirement profile in order to avoid biases and nepotism. (7-1)

Officially, hardly anyone would contradict this claim. Practical experience and observation, on the other hand, often show a somewhat different picture. In addition to those companies that rely on matching (statistical judgements) and do so in the end, there are companies that officially claim to rely on statistical judgements but in reality rely on intuitive (clinical) judgements to actually fill key positions. This can happen, for example, when decision-makers place their personal impressions and personal preferences above formal criteria. "It may well be that Mrs. Hover is closer to the official requirement criteria. Still, I am in favour of Martin getting the job. That is what my gut feeling tells me and I haven't been that wrong in the past". If this case becomes the rule, the formal measurement of talents may not be necessary. In Fig. 8.5 this case is indicated by the quadrant in the lower right area.

But there is also the opposite case. Accordingly, a company officially intends to give precedence to those candidates or to offer a key position in which interpersonal trust is placed. But as soon as the actual decision is made, the inner voice is

Fig. 8.5 Ideal and reality when filling key positions

Reality		trust	matching
matching		Ad hoc rationalisation of a decision	Formal, rational, prepared decision making
trust		Informal and trust-based decision making	Mistrust against formal decision-making

Ideal aspiration

mistrusted and rational criteria are sought. Somehow one tries to rationalize decisions for or against candidates ad hoc and to base them on matching. This is the case when decisions for or against candidates have to be formally justified, for example against a higher authority, or when there is a need to secure legal protection in order to avoid potential accusations of arbitrariness or even discrimination. This constellation is problematic because the information required for a statistical judgement is often and simply not available in the given decision-making situation. You are kind of unprepared. In the figure shown, this case is indicated by the upper left field.

Of course, decisions within the framework of talent management are only consistent if the demands and reality correspond. In Fig. 8.5 these cases are indicated by the grey shaded fields. The right upper case is sufficiently well known and is being sought in numerous companies. No less interesting, however, is the opposite approach, according to which internal appointments to key positions are not only to be made on the basis of trust, but are also to be made in this way.

> In the end, personal trust always decides what opportunities are offered to a talented candidate. We therefore create opportunities for building trust. (7-2)

From the perspective of a scientifically rooted practitioner, it takes courage to rely solely on trust. If one studies the extensive literature on the subject of talent management, one encounters above all the implicit or explicit appeal not to do so (Silzer and Dowel 2010). A possible, strong argument, which has already been hinted at above, is that at the end of the day it can still depend on trust on the part of the decision-makers, regardless of what the data situation suggests.

But if trust now plays a determining role, then it would be conceivable to adjust precisely to this and to declare clinical judgment to be the official pace. If you follow this path, you will invest less time and energy in the formal measurement of talents. Rather, from the outset, framework conditions will be created that serve to build trust. In practical terms, this can mean that decision-makers are given the opportunity to exchange ideas with high potentials. The possibilities are endless. Think of fireside chats, mentoring, reversed mentoring, action learning, informal events, executive bar camps, roundtables, the active involvement of high potentials in strategic decision-making processes, recommendations by colleagues, etc. The decisive difference is that you know an internal candidate personally and not only his or her competence profile, supplemented by a situational interview.

The Independent Talent in Its Natural Environment

There is hardly any other HR-relevant topic where the three types of Hire & Pay, central planning and control as well as people-centered enablement become as clear as with the topic of talent development. In this subchapter, the latter two were systematically compared (see Fig. 8.6 for an overview). The variant of centrally planned and controlled talent development seems to be sufficiently well known to

8.2 Talent Development

Accountability	*1-1 Company and HR* As a company, we have a responsibility to develop our most talented people.	*1-2 Employees themselves* The responsibility for the development of our employees lies with the employees themselves. We enable them for this where necessary and where desired.
Career paths	*2-1 Standardized and normative* Employees expect clear perspectives and (normative) career paths. That is why we describe and prescribes precisely as possible how one could achieve a target position in the long term.	*2-2 Individual and descriptive* There are as many career paths with us as there are employees. We offer our employees transparency and orientation about previous experiences and careers of others.
Stretch roles	*3-1 Assigned* To ensure that our high potentials learn as quickly as possible, we throw them in the deep end when and where it makes sense from the company's point of view.	*3-2 Opened* Talents search for cold water on their own and jump in by themselves. We create transparency, trust and reduce obstacles.
Mentor-mentee relationship	*4-1 Structured assignment* We assign a mentor from senior management to each talent. In doing so, we systematically pay attention to the correct fit.	*4-2 Social mediation* Talents must convince their mentors themselves. If they can't, they will have little chance to succeed in the long run.
Action learning	*5-1 Assigned, on-top-of-the-job* Our high potentials learn from and with each other on the basis of strategic tasks or learning project that are assigned to them in addition to their regular work (on-top-of-the-job).	*5-2 Part of natural work (on-the-job)* For our high potentials, learning from and with each other on the basis of strategic problems is a natural part of their daily work.
Basis for operation	*6-1 Formal Processes and Systems* In developing our most talented people, we rely primarily on objective processes, data, systems and formal assessment methods.	*6-2 Social exchange* When accompanying our most talented people, we focus primarily on personal support and interpersonal exchange.
Decision making	*7-1 Criteria Guided* The placement and promotion of a talent is based on the formal match between his or her suitability and a requirement profile in order to avoid biases and nepotism.	*7-2 Trust based* In the end, personal trust always decides what opportunities are offered to a talented candidate. We therefore create opportunities for building trust.

Fig. 8.6 Overview of all strategic dimensions of talent promotion and development

most companies. It basically reflects the most widespread best practice. However, the more agile version is completely different. Almost already when the considerations are put together, the focus here is clearly on personal responsibility of the talent, networking and interpersonal exchange, individuality and closeness to operational reality.

8.3 Expert Career

In traditional, hierarchical companies, the appreciation of an employee or manager increases with the hierarchical level to which they belong. The CEO receives the highest esteem. As already comprehensively described in Chap. 4 this is based, among other things, on the assumption that managers would be superior to those below in many respects. At the same time, it was above all those employees with professional superiority who had the greatest chances of being promoted to higher levels. This classical idea has been increasingly called into doubt during the last several decades. This development probably began with the observation that some employees did not hold a management position, but whose expertise seemed indispensable for the company even in strategic terms. Any company can report cases of this kind. These cases became problematic at the latest when it came to classifying the experts concerned into an adequate salary group. And there, higher salary groups were usually only intended for managers, but not for indispensable experts.

In more and more companies, the solution was to establish a further path parallel to the management career, namely the *expert career*. As indicated in the Fig. 8.7, the influence of a manager increases with increasing hierarchical level. For example, personnel and budget responsibility are increasing.

The influence of experts, on the other hand, results less from their formal position in the hierarchy than from the (strategic) importance of their particular expertise. The greater and more relevant the expertise of an expert, the higher is not only its resonance within the company, but also its effectiveness on decisions within the organization.

Already in Sect. 4.4 the T-concept was used to draw attention to the fact that expertise is becoming increasingly important, especially in agile organizations. While in traditional companies executives were experts and generalists at the same time, we increasingly observe a separation between generalists who maintain a broad overview and coordinate accordingly (executives) on the one hand and those

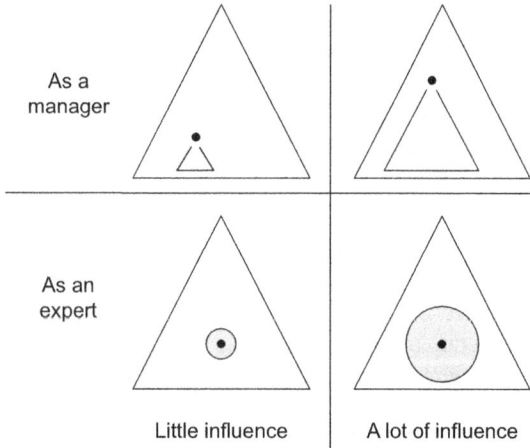

Fig. 8.7 Influence as manager or expert

employees who have a professional depth within their sphere of activity that clearly exceeds the expertise of the respective executives on the other.

The Internal Positioning of the Expert Career

There are a number of studies on the subject of specialist careers in which, for example, HR managers were asked what were the main reasons for introducing a specialist career in their company (e.g. DGFP 2012). In the broadest sense, this involves the positioning of this approach in the company and the arguments put forward for setting up an alternative career path. The following statement regularly reaches a top position in these studies:

> We want to offer important experts who seem unsuitable for a management career a development perspective and thereby retain them in the company. (1-1)

Undoubtedly, this type of strategic alignment of an expert career is an obvious variant. But you have to look twice to understand the peculiarity of this prioritization. Here a simple thought experiment helps. Imagine asking HR executives why there is a *management* career path in their company and getting the same answer, but reversed: "We have set up a management career path to offer a perspective to those employees who have no expertise but can lead well". Some would find this form of argumentation difficult to digest or even kind of odd. However, this thought experiment illustrates the special character of the above strategic statement. You want to just treat experts well, i.e. individual employees. Companies that think and act in this way are known to run the risk of accumulating a group of colleagues who enjoy special privileges because of their experts, regardless of relevant requirements. Cynical tongues also like to speak of the so-called "elephant cemetery".

A contradictory, strategic statement could focus less on the affected *persons*, i.e. the experts themselves, than on the actual needs of the company. The strategic statement regarding the positioning of the expert career could then be as follows:

> By means of expert careers, we ensure the availability of critical expertise within the company. (1-2)

The focus here is not on the expert but on the *expertise*. The central motivation for an expert career is not to just treat experts well, but to secure the internal need for expertise, wherever it may be. There is a fine but strategic difference between these two options.

Top-Class Sport Versus Mass Sport

In contrast to the just explained dimension of the strategic positioning of specialist careers, the following differentiation has considerable consequences for the operative implementation of this idea. Our own studies on this topic have clearly shown that there are apparently two extremely different variants in connection with expert careers, which differ in terms of the scope (cf. Berberich 2014). There are companies that offer *every* employee above a certain level the opportunity to pursue a specialist career, regardless of the function in which the employee works. We also call this option "mass sport":

> All employees above a certain level have the opportunity to pursue a management or expert career (mass sports). (2-1)

Other companies, on the other hand, are extremely *selective* when it comes to expert careers. The historically best-known example of this approach is provided by IBM and its Fellow Program. At IBM, a maximum of ten experts are personally appointed Fellow status by the CEO each year. These Fellows not only enjoy an extremely high reputation within the company, but also extraordinary privileges and almost limitless self-determination. Similar to professors, they are completely free to choose whatever topics and interests they wish to bring to the table. An approach like this can be described as a "top-class sport", which only provides for a selected, manageable elite:

> Only a few selected experts are deprived of expert careers with us. In this respect, we treat this possibility only very selectively (top-class sport). (2-2)

Depending on the strategic alignment, mass sport or top-class sport, the operative design and implementation is clearly different. Experience has shown that mass sport is a variant that is not only associated with significantly higher complexity and higher expenditure, but also requires more comprehensive internal communication with employees. It is not uncommon to observe that the definition of expert careers in very different functional areas leads to quite strange art products, which is reflected, among other things, in job titles that sometimes sound pretty strange.

Four Basic Types of Expert Careers

So far, two strategic dimensions have been addressed. The first dimension described the focus on experts versus expertise. The second dimension was concerned with the distinction between top sport and mass sport. If these two dimensions are combined in a four-field matrix, the basic variations of expert careers shown in Fig. 8.8 are obtained.

If companies try to build expert careers around selected individuals who have rendered outstanding services to the company, for example to please them or to retain them in the company, this would correspond to variation A. In a way, each king is built his or her own kingdom here. In practice, such careers are usually recognised when, for example, the "king" is retired and there is no replacement. The situation is different in the case of a few selected expert positions on which a company is particularly dependent and with which a strategic need for outstanding

8.3 Expert Career

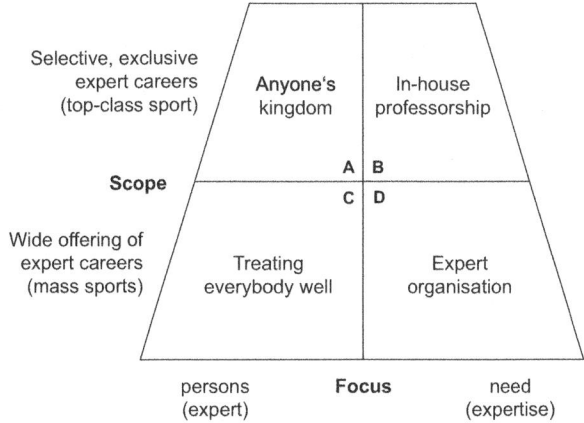

Fig. 8.8 Four basic types of expert careers

expertise is associated (B). Expert careers of this kind are best compared to academic careers (in-house professorships). According to our own studies, these two varieties are rather under-represented, at least in German-speaking countries (cf. Berberich 2014). Mass sport clearly dominates. Approximately every third company strives to somehow do justice to a broad target group of employees in the company with an expert career (C). Expert careers are not primarily geared to the needs of the company but to the requests of the employees. If an employee appears to be particularly important for the organization, but is unable or unwilling to lead, an expert career is made possible. The primary goal here is usually to retain these employees. In principle, this option is open to every employee. The most widespread variation can be described as an expert organization (D). These are organizations in which expertise counts more than leadership or is at least formally of comparable importance. This form is particularly common in research-intensive industries or in management consultancies.

Organizational Integration and Reporting Lines

A particularly exciting question in the context of expert careers is: To whom does an expert report? How is an employee who has embarked on an expert career integrated into the organization? In traditional, hierarchically managed companies in which the management career path dominates, experts usually report to regular supervisors. The management hierarchy represents the central framework within which the experts are positioned. The experts have a direct manager. They are used to agree on goals or otherwise to agree on mutual expectations. In this strategic alignment, it is particularly important to note that there is a form of vertical super-ordination and subordination.

> With us, every expert reports to a line manager, as do all other colleagues. Accordingly, objective setting is also made with experts. (3-1)

An example of this would be the labour law expert within the HR department. This employee has proven expertise that is critical for the company. He does not and should not lead any employees. Nevertheless, his or her salary grade corresponds to that of a team leader. His or her direct supervisor might be the HR director.

Things are quite different with the IBM Fellows example already mentioned. All Fellows report to the CEO. Variations such as these do not provide for subordination of experts to line managers. They should not have bosses and should be allowed to move around the company as freely as possible.

> Our experts all report to the CEO and are otherwise independent. This gives them the freedom to make a difference for the company as a whole. (3-2)

This does not mean that they are actually led by the CEO him or herself. No CEO would have the necessary time to do this. However, the experts have a manager who, however, acts less as a boss than primarily as an enabler (cf. Sect. 4.4). The manager ensures that the experts find the framework conditions they need in order to be as effective as possible in the company. Comparable constellations have always existed in top-class sport or, for example, in art. Athletes, or successful musicians also have managers. Their role is above all to ensure that the framework conditions are in place to enable the actual stars to perform successfully.

Equal Treatment of Managers and Experts

As already mentioned at the beginning, the introduction of expert careers was to reward existing experts without management responsibility fairly and adequately and to put them on a comparable level with their colleagues bearing responsibility for people. Probably the easiest way to do this is to open higher salary grades for employees without management responsibility. Managers and experts with identical grading will receive comparable salaries, possibly a company car and other privileges such as their own office, participation in strategic events, embossed business cards, etc. The principle of qualitative equal treatment can be summed up as follows:

> Experts are consistently placed on an equal footing with managers of the same level. They receive comparable salaries and privileges. (4-1)

Now there is a stereotypical notion of managers who embark on an appropriate managerial career and strive extrinsically for power, wealth and visible status. On the other hand, there is also a simplistic view of what experts may consider desirable. According to this, intrinsically motivated experts primarily want to deal with their primary topic and otherwise be left alone. Money, status and power play a subordinate role for them. Rather, experts prefer exchange with other experts, flexibility in working conditions, self-determination in the content they deal with or access to the latest knowledge (cf. Goffee and Jones 2006). The underlying idea is relevant with regard to the strategic orientation of expert careers. If different preferences are indeed assumed, it would make sense to align incentives and additional privileges with these preferences:

> Experts and managers have different preferences in terms of salary and other privileges. That is why we treat experts in a different way than their colleagues in management positions. (4-2)

This strategic alignment is closely related to a consideration elsewhere in this book related to remuneration (see Chap. 9). The question is whether an incentive is the result of work, or rather the prerequisite for work. The latter option goes in the direction of allowing experts to benefit from the incentives and privileges they need as a prerequisite for doing what is intrinsically close to their hearts.

How Experts Work

Put simply, the power of leaders is based on two possible foundations. Either they have influence because of their formal position. They get to decide because they're the bosses. The employees follow them because they cannot do otherwise. Or else, managers have influence because others listen to them. They have power over their followers because these followers want to be led by him or her. Here aspects such as charisma, past successes, social skills, reasonable views in the past etc. play a certain role.

The mode of action of experts in companies can be viewed similarly differently or even institutionally oriented. You can involve experts in formal decision-making bodies and give them a formal right to vote. Top experts are also invited to every internal management conference. Depending on the content and goal of a project, selected experts are formally integrated into the project team. Experts are generally used for certain problems and form a kind of special command. In the end, it is always a matter of formally integrating experts into the existing hierarchy and assigning them permanent or temporary formal responsibilities.

> The influence of experts in the company is formally defined. Certain experts are part of certain decision-making bodies and project groups (formal influence). (5-1)

With this approach, the effectiveness of an expert is formally assured. Other employees listen to the expert because they are officially encouraged to do so—"As long as our expert does not approve here, we won't go on". Hierarchically managed organizations will be more likely to accept this strategic alignment of expert careers than the following alternative.

There are experts not only in companies, but also wherever people are concerned about a subject, for example in professional or scientific communities. Many experts articulate their views in blogs, which they then spread via Twitter. And whoever has the most followers on Twitter also has the greatest influence in the community. In social media, the number of followers is an indicator of power. And if you want to have influence and a hearing as an expert, you have to actively win them over. You have to convince, get actively involved, be present, raise your word, etc. No one is successful in social media because a higher authority would have decided so. The mode of action of experts in companies can be understood in a similar way:

> The influence of an expert always depends on the expert him or herself. He or she must develop his or her own influence and thus his or her own acceptance (informal influence). (5-2)

Agile organizations in which the network idea is anchored in the consciousness of all players are more likely to adopt this approach than the one described first. Why should the expert have formal power and act as a boss where even the leaders avoid acting as bosses (see Sect. 4.4)? While employees in hierarchical organizations primarily feel committed to their superiors, employees in agile organizations primarily feel committed to their colleagues and customers (see Sect. 4.5). In the light of this idea, an informal mode of operation appears to be much more compatible.

When Is an Expert an Expert?

Section 8.1 already addressed the question of when a talent is a talent. The focus was on the key HR issue of talent identification. In connection with the subject of expert career, a similar question now arises: When is an expert an expert? The considerations relating to talent identification can be directly transferred here. Thus, in traditional hierarchical organizations, one will always tend to see the (top-down) nomination of an employee to the status of an expert to be the responsibility of superiors.

> An expert is only an expert if superiors see it that way. Accordingly, experts are always nominated top-down. (6-1)

The considerations in the previous section suggest an alternative orientation according to which experts can only be experts if colleagues, teams and managers see it that way. In this case one would rather speak of a *peer nomination* of experts:

> An expert is only an expert if others in the company see it that way. Therefore, experts are always nominated or at least recommended by peers. (6-2)

In the context of this distinction, one could now make the next distinction and ask how long an expert should have expert status. However, this is not to be discussed in more detail at this point. A decisive question in the selection of experts relates to competencies that are not directly related to the technical expertise, but are more of a social nature. Are we going to accept so-called nerds as experts?

Nerds as Experts?

A *nerd* is seen as a person who is significantly above average in intelligence, who shows great enthusiasm for technical problems but is socially disinterested or even socially less competent. The term nerd is less an academic, psychological term. Rather, it describes a kind of stereotype, the significance of which has gained in importance especially in the course of growing information technology. One imagines a nerd as someone who spends his life in front of the computer, avoids people, does not care about his appearance and is not interested in sports or healthy nutrition.

Such people have always been irreplaceable in numerous companies, especially in the IT industry. Companies such as SAP or Microsoft would probably not exist today if they had not also been home to numerous nerds. Technically, these people perform outstandingly. In the context of a professional career, however, the question now arises as to the extent to which so-called nerds should be officially treated as experts. A possible answer is very simple and perhaps also obvious. Expert status is decided solely on the basis of an employee's expertise. Social abilities may be disregarded.

> For us, the only thing that matters in experts is their technical expertise and cognitive capacity. Everything else is secondary. (7-1)

This approach can be pursued as long as the influence of experts is formally regulated. In this case, the organization ensures that an expert has his or her formal influence. It may be given formal decision-making powers and thus officially strengthen its otherwise weak social capabilities. However, this approach will probably fail, if it is the responsibility of the experts themselves to develop interpersonal influence within the organization, if they have to gain support or convince others, if it is their task to actively bring themselves into play. In the latter case, an expert can only act to the extent that his or her social competence and social interest allow.

> Experts without social competence ("nerds") hardly have a chance with us. They would find it difficult to get actively involved and gain the acceptance of others. (7-2)

At a first glance, the question of the acceptance of nerds seems to be a relatively insignificant one. In fact, it touches on a whole range of relevant, strategic dimensions relating to the subject of the expert career (see Fig. 8.9). From my personal experience I can say that the question "Would you accept nerds as experts?" is a very powerful entry question to understand how a company deals with the subject of the expert career as a whole.

Focus and priority	*1-1 Experts* We want to offer important experts who seem unsuitable for a management career a development perspective and thereby retain them in the company.	*1-2 Expertise* By means of expert careers, we ensure the availability of critical expertise within the company.
Scope	*2-1 Mass sports* All employees above a certain level have the opportunity to pursue a management or expert career.	*2-2 Top sport* Only a few selected experts are deprived of expert careers with us. In this respect, we treat this possibility only very selectively.
Organizational integration	*3-1 Hierarchical Integration* With us, every expert reports to a line manager, as do all other colleagues. Accordingly, objective setting is also made with experts.	*3-2 Independence* Our experts all report to the CEO and are otherwise independent. This gives them the freedom to make a difference for the company as a whole.
Equal treatment	*4-1 Qualitative Equal Treatment* Experts are consistently placed on an equal footing with managers at the same level. They receive comparable salaries and privileges.	*4-2 Orientation towards preferences* Experts and managers have different preferences in terms of salary and other privileges. That is why we treat experts in a different way than their colleagues in management positions.
Influence within the organization	*5-1 Formal influence* The influence of experts in the company is formally defined. Certain experts are part of certain decision-making bodies and project groups.	*5-2 Informal Influence* The influence of an expert always depends on the expert him or herself. He or she must develop his or her own influence and thus his or her own acceptance (informal influence).
Nomination	*6-1 Deciding Managers* An expert is only an expert if superiors see it that way. Accordingly, experts are always nominated top-down.	*6-2 Decide Other* An expert is only an expert if others in the company see it that way. Therefore, experts are always nominated or at least recommended by peers.
Relevance of social competence	*7-1 Irrelevant* For us, the only thing that matters to experts is their technical expertise and cognitive capacity. Everything else is secondary.	*7-2 Critical to success* Experts without social competence ("nerds") hardly have a chance with us. They would find it difficult to get actively involved and gain the acceptance of others.

Fig. 8.9 Overview of all strategic dimensions related to expert career

References

Berberich M (2014) The expert career. BlogIntoBook, Print on Demand

Berger LA, Berger DR (2005) Management wisdom from the New York yankees'dynasty: what every manager can learn from a legendary team's 80-year winning streak. John Wiley & Sons, San Francisco

References

DGFP (2012) Fachlaufbahnen als alternative Karrierepfade. Praxispapier 5/2012

Erikson EH (1959) Identity and the life cycle. International Universities Press, New York

Fölsing A (1995) Albert Einstein: Eine Biographie. Suhrkamp, Berlin

Goffee R, Jones G (2006) Why should anyone be led by you? What takes to be an authentic leader. Harvard Business School Press, Boston, MA

Kegan R (1983) The evolving self: problem and process in human development. Harvard University Press, Boston, MA

Lewis M (2004) Moneyball. The art of winning an unfair game. Norton, New York

Marquardt MJ, Leonard HS, Freedman AM, Hill CC (2009) Action learning for developing leaders and organizations. American Psychological Association, Washington, DC

McCall MW (1998) High flyers: developing the next generation of leaders. Harvard Business School Press, Boston, MA

Meehl PE (2013) Clinical versus statistical prediction. A theoretical analysis and a review of evidence. Echo Point Books & Media, Brattleboro, VT

Michaels E, Handfield-Jones H, Axelrod B (2001) The war for talent. Harvard Business School Press, Boston, MA

Robinson K (2009) The element. How finding your passion changes everything. Viking, New York

Silzer RF, Church AH (2009) The pearls and perils of identifying potential. Ind Organ Psychol Perspect Sci Pract 2(4):377–412

Silzer R, Dowell BE (2010) Strategy-driven talent management. A leadership imperative. Jossey-Bass, San Francisco

Stepper J (2015) Working out loud. For a better career and life. Ikigai Press, New York

Remuneration   9

At the latest when it comes to money, the current and aimed at understanding of leadership and organization of a company becomes visible. Who gets how much and why? What are the guiding principles behind answering this question? What implicit or explicit assumptions are made? Whether it is about division of labour, collaboration, leaders as bosses, coaches, partners or enablers, Theory X or Y, instruction or self-management, commitment up or left and right, conformity, individuality, hierarchical or inverse pyramids, in the end all this is reflected not only in the way in which the importance of compensation is attributed but how compensation systems are strategically aligned. In a certain way, it comes last.

At the same time, this is a topic in which companies have only limited room for manoeuvre. Probably every HR professional, every internal compensation specialist, will recognize the limits of possible changes when reading this chapter. One of the reasons for this is that no company starts by developing its own compensation strategies from scratch and every change always creates the risk of resentment, perceived unequal treatment, etc. In addition, many companies are bound by public regulation.

This chapter has a slightly different structure than the other chapters, which deal with key HR topics. This chapter begins with a general part. The topics of base pay and variable pay are then discussed in more detail. This general part on compensation policy is necessary because there are strategic dimensions in the context of remuneration, which are of a fundamental nature irrespective of whether fixed or variable salary components are to be determined.

9.1 Compensation Policy

Compensation policy is concerned with the importance of money and remuneration as a whole. This is where the company's corporate policy stance and the resulting consequences come into play. What role do money and incentives play in attracting or motivating future and current employees? What does justice mean in this context?

Traditionally, the assumption is that remuneration is the fair consideration of a company for services rendered. In this respect, remuneration is supposed to be based on the latter. We'll start by challenging this first assumption. Is work a prerequisite for a salary?

Work as a Prerequisite for Salary

In connection with the exciting topic of remuneration, a certain point of view is widespread, but it will be somewhat questioned or at least supplemented in the further course of this chapter: When employees work for a company, they deserve appropriate financial and material rewards. The focus here is on the question of *equity*, a question that is not always easy to answer in practice. Accordingly, it is assumed that *salary determination* should be based on very different factors, i.e. on qualification, responsibility within the company, performance, family status or success. It is not uncommon for factors such as the length of service with the company or the regional cost of living to be specifically taken into account. In the end, the entire bouquet leads to what is known internationally as *total compensation*, a combination of a wide variety of salary components, the amount of which is based on different factors. Jobs are evaluated and clustered into pay grades with the corresponding pay bands. Variable compensation components are based on the achievement of previously agreed upon annual targets and much more.

In fact, this is all about financial and material forms of reward. These are contractually agreed on, whether in employment or collective agreements. There is no mention of non-material forms of reward either in HR policy considerations or in the numerous HR textbooks. Almost tacitly, an attitude has crept into the practice of HR according to which remuneration is the result of work.

> Remuneration is the consequence of responsibility and performance. It is the price we pay for work. First comes work. Reward follows. (1-1)

This view is a deeply rooted in classical economic thinking, according to which work has its price. If, as a company, I want a person to do the work I want him or her to do, I have to pay a price. The higher the value of this work, the higher the price must be. Anything else wouldn't be fair. This is often based on the assumption that an employee would never voluntarily perform the work that is expected of him or her, but does so because he or she receives the money he or she needs to fulfil his or her life's desires or to cover his or her life's needs.

Salary as a Prerequisite for Work

If you ask employees what they would do if they unexpectedly won the lottery and never had to work again to make a living, you often get the answer: "I would continue to do my job". This may not be true in every case, but it reflects a fact that people see more in their work than it being a means of securing their livelihood. Rather, they implicitly recognize in their work a multitude of non-monetary incentives relevant for happiness: a meaning in life, one more reason to get up in the morning, social exchange, opportunities for personal development and growth, social recognition, structure, the feeling of being needed to name only a few aspects.

Probably for the first time these aspects became clear from a social science perspective after a team around the young scientist Marie Jahoda spent many months in the Austrian settlement of Marienthal in the 1930s to investigate the consequences of extensive sudden unemployment. One of the largest textile factories closed from 1 day to the next and many hundreds of employees and citizens became unemployed for a long time. The consequences were not only existential hardships but above all the loss of identity, social structure, meaning, social exchange or personal development (Jahoda et al. 1933). Obviously the value of work is clearly more than just the wage.

Rewards for a job usually involve much more than just material or financial reward. This is true not only in the private sphere, where most activities are not remunerated—think here of raising children, hobbies, activities in private communities, etc.—but also in the professional context.

If you look at the biographies of extremely successful people from different fields, such as sport, art, politics or science, you will see that these people have never carried out their activities primarily for the sake of money. Money was merely a welcome side effect of their activities. Exceptions are people who have considered their purpose in life and their vocation solely in earning money per se. Probably people like the American investor Georg Soros belong to this group.

Taken together, these considerations lead to a completely different view of the importance of salary in relation to the exercise of activities. I can illustrate this with my own profession. Of course I get money to write this book. However, I am not writing this book for the money. My profession is that of a professor. Professors do not receive their salary as a result of their work. That was never the idea. Professors receive their salaries so that they can do what they want to do out of their deepest intrinsic motivation: research, teaching, and occasionally writing books. They receive their salary so that they are not plagued by existential worries in the performance of their work and do not feel compelled to pursue another activity at the same time. This strategy can be summarized as follows in a strategic statement:

> Remuneration is the prerequisite for responsibility and performance. Employees receive their salaries so that they can do what they intrinsically want to do. (1-2)

Executives who tend to agree with Theory X probably will be completely irritated about this statement. They see people as lazy by nature. You only get them to work if you promise them money. And the more you promise them, the more they'll be willing to do. Leaders, however, who believe in Theory Y according to McGregor (1960), will give applause to the above statement.

Reward Versus Profit

The challenge in developing compensation systems is based on a fundamental dilemma. If this dilemma did not exist, this chapter would not have to be written. There would be no wage disputes, no strikes, no debates about money, salaries, etc. The dilemma lies in the fact that, on the one hand, employees prefer or actively demand more money. This also applies to the deeply intrinsically motivated, thoroughly enthusiastic employees, who would even be willing to pay to do their jobs. When a person is faced with the choice of accepting a lower or higher reward under *truly* equal conditions, he or she will always choose the higher reward. Anything else would be either stupid, irrational or even pathological. On the other hand, the company tries to keep salaries and thus wage costs lower in order to achieve the highest possible profit. We are dealing with a conflict of goals, a dilemma due to which people can never be equally happy.

Within this area of tension, four themes play a decisive role. They always appear when it comes to remuneration, in textbooks, manuals and, of course, in practice. They might be targets or prerequisites. It is about equity or fairness, motivation, social dynamics and acquisition and loyalty.

- *Equity or fairness*. What is the balance between the employees' contribution on the one hand and their remuneration on the other compared to different employees and jobs? How does one achieve justice and equity?
- *Motivation*. Under what circumstances do individual components of remuneration have a motivating or demotivating effect?
- *Social dynamics*. What influence does a compensation system have on leadership and cooperation within and between teams and the company as a whole? How can one ensure that functional effects outweigh toxic effects?
- *Acquisition and loyalty*. What significance does compensation have in attracting and retaining employees? How do you treat the best in terms of what they deserve?

These aspects will be discussed in more detail below. In the course of this, general, strategic dimensions are considered and discussed.

Equity or Fairness

Remuneration should be fair. Who would dare not to support that statement? But the question of what is fair or not is marked by a high degree of uncertainty and subjectivity. Attempts to explain fairness and equity usually lead to the consideration of three factors. On the one hand, there is a contribution made by an employee. On the other hand, one gets some kind of compensation. But this juxtaposition alone does not lead to an assessment of justice. At the end of the day, a third factor is also important: the comparison between employees, jobs or times (see Fig. 9.1).

9.1 Compensation Policy

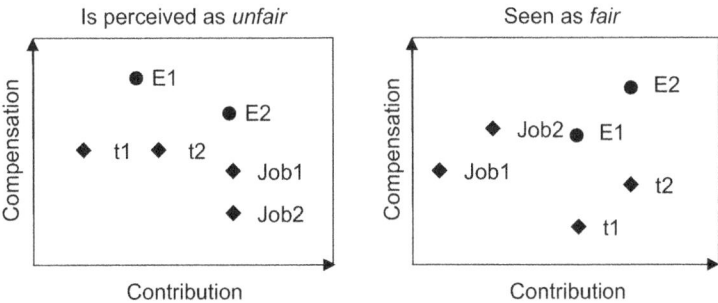

Fig. 9.1 What is seen as unfair or fair (E: Employee, t: Time)

The left side of Fig. 9.1 shows constellations that employees are likely to classify as unfair. Let's first look at the comparison between employee E1 and employee E2. E2 contributes more to the success of the company than E1, but receives a lower level of compensation. E1 is the happier one in this constellation and will only endure it if he or she distances him or herself emotionally and interpersonally from E2—"it's not my fault that E2 gets less, although she would certainly have to earn more than me". E2, on the other hand, has little choice but to perceive the situation as unfair. How E2 will probably react in motivational terms will be examined in more detail later in this chapter.

In addition to this social comparison, however, there are also comparisons between times and jobs in relation to a single employee. If an employee's expected contribution increases from time t1 to time t2, but his or her compensation remains the same, the employee concerned will find this unfair. The same can be the case when comparing two jobs. If an employee finds that two jobs Job1 and Job2 require something comparable, he or she classifies Job2 as unfairly remunerated.

On the right side of the Fig. 9.1 constellations are shown that are more likely to be perceived as fair. Here, contribution and remuneration have a positive and rather balanced relationship with regard to all three conditions.

Complexity and Simplicity

But how can fairness be achieved when it comes to the design of compensation systems? There are two possible answers to this question. Fairness can be achieved by making compensation systems as simple as possible. The other answer would be: remuneration systems can be designed fairly by considering as many factors as possible at the same time and achieving the highest possible degree of differentiation. Both answers are probably correct. At the same time, they obviously contradict each other.

A good example of a simple system is well known because it is related of football. If two teams meet, the winner gets three points and the one that loses no point. If the teams split in a tie, both teams receive one point. That is it. This system is just because it is simple. For the same reason, it is also unfair. Historical dramas have already taken place here. A team dominates their opponent for 89 min and deserves to win. In the last minute, they take the equalizer due to a bad pass. Is the scoring system fair in such a situation? The alternative would be a sophisticated system, where not only the goals but other criteria are taken into account—fouls, ball possession, shots on goal, corners, etc. These criteria and more could be evaluated and weighted accordingly. At the end of the match, both teams will have total scores that decide which one wins or loses. Imagine the dynamics that would result from this.

Compensation systems can be simple or differentiated. The reasons for a multi-layered, complex form of *pay differentiation* are endless. Those who bear a higher responsibility should also earn more. The better the individual but also the team performance, the higher the reward should be. The more successful the company is, the more the employees are supposed to earn. Employees in regions with a high cost of living (Munich, Paris) should receive a higher salary than employees in regions with cost of living (Shaftsbury, Dorset). Single earners who have to provide for families with several members should earn more than childless double earners. The salary should be based on the educational level of the employees and their market value in the external labour market. Those who hold strategically relevant tasks and jobs (key functions) also deserve more than those employees whose tasks are only of minor relevance. Employees who are difficult to replace have to earn more than employees who are easy to replace. The salary might also be based on the length of service within the company. The list could be extended at will. In order to understand how companies try to do practical justice to this diversity of factors, a glance at the current HR textbooks or relevant handbooks is sufficient (Berger and Berger 2008; Dessler 2018; Jackson and Schuler 2012).

If a company now has five million euros at its disposal and is to distribute this amount fairly among 100 employees, taking the above arguments into account, how does it proceed? I ask my students this question during my lecture to show them the complexity of fair remuneration. Companies that face this complexity tend to follow the following strategic premise:

> Fair and motivating remuneration systems must take into account as many factors at the same time as possible. We want and have to face this level of complexity. (2-1)

There are entire armies of compensation consultants who support such a strategic priority. Here complexity often leads to complicatedness, which in turn increases consulting fees. However, complex or complicated remuneration systems are never conclusively fair. They cannot be, because there is always one more level of differentiation to think about. Where do you stop? As we will see in the course of this chapter, the question of performance-related pay alone can hardly be answered fairly. What does performance mean? How do you measure it? Who will judge it? There is objectively no limit to the possible complexity in the design of such systems.

The radical counter-draft to this is based on consistent simplicity. The simplest remuneration system can be explained in a short sentence: Every employee receives the same salary. This is called *equal pay*. If you have to distribute five million euros among 100 employees, then each employee receives 50,000 euros. Is that fair? Yes and no. In fact, there are companies that practise exactly this approach. They follow the premise:

> Remuneration systems must be as simple as possible. Then everyone knows where he or she stands and we can protect ourselves from exhausting debates. (2-2)

Debates about the fairness of their remuneration system also take place in these companies. However, these discussions are of a more fundamental nature and less detailed. It is not so much a question of whether a job should be at salary level 24 or 25, but of a common understanding of values.

Pay Transparency

If everyone in the company earns the same salary, there is automatically a pay transparency. Everyone knows other people's salaries. With the question of pay differentiation, the question of transparency now also arises—a further dimension of a strategic orientation. Knowing the salary of others is not always a cause of happiness and contentment. Scientific studies show quite clearly that social comparisons are highly relevant for the assessment of one's own prosperity. For example, Luttmer (2005) showed that people who have richer neighbours are more dissatisfied with the same salary. If you have a poorer neighbour, on the other hand, this does not lead to higher satisfaction. Similar effects could be shown with regard to the job satisfaction of employees. When colleagues earn more than you do, it leads to dissatisfaction. But if one earns more than the others, this does not necessarily lead to higher job satisfaction (see Card et al. 2010). The bottom line is that social comparisons inevitably lead to lower satisfaction overall. When companies answer the question of pay transparency based on this simple insight, they logically arrive at this strategic premise:

> Individual salaries are a confidential matter for the respective employees and their managers. Anything else leads to dissatisfaction and conflicts. (3-1)

These scientific findings find their confirmation in everyday life. Even before the studies mentioned above, we knew that distribution issues could always be a source of dissatisfaction and conflict. Anyone who has children knows this all the more. When parents give a bag of chips to a group of four children, they have two options. Either they divide the contents of the bag equally and give each child what it deserves. Or you can give the bag to the children and let them negotiate the distribution themselves. There is no doubt that those parents who educate their children to maturity will choose the second option. Conflicts are fine. The main thing is that you've learned to deal with them.

In agile companies that rely on pay transparency, personal responsibility, decentralized self-regulation and transparency of performance are a top priority. A shining example of this is the American organic supermarket chain Whole Foods Market (Wells and Haglock 2005). Examples such as this show that pay transparency must always go hand in hand with an appropriate corporate culture. Perhaps there is hardly another topic where self-regulation and maturity are put to the test to the same extent as this one. As will become clear later in this chapter, this can even mean that employees determine their own salaries in the joint dispute. Agile organizations do not shy away from conflicts, but see them as opportunities for intelligent action. In this respect, it is not surprising that agile organizations, especially in the onboarding phase, attach importance to training on how to deal with conflicts (cf. Sect. 5.4).

> We strive to achieve the highest possible level of pay transparency. Transparency forces us to find solutions that are shared. (3-2)

Finally, one has to ask oneself what role job satisfaction plays. All studies on pay transparency that I am aware of consider job satisfaction to be a relevant dependent variable. Why? How desirable is it that employees are generally satisfied? A former CEO of the software manufacturer SAP once said: "Sales employees must never be satisfied with their salary". Every change, every improvement, every innovation, even every revolution had its origin in the fact that someone was completely dissatisfied and took the initiative, accordingly, to change things Constructive dissatisfaction can also be seen as the source of positive change, provided that those affected have the autonomy to change something in their situation (Inauen et al. 2015). Satisfaction can only play a role if employees find themselves in the position of being victims and attribute a low degree of self-efficacy to themselves. Only if they are satisfied with their dependence, do they remain obedient.

Motivation

Whenever a person goes to work, he or she is usually rewarded. Admittedly, this sentence contains a daring statement that is worth thinking about for a moment. Here we are deliberately talking about people and not just about employees. In addition, the term "reward" deserves special attention. When a person mows his lawn on the weekend, he or she is happy about the well-tended lawn at the end. When a person plays a piece of Mozart on the piano, he or she may be filled with the special emotional form of expressing him or herself. When a person helps another person, thankfulness, recognition and much more are given in return. Usually actions are rewarded in some form. Particularly in the private sphere, these are primarily non-material forms of reward, whereas in the professional context we usually subsume material forms of reward. The latter is due to the fact that companies traditionally regard salary as a consequence of work—pleasure follows work. This has already been discussed above. This, in turn, is based on the assumption that employees perform their work only because they receive a material reward in return. We therefore assume an *extrinsic motivation*. They do something either to get a reward "from outside" (extrinsic) or to avoid punishment by others.

> Employees work primarily for money. If you want motivated employees, you have to offer them an attractive reward. (4-1)

In the private examples mentioned at the beginning, things seem to be different. Here the reward results from the activity itself. The reward is the work and the work is the reward. We are talking here about *intrinsic motivation*. The fulfilment results from the activity itself. You do something because you want it from within. Very successful people can't help but do what they do. Their activity, their work is part of their identity.

Probably every employee has both intrinsic and extrinsic motivation. Partly one does something following an inner drive to, partly also due to external pressure or incentive. Put simply, one could say that the overall motivation of an employee is the result of intrinsic plus extrinsic motivation and the overall motivation is an important predictor of his or her performance:

Performance $= f(n \times$ *intrinsic motivation* $+ m \times$ *extrinsic motivation*$)$.

It can also be assumed that intrinsic motivation in terms of performance has a higher weight (n) than extrinsic motivation (m). As soon as a human being makes a task his own and acts (intrinsically) from the deepest inner motivation, he or she will produce a higher level of performance than if he or she works on the same task from extrinsic causes. We know this from numerous studies. For example, it could be shown that extrinsic incentives lead people to avoid risk and are more inclined to seek the easy way (cf. Kohn 1999). In the end, it is not so much the success of having mastered a task that counts, but the receipt of the extrinsic reward. In this respect, it is worth keeping intrinsic motivation high and extrinsic motivation as low as possible in order to ultimately align the motivation balance in favour of high performance.

> Of course, salary must be fair. However, we rely as much as possible on the intrinsic motivation of our employees in order to achieve the best possible performance. (4-2)

So, the question arises in the further course of this chapter as to how the design of base pay affects the intrinsic versus extrinsic motivation of employees. Above all, however, the form of remuneration that explicitly aims to motivate employees extrinsically, namely variable, contingent rewards, requires closer consideration. This is discussed in more detail below.

Talking about Money

Whenever we talk about intrinsic motivation in a business context, we will hear some voices asking why we pay our employees a salary at all. After all, they get their reward from the activity itself. Anyone who argues in this way ignores the principle outlined at the beginning of this chapter that people always prefer more money over less money. The desire for more money and intrinsic motivation do not contradict each other, even if this seems so at first glance. I can illustrate this with my own personal example.

When I give keynote speeches, I expect the highest possible fee. Anything else would be unreasonable from a business perspective. When I give an opening keynote in front of 100 international top executives at a top-class event, the fee I expect is relatively high, which rarely surprises the organizer. But if I give the same keynote in front of a charitable association in my region, I know that the organizer does not pursue any business interests and the organization is emotionally close to me due to my regional solidarity, then it can happen that I give the keynote without any fee. Anyone who knows me and has ever experienced me as a presenter knows that I give both keynotes with the same enthusiasm and energy. When I give keynotes I am always intrinsically motivated. I do not think about money on stage. I am completely blocking that out. I rarely give keynotes motivated only extrinsically.

This perspective can be used strategically by talking to employees about their salary at a certain point in time (especially during the hiring period), but then doing everything in their power to banish this issue from their daily consciousness. This is done by simply not talking about it anymore.

> Money should not play a role in daily work. We therefore try to talk about this topic as rarely as possible. (5-2)

One might wonder why money is so seldom spoken about especially in countries like my home country Germany. Sometimes it seems like chats about salaries are reprehensible. Somehow one is afraid of putting money and salaries in the foreground in interpersonal communication. Probably people in Germany implicitly apply the theory that the focus on money could give the impression of extrinsic motivation. By not talking about money, you protect yourself from that impression. The bottom line is that they are right to do so. That people think like that can be tested in a simple way. Think of the following situation followed by a simple question: There are two doctors. One is only doing his job for the money. The other is a doctor, because he likes to be a doctor from his inner drive and draws fulfilment from his work. Which doctor would you go to? Of course, it is assumed that the intrinsically motivated doctor is better, even if he bills you after the treatment.

In many companies, the increasing institutionalization of large parts of HR has led to a continuous confrontation with salary issues or associated aspects. This is particularly the case with regard to variable pay or merit increases. Here we act according to the premise:

> Money is a central issue for all involved. It is therefore more important than ever to talk about it more frequently. (5-1)

In concrete terms, this continuous discussion takes place in annual performance reviews relevant to salaries within the framework of cyclical performance appraisals. The natural consequence is that the subject of money takes up more space and good intrinsic motivation is thus literally cannibalized in favour of worse extrinsic motivation.

Social Dynamics

The third issue that is of central importance in the context of remuneration after the issues of fairness and motivation is that of social dynamics. In principle, it can be assumed that compensation systems and social interaction within an organization are mutually dependent. We had an interesting discussion about this at my university several years ago. The background to this is that the ministry makes a budget available to the universities, which may be distributed to professors by the universities depending on their performance. The universities themselves decide how this performance-related remuneration is to be paid. In addition to numerous questions, we were concerned with the question of who should assess the professors' performance at our university. It quickly became clear that this could not or should not be the dean of the respective faculties. Deans are elected by professors. Their dominant leadership role is that of the partner (see Sect. 4.4) and partners do not judge their colleagues. Whoever decides on the salary of employees, however, has power and the affected employees get into a kind of dependency relationship. We definitely didn't want this.

This small example shows the interaction between remuneration systems and social systems. Whoever has the money has the power. Especially in hierarchical organizations, this power lies with the next level supervisor or above. They use budgets to be distributed as a management tool with which they incentivise certain expected behaviours.

> Providing incentives is a management function. Higher management bodies therefore decide on the amount of the remuneration. (6-1)

This results in vertical power relations with superiority and subordination. In Sect. 4.4 four different leadership roles were described, namely that of the boss, the coach, the partner and the enabler. These leadership roles imply certain variations when it comes to remuneration systems. At the same time, they exclude others. To get right to the point: A manager who decides to a considerable extent on the salary of his employees will find it extremely difficult to act as a coach or partner because an unequal distribution of financial power institutionally stands in the way of a meeting at eye level.

Another effect affecting social dynamics has already been discussed in Sect. 6.3 (Formal judgement). If an employee's variable compensation or merit increase depends on an annual performance review and forced distribution must be adhered to, then employees become competitors who have a further incentive to weaken each other or at least not support each other.

But it is not only the question of who decides on salaries that goes along with the social dynamics in a company, but also the level of salaries themselves. Do executives enjoy power, and recognition by even the professional experts? This aspect has already been dealt with comprehensively in Sect. 8.3 related to expert career. How pronounced is the salary spread between the lower and upper levels within the hierarchy? This also communicates within an organization as to who is important and who is even more important.

The radical alternative to conventional power structures is, of course, to let the employees themselves decide on their salaries. Who has now an image of man in the sense of McGregor's Theory X will not be able to follow this idea in any way. Reflexively, this idea awakens ideas of battles in which co-workers, driven by their monetary greed and selfishness, tear each other apart. In fact, there are companies that successfully practice exactly this approach.

> As far as possible, salary decisions should be placed in the hands of employees. This avoids hierarchical power structures and resentment. (6-2)

Now you do not always have to imagine that employees get together regularly and debate their salaries together. Agile organizations have appropriate mechanisms and rules for this, which concern either the target salaries or only salary components of the colleagues. Here are three practical examples:

- *Lateral scoring.* Each employee has a points budget, which over the course of a year he or she can allocate to colleagues according to their performance and responsibility. Finally, salary increases or bonuses are based on the number of points an employee has received from others.
- *Elected Salary Commission.* A group of employees is elected to decide on salary increases at the request of the employees. These written requests must be accompanied by references from colleagues.
- *Employee recognition system.* Every employee can use a budget to assign financial or material rewards to colleagues.

Some companies even go beyond this approach and let their customers decide what variable portion an employee should receive. Dave Ulrich recently reported at a conference about an airline where frequent flyers are entitled to spontaneously issue vouchers to flight attendants should they be particularly satisfied with their performance.

If you study the current literature on the subject compensation & benefits, you will hardly find any content on leadership, cooperation, values or other social aspects. Rather, one gets the impression that this matter is merely about a mixture of finance and law seen in the light of an extremely mechanistic understanding of organization. This perspective falls far short. If companies want to strengthen or change their understanding of leadership and organization, they cannot avoid taking social dynamics into account.

Acquisition and Loyalty

In addition to the issues of fairness, motivation and social dynamics, a fourth issue plays a central role in the context of remuneration. It is about the effect of money on the acquisition and retention of employees. This is also referred to as the *acquisitive function* of remuneration. Employees decide for or against an employer because of money, among other things. This aspect has almost nothing to do with fairness or motivation. It is simply a question of how, for example, to pay an experienced software developer to seriously consider employment in a company. In the context of basic remuneration, this aspect will be discussed in more detail in the following section. Above all, it will deal with the critical question of how to deal with outstanding candidates with correspondingly outstanding salary expectations.

A Question of Leadership and Attitude

In contrast to large parts of this book, this subchapter hardly deals with technical concepts, i.e. processes, instruments, systems that describe *how* something can be done. This was all about *why*. This *why* raises questions that are primarily addressed to business leaders. The central point is: Which fundamental role does or should salary play? The traditional, economic approach always assumed that salary was the price of labour. In my view, this is rather a question of leadership and organization. As we have seen, agile organizations provide a perhaps unfamiliar response to this. Accordingly, salary is first and foremost the prerequisite for work. Pay employees well. Handle things transparently and keep it as simple as possible. Finally, make sure money is not talked about too much (Fig. 9.2).

9.2 Base Pay

Base pay could be understood as a kind of flat rate in the broadest sense. Instead of talking every month, every week or even every day about an employee's performance or contribution and then repeatedly renegotiating the appropriate remuneration, a monthly fixed salary is agreed upon, which is not contested for the time being. When determining base pay, companies usually orient themselves on the responsibility (the job) of the respective employee on the one hand and on the payment for comparable jobs in the market on the other. The higher the responsibility, the higher the base pay. And, the more you pay for a set of responsibilities in the market, the higher the basic salary must be. In practice, there is a broad agreement on that. You

Role of remuneration	1-1 Reward for work Remuneration is the consequence of responsibility and performance. It is the price we pay for work. First comes work. Reward follows.	1-2 Prerequisite of work Remuneration is the prerequisite for responsibility and performance. Employees receive their salaries so that they can do what they intrinsically want to do.
Differentiation of systems	2-1 Strong differentiation Fair and motivating remuneration systems must take into account as many factors at the same time as possible. We want and have to face this level of complexity.	2-2 Simplicity Remuneration systems must be as simple as possible. Then everyone knows where he or she stands and we protect ourselves from exhausting debates.
Transparency	3-1 No transparency Individual salaries are a confidential matter for the respective employees and their managers. Anything else leads to dissatisfaction and conflicts.	3-2 Much transparency We strive to achieve the highest possible level of pay transparency. Transparency forces us to find solutions that are shared.
Motivating effect	4-1 Extrinsic Motivation Employees work primarily for money. If you want motivated employees, you have to offer them an attractive reward.	4-2 Intrinsic Motivation Of course, the salary must be right. However, we rely as much as possible on the intrinsic motivation of our employees in order to achieve the best possible performance.
Talking about money	5-1 Frequently Money is a central issue for all involved. It is therefore more important than ever to talk about it more frequently.	5-2 Rarely Money should not play a role in daily work. We therefore try to talk about this topic as rarely as possible.
Responsibility for salary decisions	6-1 Executive Providing incentives is a management function. Higher management bodies therefore decide on the amount of the remuneration.	6-2 Others As far as possible, salary decisions should be placed in the hands of employees. This avoids hierarchical power structures and resentment.

Fig. 9.2 Overview of all strategic dimensions of remuneration policy

can also read about it in most HR textbooks. Things are no longer quite so uniform in practice if you look at how agile companies act, how granularly they classify their employees or how close their salaries are to each other.

Flexible Versus Static Grouping

When determining base pay, most companies follow a classic procedure. Accordingly, there is always a *job* to be filled at the beginning. To be more precise, this is an open position and a job is linked to the vacancy. Based on the job it is clarified what its level of *responsibility* is. If this is not clear beforehand, it will be determined

9.2 Base Pay

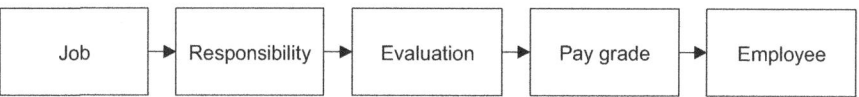

Fig. 9.3 At the beginning there is the job and at the end there is the employee

through a systematic job analysis. If you know the level of responsibility, then you are also able to evaluate the job. This is also referred to as *job evaluation*. A common system for job evaluation is the Hay system, in which points are awarded along certain responsibility dimensions (EL-Hajji 2015). The result is the so-called *job value*. On this basis, the job can now be uniquely assigned to a particular *pay grade* from which the basic salary is derived within a related *pay band*. As soon as the salary has been determined, the search is on for a suitable employee, who should finally be able to meet the predefined set of responsibility. This classical procedure is graphically summarized in the Fig. 9.3.

The logic behind this seems plausible. The basic remuneration of an employee must be based on responsibility and responsibility must be clearly defined before hiring an employee. Anything else would appear arbitrary and the danger of injustice would be very high. It would be unprofessional and irritating for all involved—companies and employees—to hire an employee, promise him or her a salary and then somehow see what he or she could contribute to the company.

> In the beginning there is always the job, the associated responsibility, its evaluation and grading. Only then a suitable employee could be hired. (1-1)

This logic sounds so reasonable and obvious that one hardly likes to doubt it. All textbooks on HR as well as all handbooks and reference books on the subject of employee compensation that I am familiar with are based on the appropriateness of this approach. Collective agreements also reflect this view. It is likely to be shared by the vast majority of HR managers and workers councils.

In fact, the practice is not always so clear. And what at first seems reasonable can in operational reality be an obstructive corset or even harmful. A simple case may illustrate this. The position of an experienced "Senior Software Developer" is to be filled. The job is evaluated, graded and finally the search for a suitable candidate is begun. It quickly becomes apparent that experienced software developers are rare. However, several promising, motivated, talented developers have applied who do not yet have the necessary experience, but have potential. So, what to do? Putting inexperienced developers on the same level as already hired, experienced developers would not be a good idea. This would carry the risk of demotivating experienced colleagues. Just downgrade the job by one or two pay grades? This will also be met with opposition. One must know beforehand what a job entails and not simply make it dependent on the applicants.

In the course of the shortage of skilled workers, cases like this are increasing in number and it seems to me that in more and more companies the call for *flexible grading* is getting louder. It is obvious that the classical approach is based on an

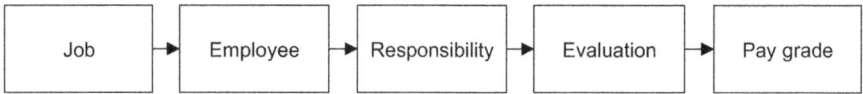

Fig. 9.4 The logic of flexible grading

oversupply of suitable candidates and that only the most suitable one has to be selected for a previously defined and evaluated position. A process in the sense of a flexible grading is shown in the Fig. 9.4.

The approach to flexible grading also begins with a job. Without the delimitation and description of a role, it would in principle be difficult to recruit employees. Responsibilities are rather roughly defined. During the phase of talent acquisition, one then looks at labour market conditions and which potential employees would be considered in principle. In orientation to the preferences, abilities and experiences of the employee to be hired, his or her responsibility is specified, evaluated and graded.

> When grading jobs, we are guided by the responsibility that an available employee can assume. This enables us to react flexibly to given labour market conditions. (1-2)

This approach does not sound that bad either. Some companies pursue this strategic orientation not only because of the shortage of talent in the labour market, but also in order to offer their own employees more flexible development opportunities within the company. Most companies shy away from internal moves if they are accompanied by promotion to the next pay grade. Internal job changes and the associated lateral development opportunities for an employee are made easier if the internal target position can be flexibly adapted to the current capabilities of the internal candidate.

Narrow and Broad Pay Bands

At least conceptually, a simpler possibility of achieving a higher level of flexibility just described is to provide for a few broad salary bands instead of many narrow salary bands. Traditionally, companies have many *narrow* salary bands. These are often laid down in collective agreements about tariffs. Companies often differentiate between 15 or more pay levels. This is primarily due to the need to do justice to differences in responsibility as precisely as possible. It is assumed that a higher level of granularity in the evaluation of jobs also leads to more fairness. You take differences in responsibility seriously.

> We differentiate according to as many (narrow) pay grades as possible. This enables us to optimally meet the respective responsibilities of different jobs. (2-1)

Once employees have learned that career development is equal to promotion to a higher salary level, narrow salary bands will be highly appreciated by those people.

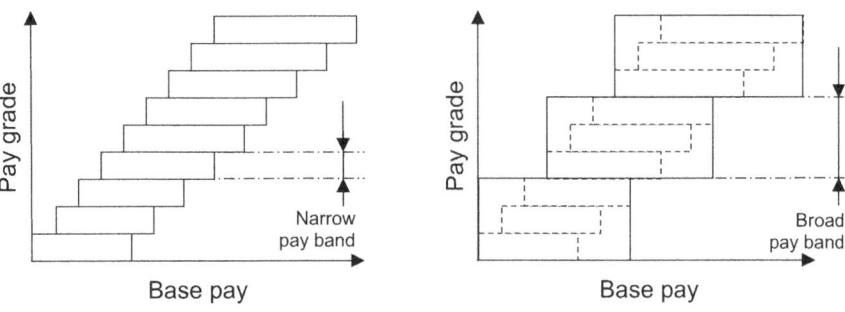

Fig. 9.5 Narrow and broad pay bands

Many pay grades offer the opportunity to make such a promotion of employees possible. And for managers, especially in hierarchical contexts, there is hardly anything better than being able to inform an employee of an upgrade to a higher pay grade.

This option is taken away when narrowly defined pay bands are combined into wider or broader pay bands. One speaks here also of the so-called *broadbanding*. Figure 9.5 shows the difference between narrow salary bands (left) and broadbanding (right). The left side shows nine salary bands and the right side only three.

Broadbanding embodies a partially radical simplification of the compensation structure. As stated earlier, simplification can also contribute to greater fairness. In most cases, employees remain in the same pay grade for many years. For professors, for example, this is the normal case.

In addition to this conceptual reduction of complexity, broadbanding has a significant psychological advantage. The continuous discussions about possible promotions are largely omitted. This prevents potential promotions from occupying a large space in ongoing debates, which in turn reduces the threat of growing extrinsic motivation. The more frequently employees and managers talk about money, the greater its extrinsic significance, which in turn leads to a loss of motivation overall. This effect has already been discussed in Sect. 9.1 above.

> We differentiate according to as few (broad) pay bands as possible. This enables us to be flexible and saves time-consuming discussions and conflicts. (2-2)

In traditional, hierarchically thinking companies in particular, there are fears associated with the change towards broader pay bands. There are fears that some control losses and associated cost developments will occur due to less restrictive structures. One fears a certain arbitrariness, because with broader salary bands one can no longer determine as precisely what jobs and their responsibilities correspond with certain pay grades. Managers have fewer formal restrictions to which they may refer. For this reason, it is still feared that employees will no longer understand why they deserve what they deserve. Empirical studies, however, indicate that these risks are overestimated. For example, Abosch (2008) reports in one of the few available international studies on this topic that not a single company that has introduced broadbanding in recent decades has regretted this step.

Top and Bottom

How much more should executives and experts earn than the regular employees and non-experts? This is another strategic question in the context of compensation, which directly touches on the question of employee appreciation. In Sect. 4.2 the concept of the *inverted pyramid* has already been introduced. In contrast to strictly hierarchical companies, the view here is that the employees are the "real heroes" of the company. Managers and executives, on the other hand, just have the task, in their role as enablers and servant leaders (cf. Sect. 4.4), of creating framework conditions that enable employees to do a good job. If this consideration is taken seriously, it means not only a higher appreciation of the employees—who are in the centre—but also a smaller salary spread between the remuneration of executives, managers and employees. The salary structure then is supposed to present itself accordingly.

> We aim to keep the differences in basic salary between upper and lower pay grades as small as possible. This reflects the esteem in which we hold our employees. (3-2)

If, however, a company is characterised by the attitude that the value of the respective position holder increases with increasing hierarchical level, then it must be assumed that the salary spread is as high as possible. This is not only tolerated but intended then.

> Employees on upper hierarchical levels must earn significantly more than employees on lower levels. This creates incentives for development and growing responsibility. (3-1)

Now there is a widespread way of describing and statistically analysing *salary differences*. Here, the so-called *Lorenz curve* is used, as shown graphically in the Fig. 9.6.

On the horizontal axis, all employees are sorted according to their basic salary and displayed in ascending order from the lowest wage to the highest wage. The vertical shows the cumulated salaries. The more unequal the distribution of salary is, the more the arc stretches into the lower right corner. If, on the other hand, all employees had exactly the same salary, the diagonal shown in the figure would result. If you now divide the area under the curve (hatched area) by the area under the diagonal, you get the so-called *Gini coefficient*, a measure for the inequality of a distribution. If this value is 1, then there is a complete equal distribution, which would indicate perfect equal pay. In the case of a Gini coefficient close to 0, absolutistic states would be assumed. The CEO, as if he or she were as the Sun King, receives everything, the employees nothing.

According to the German Federal Ministry of Finance (Bundesministerium der Finanzen 2017), this coefficient has increased continuously between 1990 and 2005

9.2 Base Pay

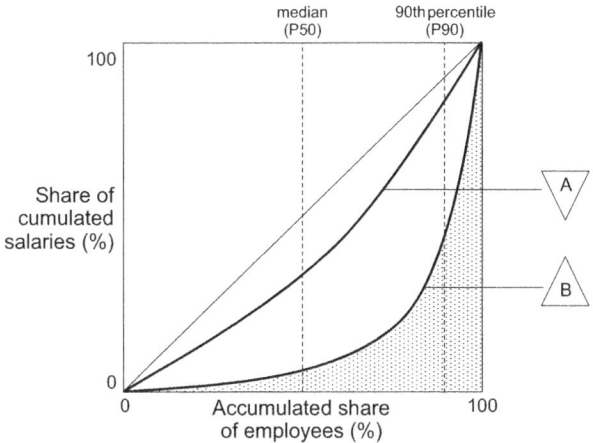

Fig. 9.6 The Lorenz curve to describe salary inequality

and has since settled at a constant level of 0.3. Somewhat less abstract and more manageable for companies is the so-called *P90/P50 relation*. Two values are set in relation to each other. The first value P90 indicates the amount above which an employee is among the top 10% in terms of compensation (90% percentile). The value P50 (50% percentile) is the median, the value that divides the total group of employees into two equal groups (see Fig. 9.6). 50% earn more than the median, 50% less. According to the OECD (2016), the P90/P50 ratio in Germany is 1.5.[1] In an international comparison, Germany is thus in the midfield.

This raises the question for companies as to what salary differences they are aiming for, whether you want to drag the Lorenz curve to the lower right corner or rather move it diagonally. Do you want to increase the Gini factor and thus reduce the P90/P50 ratio or do you rather aim for the opposite? Do you—following the figure above—want to design the compensation structure in the sense of the inverse pyramid (curve A) or rather strive to become an absolutistic state (curve B)?

Does it Cost What it Takes?

In particular, base pay plays a special role with regard to the acquisition function of remuneration described above. Every experienced HR manager, HR professional, recruiter or HR business partner knows this case: A truly outstanding candidate has salary expectations that are far above the salary level set by the respective pay grade. He or she refers to the fact that he or she receives the salary he or she expects from other companies. What do you do? Do you opt for the salary range or for the

---

[1] This value is not based on the basic remuneration but on the total remuneration including taxes and social security contributions. Nevertheless, this value should suffice as a rough guide.

candidate? This is clearly a critical situation in which the strategic alignment of a company is directly affected.

The highly successful company Netflix would have a clear answer to the above question. Netflix pursues a strategy that can be summed up as follows:

> With the best, you can't compromise. In order to win and keep them, we are willing to pay almost every salary. (4-2)

Even if current employees make new salary demands and refer to their market value in the labour market, this company gives way. Apparently Netflix can afford this strategy. In fact, Netflix sees this as a strategy to strengthen its own competitiveness and thus provides a new edition of the traditional Robert Bosch quote: "I do not pay good wages because I have a lot of money, but I have a lot of money because I pay good wages" (cf. McCord 2014). Netflix not only acts consistently in one direction, but also in the other. As soon as the company notices that an employee is no longer delivering what he or she is supposed to deliver, he or she is dismissed with generous severance payments. It is not those well performing employees who receive high salaries that are expensive, but those employees who receive salaries but do not perform as expected. This is the conviction of this special company. According to my own observations and assessments, most companies in Germany act differently. They have committed themselves to a conflicting premise, which, due to its widespread use, requires little additional explanation:

> Even with the best, we have to respect structural boundaries. Anything else leads to exhausting negotiations, exploding costs and envy. (4-1)

Both strategic options sound reasonable or at least comprehensible in their own way. There is probably hardly a strategic dimension where a decision in one direction or another is more painful. But this is precisely what strategic decisions are about. Section 3.3 details the importance of key and bottleneck functions. If a company cannot afford the best salaries in all areas—and this will probably be the norm—then it should at least think in this direction with regard to the strategically highly relevant key functions. Key functions are characterized by the fact that you need employees there who are better than the employees the competitor has in comparable functions. But those who want to have the better or even the best should possibly also be willing to pay the salary that is paid in the market for the best.

Little Room for Manoeuvre

Hardly any other topic within HR is as regulated as that of base pay. The systems and processes are accordingly cemented, for example through collective agreements on tariffs within certain industries and countries, company agreements, employment contracts, etc. In addition, salary systems are anchored in the culture and thinking of all. Most companies will think long and hard about whether and how to make

Evaluation	**1-1 Job evaluation**	**1-2 Employee responsibility**
	In the beginning there is always the job, the associated responsibility, its evaluation and grading. Only then a suitable employee could be hired.	When grading jobs, we are guided by the responsibility that an available employee can assume. This enables us to react flexibly to given labour market conditions.
Differentiation	**2-1 Narrow, many grades**	**2-2 Broad, few grades**
	We differentiate according to as many (narrow) pay grades as possible. This enables us to optimally meet the respective responsibilities of different jobs.	We differentiate according to as few (broad) pay bands as possible. This enables us to be flexible and saves time-consuming discussions and conflicts.
Differences	**3-1 Large salary differences**	**3-2 As equal as possible**
	Employees on upper hierarchical levels must earn significantly more than employees on lower levels. This creates incentives for development and growing responsibility.	We aim to keep the differences in basic salary between upper and lower pay grades as small as possible. This reflects the esteem in which we hold our employees.
Flexibility	**4-1 No flexibility**	**4-2 Competitive orientation**
	Even with the best, we have to respect structural boundaries. Anything else leads to exhausting negotiations, exploding costs and envy.	With the best, you can't compromise. In order to win and keep them, we are willing to pay almost every salary.

Fig. 9.7 Overview of all strategic dimensions related to base pay

changes to their base pay strategies. In this respect, the considerations in this subchapter and the strategic dimensions presented therein (see Fig. 9.7) are rather theoretical for most companies. However, the strategic options described here are of considerable relevance for young companies in particular.

9.3 Pay for Performance

The topic of base pay that has just been dealt with appears comparatively simple and straightforward in comparison to the following one. As will become apparent, variable pay for performance is accompanied by considerable social dynamism, which is hardly predictable even for experienced practitioners. As with hardly any other topic, naivety can lead here not only to high costs but also to considerable damage. A key focus here is the role of variable compensation with regards to employee motivation and collaboration.

Money Motivates: But Only when Paid for Doing Boring Tasks

In the business context, *pay for performance* is a true extrinsic motivator. Do this and you get that. The more you achieve, the more you get. That is how simple the logic is. This may be due to an implicit distrust of the employees concerned, even if the supporters of this form of remuneration would not say so out loud. Anyone who advocates contingent pay must implicitly assume that employees do not give their best on their own initiative, because if employees gave everything in their power, the prospect of contingent rewards can obviously have no effect. Sport is a good example. When an amateur golfer participates in a golf tournament, he or she uses to give his or her best. How could he or she not? If the golfer were promised prize money, this would not improve his or her performance unless he or she did not give his best of his own accord. There is no chance to increase capabilities by rewards. Every form of variable incentive therefore implies the implicit assumption that there is potential for an employee to perform better at a given moment, whereby exploiting this potential is merely a question of his will—his motivation—and not his ability.

> We motivate with individual, variable incentives. Those who do more should have more in their pockets in the end. (1-1)

The above assumption and the strategic alignment associated with it may be particularly true when a task assigned to an employee is highly unattractive or boring. The management mastermind Frederick Winslow Taylor (1911) has already pointed this out in an impressive way in his book "The Principles of Scientific Management", which is well worth reading. If one offers workers who have the task of shovelling material from A to B the prospect of performance-related pay, for example, then they will visibly increase their performance.

However, the situation is completely different for demanding and creative tasks. Already in Sect. 4.3 a distinction was made between tasks according to scope and complexity as well as result and process certainty. It was shown that especially in strictly hierarchical companies there is a form of division of tasks that results in extremely repetitive, pitiful tasks. These tasks not only clearly describe the results to be achieved (high certainty of outcomes) but also how they are to be achieved (high certainty of process). In such cases, a pay for performance can actually motivate because it can be assumed that the employees are not very motivated in the first place. This form of motivation is purely extrinsic. Some companies transfer this thinking to the entire company regardless of the fact that there are also attractive tasks with low result and process certainty in the same company. But how things behave in tasks with low task certainty and at the same time with high task dynamics is explained below.

Tasks for which One Gets Money Must Be Unattractive

But the opposite is also true. Money does not only motivate for unattractive tasks. Rather, employees deduce from the reward the attractiveness of the task: if you are paid for something, then the task is probably unattractive. This was already demonstrated by the early experiments of the psychologist Leon Festinger in the 1960s, although Festinger was primarily concerned with considerations regarding his theory of cognitive dissonance (Festinger 1962). The experiment is as follows:

Two groups A and B fulfil a demonstrably boring task. Group A receives an equivalent of 5 euros. Group B, on the other hand, receives 20 euros for this, a significantly higher amount. Then the participants of the groups are asked how attractive they found the task. The result is astonishing. People who receive only a small reward for a task (group A) find the task more interesting or less boring than those who received a high reward (group B). From an HR perspective, one might conclude that the higher the reward, the lower the degree of job satisfaction. However, this result shows a contrary effect. Two explanations of this frequently replicated finding are of importance here:

– When employees receive an attractive salary for a task, this strengthens their extrinsic motivation. They actually learn or become aware of performing a task primarily for the sake of money, regardless of what their motivational situation was like before. At the same time they accept the boring nature of a task.
– Fulfilling a boring task and at the same time receiving only a small reward for it creates a kind of inner conflict in people. Things do not go together. This is also called cognitive dissonance. By upgrading the task, people recognize the possibility of overcoming this conflict. "There was hardly any money paid for it, but the task wasn't actually so bad."

For companies, this means that in the case of boring tasks, it is better to pay only a small salary in order to perhaps cause thereby a cognitive upgrading of the task. This approach is unlikely to be realistic in practice. The other case seems more realistic: one pays employees a reasonable salary for the fulfilment of boring tasks and thus accepts the purchase of purely extrinsically motivated employees.

Contingent Reward Kills Motivation and Cooperation

Children like to paint pictures. They do this because they derive a natural joy from it. If you start rewarding them for painting pictures by giving them a cookie for each picture, for example, they will stop painting pictures if you decide at some point to no longer give them the reward for painting pictures. There is hardly any other effect in social science that has been replicated and confirmed more frequently than this one. It is referred to as the *overjustification effect* (Lepper et al. 1973). Intrinsic motivation is transformed into extrinsic motivation, which then is destroyed when the extrinsic motivator is removed. *Intrinsic motivation* describes an inner drive to do something out of one's own desires. You do something because you want to do it yourself. The task itself is the reward. *Extrinsic motivation*, on the other hand, describes the drive to do something to obtain a reward offered "from outside" or to avoid threatened punishment. You do something because someone else wants you to.

The tragic thing is that extrinsic motivation tends to lead to lower performance than intrinsic motivation. As described above, the shift from intrinsic to extrinsic motivation is at the expense of the overall motivation balance, resulting in lower performance. Now, from an entrepreneurial point of view, one might argue that this does not matter as long as the employees fulfil the tasks assigned to them–"Intrinsic, extrinsic, I do not care. As long as people do their job". This way of thinking may be appropriate with a high degree of task certainty. However, if there is a low degree of task certainty, it is not, because it is not really clear what the job consists of. Neither the results nor the ways to achieve them are clear and require a high degree of creativity on the part of the employees. Countless studies have shown that performance decreases especially in tasks of this kind as soon as employees are rewarded according to their performance (cf. Pink 2009). This is how the great author Alfie Kohn (1999, p. 67) sums it up: "Do rewards motivate people? Absolutely. They motivate people to get rewards". As soon as employees learn that they will get *this* when they do *that,* they no longer focus on *that* but on *this*. The task itself moves into the background.

In addition to task certainty, task dynamics also play a decisive role in this context. As already mentioned in Sect. 4.5, task dynamics are concerned with the mutual interdependencies of tasks. Is there a strict division of labour in which the initially independent work results of several employees add up to a total product or service? Or does this result from a reciprocal, dynamic interaction of several interconnected tasks and people—galley or football team? In agile organizations, the latter is of course closer to reality. You think in teams and networks. In such a setting, individual performance incentives can have a toxic effect. As already explained in the context of formal assessment (Sect. 6.3), it is precisely the use of forced distribution or forced ranking that carries the risk of turning colleagues into competitors. When there are few places on the podium, the individual loses interest in strengthening others. In summary, the following applies in agile organizations:

> With us there is no individual bonus. This would only come at the expense of intrinsic motivation and lateral cooperation. (1-2)

Companies such as Robert Bosch GmbH, for example, have shown how a large corporation has completely abolished individual bonuses worldwide for precisely these reasons. A number of other large companies are currently and consistently pursuing this idea.

One-Time Bonuses

When Richard returns to his desk after several very strenuous but all the more successful days at the fair, he finds two concert tickets—for him and his wife—accompanied by a hand-written card. With very nice words the team thanks Richard for his special commitment. Richard will probably tell this story years later. At least he will remember it in a very positive way. An alternative monetary way is for managers or colleagues to award spontaneous *one-time bonuses*.

Interestingly, this form of personal recognition has a motivating effect on employees. This is initially due to the fact that recognitions of this kind take place

9.3 Pay for Performance

immediately. Above all, however, its motivating effect is due to the fact that it comes suddenly and without prior notice in an unsolicited manner. Imagine the above event in a different light. Richard's manager promises Richard two tickets and a handwritten card if he agrees to work overtime at the upcoming fair. This approach would follow the classic pattern of "Do this and you get that". Here—as explained above—there would rather be the danger of questioning Richard's intrinsic motivation and ultimately diminishing it.

> One-time bonuses are always awarded on the spot and unexpectedly for employees. This is the only way to maintain intrinsic motivation. (2-2)

At the same time, the sudden, unplanned and spontaneous awarding of bonuses always entails the risk of arbitrariness. Some see in it the beauty of human surprises as part of an unforeseeable life that occasionally brings unexpected joys. Others miss a clear process and fair rules. According to which criteria are one-time bonuses awarded and who decides? How do we create fairness in this respect and prevent injustice? Is there not a need for more transparency instead of a reward in the manner of a generous ruler? Questions and concerns of this kind point in the opposite direction:

> Employees must know in advance why they are receiving a one-time bonus. Otherwise there would be the danger of arbitrariness and injustice. (2-1)

If a company primarily strives for equity in the distribution of incentives then it will always look for rules. Those companies that are very serious about this often orient themselves on rare individual cases of possible injustices that need to be avoided with comprehensive rules. Ultimately, however, it must be noted that well intentioned avoidance of injustice in the distribution of incentives can destroy exactly what the incentives were originally implemented for.

Sharing Profit Among Employees

In addition to contingent rewards, there are also known forms of performance-related remuneration. While the first component of variable remuneration is based on the performance of individuals or teams, another variable component is based on the performance or success of the company as a whole or of large, higher-level organizational units (Blasi et al. 2003). The variety of conceivable ways here are numerous. It is about *profit sharing*, *employee stock ownership*, *employee stock options* to name only the most important ones. The functioning of these models is not discussed here. The most important reasons why companies decide to let their employees participate in the company's success are of particular relevance here. Subsequently, it can be evaluated to what extent sharing success is an option in companies, which are led in a more hierarchical or agile manner.

- At the latest, when employees participate in the success, they deal more intensively with the development of their company's business situation. As a shareholder of your own company, you will check your share performance more frequently than if you do not own any shares. The success of the company is thus continuously brought to the attention of the employees. They adopt the status of the company as their own, which can be a desirable effect for companies in order to increase employees' commitment.
- Sharing success with employees has the consequence that the employees recognize themselves more as a kind of *performance community*. Success as a group comes more to the fore than individual contributions and incentives. You are in the same boat, so to speak. Accordingly, a certain incentive for lateral cooperation and cooperation is assumed. Conversely, individual actions that are seen by others as detrimental to overall success are socially sanctioned without intervention from the top.
- Sometimes, the term "*breathing company*"is also used in connection with profit sharing schemes. If the company is doing well, the employees benefit accordingly. If, on the other hand, the company is not doing so well, the employees also have to accept losses, at least to a certain extent. In the positive case, the company will have to cope with paying out additional amounts. In the negative case, additional loads are avoided. Responsibility and entrepreneurial risks are thus distributed among the employees.
- If candidates are promised a profit share paired with a lower basic salary, this also has a kind of selection function. In particular stock options appeal above all to those target groups who are able to deal with uncertainties, who believe in the future of the company at the same time and demonstrate a certain entrepreneurial willingness to take risks.

The argument that employees would try harder because of their prospect of a profit-sharing bonus would be naive. This may be the case for very small companies. In large corporations, on the other hand, the individual performance of an individual employee with regard to the success of the company as a whole is of little significance, and the people concerned know this.

To sum up these considerations, the models described above are about identifying employees with the company's success, working together to achieve overarching goals, flexibility based on the business situation, shared responsibility and entrepreneurial thinking, and attracting employees who are willing to take risks, who are optimistic, and adaptable. All this sounds very compatible with the principles of agile leadership and organization. Although there are currently no reliable empirical findings, one can assume that those ideas are more widespread in agile companies than in other companies. In this respect, the opposite poles of a strategic orientation in this question are comparatively simple. Either a company shows a tendency to share success with its employees:

> We share success among our employees in order to attract the right employees, strengthen flexibility, cooperation and orientation towards overriding goals. (3-2)

Or one tends to dispense sharing success among employees:

> We pay fair salaries. In addition, we do not share success among our employees. It is the sole responsibility of entrepreneurs and shareholders to dispose of profits and value developments. (3-1)

If a company opts for the latter premise, things are relatively simple. However, as soon as a company moves in the direction of sharing success, it faces the problem of deciding on the appropriate model and structuring it operationally. This raises a number of open questions regarding the amount and nature of distributions. From a legal point of view, companies have considerable room for manoeuvre here in many countries. For example, the question arises as to which organizational unit should be taken into account when measuring corporate success. Is it about the success of the department, the division or even the entire group? What does corporate success actually mean? Questions of this kind are not dealt with further at this point. More fundamental, however, is the question of how to proceed in the development and operational design of these models.

Active Involvement

The classic approach to the development of any kind of success-sharing models is probably that an internal project group with the support of external consultants—management consultants with a focus on compensation models, tax consultants, bank consultants, lawyers—develop a model and then proudly presents it to the employees.

> The model for sharing success is developed by an internal project group with external support. The model is then rolled out internally. (4-1)

This approach may seem professional at first. The main advantage is that you can achieve a conceptual result comparatively quickly and avoid rumours or uncertainties on the part of employees at an early stage of development. On the other hand, measures that affect the income of employees always trigger a certain social dynamic—a complex, unpredictable mixture of joy, acceptance, rejection, envy, resentment, sense of justice, feelings of revaluation or devaluation, etc.—which is why the measures are not always designed to be a positive and effective way of dealing with the situation. Later in this book (in Sect. 11.1) it is argued in more detail that anticipation of social dynamics should always lead to the conclusion that the employees and managers concerned should play an active part in the design of any measures. In this case it is a question of participation and active involvement.

> When designing our model of sharing success, we actively involve the affected employees and managers. We regard sharing without participation as a dysfunctional contradiction. (4-2)

Contingent reward	1-1 Individual bonuses We motivate with individual, variable incentives. Those who do more should have more in their pockets in the end.	1-2 No individual bonuses With us there is no individual bonus. This would only be at the expense of intrinsic motivation and lateral cooperation.
One-time bonuses	2-1 By arrangement Employees must be clear in advance why they are receiving a one-time bonus. Otherwise there would be the danger of arbitrariness and injustice.	2-2 Suddenly One-time bonuses are always awarded abruptly and unexpectedly to employees. This is the only way to maintain intrinsic motivation.
Sharing success	3-1 No sharing We pay fair salaries. In addition, we do not share success among our employees. It is the sole responsibility of entrepreneurs and shareholders to dispose of profits and value developments.	3-2 Strong sharing We share success among our employees in order to attract the right employees, strengthen flexibility, cooperation and orientation towards overriding goals.
Conceptualization	4-1 Top-down The model for sharing success is developed by an internal project group with external support. The model is then rolled out internally.	4-2 Involved When designing our model of sharing success, we actively involve the affected employees and managers. We regard sharing without participation as a dysfunctional contradiction.

Fig. 9.8 Overview of all strategic dimensions of pay for performance

The question of how the active participation of employees and managers is possible cannot be answered in general terms. This depends not only on the type and size of the company but also on its culture and past experience with projects of this kind. A more in-depth consideration of this aspect is given in Chap. 12 (Managing change and transformation).

Fewer Bonuses, More Participation

The topic of variable pay can be summarized comparatively easily. If one takes a fresh look at the strategic dimensions in the Fig. 9.8, which are juxtaposed in an overview, it becomes clear that there are simply no individual bonuses in agile organizations, at least not in their classic "do this and you get that" form. On the other hand, the focus is much more on a broad-based participation of employees in the company's success.

References

Abosch KS (2008) Broadbanding. In: Berger LA, Berger DR (eds) The compensation handbook. A state-of-the-art guide to compensation strategy and design. McGraw-Hill, New York, pp S 159–S 166

References

Berger LA, Berger DR (2008) The compensation handbook. A state-of-the-art guide to compensation strategy and design. McGraw-Hill, New York

Blasi J, Kruse D, Bernstein A (2003) In the company of owners. The truth about stock options and why employees should have them. Basic Books, New York

Bundesministerium der Finanzen (2017) Einkommensungleichheit und soziale Mobilität. Gutachten des Wissenschaftlichen Beirats beim Bundesministerium der Finanzen 2017/1

Card D, Mas A, Moretti E, Saez E (2010) Inequality at work. The effect of peer salaries on job satisfaction. Working paper 16396. National Bureau of Economic Research, Cambridge, MA

Dessler G (2018) Human resources management. Pearson, Boston

EL-Hajji MA (2015) The Hay system of job evaluation: a critical analysis. J Hum Resour Manag Labor Stud 3(1):1–22

Festinger L (1962) Cognitive dissonance. Sci Am 207(4):93–106

Inauen A, Jenny G, Bauer G (2015) Discriminating five forms of job satisfaction: investigating their relevance for occupational health research and practice. Psychology 6:138–150

Jackson EJ, Schuler RS (2012) Strategic human resource management. Blackwell, Malden

Jahoda M, Lazarsfeld PF, Zeisel H (1933) Die Arbeitslosen von Marienthal. Ein soziographischer Versuch über die Wirkungen langandauernder Arbeitslosigkeit. Hirzel, Leipzig

Kohn A (1999) Punished by rewards. The trouble with gold stars, incentive plans, A's praise and other bribes. Houghton Mifflin, New York

Lepper MR, Greene D, Nisbett RE (1973) Undermining children's intrinsic interest with extrinsic reward: a test of the "Overjustification" hypothesis. J Pers Soc Psychol 28(1):129–137

Luttmer EFP (2005) Neighbors as negatives: relative earnings and well-being. Q J Econ 120(3):963–1002

McCord P (2014) How Netflix reinvented HR. Harv Bus Rev 2014(January/February):60–77

McGregor D (1960) The human side of enterprise. McGraw-Hill, New York

OECD (2016) OECD-Wirtschaftsausblick, Ausgabe 2016/1. OECD Publishing, Paris

Pink D (2009) Drive. The surprising truth about what motivates us. Riverhead Books, New York

Taylor FW (1911) The principles of scientific management. Harper & Brothers, New York

Wells JR, Haglock T (2005) Whole foods market. Harv Bus Sch Case 705-476

Engagement and Retention 10

In the scientific literature, one searches in vain for a common definition of what is internationally understood by the term *employee engagement* (Byrne 2015). Somewhat more tangible is the construct of loyalty. Nevertheless, from the company's point of view there is somehow agreement that engagement and loyalty seem to be positive and important, at least to some extent. Engagement in particular is something that is seen in connection with employees and can be specifically influenced. This brings this elusive concept closer to the field of HR. The present chapter deals with three topics which—possibly somewhat arbitrarily—are assigned to this overarching theme of engagement and loyalty. On the one hand, the first sub-chapter deals with working conditions as an essential component and factor of employer attractiveness. Hardly anyone seriously denies that working conditions and the associated attractiveness as an employer have an influence on the engagement of employees. The special focus will be on the aspect of flexibility at work.

Furthermore, this chapter deals with an approach that has been taken into consideration for many decades when the entrepreneurial interest is focused on the topics of engagement or satisfaction. We are talking about employee surveys. The chapter concludes with a differentiated and strategic consideration of the topic of employee retention. The direct reference to the concept of loyalty is evident in this area in particular.

10.1 Working Conditions and Employer Attractiveness

Employer attractiveness is certainly an extremely complex construct. If you ask yourself what does *not* matter in terms of employer attractiveness, you will find it difficult to find concrete aspects. Somehow, all the topics covered in this book are related in some way to the question of how an employer is seen and evaluated by an employee or external candidate. Think of salary, development opportunities, working conditions in general, leadership, culture, etc. Nevertheless, this subchapter will first attempt to sort out relevant aspects around this topic. In the course of this, however, there is a focus on physical working conditions, which are ultimately about working place and working time.

Garbage Men, Soldiers and Mountaineers

There is a perspective on the issue of employer attractiveness that is probably very widespread. One could outline this view as follows:

> Employees are particularly productive and satisfied when they are in an attractive working environment. It is therefore always an advantage to be as interesting as possible as an employer. In addition, employer quality increases the number of applications received and reduces voluntary turnover. Only those who are substantially attractive as employers have realistic prospects of doing well in the war for talent and of developing a positive employer image in the long term.

Who would seriously disagree with this statement? It sounds amazingly plausible. At least the opposite of this statement seems hardly desirable at first glance. Companies that commit themselves to the view just outlined follow this premise:

> We want to be known as an attractive employer overall and are always striving to be one. (1-1)

In 1914, the legendary expedition leader Sir Ernest Shackleton sailed to the Antarctic Ocean with a crew of more than 20 men. Their ship, the "Endurance", was eventually stuck in the ice, crushed, and the crew had to endure many months of deprivation in the total isolation of the Arctic ice. In the end, they all survived. The following job advertisement is attributed to this expedition (Watkins 1959): "Men wanted! For hazardous journey, low wages, bitter cold, long hours of complete darkness. Safe return doubtful. Honour and recognition in case of success". What Ernest Shackleton promised here didn't sound very attractive in many respects. However, it is reported that he was overwhelmed with thousands of applications. How can such extremely unattractive conditions nevertheless appear attractive?

Some time ago, I gave a presentation on employer branding to HR managers at a conference for municipal companies. At the end one of the HR managers commented on my keynote as follows: "Your idea of employer branding sounds interesting. However, you should note, that we are looking, among other things, for city cleaners [so-called "garbage men"]. This job is not attractive. What are you promising as an employer here?"

Many jobs seem anything but attractive in many respects. Working in nursing care for the elderly is extremely stressful. In retail you are supposed to work at weekends. In management consultancies you work 60 h and more per week. Military combat, fire brigade operations, medical emergency operations are not only life-threatening but also extremely stressful psychologically.

What is special about all these occupational fields, which have just been mentioned, is that although they appear to be unattractive in many respects, in the end they contain something that attracts certain target groups to a particular degree. Employees in these areas work towards the special moment. Climbing Mount Everest is certainly anything but attractive. At the very least, one enters working conditions that would hardly have a chance of winning a "Best Place to Work" award. But to climb the summit means the highest possible feeling of happiness, which has been worked towards for months and months of cross-border deprivation.

Companies that recognize this deal differently with the issue of employer quality. They accept that many jobs are not attractive and never will be. They deal with this openly, but refer to the special or sometimes even magic moment, which is why it is nevertheless worthwhile to stand up for a task.

> We do not want to and cannot be an attractive employer in everything and for everyone. We also deal with this very openly and authentically. We focus on those moments that are worth working for. (1-2)

Fortunately, another HR expert from a municipal company supported me in the above-mentioned keynote and explained: "Yes, working as a city cleaner is very demanding. These men [most of them are men] know that. But if you ask the men if they like doing their job, they will usually agree with you. Most of them are very proud of their task and appreciate the hardness and cohesion. They often cannot imagine doing anything else".

Objective and Subjective Attractiveness

The previous considerations were based tacitly on the assumption that there were such things as attractive or unattractive working conditions. In fact, for decades there has been a question in ergonomics or management theory under which conditions employees are not only efficient but also their well-being can be ensured. What are ideal working and break times? What are ideal lighting conditions at work? What role does the social context play? What level of diversity is ideal for solving problems in teams? In the end, these efforts tend to focus on the question of what objectively constitutes an ideal employer. Finally, this leads to a *generalization* of objective criteria concerning employer attractiveness. This results in concrete recommendations for practice.

Questions of this kind became particularly visible when it came to the preferences of certain target groups, as in previous years, for example, in relation to *generation Y* (all those born between 1980 and 1995) or, more recently, to *generation Z*, the next generation (e.g. Tapscott 2008; Combi 2015). This is also based on the assumption that an employer is only attractive for the representatives of various generations if certain general criteria are met.

Even some employer competitions or awards, in which particularly attractive employers are awarded annually, are usually based on clear criteria: if this or that is fulfilled, then an employer is seen as an attractive employer. If you follow this point of view, then you start from recognized standards, which you try to live up to as far as possible.

> In developing our attractiveness as an employer, we are guided by objective, (scientifically) recognized standards. We try to implement these throughout the company. (2-1)

On closer inspection, this strategy is also an attempt to deal with people or target groups without really dealing with them. In the end, it is the average that decides. "On average, people of generation Y want a high degree of work-life balance and safety. Money, on the other hand, is not so important to them". These findings describe averaged, generalized tendencies. What the individual expects, on the other hand, is literally ignored.

But is it not rather the case that people have very individual needs because people are different? Is it not the case that one person would prefer to work in solitary seclusion, while the some other person would see this as a form of torture, as social deprivation? Don't you know those colleagues who like to get up early and want to get as much of their work done before the dew on the meadows disappears, while some other colleague prefers the inspiring silence later in the evening?

If one agrees with these considerations of personal differences, one will strategically arrive at a somewhat different understanding of employer attractiveness. What is attractive and what is not always depends on the preferences of individuals. Employer attractiveness is thus seen as a rather subjective construct. Instead of generalization, this strategy follows the idea of *individualization*.

> Employer attractiveness is an individual, subjective matter. Therefore, we can only be attractive if we create space for the needs of the individual. (2-2)

As obvious or understandable as this strategic priority may seem, it may cause many executives or HR professionals to ponder. Can you really please every single employee? Is this even advisable? If working conditions or special privileges are approved or granted by superiors, there is always the danger of paving the way for injustice or patronising behaviour. Not only is there the potential for one employee to demand the same as the other—"but I am entitled to do the same". Rather, it can happen that one manager grants his employees more privileges than the other manager. In the end, there are the good and the bad.

If one really wants to meet individual needs and at the same time avoid injustice and patronizing behaviour, then only two further strategies remain. Firstly, all employees are given the same flexibility to decide for themselves what suits them best or not. The second is to allow employees to decide for themselves who is entitled to what privileges and who is not. Both strategies have to do with making work more flexible.

Place and Time

Making work more flexible is probably one of the most central issues when it comes to employer attractiveness. In the following, the focus is on two dimensions, namely the flexibility of the workplace on the one hand and the flexibility of working hours on the other. Much has already been published on this, so the concrete concepts will not be discussed here (see e.g. Jackson and Schuler 2012). Almost all HR textbooks describe the common approaches—flexitime, trust-based working hours, teleworking, home office, job-sharing, working time accounts, etc. This topic will also be considered from a more fundamental, strategic perspective. To achieve this, it is worthwhile to first take the perspective of an exemplary employee.

Suppose an employee—let's call him Thomas—sits at his desk on a Tuesday afternoon at 4.55 p.m. and prepares the offer for a customer. Three questions now arise:

- Why is Thomas working at 4.55 p.m.?
- Why is Thomas sitting at this desk of all places?
- What could Thomas have done not to have to work or sit at this one desk at that time?

The complete spectrum of strategic dimensions in relation to flexible work arrangements can be identified on the basis of these three questions. We start with a very common, possible answer:

> Thomas works at 4.55 p.m. because his working hours do not end until 5.00 p.m. So he's got five more minutes to go. He's sitting at this desk because he's been assigned to it. He could hardly have changed this in advance, unless he had convinced the management of the importance of an alternative working hour model and successfully asked for a different place to work from.

In many countries and industries, numerous employees would answer the above questions in exactly this or a similar way. We are dealing with rigid or fixed working conditions. Let us come to the second answer, as it would be conceivable under flexible conditions:

> Thomas works at 4.55 p.m. because the offer has to be sent the next day at the latest and he wanted to allow some time for it. He's sitting at this desk because it was unoccupied. In order not to have to work at this time any more, he should have started earlier with the preparation of the offer, for instance by investing one hour the day before in the evening or getting up earlier today. He could have done it from home, but he enjoys the privacy of the office (two children demanding attention are waiting at home).

In the first case, the place and time of work are clearly regulated by the company and the employee has no option but to follow this regulation. In the second case, the focus is on the service to be provided. When and where Thomas will do this is up to him. The regulation of place and time can also be described as a regulation of first order. It regulates when and where work is to be done.

Regulation of First Order

Regulations relating to working hours are described in so-called *working hours models*. In addition to the working time volume, they also clarify the time distribution over the course of the weekdays and the degree of flexibility. These models and their different variations are described sufficiently in almost every HR management textbook. For companies, the fundamental question is how much *working hours flexibility* they want to grant their employees. The spectrum ranges from rigid or fixed working hours to *trust-based working hours*. In the latter case, the employees themselves decide when to work and when not to.

Fixed working arrangements are justified by at least two factors. On the one hand, the work itself may require certain fixed working hours for objective reasons. Just think of the infrastructure to be used, such as machines that have to be fully utilized on the one hand and on which only one employee can work at a time. A clear allocation of the space of work usually goes hand in hand with this because the infrastructure is immovable. In other areas, interaction with customers may require specific working hours and locations. Just think of the stationary retail trade. When the store opens, employees should have a local presence in the store.

The other factor has more to do with leadership and cultural conditions. If it is assumed that employees are reluctant to do their job, they actually do so only because they receive money for it. So if you believe in Theory X, you will force employees to be present. And during this time of presence, the human resource is available to the company in a certain way. The employees have to do what they are told in the given time. If you think in this direction, rigid working times simply have a control function. Both factors lead to the following strategic premise:

> We prefer fixed working conditions. This ensures clarity and control. Deviations towards higher autonomy are rather the exception. (3-1)

You can experience this leadership culture as an outsider when you are standing in a traffic jam in times of so-called "rush hour". For many car-driving employees it would have made more sense to leave the office an hour or earlier or to stay longer in the office in order to avoid the volume of traffic. Many of those affected only need a mobile infrastructure—computer and telephone—for much of their work. Basically, they have their office in their pockets. So if they torture themselves through the traffic at 5 p.m. of all times, it is probably only because they are not allowed to do otherwise. Slaves on the streets.

For employees and teams whose main task is to think and communicate, rigid working conditions seem rather absurd. There are studies that have investigated the question of where and when employees have good, professionally relevant ideas. The scientific value of most studies I know of is rather limited. Nevertheless, they all arrive at fairly clear results. The best, professionally relevant ideas do not emerge during so-called working hours or at the so-called workplace. Rather, they arise when running, mowing the lawn, going for a walk, falling asleep, reading, taking a shower, etc. By the way, boring meetings lead to more ideas than exhausting meetings. Almost when these very plausible and subjectively understandable results are put together, one must conclude that traditional working conditions prevent people from doing what they are paid for, especially when their work is essentially about thinking.

Where thought and communication are predominant, traditional notions of working time and the workplace lose their original meaning. What is a *workplace* when you primarily need your brain to work? Future generations will probably no longer understand this word "workplace". "Is work something you go to?" The antithesis to rigid working conditions is flexible working arrangements. Flexibility in terms of place and time is, so to speak, the default setting from which narrower targets are set where they appear necessary and not vice versa.

> We place a high degree of autonomy and sovereignty on working conditions. Narrower specifications only exist where they appear to make sense. (3-2)

Local, physical framework conditions play an important role, especially with regard to the innovative capacity of companies. Presumably one can already recognize from the *architecture* of a company what degree of innovation is possible there and what understanding of leadership and organization prevails. Strictly hierarchical, static companies with a divided labour can usually be identified by long corridors with clearly defined offices. You can really see those as organizational silos. Agile, innovative companies, on the other hand, rely on architecture that is basically reminiscent of monasteries. The floor plan of the former Benedictine monastery Blaubeuren in Germany is shown here as an example (see Fig. 10.1).

The above statement may at first seem surprising. What do monasteries have to do with innovation? In fact, empirical evidence has shown that innovative companies offer their employees different, spatial work zones, as is the case in monasteries (Allen and Henn 2007). This includes areas for collaboration and spontaneous exchange and encounter as well as spaces for retreat and concentration. Monasteries also offer spaces of inspiration. In the end, the employees decide which physical

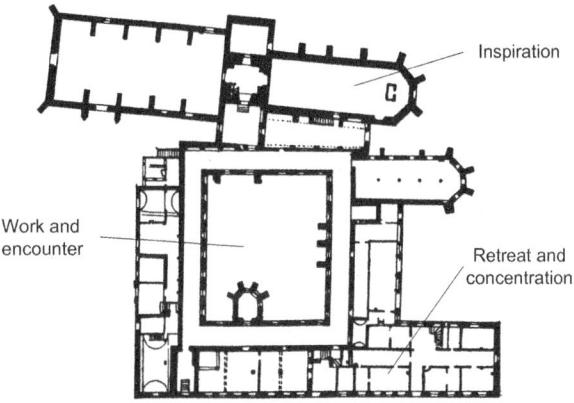

Fig. 10.1 Areas within the monastery Blaubeuren. Source: Wikimedia Commons (2018). Grundriss Blaubeuren Ehem. Benediktiner-Kloster

environment suits them best in a given situation, depending on their current tasks and personal preferences.

Regulation of Second Order

First imagine the following simple situation: The members of a team have complete freedom to determine their own working hours and places—trust-based working hours and trust-based working place. There are no permanently assigned offices or desks, nor are there working hours that would be prescribed or tracked in any way. However, over time, colleagues decide to regulate their places of work in some way. At the end of the day, every employee sits permanently in the same place. Fixed structures also develop over time with regard to working hours. The employees agree to be present on certain days at certain times, because from their point of view this is good for cooperation and communication.

So, we have a situation in which formally there are extremely flexible working conditions, but the team has imposed a certain restriction or fixation on itself. Do flexible working conditions prevail or not? Kind of, but kind of not either. Obviously, the consideration of regulations on two levels is necessary here. We are talking here about regulations of first and second order.

In the literature and in practice, an examination of flexible working conditions takes place primarily at the conceptual level. It is explained what you can do—trust-based working hour, non-territorial workspaces, job-sharing, etc. But the really decisive question is who you mean by "you" in concrete terms. Most people implicitly assume that we are talking about the company here represented by its management. The company decides what the working conditions are like.

First-order regulations describe how working conditions are now regulated. *Second order regulations* describe how these regulations arise and, above all, who decides on first order regulations (the "you"). In a way, these are meta rules, rules about the regulation of rules. A central facet of second-order regulation is the question of who is responsible for the development of rules. Who makes the rules? Who can change it? At this point, another strategic dimension opens up. Is it the employees themselves or is it a higher central authority, such as the company management, the workers council, the HR function or all together? If first-order regulations are compared with second-order regulations, the constellations shown in Fig. 10.2 is the result.

The common, implicit notion with regard to the second order regulation probably assumes that a higher authority has the regulation of working conditions (first order regulation).

> A higher authority (e.g. company management) decides about the regulations of the working conditions. (4-1)

One extreme case *A* describes a situation of centrally *prescribed rigidity*. Management, for example, stipulates that employees must be present at a certain place at

10.1 Working Conditions and Employer Attractiveness

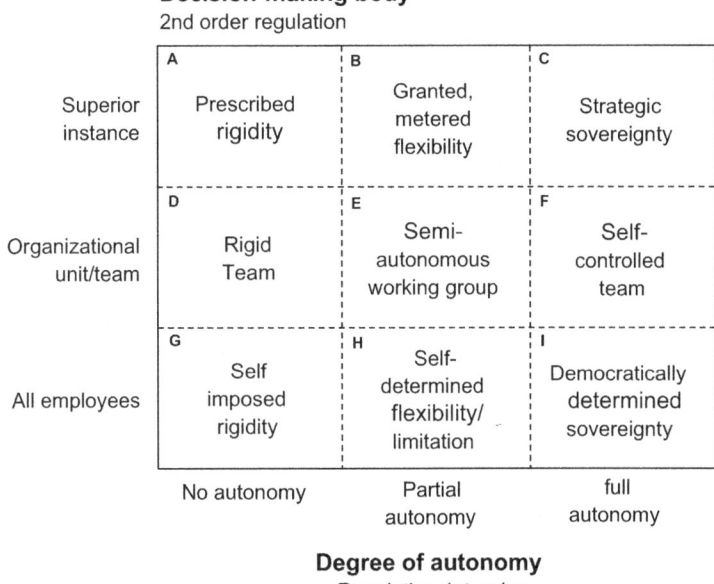

Fig. 10.2 First and second order regulation concerning the flexibility of working conditions

certain times. This situation is offset by working conditions in which, for example, the CEO has decided that comprehensive flexibility should prevail. In the case of *strategic sovereignty (C)*, it is important to management to avoid any form of rigidity. Flexible working conditions do not exist because employees want them to, but because management wants them to. Here, CEOs act as guardians of freedom.

The constellations *G* to *I* describe situations that are as they are because the employees want them to be this way. It is not necessarily to be assumed that employees voluntarily prefer the status of unlimited freedom at all times. Also colleagues can be suspicious, or even call for rigid rules. In the case of *self-imposed rigidity (G)*, fixed working conditions prevail because the employees want this, while in the case of *democratically determined sovereignty (I)* there is room for manoeuvre in terms of place and time because the employees themselves have spoken out in favour of it and have jointly decided so.

> Our employees themselves decide on the regulations governing working conditions within the framework of a democratic process. (4-2)

In addition to these extremes, which have just been described, there are, of course, intermediate forms which will not be discussed in detail here. For example, a second order rule may be to leave the rules on place and time of work to the organizational units. The teams themselves are responsible for how they sort things out. A widespread variant, which has been intensively discussed since the 1980s, is the so-called *semi-autonomous working group (E)*. It is up to the teams themselves to regulate, at least in part, their presence, distribution of tasks, holidays, etc. (e.g. van Mierlo et al. 2001).

A closer look at the above classification of conditions of sovereignty may reveal a lack of individual sovereignty, according to which employees not only decide for themselves when they work and where, but also give themselves the power to dispose of this degree of autonomy. This form of absolute, individual independence may exist in one-man companies, in freelancers, writers, artists, etc., but it is also a form of independence that is not only a matter of the individual. Organizations do not have this. Institutionally, it is simply inconceivable.

Why Agile Organizations Do Not Win HR Awards

Agile organizations rely above all on the sovereignty or autonomy of their employees and teams. This is a natural consequence of a multitude of assumptions and prerequisites. As discussed in detail in Chap. 4 employees and teams are regarded as responsible people who themselves have the best knowledge of how to meet their obligations to their customers—not their bosses. Iterative, short-cycle processes require flexible action. The combination of necessary collaboration, communication, spontaneous encounter, exchange but also necessary concentration, the possibility of retreat can hardly do justice to a rigid working world. Agile organizations know that you can't put employees in certain cage-like offices at certain times in the hope of finding innovative solutions.

Traditional, hierarchical companies that face the threat of disruption increasingly understand this aspect and are working hard and eagerly on new, more flexible models of working hours and premises that are more reminiscent of those assumed to be in place in Silicon Valley. For them, small changes often have the character of revolutions. What has always been a matter of course in agile companies often has to be laboriously fought for in traditional companies. While in agile organizations, for example, no one would question the fact that one is constantly and everywhere informed and in some way trained, in hierarchical companies one argues with workers' councils about whether one can encourage employees to watch professionally relevant TED[1] videos even during their spare time.

After all, when one of the countless prizes for special, innovative achievements in HR is ceremonially awarded again in glittering events, a hierarchical company always wins. This is because for them any change towards greater flexibility is a prize-winning achievement, while flexibility has always been lived and taken for granted in agile companies. Nobody there would come up with the idea of trying to win an award for it.

---

[1]TED is a platform for speeches and presentations by leading thought leaders that is recognized in the community worldwide as a source of inspiration for professionally relevant content. A so called TED Talk continuously maximum 18 min (https://www.ted.com/).

Work-Life Balance

When you think of *work-life balance*, you automatically think of flexible working conditions and possibly vice versa. With this term a discussion often follows about whether or not this term reflects the right idea. Yes, work and life do not have to be two separate things. But for some people that is exactly the case. And yes, there could be terms for it, such as "work-private integration" or "work-life blending". However, these are not so much better either. At the end of the day it is a matter of a healthy combination of what could be described as work on the one hand and private life and family on the other.

In principle, it is agreed that work-life balance requires flexible working conditions. Only then can one, on the one hand, pursue one's professional obligations and turn appropriately to one's children, friends or private community. In this respect, the tendency to treat work-life balance as a structural issue can be observed. It needs formal rules to live up to this claim. Work-life balance is something you should design, manage and perhaps also measure. The well-known and much quoted HR thought leaders Wayne Cascio and John Boudreau therefore define work-life balance as "any employer-sponsored benefit or working condition that helps an employee to balance work and non-work demands" (Cascio and Boudreau 2008, p. 153). Then they list them: Childcare, flexible working conditions, parental leave, sabbaticals, etc., the usual structural measures.

> In order to achieve work-life balance, we rely on appropriate programs and structural measures (e.g. flexitime, job sharing, company kindergarten). (5-1)

To think this way reflects a strategic alignment in relation to this particular issue. However, this mindset, represents only one position on a broader strategic spectrum. This becomes clear when one considers a number of common phenomena:

- There are companies that allow their employees trust-based working hours and a flexible choice of work location, but at the same time employees suffer a series of burnouts and in a certain way neglect their private lives.
- Some companies have decided to offer instruments to promote work-life balance (e.g. company kindergarten)—often at the requests of employees—and finally find that these are not made use of by employees.
- Some employees recognize that fixed structures are the very basis for separating work and private life or for reconciling work and private life. For them it is clear when work ends and when family begins, they can rely on it and build on it.
- The merging of work and private life (e.g. checking professionally relevant e-mails shortly before falling asleep), which goes hand in hand with greater flexibility, leads to so-called *spill-over effects*. Because somehow work is always done, in a positive and negative sense, work-related emotions and thoughts radiate (spillover) into the private context (Edwards and Rothbard 2000).

Work-life balance obviously requires more than just a structural framework. Flexible working conditions can be a prerequisite for this form of compatibility. However, they're, no guarantee for that. In this context, not only structural conditions but also cultural conditions are decisive.

How does a manager react when he or she realizes that Thomas, who has already been introduced, does not write his offer on weekdays at 5 p.m. but on weekends? Is Thomas seen as a role model or as an example of how it should not be? Does the manager think: "Thomas is a true role model. He's ready to sacrifice his private time for the company. He's showing you how to walk extra miles?" Or he or she thinks: "Apparently Thomas does not have himself and his work under control. He should better plan and learn how to use his resources. Saying "no" would be better sometimes. Doesn't he have any friends? Doesn't he have a family? Maybe we have to help him to take more responsibility for himself and his private situation". Work-life balance is also a cultural issue and is therefore largely the responsibility of leaders (McCarthy et al. 2010). Companies that think this way go beyond structural measures and commit themselves to a broader premise:

> To achieve work-life balance, we tell our employees that family and friends are more important than work. (5-2)

In the case of this strategic alignment, their CEOs convey a clear message that we want people to live a healthy life as employees. This includes family, friends, private interests, possibly a spiritual faith. Life is bigger than work. Only those who are able to take responsibility for their lives are able to take responsibility for customers and colleagues. Work is interchangeable, family and friends are not.

Work-Life Balance = Diversity, Diversity = Work-Life Balance

In contrast to the HR thinkers Cascio and Boudreau just mentioned, work-life balance should be defined less in structural HR terms. In essence, work-life balance is nothing more than the *appreciation of individual life plans* by the company, its executives, colleagues and ultimately by the employee him or herself. Life plans include friends, family, work, religion, hobbies, etc. At the same time, life plans are always to be understood as *individual* life plans. No life plan of a human being is the same as the life plan of another human being.

Already in Sect. 4.2 a similar definition was presented. It was about the concept of diversity. It was made clear that diversity is nothing else than the appreciation of individuality. Here we come full circle. Work-life balance and diversity are essentially one and the same concept, at least they are based on a common, fundamental understanding. This consideration can be illustrated, for example, by the question of how it is possible to achieve a higher proportion of female executives in management.

Traditionally, this topic has been dealt with under the heading of *gender diversity*. This means that equality between men and women is at stake, which in turn could be measured by the relative proportion of women in managerial positions. The extent to which equality can actually be achieved, however, has much to do with the appreciation of individual life plans. Men in leading positions usually have different life plans than their female colleagues. Traditionally, managers have been required to be fully committed to the company, to override the interests of the company to all other interests, to demonstrate limitless mobility, to be the first to board and the last to leave the ship. For men, this understanding of leadership was feasible for many decades. They could afford the accompanying life plan because it provided for a partner who took care of the family in the meantime. If a woman takes on a leadership role under these circumstances, she either has the option to do this without a family—about 70% of all female managers do—or to switch roles with her partner (Collinson and Hearn 1995). She works and he stays home taking care for the kids. Another alternative would be to outsource family affairs to grandparents, nannies and the like. On the surface, a high quota of women can be reached by accepting there being an increasing number of masculinized women. However, this has little to do with true diversity.

Genuine diversity can only be achieved if a company manages to value individual life plans and preferences. Fortunately, there are more and more men who want to see their children grow up. They regard the life plans of a majority of male executives as antisocial in a way, because they offer only limited space for family and friends—for what really counts in life. Fortunately, there is also a majority among women who are apparently not prepared to adopt masculine lifestyles that are far remote from actual living. Diversity would mean valuing not only their individuality but also their individual life plans. Perhaps it is precisely those people who are better leaders, who are ready and willing to take responsibility for children, family and friends in their private lives, too. Therefore, it is not surprising that more and more modern thinking companies are working on alternative models. At SAP, for example, part-time leadership is encouraged. Other companies in turn rely on job sharing at management level. It will be interesting to see what exciting concepts the practice will produce in the coming years.

Structure Versus Individuality

This sub-chapter has been based on the assumption that employer attractiveness is primarily a question of working conditions. In doing so, we deliberately avoided presenting what it is that makes an employer attractive. Rather, the focus was on the aspect of *how* working conditions are designed and *who* is responsible for them. A corresponding overview of all strategic statements and dimensions is provided by Fig. 10.3. When these two sides are considered together, it becomes clear that the issues of working conditions and employer attractiveness can either be viewed structurally. That would be the left side. This is about rules and conditions that are structurally defined in the company, mainly top down. Or one understands working

Priority related to employer attractiveness	1-1 General attractiveness We want to be seen as an attractive employer overall and are striving to be so.	1-2 Realistic attractiveness We do not want to and cannot be an attractive employer in everything and for everyone. We also deal with this very openly and authentically. We focus on those moments that are worth working for.
Understanding employer attractiveness	2-1 Objective, based on standards In developing our attractiveness as an employer, we are guided by objective, (scientifically) recognized standards. We try to implement these throughout the company.	2-2 Subjective and individual Employer attractiveness is an individual, subjective matter. Therefore, we can only be attractive if we create space for the needs of the individual.
Regulation of working conditions 1st order	3-1 Fixed working conditions We prefer fixed working conditions. This ensures clarity and control. Deviations towards higher autonomy are rather the exception.	3-2 Sovereignty We place a high degree of autonomy and sovereignty on working conditions. Narrower specifications only exist where they appear to make sense.
Regulation of working conditions 2nd order	4-1 Superordinate levels A higher authority (e.g. company management) decides about the regulations of the working conditions.	4-2 Employees and teams Our employees themselves decide on the regulations governing working conditions within the framework of a democratic process.
Work-life balance	5-1 Structural measures In order to achieve work-life balance, we rely on appropriate programs and structural measures (e.g. flexitime, job sharing, company kindergarten).	5-2 Attitude and culture To achieve work-life balance, we tell our employees that family and friends are more important than work.

Fig. 10.3 Overview of all strategic dimensions on working conditions and employer attractiveness

conditions and employer attractiveness more as a question of individuality. What does the employee want? How sovereign is he or she in shaping his or her conditions? Which individual life plan can he or she realize? In the end, employer attractiveness in the sense of individuality always arises from the experience of the individual employee.

10.2 Employee Survey

For many years, the American analytics firm Gallup has been announcing the horror news that the vast majority of employees worldwide are either not engaged or actively disengaged. This Gallup finding is almost always quoted when there is talk of *employee engagement* somewhere. Interestingly, however, hardly anyone who quotes this knows how it actually came about. Gallup itself also makes a secret of it. Presumably, this claimed ratio is a pure artefact, used for mere marketing

Fig. 10.4 Cycle of a classic employee survey

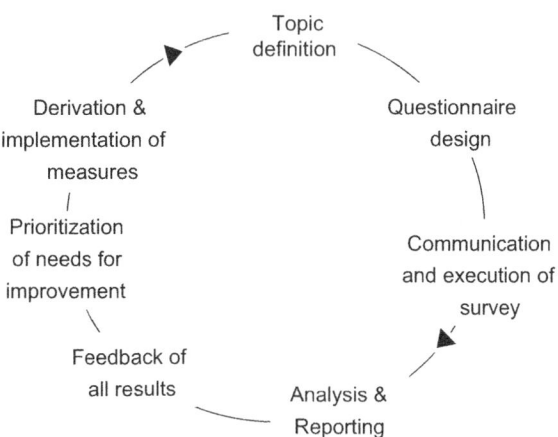

purposes.[2] They hit a nerve. Which CEO does not want to know how engaged his or her employees are? After all, it is assumed that satisfied, motivated employees perform better, as researchers at Gallup believe they have scientifically proven (Harter et al. 2002), once again confusing correlation with causality. As with Gallup, the widespread basis for determining employee engagement have always been the so-called *employee surveys*.

In the further course of this subchapter, the most widespread, classical approach of employee surveys and its strategic alignment will first be presented. This approach is then contrasted with a more agile approach.

The Classic Approach of an Employee Survey

Classic employee surveys follow a cycle of one or more years. This cycle provides far more than the term employee survey suggests. In fact, it is not only about surveying itself, but about an on-going process that is designed to develop an organization into a better state through surveying, feedback and improvement. The typical procedure is shown in the Fig. 10.4. The individual steps are briefly described below.

If an employee survey is the solution, what is the problem? The problem is neither a presumed lack of motivation nor low satisfaction on the part of the employees, but simply a lack of knowledge. One would like to know how the employees see things, how they are doing, but one does not know this. A study helps in such situations. At the end, a study provides insights into previously unknown facts. But who has this

---

[2] A more differentiated review of Gallup's misleading approach to measuring employee engagement can be found in my blog: http://www.armintrost.de/en/are-gallups-engagement-numbers-fake-at-least-they-are-heavily-cited/

problem? Within the framework of classical employee surveys it is stated that everyone has this problem, the executive board but also all managers and their teams at all levels. The CEO gains insights into the company as a whole. Team leaders learn about the state of mind and the perspectives of their teams.

> Very different stakeholders benefit equally from our employee surveys. (1-1)

Traditionally, it is those topics that are taken into consideration, which are assumed to relate to employee satisfaction, motivation, performance and commitment. It is primarily about the satisfaction of the employees with their work, their salary, their internal career perspectives, their cooperation with others, their direct superiors, the company strategy, communication, their working tools, etc. If the results are finally on the table, you can determine where things are going well and where they are not. On this basis, priorities for future measures can then be reached.

> We consider a wide range of topics. From the results of an employee survey, we then draw conclusions about the need for improvements and derive priorities. (2-1)

The employees are asked by means of anonymous, structured questionnaires. This ensures that the employees can respond fearlessly and thus honestly. The structured nature of the questionnaire enables comparability inwards and outwards. There are pre-formulated questions with standardized answers.

> Honest answers require anonymity in an employee survey. That is why we use structured questionnaires, which also makes it possible to compare the results. (3-1)

In most of these employee surveys all employees are invited to participate, without exception. This would not be necessary for scientific procedures, as sampling would also be sufficient to arrive at the same findings. However, particular importance is attached to the active involvement of employees. One would also not want to rely on a sample in a democratic election. In fact, employee surveys have their roots in *organizational development* and the associated action research. "Turning those affected into active players" was the principle that led to the so-called *survey feedback method* (Bowers 1973).

> During employee surveys we always survey all employees. Our aim is to ensure the broad involvement of all employees. (4-1)

Such classic forms of employee surveys are quite costly in terms of preparation, implementation and operation, especially in terms of reporting all the results and deriving appropriate measures from them. There is an explicit demand to mobilise organizational units in all areas and at all levels. It therefore makes sense to conduct employee surveys at the most once a year.

> We conduct employee surveys in (multi)annual cycles. Anything else would be unacceptable in terms of effort. (5-1)

10.2 Employee Survey

For employee surveys, the unwritten law applies that the results must never disappear into the much-quoted drawer, regardless of how the results turned out. In recent years, most companies have even gone well beyond this requirement. Each business unit, each department, each team receives its own report with aggregated representations of the statements of its respective employees. In this context, large corporations are experiencing real avalanches or reports.

> The results of an employee survey are intended for all employees and managers at all levels. A differentiation is made according to organizational units. (6-1)

Then the actual work begins. Within the framework of so-called *follow-up processes*, all divisions, departments and teams are encouraged to look at their own results, reflect on them and derive needs for improvement. The results of your own organizational unit are compared with those of higher-level units and any deviations are evaluated and prioritized. This is based on the conviction that the follow-up processes will decide whether the whole effort of the survey was worth it. Only if something changes noticeably for the employees will they be ready to participate in the next employee survey again in 2 years' time.

> We regard follow-up processes as the most important part of an employee survey. The survey must lead to visible consequences at all levels. (7-1)

That is how employee surveys are presented in most companies these days. Almost 20 years ago, together with colleagues at the University of Mannheim in Germany, I wrote a book on employee surveys in which I presented exactly this classic view (Trost et al. 1999). I wouldn't write that book like that today. In large parts, I had been wrong. In addition, it became clear to me that this approach corresponds to a deeply hierarchical understanding of leadership and organization.

The following sections will therefore present an alternative view. It becomes clear that classic employee surveys have limitations and rarely deliver on what they promise. This is the case in hierarchical companies and especially in agile ones. However, the strategic alternatives outlined in the following are primarily compatible with agile framework conditions.

Only What Was Important Before Is also Important Afterwards

In the course of my career, I have often had the opportunity to present employee survey results to executive boards. I'll never forget one moment, though. I was standing in front of the management of a large IT company presenting bar charts, pie charts on various questions of the employee survey just conducted. "And here you can see the satisfaction of your employees with their working conditions". "This slide shows the distribution of answers to the question of satisfaction with communication" etc. So it went on for half an eternity. Anyone who knows me knows that I am quite capable of inspiring listeners. But in this situation, I had real trouble. "And here you see the results on the question: Could you explain our Internet strategy to a new hire? 48% agreed. The rest did not". Suddenly there was tension in the room. Everyone was totally awake. The CEO suffered some kind of choleric seizure, "If this result is correct, then we can close our company in a few years" he shouted.

What had happened? This result, which was based on knowledge of the Internet strategy, was not only somehow interesting (in the best case) for the members of the executive board present, but also highly relevant—a decisive difference. For a person or a group, survey results are relevant if they are directly related to their objectives. Otherwise they are at best only interesting.

And there is something else I have learned from many years of practical work with employee surveys: What is not important before a survey is not important after the survey—regardless of the results. I now consider this the golden law of employee surveys.

> In employee surveys, only those topics are taken into consideration that have a high priority even before the survey. Only what is important before the survey is also important after the survey. (2-2)

This law has direct implications for the choice of survey topics. It does not seem to be a good strategy to ask a wide range of topics and then to see what the results will be. Rather, it is better to consider those topics in a survey for which one already has respect in advance for the results. This significant difference is graphically depicted in the Fig. 10.5.

In the upper part of this figure, the classical approach is indicated, according to which an open spectrum of topics is first considered. This is usually the result of the standard questionnaire of the consultant carrying out the consultation. Then, *after* conducting the survey and analysing the results, priorities are derived. The alternative, on the other hand, shows comparable steps, but in a different order. It starts with the priorities from which the really relevant contents of the survey are derived. They're determined *beforehand*. The rest will follow.

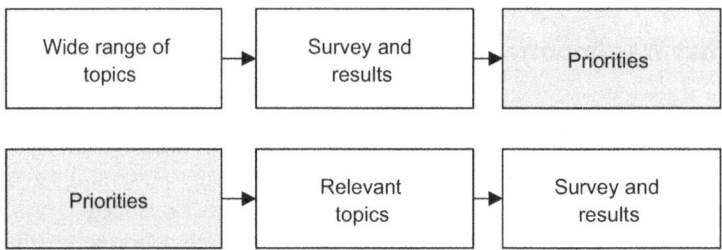

Fig. 10.5 Priorities before and after the survey

Who Is the Customer?

Now different survey contents are also of different relevance for different stakeholders in the company. The upper management team deals with other issues than operational teams. For IT support, which wants to know the degree of satisfaction of its internal customers, other content is relevant. In the Fig. 10.6 different contents and survey formats are indicated in relation to possible target groups.

A central question when conducting an internal survey is therefore the question of the respective customer. A survey should then also concentrate on their focal points.

> In employee surveys, we concentrate on the focal points of a particular customer (stakeholder). (1-2)

If, on the other hand, an attempt is made to serve a wide variety of stakeholders at the same time with *one* approach, this usually leads to the fact that the interests of no one are consistently addressed. In the end, this may mean that different stakeholders also need independent surveys with different formats. The classical approach of the employee survey as described above does not do justice to this principle. It tries to cover the interests of different target groups at once, an attempt that must fail. Therefore, the following strategic premise should apply to the results:

> The results of an employee survey are only relevant to those stakeholders who are responsible for the content under consideration. (6-2)

Accordingly, it is not necessary to reflect on all results with all employees, differentiated according to organizational units, but exclusively to the respective internal target group. Survey participants should be informed about the results. But asking everybody to work with the results is usually anything but effective.

Stakeholder	Relevant survey contents	Survey format
Upper Management	Strategic contents, commitment to strategic priorities, transformations and the capability of employees to contribute to them	Strategic pulse survey
Internal service providers	Internal satisfaction with internal company services, suggestions for improvement, evaluation of customer preferences	Internal customer survey
Middle Management	Management quality, prioritization and evaluation of (potential) measures, strategic content, evaluation of cooperation and communication	Management assessment, 360-degree assessment, pulse survey
Operational Teams	Satisfaction with working conditions, cooperation and communication within the team, evaluation of measures and proposals	Simple team survey

Fig. 10.6 Different survey contents and formats for different stakeholders (customers)

Pulse Surveys

As shown in Fig. 10.6, *pulse surveys* are referred to as a possible survey format at various points. Pulse surveys have established themselves in recent years as valuable alternatives or supplements to traditional employee surveys. A simple example may illustrate the idea behind this approach.

Let's assume that the management of a company has recognized and defined the topic of digitization as a strategic topic. It sees itself under time pressure and is convinced that this topic only has a chance of success if the entire organization is committed to this particular topic within a few months. In this case, a strategic pulse survey would be appropriate, in which a sample of employees is surveyed monthly on this topic. Possible questions could be:

- Are you convinced that the topic of digitization is of great importance for the future of our company? (commitment)
- Do you understand what digitization means for you and the colleagues your are working with on a daily basis? (purpose and meaning)
- Do you actively contribute to the success of our digitization strategy in your daily work? (engagement)
- Do you get the necessary support and opportunities to contribute to our digitization strategy? (capabilities)

If digitization is an issue of high strategic importance, management will be concerned about the results of the survey on a monthly basis and will act promptly depending on the results. The results are also reported exclusively to the management. At best, the respondents will be informed accordingly.

Fast and Minimally Invasive

Pulse surveys are a good example of agile survey methods. They're fast. They address the needs of limited target groups without wastage. Moreover, they concentrate on the essentials. The costs for pulse surveys are low compared to those of classical employee surveys. This is not so much a matter of broad employee involvement or democratic decision-making processes, but merely of rapid feedback. Samples are best suited for this and save money.

> Only samples are needed in employee surveys. This is sufficient to obtain representative results. (4-2)

Pulse surveys can therefore also be carried out on a short-cycle basis, monthly or on demand. Modern survey instruments allow fast surveys to be carried out within a few minutes. At least this is technically the case. The extent to which any coordination with workers councils and other coordination loops will cost time is not to be discussed further here.

10.2 Employee Survey

> We conduct employee surveys as often as necessary, if necessary continuously, every day. (5-2)

Amazon, for example, surveys its employees on a daily basis. Each employee is asked a single question at the beginning of the working day. The questions vary from employee to employee. Responses are given via a mobile device. In total, the answers provide a continuous barometer of the employees' views.

Just as I can conduct a spontaneous survey as part of my lecture, so teams and departments can also do this, for example, as part of meetings or closed conferences. These so-called instant surveys, in which the acute content needs and questions of those affected are addressed, are usually of greater relevance to the participants than standardized result reports, which are washed ashore once a year in the context of classical employee surveys.

On-Going Feedback

Classic employee surveys are usually experienced by employees and managers as singular and isolated events. "What, the next employee survey is coming up? Two years have passed again?" This is worth mentioning in so far as the figures of other controlling systems are worked with rather continuously. Just think of revenue, costs, quality indicators, accident ratio, etc. This is hardly the case for figures generated from classic, long-cycle employee surveys. Classic employee surveys come and go. In view of this, companies might be faced with the question of how employee surveys are designed and carried out so that they become the subject of continuous consideration and decision-making.

> The results of employee surveys must be a natural part of continuous decision-making processes. Otherwise, they eke out a shadowy existence. (7-2)

Continuity is not necessary just for the sake of continuity. As a good patient, you only go to the dentist every 6 months. And if everything is all right, you can let the matter rest for another 6 months. If, however, a topic is to be worked on seriously and one is faced with continuous uncertainty, then continuous attention is required, which classical employee surveys hardly offer.

Talk to Each Other

From time to time I talk to CEOs about employee surveys. Usually he or she is concerned with the question of whether or how they could or should conduct an employee survey. Especially in small and medium-sized companies, I tend to respond with the question "Why do not you just talk to your people?" I am of course aware of the concerns. Do the employees really say what they think? What about the objectivity and comparability of the statements? After all, structured surveys provide figures that can be compared in all directions.

But I do not know any CEOs and executives who regularly invite groups of employees for breakfast, a fireside chat or other occasions, and who have then ever regretted it. Of course, these formats require trust, just as leadership requires trust overall. If such conversations are not possible, there seems to be a more fundamental problem in the organization. It remains to be seen whether an anonymous employee survey will lead to better results.

> Honest answers within the scope of an employee survey are obtained above all through direct, trusting dialogue. That also conveys honest interest. (3-2)

In classical employee surveys it is not uncommon that even teams of less than ten employees receive their own report with the aggregated statements of the team members. As already mentioned, these teams are then asked to work with their results in the follow-up processes. I myself have too often experienced such employee survey follow-up workshops. I never doubted that a simple, spontaneous, moderated map query would have been more productive. "What is going well? What should we do better in the future?" All this paired with prioritization and an action plan. That would certainly have been much more effective and efficient each time.

Compatible Questions

The previous comparison of conventional employee surveys with their more agile alternatives of pulse surveys may have given the impression that the second variant is superior to the former in every respect. In fact, I have a critical view of the classic form of employee surveys, but I am of the opinion that questions are basically not disadvantageous as long as there is an honest interest in them and conclusions are drawn from the answers.

If a company now adheres to its classic form of employee survey, then it should at least align the contents of the survey in such a way that they are compatible with the desired understanding of leadership and organization. Because even the questionnaire and the questions it contains convey to the employees what is deemed to be important in a company and what is not. A common item in employee surveys, for example, is: "I receive clear instructions from my direct manager". Is it really the role of managers to give clear instructions? This question suggests that bosses are desirable in this company (see Sect. 4.4). Is that what you want? Almost all questions of Gallup's internationally popular Q12 have a hierarchical character. They are reminiscent of early phases of industrialization. Consider, for example, the question: "Last year I had the opportunity to learn and develop in my company". In any even rudimentarily agile company one will be surprised at this question. There they would perhaps be formulated as follows: "I have already learned something new today". So, do we need "opportunities" for learning? Work in itself is an opportunity. What does the period "in the past year" signal—apart from the fact that this period is understood differently depending on whether the question is asked at the beginning, in the middle or at the end of a calendar year? How can it be that someone hasn't learned anything in the past 24 h?

External consulting firms and institutes that offer their support as partners in the implementation of an employee survey almost always claim to accommodate their standard questionnaire. They do this because a lot of money can be earned with external comparisons (benchmarks). Often, however, these questionnaires have their historical origin in a time when one did not even know how to spell the term "agility". The practical, concluding hint is therefore to first talk to an external consulting firm about their understanding of leadership and organization and to clarify whether they are on the same page here.

Dinosaurs and Minimally Invasive Measures

There are two analogies that are often used and immediately understood by CEOs when comparing classic, traditional employee surveys with the type of alternative presented here. In the classic variant, there is often talk of "dinosaur surveys", not because dinosaurs are surveyed here, but because these measures are extremely costly and massive in relation to almost everything. All employees are asked about any conceivable content. Everyone receives reports that everyone can and should work with them. I want everyone to benefit somehow. In contrast, the alternatives presented here (see right side of Fig. 10.7) have a "minimally invasive" character. Here we focus on the essentials, quickly, flexibly and simply, without any noticeable side effects.

10.3 Employee Retention

With hardly any other HR-relevant topic is it so obvious which problem is addressed by it. Losing a high-performing, valued colleague to another company can be extremely painful for the team, or the entire company. At the same time, the costs of voluntary turnover can be determined relatively clearly. It is estimated that loosing an employee is approximately 0.5 to 3 times his or her annual salary (Phillips and Edwards 2009). The figure for the low-skilled is more likely to be 0.5 and for the high-skilled closer to 3. Sometimes the loss is dramatic, especially in key positions. Bill Gates once said about Microsoft: "Take out twelve specific people and Microsoft becomes a meaningless company" (Bartlett 2001).

At the same time, this topic seems difficult to grasp. At least I haven't met a company that would have an employee retention department in addition to training & development, compensation & benefits, recruiting or other typical HR functions. We know clear, practical approaches and concepts in almost all HR functions. Think of employer branding, assessment centres, compensation structures, performance potential matrix, etc. We do not have this in the context of employee retention. Nor do I know of a Head of Employee Retention. Even if he or she existed, what would his or her job description include? Intuitively, we know that employee retention has

Customers of the survey	**1-1 Broad group of stakeholders** Very different stakeholders benefit equally from our employee surveys.	**1-2 Selected stakeholders** In employee surveys, we concentrate on the focal points of a particular customer (stakeholder).
Priorities in terms of content	**2-1 Depending on results** We consider a wide range of topics. From the results of an employee survey, we then draw conclusions about the need for improvements and derive priorities.	**2-2 Pre-defined** In employee surveys, only those topics are taken into consideration that have a high priority even before the survey. Only what is important before the survey is also important after the survey.
Formats	**3-1 Anonymous and structured** Honest answers require anonymity in an employee survey. That is why we use structured questionnaires, which also makes it possible to compare the results.	**3-2 Open and interpersonal** Honest answers within the scope of an employee survey are obtained above all through direct, trusting dialogue. That also conveys honest interest.
Participants	**4-1 All employees** During employee surveys we always survey all employees. Our aim is to ensure the broad involvement of all employees.	**4-2 Samples** Only samples are asked to participate in employee surveys. This is sufficient to obtain representative results.
Time	**5-1 Long cycle** We conduct employee surveys in (multi)annual cycles. Anything else would be unacceptable in terms of effort.	**5-2 Continuous, on demand** We conduct employee surveys as often as necessary, if necessary continuously, every day.
Target group	**6-1 All employees at all levels** The results of an employee survey are intended for all employees and managers at all levels. A differentiation is made according to organizational units.	**6-2 Responsible for content** The results of an employee survey are only relevant to those stakeholders who are responsible for the content under consideration.
Dealing with results	**7-1 Complex follow-up processes** We regard follow-up processes as the most important part of an employee survey. The survey must lead to visible consequences at all levels.	**7-2 Part of regular processes** The results of employee surveys must be a natural part of continuous decision-making processes. Otherwise, they eke out a shadowy existence.

Fig. 10.7 Overview of all strategic dimensions of the employee survey

something to do with everything: with leadership, with corporate culture, career perspectives, salary, teamwork, working conditions and much more. In this respect, there is only a very small degree of institutionalization in most companies with regard to this topic in particular.

It seems all the more crucial to at least develop an attitude on how to deal with *voluntary turnover*. Indeed, there are significant differences between companies here. You could retain your spouse by locking him or her up or by loving him or her. Employees who voluntarily leave the company can be seen as traitors or as opening up an opportunity. One can erect walls around employees or assume at the interview that they will of course move on after several years anyway. This subchapter deals with contrasting perspectives of this kind. It becomes apparent that depending on the perspective, depending on the attitude, different practices are the obvious result.

Individual and Universal Preferences

Retaining employees means making an effort to attract employees. The bottom line is to experience more attractive conditions in the current company than with another employer who keeps the door open. What is attractive and what is not is decided solely by the individual employee as it was outlined in Sect. 10.1. Average observations, as they are common in science or in the context of people analytics, only do little justice to the individuality of personal preferences and life situations. So anyone who wants to retain employees must understand what is important to them in detail and to what extent an employer can relate to this. Industrial and organizational psychology refers here to the so-called *psychological contract* (Rousseau 1995). There is a give and take between employee and employer that must be attractive for both sides. This is not only about the formally agreed upon things, such as working hours, salary, etc., but primarily about unwritten things, such as meaningfulness, trust, learning opportunities, social relations, opportunities for development, contents that would hardly be recorded in a written contract, but which nevertheless play a decisive role in the thinking and experience of the employees.

Because dealing with the individual preferences of employees can be very time-consuming, many companies tend to concentrate on those employees for whom this effort seems to be worthwhile when it comes to employee retention. The guiding question in the selection of these employees is: "Who do we not want to lose under any circumstances?"

> When it comes to employee retention, we concentrate on those employees who are of above-average value to the company and difficult to replace. Anything else would be a waste of time. (1-1)

In fact, the return on investment is highest here. We know that it is more the high-performing employees who voluntarily leave a company (Livingstone 1994). At the same time, the *turnover costs* for high-performing employees, particularly talented high-potential employees, and employees in key positions, are higher than for other employees in the same organization.

Nevertheless, we can assume that certain things are important to everyone. We accept universal preferences. People want recognition. People search for meaning. More money is more attractive than less money. People prefer a trusting social environment to a social context marked by resentment. If a company sees things that way, it will come to somewhat different conclusions with regard to employee loyalty:

> Individual, particularly important employees can only be retained in the company if all employees are treated well. (1-2)

For some companies, focusing on certain groups of employees is inherently strange. They regard their companies as a system of interdependent tasks and roles (see Sect. 4.5). The workforce views them holistically as a team that either loses together or fails together. These companies therefore concentrate on the cultural and structural framework conditions as a whole:

> Employees remain with the company if the cultural and structural conditions of the company as a whole are right for them. (2-2)

A particular focus in this company is on the social relationships between employees and teams. This is based on an assumption that seems very powerful, but at the same time has received little attention in the literature on employee retention. Many advantages of an employer are basically interchangeable. If an employee moves from one employer to another, the employee takes his or her salary with him or her. He or she exchanges one responsibility for another or a comparable one. He or she had a company car before and after. Frequently, it is not even necessary to change location. But what an employee can never take with him or her are the social relationships he or she has established with his or her previous employer. Those who change companies leave their colleagues—often friends—behind. What remains are social contacts on LinkedIn and the intention to "stay in touch somehow". In reality, this intention is rarely fulfilled to the extent that it was initially aimed for. Most people know that.

Hierarchically thinking companies, on the other hand, delegate employee retention to their managers and thus reduce social relationships to the one between the employee and his or her direct manager. It is precisely in these companies that one repeatedly hears what is probably the most quoted "wisdom" on the subject of employee loyalty: "People join companies and leave bosses".

> Employee retention is a matter for the direct manager. At this level, our investments pay off. "People join companies, and leave bosses." (2-1)

Whether a company focuses on individual or universal preferences, whether it focuses on individuals or on the overall framework, whether it holds the CEO or the individual supervisor accountable, there are no conflicting options. One can certainly combine these perspectives. However, it is worth becoming aware of these options as a company and reflecting on how much one would like to adopt from which point of view.

The Analysis Versus Forecast of Voluntary Fluctuation

One of the few very common best practices in connection with employee retention is the so-called *exit interview*. Once an employee has voluntarily resigned, he or she is asked to answer questions about his or her resignation. This is done either by means of a questionnaire or a structured interview with a third party. The idea behind it is simple. You want to understand the reasons for the termination and know where the employee is going and why. One learns something about competition in the labour market and in the best case can derive improvements for one's own working conditions. This is an attempt to live up to the claim of being able to derive consequences for avoiding future fluctuation.

> When an employee leaves us (suddenly), we want to understand the reasons for this step. This is why we conduct exit surveys, among other things. This helps us to avoid turnover in the future. (3-1)

As obvious as this method may seem at first, it is problematic. This scenario has a somewhat derogatory character, especially when the exit survey is carried out using questionnaires. Imagine a man who has been abandoned by his wife and he sends her a questionnaire. A separation may deserve a little more attention and dialogue—in private as well as in professional life. The even more significant problem with this approach, however, is that the survey simply takes place too late, namely after the employee has already quit. An earlier interest could even have prevented the termination.

It is often more important to know, or at least to have a hunch, who wants to leave the company in the future or who actually does in the end. In contrast to looking back with exit interviews, there are a number of very different types of prognosis. A simple method of risk assessment is to classify all employees of a team or department, for example, according to the probability and damage of voluntary turnover. A result can then be displayed as indicated in Fig. 10.8.

Employee A is an employee whom you do not want to lose under any circumstances, but who at the same time is assumed to be very loyal to the company.

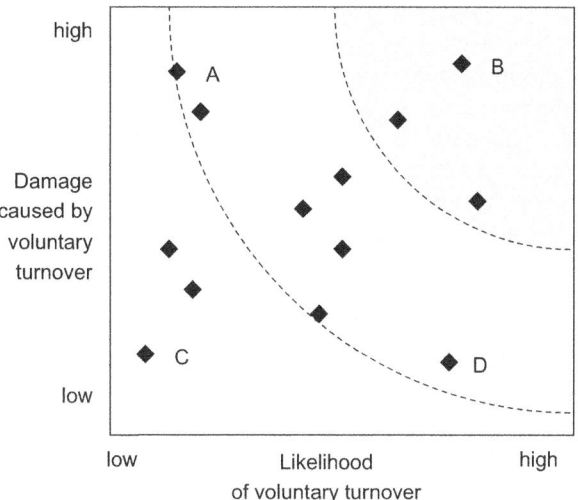

Fig. 10.8 A simple form of risk analysis

It is more risky with employee B. He or she is assumed to have a high *turnover intention*, sometimes referred to as *flight risk*. At the same time, the consequences of him or her quitting his or her job would be dramatic. With C you do not have to worry and with a voluntary departure of employee D you could probably live.

The exciting question now is how to assess the probability of individual flight risk. In some companies this is done in an empathetic way. You know the people. You tal to them. There may be openness about their future plans and visions. However, experienced managers are also aware of the specific signs of upcoming voluntary turnover. One thinks here of performance slumps, the constant praise of other companies, voluntary social separation etc.

> When an employee quits his or her job, it should never surprise us. Such a step is announced beforehand. We know about it a long time in advance and talk about it openly and constructively. (3-2)

This strategic statement suggests an attitude that regards an imminent voluntary termination as an interpersonal matter. Here a person intends to change a professional relationship with other people. Companies that think and act in the categories of networks, teams, mutual trust, leadership based on partnership cannot and will not do otherwise and avoid formal tools that convey the superficial impression one should be interested in the concerns of employees but at the same time keeps a distance to them.

> We regard an imminent voluntary turnover as a matter that we want to deal with in an interpersonal and cooperative manner. (4-2)

On the other hand, the current discussion on the significance of digitization and artificial intelligence in HR takes a completely different view. Anyone who is currently involved with *people analytics* will inevitably come across a typical application example with regard to employee retention. By accessing a large amount of employee-related data (big data), algorithms are developed that can use machine learning to increasingly accurately predict when which employee will quit his or her job voluntarily. A wide variety of data can be considered relevant here: the new profile picture on LinkedIn, absences due to brief illnesses on Mondays or Fridays, visits to job boards on the Internet, the quantity and quality of communication with colleagues and much more.

> Our aim is to be able to predict who will leave us and when by using extensive data (big data), artificial intelligence and algorithms. (4-1)

It is astonishing with what unrestrained euphoria more and more protagonists of the new discipline people analytics rave about such scenarios. Hierarchically thinking companies may share this excitement.

Is Voluntary Fluctuation Really a Problem?

There are numerous companies with extremely low *turnover rates*—less than one per cent. This reflects the amazingly high loyalty of the employees to "their" company. Employees who spend their entire working life in one and the same company are completely normal there. CEOs of these companies are not always completely happy about this circumstance. "Most employees have never seen anything other than our company," they say. Or: "A healthy fluctuation would actually be not too bad", whatever the term "healthy" might mean in this regard. The language then often comes to the much quoted "fresh blood", impulses and perspectives from outside.

> We benefit from fresh perspectives and ideas from new employees. Therefore, we consciously want to allow, and cope with, a "healthy" level of voluntary turnover. (5-2)

Things are quite different for other companies. They see voluntary fluctuation as a threat or even a disease that needs to be combated. You can hear them say in times of shortage of skilled workers: "Our problem is not recruiting good employees. Our problem is to retain good employees".

> We benefit from the many years of experience of our employees. That is why we want our employees to stay with us as long as possible. A low turnover rate is a good turnover rate. (5-1)

This attitude is more than understandable in view of the sometimes high turnover costs. Companies experience the situation particularly dramatically when they have to cope with their departure after many years of investment in the training and further education of their employees.

In addition to this financial, objective view, however, emotional perspectives also seem to play a role. Especially in extremely hierarchically managed companies, managers implicitly claim that their employees belong to them. This is dominated by a kind of dependency relationship between employees and their employer. In a way, employees are expected to be grateful that they have been accommodated in the company. From the payment of a good salary, managers infer the right to dispose of their employees. Admittedly, this is a very traditional view. My impression, however, is that at least traces of the same can still be found in many companies. Executives who actually think this way expect loyalty from their people. This is the implicit content of the psychological employment contract. If this contract is broken by the employee, the relationship is terminated forever. These employees may not necessarily be directly referred to as traitors. In the treatment of these employees, however, this is the view and attitude that shines through.

> We expect loyalty from our employees. When employees move to competitors, we consider permanently terminating the relationship with the respective employee. (6-1)

While in one company leaving employees are interviewed by independent third parties about the motives of their decision within the framework of an exit interview, in another company the CEO invites the future ex-employee to a personal interview. It is less a matter of the employee's motives for terminating his employment than of the possibilities for future cooperation. Admittedly, this conversation is only scheduled if a corresponding future potential for collaboration is assumed possible.

Management consultancies have always had an extremely high turnover rate, which is understandable. Many young consultants never intended to work in this industry for more than 3–5 years, especially if they want to see their children grow up at some point. Management consultancies know this and adjust to it. When consultants voluntarily leave their company, they often move to current or potential customers. This is precisely where there is an outstanding opportunity to establish and maintain diverse contacts with the industry, for example via an *alumni network*. I myself am part of the SAP Alumni Network, a wonderful community of former SAP colleagues from whom SAP itself probably benefits the most.[3] Here employees, customers, partners, suppliers or simply multipliers meet regularly.

> We see an opportunity in every employee who voluntarily leaves us. They become valuable partners, customers, suppliers or multipliers. We systematically maintain contact with them. (6-2)

One of the best things that can happen to an employer are employees who leave the company and return after a while. These employees come back more mature than when they left. Basically, this is a free form of continuing education. Companies that actively promote the recovery of former employees now speak of so-called *boomerang hiring*. The easiest way to do this is to agree a return guarantee, coupled with a clear plan of how to stay in touch.

Retain Employees by Letting Them Go

If an employee voluntarily resigns from Amazon, he or she receives a bonus of several thousand euros regardless of his or her function or pay grade. Measures of this kind are also referred to as *paradoxical interventions*. Why should an employer reward a quitting employee for something that harms the company? Other companies pay a retention bonus to retain employees. Wouldn't that be more appropriate? From a psychological point of view, Amazon's approach is quite interesting and comparatively smart. It gives employees the message that they are free people and are not forced to stay with their current employer. "You are free and that is good." At the same time, this strategy conveys the idea that the well-being of people is a fundamental concern, even when it comes to leaving the company. The actual effect of this measure, however, is that it addresses the intrinsic motivation of the employees. Those who remain in the company obviously do not do this just for the sake of money. After all, every employee who stays, decides against this, quite large amount of money.

---

[3] https://alumni.sap.com/

10.3 Employee Retention

> We support employees who want to leave us voluntarily. Those who decide to stay do so because they really want it and from intrinsic drive. (7-2)

The classical approach works exactly the other way round. Think here of common forms of *Long-Term Incentives* (LTI). Here, attractive bonuses are offered to executives in particular if long-term performance targets are achieved. However, the real intention of these LTIs is to draw the attention of decision-makers to long-term rather than short-term goals. A desirable side effect is to keep managers for a relatively long period of time. The fact that executives who actually want to leave the company are consciously motivated to just serve their time is thereby consciously accepted. In my circle of acquaintances I know of enough such cases—"actually I should have to quit immediately, but I am still taking these damn LTIs".

> We offer employees (extrinsic) incentives. In this way, we try to compete successfully against our competitors in the labour market. (7-1)

However, extrinsic and intrinsic ways of retaining employees are not limited to financial incentives. On closer inspection, a multitude of other methods can be found in practice. Thus, there are still companies in which above-average activity on platforms such as LinkedIn is already interpreted as a latent violation of loyalty, while in other companies employees without such activities are not even hired. Many companies shy away from publicly presenting their teams on their websites because they fear attacks from headhunters.

> We specifically try to keep career opportunities away from our employees from the outside. (8-1)

There are companies with sophisticated defence strategies against executive search consultancies. This already begins with the training of receptionists, who must learn to recognize headhunters at an early stage and to keep these outside threats away from them. Other companies do not even try to erect walls around the workforce. They are deliberately open, partly for strategic reasons.

> We cannot and do not want to hide our employees from the outside, on the contrary. We can't hold those who intent to go anyway. (8-2)

They follow the attitude that good people who want to leave cannot be deterred by this. Here you often hear the motto: Retaining people by letting them go.

Threat to the Company Versus Interpersonal Confrontation

As the strategic options described above (an overview is provided in the Fig. 10.9) have shown, there are two conflicting attitudes when dealing with these issues. Some companies see voluntary turnover primarily as an entrepreneurial threat. Fluctuation is bad. You have to protect yourself from it. The main responsible persons are the

Focus	1-1 Employees of much value	1-2 All employees
	When it comes to employee retention, we concentrate on those employees who are of above-average value to the company and difficult to replace. Anything else would be a waste of time.	Individual, particularly important employees can only be retained in the company if all employees are treated well.
Accountability	2-1 Direct manager	2-2 Companies
	Employee retention is a matter for the direct manager. At this level, our investments pay off. "People join companies, and leave bosses."	Employees remain with the company if the cultural and structural conditions of the company as a whole are right for them.
Understanding Turnover	3-1 After a notice of termination	3-2 Anticipating
	When an employee leaves us (suddenly), we want to understand the reasons for this step. This is why we conduct exit surveys, among other things. This helps us to avoid turnover in the future.	When an employee quits his or her job, it should never surprise us. Such a step is announced beforehand. We know about it a long time in advance and talk about it openly and constructively.
Prediction of voluntary turnover	4-1 Based on data and analytics	4-2 Interpersonal
	Our aim is to be able to predict who will leave us and when by using extensive data (big data), artificial intelligence and algorithms.	We regard an imminent voluntary turnover as a matter that we want to deal with in an interpersonal and cooperative manner.
Dealing with voluntary turnover	5-1 Fluctuation as a problem	5-2 Fluctuation as an opportunity
	We benefit from the many years of experience of our employees. That is why we want our employees to stay with us as long as possible. A low turnover rate is a good turnover rate.	We benefit from fresh perspectives and ideas from new employees. Therefore, we consciously want to allow and cope with a "healthy" level of voluntary turnover.
Future relation to those who leave	6-1 Banishment	6-2 Networking
	We expect loyalty from our employees. When employees move to competitors, we consider permanently terminating the relationship with the respective employee.	We see an opportunity in every employee who voluntarily leaves us. They become valuable partners, customers, suppliers or multipliers. We systematically maintain contact with them.
Reaction on voluntary turnover	7-1 Extrinsic avoidance	7-2 Support
	We offer employees (extrinsic) incentives. In this way, we try to compete successfully against our competitors in the labour market.	We support employees who want to leave us voluntarily. Those who decide to stay do so because they really want it and from intrinsic drive.
Openness and demarcation	8-1 Protective wall	8-2 Opening
	We try to keep career opportunities away from our employees from the outside.	We cannot and do not want to hide our employees from the outside, on the contrary. We can't hold those who intent to go anyway.

Fig. 10.9 Overview of all strategic dimensions concerning employee retention

direct managers. Voluntary turnover results in banishment. An individual discussion before and after the dismissal hardly takes place. Other companies see career change as something normal. They respect this and see opportunities in it, even if they are not always happy about the departure of a valued colleague.

References

Allen TJ, Henn GW (2007) The organization and architecture of innovation. In: Managing the flow of technology. Butterworth-Heinemann, Burlington, VT

Bartlett CA (2001) Microsoft. Competing on talent (A). Harvard Business School, Boston, MA

Bowers DG (1973) OD techniques and their results in 23 organizations. J Appl Behav Sci 9(1):21–43

Byrne ZS (2015) Understanding employee engagement: theory, research, and practice. Routledge, New York

Cascio W, Boudreau J (2008) Investing in people: the financial impact of human resource initiatives. Pearson Education, Upper Saddle River, NJ

Collinson DL, Hearn J (1995) Men managing leadership? Men and women of the corporation revisited. Int Rev Women Leadersh 1(2):1–24

Combi C (2015) Generation Z: their voices, their lives. Hutchinson, London

Edwards JR, Rothbard NP (2000) Mechanisms linking work and family: clarifying the relationship between work and family constructs. Acad Manag Rev 25:178–199

Harter JK, Frank L, Schmidt FL, Haye TL (2002) Business-unit-level relationship between employee satisfaction, employee engagement, and business outcomes: a meta-analysis. J Appl Psychol 87(2):268–279

Jackson EJ, Schuler RS (2012) Strategic human resource management. Blackwell, Malden, MA

Livingstone W (1994) Another look at the relationship between performance and voluntary turnover. Acad Manag J 37:269–298

McCarthy A, Darcy C, Grady G (2010) Work-life balance policy and practice: understanding line manager attitudes and behaviors. Hum Resour Manag Rev 20:158–167

Phillips JJ, Edwards L (2009) Managing talent retention. an ROI approach. John Wiley, San Francisco

Rousseau DM (1995) Psychological contracts in organizations. Understanding written and unwritten agreements. SAGE, Thousand Oaks, CA

Tapscott D (2008) Grown up digital: how the net generation is changing your world. McGraw-Hill, New York

Trost A, Jöns I, Bungard W (1999) Mitarbeiterbefragung. Weka, Augsburg

van Mierlo H, Rutte CG, Seinen B, Kompier M (2001) Autonomous teamwork and psychological well-being. Eur J Work Organ Psy 10(3):291–301

Watkins J (1959) The 100 greatest advertisements 1852–1958: who wrote them and what they did. Dover, New York

HR Operation 11

Successful HR requires institutional framework conditions and an infrastructure. This includes, among other things, an adequate HR organization, a functioning information technology and appropriate usage of key figures. That is what this chapter is about. In this respect, the following pages are less concerned with approaches and concepts that contribute to solving HR-related challenges as described in the previous chapters. Rather, this chapter deals with the question of who is responsible for implementation and operation, what role digital technology or digital HR plays in this and to what extent key figures and people analytics are essential for success. What is crucial here is that these institutional framework conditions and the infrastructure in agile organizations are set up and used in a completely different way than is the case in organizations striving for stability.

11.1 HR Organization

This subchapter focuses on the question of who is responsible for HR-related questions, challenges and tasks in a company. While the previous chapters dealt with key HR topics and their possible strategic alignment, in the following we turn to HR organization, a topic that concerns infrastructure. In this respect, we are moving from this point in the book to another level. In the following, a widespread and traditional view of HR organizations will be presented. In the course of this subchapter we then move on to an alternative view.

Personnel Department

There is a widespread idea of what constitutes an HR organization that can be described as naive, even though it may still apply to some small and medium-sized enterprises. Accordingly, the HR organization includes all those employees who work in the *personnel department*. If you want to visit someone from the personnel department, you have to go to the administration building, second floor, back left. There you'll find the nice colleagues (mostly woman) from the "personnel office" or "payroll office". The people there just take care of everything administrative that somehow has to do with personnel: Payroll, new hires, employment contracts, etc.

The guiding principle in distinguishing the HR department from the rest of the organization has always been to keep all HR-related matters away from those who contribute in the real business, the business line. Each area is supposed to takes care of its own affairs. The marketing department takes care of advertising, the accounting department everything to do with money, the purchasing department procures what you need to work and the personnel department takes care of everything that revolves around people.

> HR-relevant tasks are a matter of the personnel department. In this way, it provides the business with the freedom to carry out their tasks. (1-1)

This requires experienced professionals, colleagues who, for example, have focused on HR during their studies or have gained experience in this profession over many years. There is a similar, widespread opinion with regard to HR as there is with regard to marketing, according to which somehow everyone can do this and in fact everyone has something to say. However, when it comes to labour law details or aspects of compensation systems, most colleagues outside HR tend to react narrowly. The professional development of an employer brand requires skills that are not acquired overnight. The same applies to the development of a talent management system and other comprehensive HR concepts. As in other functional areas, professionals are needed to cope with complex challenges.

> As in other functions, we also need HR experts with many years of experience in a specific subject area. (2-1)

So it is not surprising that whenever a more complex HR-related concept is to be discussed in a workshop, for example, HR experts—professionals—usually meet among themselves. *Inside-out* is the predominant principle in the development and implementation of new concepts. At first, ideas, processes, systems, rules, instruments, for example in connection with compensation systems or talent management systems are thought through to the end. They are then rolled out into the organization. You mainly think from the inside out.

Dave Ulrich and the Three-Pillar Model

Then, in 1997, Dave Ulrich appeared on the scene and with his book "Human Resources Champions" brought the HR world another step forward (Ulrich 1997). He argued that HR must provide both strategic thinking and administrative excellence. He further argued that different HR-related challenges also require different

11.1 HR Organization

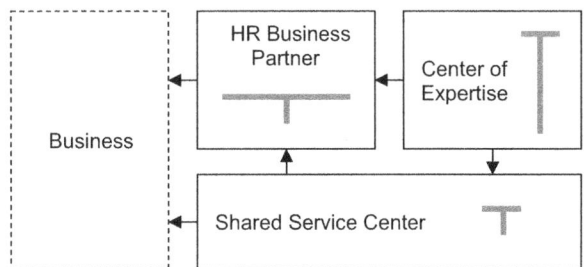

Fig. 11.1 The three-pillar model of personnel organization

functions within an HR organization. Some take care of administrative things while others take care of strategic matters. Finally, Ulrich's valuable impulse led to the well-known *three-pillar model*, which became a blueprint of their HR organization, especially for larger companies (see Fig. 11.1).

All in all, the business line is seen as a kind of customer of the HR organization. They are initially served by the so-called *HR Business Partners*. They are regarded as contact persons for all HR-relevant questions and challenges on a predominantly strategic level. In the sense of the T-concept, they have above all a very broad spectrum of knowledge and experience (horizontal bars), which is why they were also aptly described as HR generalists in earlier times—although HR generalists and HR business partners are not identical in their understanding of roles. The *Center of Expertise (CoE)* comes into play as soon as complex topics appear on the agenda that above all require technical or factual depth (vertical bars). Here you will primarily find specialists who are particularly well versed in one or a few areas of HR—specialists in labour law, variable compensation schemes, expatriation, employer branding, executive development, etc. Normally, the CoE does not have direct access to the business line. Rather, they pass the balls on to the HR business partners. In addition to supporting HR Business Partners in special matters, they have an influence on what is done in the *Shared Service Center*. The latter take care of all standardized, administrative, repetitive tasks in the context of HR (payroll, applicant management, etc.). In this way, they provide services to employees and managers in the business line as well as to HR Business Partners. In order to take advantage of economies of scale, these tasks are usually bundled for several business units or countries and finally shifted to low-wage countries. Here the principle of cost efficiency applies primarily.

> As in other functions, we also pursue a division of labour and separation of tasks in HR. This enables us to achieve professionalism and efficiency. (3-1)

For many companies, this step towards the three-pillar model represented a significant milestone towards a new level of professionalism. However, this was not the final answer to the question of how to operate internationally with personnel matters, even if parts of administrative personnel work had already been bundled across countries (cf. Sect. 3.6, International HR strategies).

On the Way to Global HR

In many companies, a history from being a local to a global player often repeats itself according to the same pattern (see also Bartlett and Ghoshal 1998). In the early days, companies usually operated locally. The founder of Amazon Jeff Bezos also started locally by delivering books personally and by bike. SAP's first customer, the chemical fibre plant ICI, was located in the small German village Kraichgau, not far from the company's headquarters in Walldorf. As soon as a company supplies customers beyond the national border, it becomes *international*. One acts increasingly into the world, however from a central homeland focus. Resources, such as products, ideas and values, are carried out from an experienced centre. Companies that are in this phase will eventually have colleagues dealing with "International HR". However, their main task is first and foremost the administration of foreign assignments or expatriations—one notices that the word "foreign" is still used in this phase.

Over the years, small HR organizations have been set up in various countries to deal with local HR-related issues. In most cases, this involves purely administrative tasks relating to the recruitment and remuneration of employees—Hire & Pay. In the company headquarters, one is glad that colleagues on site take care of all these matters. You leave them alone and let them go and do things. Often the HR managers in the headquarter do not even know the HR managers in the branches, but this is not regretted either. In this phase, a company acts *multinationally*. The units act autonomously and thus do justice to the principle of local differentiation. All this is changing in the course of a more global orientation of the HR organization. Once HR gets *global*, the principle of global integration is followed. The company is now seen as a single unit in which one tries to define common, uniform approaches in a spirit of partnership, usually moderated by representatives of the headquarters.

The development from an international to a multinational company is usually gradual, while the leap to a global company for HR requires special, strategic efforts.

The Leap to Global HR

Very often I hear statements such as "We already have a functioning talent management system at our headquarter. Now it is a matter of getting the concept to run worldwide". An employer positioning has already been developed for Germany, but everyone still does what they want in the countries. The internal learning platform is already being well used at the headquarters. In the local branches on other continents, this platform is literally ignored. There are very different forms of annual performance appraisals in the group worldwide. Then one hears globally thinking HR managers saying: "Our problem is the lack of uniformity". Countless times, however, I have also discussed HR strategies with decentralized HR teams in a business unit and have learned almost as often that certain things cannot be regulated differently because this or that is prescribed by the corporate headquarters.

Section 4.4 dealt intensively with different leadership roles. It became clear that the roles of boss, coach, partner and enabler can be distinguished. This distinction

11.1 HR Organization

has been developed and described in relation to managers and how they interpret their way of acting. However, you can also extend the scope of these roles and apply them to central units within a global HR organization. Specifically, this raises the question of what role, for example, a corporate HR function plays in the headquarters of an internationally operating company. In hierarchically managed organizations, central HR units seem to have a tendency to act as bosses for HR teams in countries and divisions. More or less they dictate to the decentralized units how they have to do their HR-related work. They do not do this because they think they are better, but because there are some good reasons:

- Executives and project managers with internationally distributed teams leading employees in different countries want uniform HR-relevant processes, tools and services.
- Some external target groups and internal target functions are global in nature. Thus, in the context of talent acquisition for some global positions in the company, suitable candidates will be sought globally. Executive development will have to be carried out globally on the upper levels because the topic and the participants are international.
- Global bundling and standardization of processes and services generates economies of scale and thus contributes to efficiency.
- In some cases, there are already global regulations and policies that have to be met in HR, regardless of HR-relevant issues. Compliance rules are an example here.
- It is not uncommon for a company to be forced to agree on uniform standards when introducing information technology. Cloud solutions in particular allow little room for local customization (see also Sect. 11.3).

All these arguments have led many companies in the past to commit themselves to the following premise:

> We centralise HR-relevant tasks and responsibilities as far as possible. This enables us to achieve efficiency and uniformity. (4-1)

The extent to which companies act in terms of regional differentiation or global integration in their HR work is rarely decided by HR alone. The balance of power between local units and the company headquarters is of overriding importance (cf. also Bartlett and Ghoshal 1998). Globally thinking companies act fundamentally differently than multinational or international companies. However, this applies not only to HR but also to other disciplines such as marketing or finance.

Obligated to the Head of HR

A characteristic of HR organizations within hierarchical and static companies is that they themselves are hierarchically structured. Even if the HR Business Partners serve as strategic partners to their internal customers in the business line, they often report to the Head of HR Business Partner, who in turn reports to a higher-level HR Executive, who eventually reports to the *CHRO*. A direct exchange between HR and the head of a business unit is only possible at the highest level, for example in the executive board. Section 4.5 dealt in detail with the question of who employees and teams are committed to. It became clear that especially in hierarchical companies a primary obligation towards the next higher management level is the default setting. Not only the orders or instructions come from there, but also the consequences for successful and less successful work. In hierarchical HR organizations, this is precisely the case.

> Employees in the HR department are first and foremost committed to their next higher management and finally to the management. (5-1)

So if, for example, employees in HR marketing develop a new campus recruiting campaign or colleagues in training and development work on a competence management project, they will discuss their results with their higher boss within HR until he or she is satisfied. Only then can he or she carry the results to his or her boss, who in turn to his or her boss and so on. For employees who have been socialized in hierarchically thinking companies, this logic is completely normal.

HR Organization in Agile Companies

Now, more and more so-called thought leaders are appearing on the stage who are of the opinion that HR should be completely dissolved as a separate function and all HR-relevant tasks should be transferred to the business line. Even if there are companies that practice this successfully, this book will only take up this approach as an extreme, radical variant. For most of the companies I have in mind, this approach would be too radical. Nevertheless, the premise of agile companies stretches towards this idea:

> HR-relevant tasks are taken over as far as possible by the business lines themselves. They know best what is good for them. (1-2)

This raises the question of what can actually be taken over by the business lines and what cannot. As always, the answer here is: It depends. In the following, therefore, a model deviating from the one proposed by Dave Ulrich will be presented that might function better in a more agile context and under the assumption of responsible employees and managers. Two factors will be taken into account when designing a modern HR organization. Both factors are discussed in detail below.

The first factor deals with the *social dynamics* associated with HR-relevant tasks and approaches. Here, for example, the difference between HR and logistics becomes clear. Packages do not think and feel. But employees do. The latter react in their own way to everything we do in the HR context and these reactions can be functional but also dysfunctional. The second factor deals with the *factual complexity* of an HR-related topic, activity or challenge. There are activities in HR that are very simple, such as posting a job advertisement. However, there are also topics and activities that can only be understood and carried out by real, experienced professionals because they are particularly complex, dynamic and interwoven. Both factors, social dynamics and factual complexity, are considered in more detail below. Finally, implications for the design of an HR organization are derived according to these two factors.

Social Dynamics

It is in the nature of what we do as part of HR that people are affected by it. These employees and managers are not only objects of HR but also thinking, feeling and acting players. Regardless of whether compensation systems are developed or changed, talents identified and promoted, applicants selected, employees retained, employees transferred, promoted, trained, rewarded, in the end everything you do always leads to a kind of social dynamic. It should not get immersed here too deeply into the world of system theories. Everyone who has worked in an organization knows from experience that HR-related activities, measures and programs always trigger emotions, fears, envy, resentments, hope, resistance, happiness and much more. All actions and reactions that take place on the basis of interpersonal relationships are called *social dynamics* here. Anyone who wants to be successful in the context of HR, even if only to a limited extent, must not only understand this particular dynamic, but also take it into account. It is certainly not always easy.

If you have seen many extensive HR concepts over many years, in numerous companies of different size and industries, then you must come to the almost tragic conclusion that HR concepts never work as they are supposed to work. I haven't seen an employee survey that has completely lived up to its promise. I do not know of any other company where the annual performance appraisal was accepted and implemented in the way it was intended to in HR. I do not know of any talent management that presents itself in reality the way it does on the slides of the HR manager and his consultants. Where did variable compensation systems motivate to the degree that was hoped for? Where are all those managers who are able to objectively assess competences in the way that competence management theoretically assumes? The list is infinite. A major reason for this is that the social dynamics associated with such concepts and ideas are rarely understood or predicted sufficiently well.

Not all tasks and challenges in HR involve a high degree of social dynamism. Numerous tasks are even of amazing simplicity. One thinks here of the posting of an existing job advertisement on one of the usual job boards on the Internet or the monthly payment of a long agreed monthly salary. These things must or can simply be done. They do not cause social turmoil or any other excitement from anyone in the organization.

However, other tasks are accompanied by very a high degree of social dynamics. This is always the case when employees are affected by existential issues or when it comes to the revaluation or devaluation of people—in whatever form. Examples of this are the relaunches of compensation systems, the implementation of management tools, the implementation of extensive organizational transformations, and the large-scale downsizing of an entire company. Sometimes measures lead to a social dynamic, which one would not have expected, because the matter seems marginal at first. A classic for such cases is the change in company car policies or the introduction of a transgender restroom.

This leads us to the first important principle of HR organization: You can only deal successfully with social dynamics if you make those affected responsible. This requires insiders who are familiar with the unwritten laws within an organization and thus have the necessary level of empathy for those affected. The higher the level of expected social dynamics, the more active the role of the business line must be in design, implementation and operation of any HR-related concept.

In many places, as in this book, I have repeatedly argued that an essential trap of HR is to start with a solution without knowing the problem and without considering the business context. This widespread HR trap is one cause of the failure of many concepts due to this special kind of ignorance. This, however, is not the focus of this subchapter. One possible cause that is to be examined here is the organization of HR itself. Dave Ulrich in particular stressed at the time that HR organizations must be able to do both administration and strategy. He also argued that there must be units within the HR organization that take care of one and the other units that take care of the other. This laid the foundation for a division of labour that led to the three-pillar model described above. Over the past 20 years, numerous companies have made considerable efforts to put this model into practice. Today, increasingly critical voices are being raised. The central problem of the three-pillar model is precisely that the business line does not appear in it. Basically, Dave Ulrich has structured HR silos with all its, partly dramatic, consequences, as indicated above. Of course, the three-pillar model assumes the employees and managers within the business line as customers, with whom the HR Business Partners in particular work in partnership. However, an active role of the business line with regard to HR-relevant issues is completely left out. So, the three-pillar model does not only manifest its own silo in differentiation from the neighbouring departments. Rather, the three pillars are also sometimes experienced in practice as three silos—one could also speak somewhat cynically of Dave Ulrich's "three-silos model".

Factual Complexity

In addition to social dynamics, *factual complexity* is another important and decisive dimension. There are tasks in HR whose completion requires only a low level of expertise or technical depth. They can be carried out without any problems after a short introduction. This includes posting (not developing) a job advertisement. Operating certain functions of HR software, creating (not negotiating) an employment contract, organizing (not conducting) a hiring interview. Accordingly, however, there are also questions and challenges that are characterized by a very high degree of factual complexity. For their treatment professionals, experts are necessary, who look back not only on an adequate education in their profession but also possess years of experience. This is where problems from a wide variety of disciplines, such as international law, technology and finance, can come together. Typical examples of challenges with a high degree of factual complexity could be the worldwide introduction of an IT system in HR or the development of a new remuneration system in an international corporation. But one also thinks, for example, of an expatriation with all their technical, legal and logistical aspects.

This leads us to the second elementary principle of modern HR organization: Experts are required to deal with issues of high factual complexity. These are people who can show real depth in a matter, which they have acquired through appropriate training and, or through many years of gaining experience. Sometimes you hear people say HR can be done by anybody. Especially in cases of high factual complexity, this hypothesis is just as wrong as the statement that anyone can transplant a human heart.

Roles in an Agile HR Organization

Combining the two dimensions of social dynamics and factual complexity results in a simple scheme, as shown in the Fig. 11.2.

Within this scheme, roles of an agile HR organization are outlined. We'll start at the bottom left. This area is comparable with the well-known Shared Service Centres. Here, simple, recurring and standardizable tasks, which are associated with low social dynamics, are performed according to defined performance

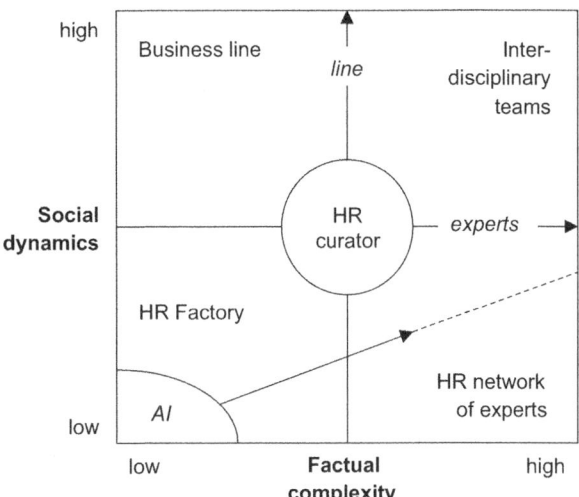

Fig. 11.2 Roles within an agile HR organization

standards. The term *HR factory* could well be used to describe this area. In addition, traditional HR information systems are used here to automate HR processes. Classic examples are payroll or the administration of incoming applications using so-called Applicant Tracking Systems (ATS). *Artificial intelligence* will increasingly assume tasks at this point. In the case of the HR factory, the question arises to what extent it should or must represent an internal unit of the company or whether this area can also be outsourced.

The lower right area represents the *HR network of expert*. This has a certain relationship to the CoE in the sense of the three-pillar model. However, the network of experts should deliberately not be understood as a kind of closed unit (centre), but as a network of internal and external specialists who can be deployed flexibly when and where they are needed. Just think of the external labour lawyer, the internal sourcing specialist or the executive coach. Nor should the impression be created here that these experts are part of the HR department. The organizational assignment is completely open here.

HR-relevant tasks, questions or challenges which have a high social dynamic, but which only require a manageable amount of expertise, belong to the *business line*. If you look at the activities of successful executives and CEOs, you will see that they spend most of their time dealing with HR-relevant issues anyway. The wonderful founder and former CEO of SAP, Dietmar Hopp, has always emphasized this by saying that he is the top HR manager in the company. Bill Gates has always considered it his primary responsibility to attract the most talented people to the company. Jack Welch, the legendary and former CEO of General Electric, essentially describes HR topics in his autobiography, which is well worth reading.

The upper right area of the figure above represents topics that are associated with a high degree of social dynamism and at the same time involve a high degree of factual complexity. Basically, this segment is comparable to the segments just described. Tasks that fall into this segment also belong to the business line. However, they certainly require the active support of experts from the HR network of experts already described. *Interdisciplinary teams* or project groups should therefore assume responsibility here. A closer look will reveal that the HR organization described above essentially consists of the HR factory and the HR network of expert. That is all.

> We primarily view the HR organization as a network within a broader corporate network. This way we avoid silo thinking. (3-2)

If companies are now striving to completely dissolve their HR department, then on the one hand they are considering an external HR factory, i.e. an administrative outsourcing partner, and on the other hand the demand-oriented commitment of external experts to complex technical issues. The rest belongs to the business line. What remains in the end is possibly an internal instance that coordinates the interaction of line, HR factory and network of expert in a certain way. One could speak of an *HR curator* here. It is possible that the HR curator will in future be the new role of the HR manager or what has been described so far as the HR Business

Partner. Based on this model, a number of important principles of HR organizations in an agile context are as follows:

- *People over Processes.* Interpersonal coordination is faster and does justice to social dynamics but also to factual complexity rather than rigid processes.
- *Simplicity.* What we do in HR should be as simple as possible, otherwise it will not be understood and lived by the relevant players in the business line.
- *No internal monopolies.* If the organization is dependent on only one HR function, this would result in a passive attitude in the HR function.
- *Consequences.* HR-relevant decisions should be made by those who ultimately have to bear the consequences of the decision.

In the following paragraphs these principles will be explained in more detail.

People Over Processes

In 2001, a prominent group of software developers published and signed the so-called *Agile Manifesto*, which has since been recognized and much quoted from as a kind of Ten Commandments for agile software development.[1] An essential element of the well-known Agile Manifesto is: *People over Processes.* This principle is comparatively simple. It propagates personal cooperation, fast, social coordination. It also assumes that social processes are faster and more adaptable than static processes can ever be. Dealing with social dynamics requires social exchange, from person to person, from team to team. It is remarkable that especially software developers, engineers of IT-supported processes, put this aspect so prominently in the foreground. One might rather suspects a high nerd density here.

According to my own observations, in HR, especially in large companies, HR managers tend to focus primarily on *processes*, especially on their colleagues from the traditional CoE (Center of Expertice)—one of the silos within the three-pillar model. This poses a real structural problem. In most cases, the employees from the CoE are organizationally separated from those social systems whose behaviour they want to determine by means of sophisticated processes. I have seen numerous companies where the HR Business Partners in particular make sure that their colleagues from the CoE do not come too close to the specialist departments. Obviously, territorial disputes can come into play here. This can have dramatic consequences for HR concepts. After all, it is usually the CoE in which complex HR systems are devised in connection with performance management, talent management, succession planning, competence management, job architectures, remuneration systems, etc. The complexity or complicatedness of these systems has already been discussed in Sect. 2.2.

---

[1]However, not ten commandments but only four premises are proposed here. The Agile Manifesto can be reached via the following link: http://agilemanifesto.org/ (Last viewed on April 30, 2019).

Sketching processes, systems and tools on PowerPoint slides is comparatively easy. However, it is extremely difficult, and for someone who is not part of the affected system is almost impossible, to understand its impact with regards to the social dynamics. A failure of the processes that are developed in CoE is extremely likely because the consequences of social dynamics are overlooked or underestimated due to a lack of involvement of the business line and a lack of interpersonal cooperation and coordination.

Simplicity

Experience has shown that HR managers who have been socialized in traditional organizations find it difficult to shift topics such as talent management, performance management, learning, succession planning and personnel recruitment all that easily to the business line. One might argue that a professional would have to take care of these things permanently. And, the topics are too complex to allow managers and employees to take responsibility for them on a permanent basis. First of all, the abilities of the line should not be underestimated. Secondly, as mentioned above, they are in a better position to cope with social complexity. Even if a high degree of social dynamic must be taken into consideration when developing a HR-relevant solution, the result, i.e. the solution itself, should be as simple as possible, otherwise it might not work in practice. This is another important principle. As soon as the logic and application of talent management, for example, appears to require too extensive explanations to managers, it has already failed. Topics and solutions are not introduced into the line because they are simple, but they must at least be simple at the core so that they are workable in the line at all.

No Internal Monopolies

In most cases, traditional personnel departments have a kind of monopoly position in their company. The business line has no choice but to make use of the services of this one department, and colleagues in HR are implicitly or explicitly aware of this. This may be one reason why it is actually wrong to speak of "customers" in this regard. After all, the latter have no choice. Every additional task or every additional project must appear to the HR departments as a burden that comes on top of the already existing work. The situation is quite different for external service providers. For them, every additional project is a new order, which of course is not only accepted, but also fought over. Monopolies have no competitors and those who have no competitors have no chance to really win. This structural problem can be solved at least in part by either outsourcing tasks from the HR department or by managing units in the HR organization as cost centres, which also includes the option that the business line can opt for the services of other, external providers.

One path that agile companies are increasingly taking is to shift HR-relevant tasks to the line. This has already been outlined in the above proposal. So that those employees who take care of these tasks within the line do not feel that they are permanently in a safe haven, they either take on this responsibility only for a certain period of time—2 or 3 years—or they take on this role only part-time. As already mentioned above, this approach also has the advantage that the employees concerned do not run the risk of losing sight of business reality. For those companies the premise is:

> It is important to us that employees only deal with HR issues for a limited period of time. Otherwise they tend to lose sight of business reality. (2-2)

This premise essentially applies to the line and the interdisciplinary groups outlined above. The situation is usually different for employees from the HR factory and for members of the HR expert network. It may also be advisable that these employees spend time in the line and spend some time in the shoes of the customers. This contributes to the internal customer orientation and to a stronger experience of the sense of their own activity.

Bear the Consequences of Your Own Actions

As already explained in detail in Sect. 4.5 an essential principle of agile enterprises is that employees and teams directly experience the consequences of their actions and decisions. This offers the opportunity to learn, and it also promotes responsible, customer-oriented outcomes. It is precisely this principle that is largely not adhered to by traditional HR departments. The opposite rather applies. Who bears the consequences of wrong selection decisions in the context of recruitment and selection? None other than the employees who ultimately work with the newly hired employee. Who will bear the consequences for talent management that may put the wrong candidates into leadership positions? Not the HR department. Who has to live with the deficits if the transfer of knowledge from training into everyday life is not successful? Not HR. This problem has structural causes in the way HR is organized and positioned in most companies. As already mentioned, HR managers in hierarchically thinking companies are primarily committed to their higher management bodies (e.g. to the CHRO). It would be advantageous if they received recognition from the line if they performed well and the opposite if they performed poorly. However, as soon as HR-relevant tasks are integrated into the line, this changes.

> Employees and teams involved in HR-related tasks are primarily committed to their internal and external customers. (5-2)

Employee referral programs, for example, are a common approach to talent acquisition that embraces this principle. They work so well because those colleagues who recommend their friends or acquaintances know that they have to live with the consequences of their recommendation. Recommending a candidate who later turns out to be a C-player can have negative consequences for the credibility of the recommender, which is why these programs are applied by employees in a very responsible manner. However, employee referral programs are only one example of how responsibility can be brought into the line. In addition, the following simple cases should be taken into account: Within a larger project group or a unit in the company, three employees declare their willingness to ...

- actively search for new employees in the labour market, to approach them and to attract them for their team
- take care of the successful integration of newly hired employees
- set up a development program to address a commonly identified learning need inside their team
- develop ideas on how variable bonuses can be distributed in the team in the future
- set up a kind of employee survey for the next strategy meeting, which should take into account critical aspects of the team's success.

What are these three employees like when they do not deliver to the satisfaction of their colleagues? There is no exit strategy here. They have to live with the consequences of their actions, which will inevitably spur them on to high performance. In addition, a constellation like this offers seeing the meaning, and it also gives the chance to learn from having experienced the consequences.

As Little Central as Possible

In the world view of employees in agile organizations who are concerned with HR-relevant questions, challenges and tasks, a central, higher-level HR function anchored in a headquarters hardly occurs. This is a logical consequence of the point explained above, lateral obligation. In hierarchical organizations, things are completely differently. Here, instructions come from the headquarters and the local HR managers feel obliged to follow the instructions from there. As already explained in the course of this subchapter, the focus here is on the tension between global integration and local differentiation (cf. also Sect. 3.6, International HR strategies). An example related to *employer branding* can be used to illustrate this. The diagram in Fig. 11.3 shows two relevant dimensions.

The *brand responsibility* dimension indicates who is responsible for the development of an employer brand, the headquarters (global, central) or the local units, countries or divisions (local, decentral). A distinction is also made between differentiated and uniform employer positioning (see also Sect. 5.1 on Employer branding).

In a hierarchically managed HR organization, only constellations A and B are considered. Either the headquarter develops a central employer positioning and defines the type of communication across all units (B). Or it makes the matter a little more elaborate and tries to take local peculiarities into account from a central point of view (A). In the end, it is all in the hands of a central instance. However, in

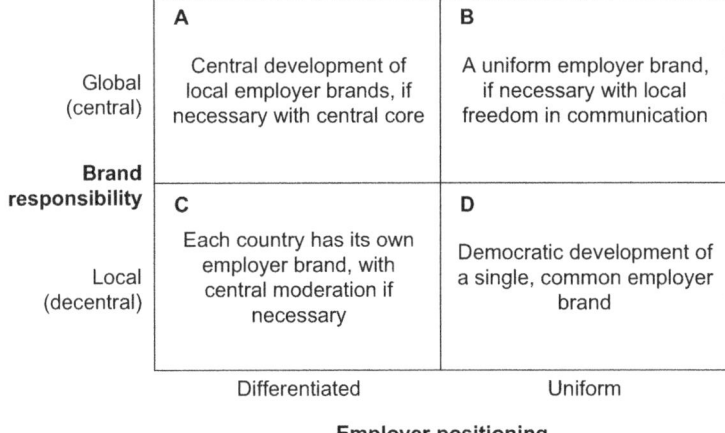

Fig. 11.3 Types of employer brands between central uniformity and local differentiation

an agile organization, this would be inconceivable. Here you act according to the principle:

> We only centralise tasks and responsibilities if this is desired from all or most decentral units. The headquarter sees itself as an enabler of decentralized instances. (4-2)

In the context of developing an employer brand, responsibility lies with the decentralized units. The consequence can be numerous employer brands under one common umbrella, which may be moderated and supported by a central unit—if the local units want (C). It does not have to happen. My own experience has shown that decentralized units also want something overarching and uniform overall. They often want a joint appearance because this leads to synergy effects and can save money in the end. Scenario D therefore offers an alternative. Here a common solution is developed according to democratic principles. In the end, the challenge is to develop a single employer positioning that is supported by all or the majority of all decentralized units.

With a little imagination, this example can be transferred to other HR-related issues, be it the development of a compensation system, talent management or, for example, the design of a global executive development program. The central CHRO, for example, has less of a determining, guiding function than a moderating role, which is much more difficult.

Back to the Business Line

In the course of the agilization of organizations, the trend towards shifting HR-relevant tasks to the line is clearly discernible. Most of the strategic dimensions discussed in this subchapter (see Fig. 11.4) point in this direction. However, the

Responsibility for personnel tasks	1-1 Primary HR department	1-2 Business line
	HR-relevant tasks are a matter of the personnel department. In this way, it provides the business with the freedom to carry out their tasks.	HR-relevant tasks are taken over as far as possible by the business lines themselves. They know best what is good for them.
Duration in HR function	2-1 As long-term as possible	2-2 Time limited
	As in other functions, we also need HR experts with many years of experience in a specific subject area.	It is important to us that employees only deal with HR issues for a limited period of time. Otherwise they tend to lose sight of business reality.
Organization of the HR Function	3-1 Division of labour	3-2 Network
	As in other functions, we also pursue a division of labour and separation of tasks in HR. This enables us to achieve professionalism and efficiency.	We primarily view the HR organization as a network within a broader corporate network. This way we avoid silo thinking.
Centralization	4-1 Maximum centralization	4-2 Minimum centralization
	We centralise HR-relevant tasks and responsibilities as far as possible. This enables us to achieve efficiency and uniformity.	We only centralise tasks and responsibilities if this is desired from all or most decentral units. The headquarter sees itself as an enabler of decentralized instances.
Obligation	5-1 Vertical	5-2 Horizontal
	Employees in the HR department are first and foremost committed to their next higher management and finally to the management.	Employees and teams involved in HR-related tasks are primarily committed to their internal and external customers.

Fig. 11.4 All strategic dimensions of HR organization at a glance

above remarks are far removed from the ever louder becoming appeal to abolish HR departments altogether. Even in highly agile organizations, there will always be colleagues who deal exclusively with HR-related tasks. In the case of challenges with high social dynamics and pronounced factual complexity, we will have to deal with other forms of team formation than we have done in recent years. Responsibilities move closer to the line. We will rather think in mixed networks where the lateral commitment to a vertical orientation will count more.

11.2 Key Figures and Control

It seems as if there has been a continuous hype about the topic of key figures in HR for years. HR managers report on situations in which they look enviously at their colleagues from the finance department and ask themselves: "Why can't I present our work so vividly on the basis of numbers?" The argument that HR is about people (not measurable) and not about things (measurable) has long since lost its weight. But also in the areas of finance, marketing or sales, assumptions are often made and the figures that are used or presented there are by far not as reliable as one might think as a naive student of business administration. So why does HR lag so far behind when it comes to the quantitative depiction of its own work? When the logistics manager is asked how many M8-30 recessed head screw he has in stock, he asks his system and knows the answer—2376. The HR manager, on the other hand, cannot even indicate how many employees in the company have English skills at a certain level. I even know HR managers who have to admit not knowing when asked about the number of employees in their company.

What You Can't Measure, You Can't Manage: Really?

Behind the perceived necessity of operating with key figures in HR there is a kind of overarching dogma that is unfortunately far too rarely called into doubt: "What you cannot measure, you cannot manage". That sounds logical at first. Managing means target-oriented and controlled action. And if you want to act purposefully, you need measurable goals supplemented by a control loop. Where am I going? Where are we at the moment? Are there any deviations? If so, what to do? All dynamic systems function according to this simple principle of cybernetic control loops. If you do not measure something, it indicates that you do not really have your thing under control.

> Professional HR requires extensive use of key figures. After all, you can't manage what you can't measure. (1-1)

This is why, in recent years, companies have put considerable effort into introducing, for example, a *balanced scorecard* in the sense of Kaplan and Norton (1996). This Balanced Scorecard provides four different fields to be considered equally (balanced): Processes, customers, finances and also the area of people (employees). For HR, it is a matter of defining specific objectives with regard to the people and of consistently substantiating these with *key performance indicators* (KPIs).

This dogma must be countered by another law, according to which most things can only be measured with considerable effort. A simple and at the same time obvious indicator is the number of employees in the company. Every company should know how many employees it employs. Hardly any annual report can do without this particular information. But if you want to determine this key figure, you have to know what an "employee" actually is. In the international context this is not so easy to define. Here one would have to be familiar with the very diverse, legal conditions of the most different countries and clearly limit which form of employment relationship is meant in the respective regions. What about freelancers? What about temporary workers? What about the long-term sick? To be an "employee", does this require a contractual agreement? So this number is determined in a pragmatic and in the usual way for headquarters. One sends one of the too many Excel templates to the respective contact persons in the regional branches and simply asks for the number of employees. While the colleague at the headquarters then consolidates the figures at some point, the colleagues in the countries hope that there will be no more scrutiny. But as they know, that happens very rarely. You always end up with a number, somehow.

I like to ask my students during my lecture: "Define application". Nobody knows what it really is. In many companies, HR professionals and recruiters will refer to the online recruiting system and count as an application everything that has been received there. But what about the numerous fake applications? Shouldn't inquiries and expressions of interest sent by e-mail directly to the departments also be included? What if a candidate knocks at the door by simply sending his or her LinkedIn profile via Facebook? "Hello, I would be interested to work with you. Here's my profile. Looking forward hearing from you. Greetings, Robert".

The valid determination of the famous *cost-per-hire* is almost impossible. Many years ago, I had the responsibility at SAP to determine this internationally. This turned into a project lasting for several months, although SAP was known to have a helpful SAP system in use. What do you consider when determining the cost-per-hire and where do you get the relevant information from? Figure 11.5 shows a number of possible components.

Of course, it is possible to allocate several costs directly to specific positions and their recruiting activities. This includes costs for job advertisements, executive search consultants, the use of selection tools, etc. However, general costs are not insignificant. In the broadest sense, these are fixed costs. Think of the development of an employer brand, the salaries of recruiters and all those involved in recruitment and selection. These costs would have to be allocated to all settings. After all, it is very difficult to estimate or even delimit additional intangible costs and losses.

Job-related costs	General expenses	Intangible losses
Advertising costs	Personnel costs for employees in the recruiting department	Opportunity costs related to those involved in the selection process
Travel expenses of the candidates	Share of personnel costs for managers involved in the selection process	Loss of coordination during coordination during the selection process
Costs for executive search		
Costs for the use of selection tools	Costs for recruiting team offices	Image losses due to rejections and bad candidate experience
Bonuses in the context of employee referral programs	Costs for technical recruiting infrastructure (license and support)	Loss of motivation due to hiring unsuitable candidates (alpha error)
Sign-on bonuses	Costs for labour market and target group studies	
Relocation expenses		
Costs for training new employees	Costs for the implementation of employer branding campaigns	
	Cost of participation in employer competitions and rewards	
	Costs for the development of an employer brand	
	Costs for the development of selection tools	

Fig. 11.5 Possible components of a cost-per-hire

11.2 Key Figures and Control

Even these seemingly simple variables "number of employees", "number of applicants" or cost-per-hire are obviously difficult to measure. The really important and best things can often not be measured at all. Talent can hardly be measured validly. The same applies to motivation, the innovative strength of a team and much more. Of course, you could measure these things *somehow*. I am scientifically socialized. In my academic career I have always dealt with the possibilities of measuring things, be it in my diploma thesis (The measurement of customer satisfaction in consulting projects) or in the context of my doctoral thesis (The measurement of lateral cooperation). I am convinced that with enough imagination and creativity you *could* measure almost anything somehow. At the same time, I am convinced that very little *can* really be measured in a sufficiently valid manner.

> The best and most important things in HR cannot be measured and we do not do it either. To try it nevertheless leads to inadequate simplifications. (1-2)

One of the most successful teams in human history was The Beatles. I've studied The Beatles up and down and read numerous biographies of their members. I never found a clue that the Beatles ever measured anything intentionally. At the most, they took notes of some things (sales figures, TV viewers, hit list rankings, etc.). The best things can often not be measured. If you try to do it anyway, you run the risk of reducing things, limiting them to a few indicators, and obscuring the whole picture. Personality is far more than what the personality test measures. Culture in a company is much more colourful, multi-layered, dynamic and complex than what a culture questionnaire reveals.

In the End, It Is All About Trust

A friend of mine who I greatly appreciate told me a wonderful story recently. I truly wish it had been my own story. When he had an appointment with his client, he paid a short visit to the HR department. He found some colleagues there, who rolled hundreds of personnel files into a meeting room. When he asked what they were doing, he got the answer: "We have to find out how many employees studied at Furtwangen University and because we do not have this information in the system, we now have to search through all personnel files". "And why do you want to know?" my friend curiously replied. "Our CEO asked for it. We do not know why." Then my friend met the CEO at lunch and he asked why he wanted to know how many employees studied at Furtwangen University. "I will soon be giving a lecture at Furtwangen University and I would like to mention how many graduates of this university we employ," he replied. My friend asked him how many engineers he employed. "About 150, I guess." "And how many employees come from this region?" "About a third." "Then I estimate that you employ about 30 graduates from the Furtwangen University," my friend said. "30?" the CEO replied in surprise. "I thought it might be around 40." Then my friend says, "You are right, it is probably 38." "That is right, 38. That should do it," the CEO responded with satisfaction.

Then my friend went back to the HR department and announced that the matter was now settled. You could now clear away the mountains of personnel files and go back to real work.

Scientific validity in the operationalization of an HR-relevant issue is one thing. Trust in one indicator is another. Of course, indicators are officially there to enable rational action based on objective knowledge. This is at least taught to our students in textbooks and at business schools. Reality is often completely different, as the above story shows.

Feedback or Control

Probably the question of *how* to measure something is overestimated. Much more important is the question of *what for* and *for whom*. This is followed by the distinction as to whether the use of a key figure is about feedback or about control. Unfortunately, it is precisely this aspect that is neglected in the practical discussion much too often. A simple example is given to illustrate this.

A recruiting team that deals with the task of hiring professionals pursues the goal of a low time-to-fill. Specifically, the period between the time a job is posted and the signing of the employment contract should not exceed 50 days. It is now less important how this key figure is measured and how meaningful it is. The decisive factor is rather who gets this figure and why. If the higher-level HR executive or even the executive board requests this key figure, then we are dealing with *control*. If this figure remains in the recruiting team and the recruiting team wants to know for itself how well it does its job, then using this figure is about *feedback*. HR organizations based on control pursue the premise:

> Key figures help executives at higher decision-making levels to control activities, processes and measures within HR. (2-1)

In hierarchically thinking organizations this view is self-evident. In most cases, the pressure comes from the top with regard to the use of key figures. However, it must be known that control can always result in a social dynamic that is in some way toxic or dysfunctional. To stick to the example above: If the work of a recruiting team is measured by *time-to-fill*, then the probability of the alpha error will automatically increase (see Fig. 5.9). One might accept mediocre B-candidates in order not to threaten the time-to-fill. In itself, this action is reasonable. Finally, one orients oneself towards the previously defined target values. All in all, other things that are not measured are excluded and loose importance. If you measure one thing, then you should also measure all other things that also somehow are significant. However, this is neither possible nor practicable. Here the unspoken principle applies, according to which a higher management level always receives the key figure that it demands, regardless of how good the performance represented by it actually is. On the left side of the Fig. 11.6 this mechanism of control is graphically indicated.

11.2 Key Figures and Control

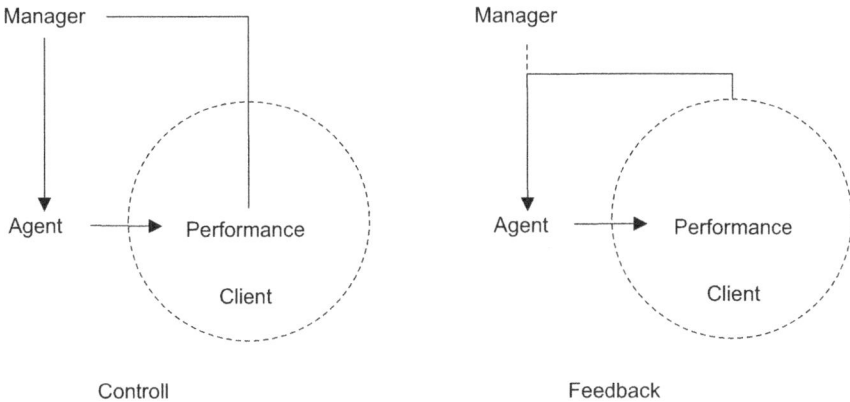

Fig. 11.6 Feedback and control

An agent (e.g. a team, a department or an employee) provides a service on the part of its client. This in turn is determined or measured by the agent's manager. The manager uses this insight to assess the performance of the agent. Here, control takes place on the basis of a key figure.

The right side of the figure shows the feedback mechanism. Here, too, the agent provides a service to the customer and then obtains feedback from the customer. The manager's task is merely to stimulate or ensure that this happens (see also Sect. 6.2, about Feedback).

> By means of key figures, teams that deal with HR-related issues independently reflect on the success of their work. (2-2)

Feedback leads to a completely different dynamic than control does. As already mentioned elsewhere, feedback works above all when the feedback recipient—here the recruiting team—collects his feedback itself, owns it and does not have to expect any external judgment and consequences.

Interesting and Relevant Key Figures

If you have previously summarized and documented key figures in a document, you would call it a "report". That sounds too bureaucratic to some ears. Today, modern companies prefer to speak of a so-called management cockpit—the dream of every executive. In fact, providers of business software advertise this specifically. They show astonished board members what they are able to see on their tablets at the tip of their fingers, in boundless granularity: ratio of women in management positions, offer acceptance rate, average span of control, takeover ratio after probationary period, promotion rate, number of applications per year, interviews-per-hiring, cost-per-hire, employer ranking, revenue per employee, turnover rate, average base pay, proportion of temporary employees, employee satisfaction, personnel expenditure rate, applicant satisfaction, transfer rate, employee referral rate, sick leave, training days per employee and year, time-to-fill, hiring rate, absenteeism rate, training expenditure per employee, hiring manager satisfaction, average length of service, internal placement rate, (early) turnover rate in the probationary period to name just a very few. Companies that want to do so probably also agree to the following strategic alignment:

> We use a broad spectrum of possible indicators because we want to map HR-related aspects as comprehensively as possible. (3-1)

Top decision-makers in these companies want a management cockpit that is as densely packed and as full as possible. Cockpits of this type convey control, overview and thus the feeling of security.

Now the question of the relevance of survey results has already been dealt with in connection with the subject of employee surveys (Sect. 10.2). It has been argued that results are only relevant—and not only interesting—when they are linked to concrete objectives that really matter. This consideration can be applied to figures in HR as a whole. Companies that want to focus on *relevance* (not just on what seems interesting) want a cockpit that is as empty as possible. If it were possible without any figures, that would be the ideal situation. They ask themselves three questions for each figure that arises wherever and whenever:

- Is there a concrete goal linked to this indicator?
- Is there a specific customer for this metric (e.g. a project manager, a team, a manager) who is responsible for the goal associated with the metric?
- In particular, do negative deviations in this figure lead to corrective measures in any case?

If even one of these questions were answered with "No", the figure would not be relevant, i.e. meaningless, and one could dispense with it with a clear conscience. Companies that take this idea seriously rely on this premise:

> We use as few relevant key figures as possible. Anything else leads to comprehensive reports that no one attaches any importance to. (3-2)

As already indicated in connection with the question of the measurability of facts, the regular determination of key figures can involve considerable effort. This is something that managers at upper levels in particular are not always aware of. One has to realize that this generation of key figures causes trouble but is not work in the true sense of the word. After all, no customer is willing to pay for this effort. Agile organizations do without key figures as far as possible. Even if a key figure is required in a critical phase, it is waived again when the storm is over. No sensible person would measure his body temperature several times a day. This is only done on days when you are plagued by fever. Some companies act as if they have or fear continuous fever.

Investment Calculations in HR Management

For a long time now, one has been hearing the appeal again and again that HR should speak the language of the CFO. For every Euro we invest in an employer brand: how much, in Euros, will be left at the end, after deduction of the costs, for the measure itself? What is the financial benefit for the company if it invests 20,000 euros per executive in their development? To what extent are HR executives able to answer such questions to the CEO *and* CFO? It is in line with the strategic alignment of HR to expect this in principle.

Of course, there are methods of how *investment calculations* can be carried out in the context of HR. In my book "Talent Relationship Management" I dealt with this topic quite extensively (Trost 2014). An important basis can be the *Human Capital Value Added* (HCVA, cf. Fitz-Enz 2009), which can be calculated comparatively simply on the basis of annual revenue, total costs, personnel costs and the number of employees in terms of full time equivalents (FTE):

$$HCVA = \frac{Revenue - (Total\ Costs - Personnel\ Costs)}{Full\ Time\ Equivalents}$$

The HCVA describes what an employee contributes on average to the value creation of a company. If you now assume that a development measure increases the productivity of a certain group of employees by 5%, you can calculate what this measure may cost. At SAP, I once argued that an employer brand would mean that the people we would attract as new hires would be 1% more productive than the people we would get without an employer brand. In view of the planned number of recruitments, the measure could not exceed one million euros per year. Investment calculations can therefore be carried out in the context of HR and these can be used as the basis for a decision that is as rational as possible.

> Investment calculations form a rational basis for investment decisions on a strategic level. (4-1)

At first glance, this strategic premise seems reasonable and rational. Probably whole armies of students of business administration learn that strategic investment decisions have to be justified in this way. With a view to practical reality, however, the question arises as to how decisions at the strategic level are actually prepared by means of investment calculations and how they are actually evaluated by decision-makers. In theory, an investment calculation is prepared in a neutral manner, taking into account as much relevant information as possible. Decision-makers are then in a position to interpret this investment calculation intelligently and evaluate it objectively. This results in a rational decision for or against a possible investment.

Evidence-Based Management

The company Safelite is a leading provider of windshield repair services in the USA. At the end of the nineties, the new CEO opted for a completely new form of remuneration. Instead of paying employees on an hourly basis, employees should in future be remunerated according to their actual performance. Basically, this is a piecework wage. The economist Eduard Lazear (2000) from Stanford University accompanied this measure scientifically. In fact, the performance and productivity of the employees could be significantly increased on the basis of this measure. Wages increased to a lesser extent than performance.

This example shows how the effect of HR-related measures can be scientifically tested. By means of so-called *evidence-based management,* attempts are made to make management decisions on the basis of empirical findings, a way of thinking that appears to be taken for granted in medicine or engineering, for example (Pfeffer and Sutton 2006). No reasonable doctor or patient would trust a drug whose effect has not been scientifically proven. However, at the same time it must be stated that HR in particular often makes decisions for measures whose effect is not scientifically, empirically evident. Does an employer brand lead to an increase in the number and quality of applicants? Are diverse teams really more productive? Does performance appraisal lead to a better relationship of trust between employees and managers? Do individual bonuses really prevent collaboration among colleagues? Questions of this kind are seldom based on one's own or already available scientific findings. But modern protagonists of evidence-based management demand, that exactly this must be done in order to be able to make really meaningful decisions (Morrell 2008). Companies that follow this claim therefore represent the strategic orientation:

> Wherever possible, we make evidence-based decisions on the basis of empirically tested effects. Anything else would just mean gut feeling based decisions. (5-1)

This claim is not new. Strictly speaking, t this approach led to the Renaissance of *scientific management* after it was developed by Frederik Winslow Taylor over 100 years ago. There are simple reasons why evidence-based management only has an extremely limited practical impact; the most important of which are methodological and pragmatic. For example, companies can only rarely carry out controlled and thus real experiments with randomised experimental and control groups. Therefore, in practice, but also in scientific publications, the application of regression statistical methods dominates, which regularly leads to confusing *correlation* with *causality.* Just because A correlates statistically with B does not necessarily mean that A is the cause of B. Just because there is a statistical connection between the conduct of performance appraisals and corporate performance does not mean that performance appraisals are the cause of corporate success. Often the cause-and-effect relationships indicate exactly the opposite or there are third variables and moderator variables that are responsible for the statistical relationship found. In addition, corresponding efficacy studies usually require more time and effort than appears practicable in reality. If the shortage of skilled workers is depressing and open vacancies cause acute pain, only a few companies will take the time to research the effectiveness of active sourcing strategies first.

A Profound Debate

However, a deeper-seated problem of evidence-based management lies in the fact that, on the one hand, the concepts and theoretical constructs examined often remain unclear and the question of the theoretical explanation of found effects is ignored. If, for example, a meta-study finds out that diversity only has a positive or negative effect on team performance under certain conditions, the first question is what is meant by diversity and what is meant by team performance (van Dijk et al. 2012). Secondly, it should be of interest, which theoretical cause-effect relationships are suspected, i.e. the question of "why". After all, good scientific work does not mean proving effects, but testing theories (Gadenne 1984).

In this respect, the discussion of theories leads to the opposite of evidence-based management. Advocates of the evidence-based approach persistently repeat that the opposite of evidence-based decision-making is to rely only on a diffuse gut feeling, to copy best practices without reflection, or to blindly follow trends. But they do a deep injustice to all those who do not make evidence-based decisions. Between evidence-based decision-making on the one hand and blind, not reflected reliance on intuition, best practices and trends on the other, there is a very common alternative that simply consists of dealing with a matter intensively, controversially and on the basis of assumptions made in the run-up to a decision.

> Measures and investments are decided on when we are convinced of their content. These decisions are preceded by controversial debates. (4-2)

Almost all considerations in this book are not evidence-based. For many of the statements and assumptions in this book, I cannot provide empirical evidence. When I argue in Chap. 5 for example, that the development of an employer brand and the implementation of a widely visible brand campaign makes no sense with narrowly defined target groups and a low budget, then this argument is not based on empirical findings, but on (hopefully) plausible considerations with deliberate consideration of various factors. This is an example of a theoretical examination of cause-effect relationships. Many HR professionals think that way—which I again cannot prove empirically, but I take the freedom to make these claims based on conclusions attained from my continuous dialogue with many practitioners.

Pre-mortem Analysis

A very effective and practical method for in-depth analysis is the so-called *premortem analysis*. From social psychology we know a group-dynamic effect, which endangers critical and controversial arguments. We are talking about groupthink. The psychologist Irving Janis (1982) pointed out in the 1980s that closed groups with charismatic leaders show a natural tendency to shut themselves off from critical arguments and tend to make surprisingly irrational decisions in the ecstasy of invulnerability. Some will confirm this from their own experience. One has worked so long and hard on an idea, on a concept, that one categorically excludes an error. "This thing has got to work. It can't be any different". In this way, thousands of projects and business ideas have probably already failed after hard work. A practical example of a method will illustrate how to force teams to reflect critically.

When an idea fails, it is not uncommon for voices to be raised in retrospect which say that one had somehow guessed this would happen beforehand, but didn't dare to speak out. It is said that in retrospect one is always smarter, but even before the failure there was enough intelligence to anticipate the failure upfront. This can be done in the form of a so-called *pre-mortem analysis*. This method requires considerable courage and openness. Members of the project team and people who do not belong to the project lock themselves in and develop reasons why their project would fail. Like with brainstorming, anything is allowed. It is about mercilessly dismantling an idea, a concept, a project and burdening it as much as possible with critical arguments. Why does the employer branding project become a failure? Why will broadbanding not work as a new model of remuneration? Why won't the employee survey help? Why will the new form of talent identification fail? Basically it is about the anticipated answer to the question why the often referred to emperor wears no clothes. In the end, it will be a question of dealing with the critical arguments. The risk, of course, is that at the end of this analysis there will be such strong doubts about the idea that it will have to be buried—now rather than later. If the idea survives, it will emerge stronger, but never unchanged, from this exercise.

Strategic Decisions at 30-Minute Intervals

Basically, given the great responsibility they carry on their shoulders, executives on C-level deserve a great deal of respect. Nor should any attempt be made here to question the competences of top decision-makers in any way. But when it comes to the way decisions are made at the highest corporate level, one should not indulge in the naïve belief that everything here is based on a solid foundation of pure rationality. It is not uncommon for the long working days of senior executives to be paved over with meetings every 30 minutes. Every half hour another project group appears, with sophisticated slides, on which complex topics are represented, paired with extensive investment calculations. In such situations, no experienced top manager relies on the beautiful calculations of these teams alone. There are other things that come into play here.

Already in the development of an investment calculation not only do objective considerations play a role but also political interests. Thus the textbook authors

11.2 Key Figures and Control

Brealey et al. (2007) justified their *"second law"*[2] according to which the number of proposed projects with desired returns always remains the same, regardless of how high the desired returns are. In other words, investment calculations tend to produce what has to come out. Experienced top decision-makers know this, or at least suspect it.

The HR marketing team of a large corporation recently told me how they tried to convince their CHRO based on cost-benefit considerations that an extremely expensive employer branding campaign may not pay off. The CHRO, on the other hand, insisted on this. After the meeting, his executive assistant explained to the team how the CHRO had stood astonished in front of a competitor's mega-poster at the airport several weeks before and at that moment had sworn: "I want that too". That is the way it sometimes works on these levels. In fact, conversely, it can help to convince a board of directors of a matter by holding a shining example of the competitor in front of them. Board members are fighters who want to hold their own in competition. This fighting spirit can also lead to irrational decisions.

In his legendary work "Administrative Behavior" Herbert S. Simon put it in a nutshell: "It is impossible for the behaviour of a single, isolated individual to reach any high degree of rationality" (Simon 1947, p. 92). With his work Simon became one of the most important pioneers of descriptive decision theory. In 1978 he was awarded the Nobel Prize for Economics for this. The central finding of descriptive decision theory is that decision-makers in companies do not make purely rational decisions. Irrationality follows psychological laws, some of which Simon sketched out. The psychologists Amos Tversky and Daniel Kahnemann put it in much more concrete terms several years later. The latter was also awarded the Nobel Prize for Economics in 2002. One of their central constructs was that of *cognitive heuristics*. Cognitive heuristics are simple rules by means of which decisions are made under uncertainty and thus absorb only a small amount of mental capacity (Kahneman 2011). One can assume that top decision-makers make decisions for or against an investment on the basis of heuristics. How much does the proposed concept recall successful concepts from the past? Does a proposal appear in the light of possible profit opportunities or in the light of possible loss risks? Do the slides look good? What is the personal and professional impression of the person presenting the proposal? What is the external appearance of the responsible project manager?

In addition to the use of heuristics, the *intuition* of the decision-makers plays an important role. To advocates of evidence-based management, intuition and gut feeling are an insult and mean the opposite of rational, good decision-making. In fact, the use of gut instinct can lead to more superior decisions than the conscious use of as complete an information as possible in the context of a "rational" decision-making process (Gigerenzer 2008). Comprehensive experience is a prerequisite for this. To reiterate the analogy with medicine, as used by advocates of evidence-based management: many experienced physicians actually use a high degree of intuition in

---

[2]Interestingly, the authors mention that they refer to "Second Law" as "Second Law" even though there is no "First Law". "Second Law just sounds better".

their daily work. They make diagnoses and decisions without being able to explain them directly and rationally. "Why do I think you have a liver problem? I just see that." And the more experienced a doctor is, the more he relies on this gut feeling in the first place (cf. Gladwell 2006).

Experimenting, Trying, Piloting

Agile organizations recognize the irrationality of decisions. They accept that the social dynamics described in Sect. 11.1 go hand in hand with HR-related concepts, are hardly predictable. They lack the time and resources for an evidence-based approach. After all, one does not want to have to write a doctoral thesis before every decision is made for or against a measure. Therefore agile organizations rely on a simple premise:

> If we are uncertain about a measure (we usually are), we simply try it out. We regard early failure as part of progress. (5-2)

This strategic orientation reflects the principle of iterative thinking and action described in Sect. 4.3. While in hierarchical organizations there is a natural tendency to always think things through first, to explore them extensively and then to act, agile organizations start as quickly as possible with a first attempt. Rapid trial and error and piloting offers the chance of early failure and thus the chance to save resources and learn early on. In the positive case, the first attempt holds the prospect of a scaling of the approach. In addition, there is hardly anything more convincing in a company than proven success, even if this success was initially observable only on a small scale. This is exactly what has been described in Sect. 7.3 in the context of continuous learning. Accordingly, learning takes place as a result of irritation within the framework of cyclical reflection. Learning = working, working = learning.

Several years ago, I conducted a study on *employee referral programs*. In this context, I came into contact with two stories that could hardly be more different. The first story takes place in a rather agile company. A project team had a job to fill and was desperate. The HR department did not seem to be in a position to supply suitable candidates with its established methods. Now a colleague had the idea that everyone in the team could check his or her professional network whether there were suitable candidates there who could be approached. The project manager reinforced this suggestion by spontaneously offering 2000 euros to the person who would bring the future new employee on board. Everyone agreed—"All right. Let's go." A few weeks later, the position was successfully filled and one colleague was 2000 euros richer. This thing really worked. The design and implementation of this employee referral program took just a minute.

Now to the second story: It takes place in a large German chemical company. A project group developed a concept for an employee referral program. There were more questions to answer than initially thought. How high should the bonus be? When do you get the bonus? Who can make recommendations? For which positions should the program apply? Who is informed, how and when about the respective status in the process? What is the technical support like? etc. Numerous workshops were held with various stakeholders worldwide—HR business partners, managers, employees, executives and, of course, the workers council. After several months of intensive work, the concept was presented to the board and failed completely. The critical moment in this presentation, when the concept was literally shot down, was one sentence voiced by a single executive board member: "Where are we headed if we also start paying bounties for enticing away employees?" That is it. The real reason for the failure was probably that a good idea was presented on too high a level and thought about too broadly from the beginning, before one was ready even to take a small step. How different the board presentation would have been had one already been able to tell success stories. "We're already doing this in a number of areas and it is going better than anything. We can now decide whether we want to expand on this or limit ourselves to the less promising approaches we have seen so far".

If employees neither with permission nor with an order from above work on something and further develop ideas, this holds considerable opportunities for a company. This is also referred to as *bootlegging* (Augsdorfer 2008), which is of course prohibited in hierarchical companies. After all, working time is a resource paid for by the company and only available to the company.

Digitization = More Data and Key Figures?

Anyone who has looked closely will have noticed a kind of paradox in this subchapter. In general, one might think that increasing digitization would fuel the use of key figures. After all, digital technology in particular provides the long-awaited foundation for this. In this subchapter the arguments were completely different. We have assumed that agility creates competitive advantages in times of digitization. This assumption underlies this book as a whole. If you take a closer look at agile teams and companies, on the other hand, you will notice that managers and teams do without key figures as far as possible. If you look at the strategic options on this topic in an overview (see Fig. 11.7) and take a look at the right-hand side, you will see that there are fewer key figures, but more interpersonal exchanges, more feedback (not control, etc.). Finally, in an agile context, an attempt is made to convince others (e.g. superiors) of one's own performance or the effectiveness of good ideas instead of just relying on key figures or investment calculations.

11.3 Digital HR and People Analytics

If I had written this book several years ago, this subchapter would certainly have received a different title. Maybe I would have called it *Human Resources Information Systems* (HRIS) at the time. In the course of digitization, a different understanding of the role of such systems has developed in the meantime. This has led to the emergence of new concepts. It is no longer just a question of mapping previously

Attitude towards key figures	*1-1 Required in Management* Professional HR requires extensive use of key figures. After all, you can't manage what you can't measure.	*1-2 Avoidance of key figures* The best and most important things in HR cannot be measured and we do not do it either. To try it nevertheless leads to inadequate simplifications.
Purpose of key figure usage	*2-1 Control* Key figures help executives at higher decision-making levels to control activities, processes and measures within HR.	*2-2 Feedback* By means of key figures, teams that deal with HR-related issues independently reflect on the success of their work.
Width of key figure usage	*3-1 As widely as possible* We use a broad spectrum of possible indicators because we want to map HR-related aspects as comprehensively as possible.	*3-2 Focus on what is relevant* We use as few relevant key figures as possible. Anything else leads to comprehensive reports that no one attaches any importance to.
Decision-making basis	*4-1 Investment calculation* Investment calculations form a rational basis for investment decisions on a strategic level.	*4-2 Conclusion and strong debates* Measures and investments are decided when we are convinced of their content. These decisions are preceded by controversial debates.
Tracking success	*5-1 Based on empirical evidence* Where possible, we make evidence-based decisions on the basis of empirically tested effects. Anything else would just be gut feeling.	*5-2 Attempting and learning* If we are uncertain about a measure (we usually are), we simply try it out. We regard early failure as part of progress.

Fig. 11.7 All strategic dimensions of key figures and controlling at a glance

physical and analogue processes into IT processes, but rather of an intelligent (smart) use of existing data in the HR context and new business models. Accordingly, *HR analytics*, *predictive analytics* or *people analytics* was suddenly mentioned as part of a *digital HR*. The nice thing about it is that these terms sound far more exciting than the term HR information system.

Making Life Easier for HR Professionals

But let's go back a few decades. For example, when SAP started to develop an HR module, it was a simple question of how to make the lives of HR professionals easier. The desired added value was obvious. In fact, the first step was the development of electronic payroll. One does not dare to imagine how the salaries of thousands of employees were calculated, documented in pay slips, paid out and controlled every month before this time. This new module represented a considerable boost in terms of efficiency and quality. In addition, processes could now be dovetailed and integrated with interfaced business functions, such as accounting. The time-consuming back and forth of documents was no longer necessary. Further application examples followed. Just think of applicant management, so-called

Applicant Tracking Systems (ATS). Such systems also made the lives of the recruiters and hiring managers easier. Now all applicant information was available electronically, it could be routed internally, evaluated and the communication with the applicant automated. And finally, in the case of recruitment, not all personal data had to be re-entered.

When software vendors developed and implemented their solutions, they primarily talked to HR people. How are you going to do that? How do you want that? Does that suit you? HR professionals are seen as customers of HR management solutions. This orientation towards the needs of HR is still noticeable today and has a formative influence on what can be seen in practice.

We use information technology to make the lives of HR professionals easier. (1-1)

In the course of the nineties, so-called *Employee Self Services* (ESS) or *Manager Self Services* (MSS) emerged. Now, for example, employees could create and send their leave request directly through a system. Bank data, home address, family status and much more was from now on maintained by the employees themselves. The term "Employee Services" was used to convey the impression that the employees received a service. In fact, services that were originally the responsibility of HR professionals were now taken over by the employees themselves in order to relieve the HR colleagues in the end. Of course, the employees themselves benefited from the flexibility and speed this brought with it. But the big winner was the HR department. The banks were no different. ATMs are certainly a blessing for bank customers. But the bank employees were also relieved. Guess, what the actual driving force behind such solutions was.

An attitude, namely to make the life of HR easier, dominates to this day. Later in this subchapter, we will look at how digital HR should be designed in order to to make the lives of employees, teams and managers easier. However, developments that have gained momentum in this context in recent years are to be described beforehand. From there, a look into the future will be taken and strategic options explored.

Mobile, BYOD, Social and Cloud

In recent years, power has increasingly passed to users in the development of software solutions. What works for the user seemed to be the best choice. Apps are only successful if the users accept them. In order to guarantee the most user-friendly experience possible, a number of principles have now been established for the development and provision of appropriate solutions and services.

Just a few years ago, visitors to relevant conferences, such as the leading European HR technology trade fair HR Tech, had to be explicitly convinced that users "go online" via mobile devices. Today it has become clear to everybody that data is created and used on a *mobile* basis. Not only smartphones and tablets should be considered, but also wearables, portable components such as smart watches, cars, or clothing equipped with sensors (smart clothes). Data is created and used where the user is and not where the Internet-enabled device—the PC—is located.

Many users take it for granted that they are always equipped with the latest technology. Hardly any smartphone in current use is probably older than 4 years. A device is replaced at the latest when it is technically no longer able to cope with the latest update of the required operating system. Some employees therefore live in two worlds. In the professional context, they are often encouraged to work with systems that are hopelessly out-dated compared to their private infrastructure. Privately the newest iPhone, and the Blackberry at work. The latest office version at home while the company is still struggling with the introduction of the penultimate update. So it was no wonder that more and more companies, under pressure from employees, were thinking about enabling the use of private technology in the business context, *Bring Your Own Device* (BYOD).

Furthermore, it can be observed that more and more IT applications in the HR context enable the usage of social networks among employees and beyond. In this respect, applications increasingly have the quality of being *social*. Think here of simple apps such as the Yellow Pages, but also of platforms that promote learning from and with one another or the lateral exchange of knowledge in the sense of knowledge management. Enterprise social networks also fall into this category. Modern feedback apps allow you to give and receive feedback not from the direct manager but from colleagues (peers) and even customers. Some applications even go beyond that and include the external networks of employees. These include apps that support employee referral programs. Such apps are able to even integrate data from platforms like LinkedIn.

Now it happened that very different users with different devices had to access the same data from different locations. What used to be managed in *one* system was now distributed across very different systems. Synchronization and the exchange of data became a serious challenge, which eventually led to so-called *cloud solutions*.

Of course, all these developments were associated with strategic decisions on the part of the companies. The question was whether to jump on the bandwagon of modern developments or not. In the end, most people apparently had no other choice. While in recent years the above-mentioned topics have been among the most frequently propagated trends, in the recent past another trend has appeared almost overnight on the horizon. We are talking about *Artificial Intelligence* (AI) in connection with *Big Data*. As will be shown immediately, this results in very far-reaching political and strategic options—in contrast to the trends towards mobile, social, cloud or BYOD.

Big Data and Artificial Intelligence

Every user, every employee produces and leaves data in almost every moment. Transaction data, communication data, clicks, downloads, usage intervals on different platforms, pages or apps. In the course of the increasing connectivity of objects

11.3 Digital HR and People Analytics

(Internet of Things) and the rapid increase of sensors in almost everything, we are experiencing a further explosion of data volumes. These data are initially largely unstructured and distributed. But as soon as you start to use these immense amounts of data in an intelligent way, you talk about *Big Data*. One knows this for example from modern, mobile navigation applications. From the movement data of millions of smartphones, current traffic jams are reported and future traffic volumes on any route are forecast. Google can already tell me today how much time I should calculate the day after tomorrow from 4.00 p.m. on the route from my hometown Tübingen to Furtwangen, the location of my wonderful university. This is just one simple example out of many.

Systems can predict user behaviour better and better. Amazon already knows our purchasing decisions at a time when we are not even aware of them and prepares everything logistically so that the delivery only takes a few hours or minutes after the moment of the actual purchase click. Self-driving cars predict the behaviour of other car drivers and act accordingly. Errors happen in the process. Systems can be wrong. However, they are continuously improving in what they predict. We speak here of *machine learning* based on corresponding feedback loops.

So it does not come as a surprise that for some time now, even in the HR context, people have been thinking about possible scenarios for the application of artificial intelligence. Some scenarios have already been discussed in this book. Here is a selection of the most well known:

- *Learning and the use of learning resources.* Based on previous learning behaviour and employees' previous usage of learning resources, their jobs, projects and social relations to colleagues, learning units are proposed to employees on a learning platform that might appear relevant to employees at the current moment. In addition to static learning resources, employees receive recommendations about who in the company they could talk to about something in order to learn from each other in a direct and personal exchange.
- *Candidate search.* On the basis of information available online about people, candidates are searched for and suggested based on current and future workforce demands, who can then be actively approached in a further step. By means of self-optimizing algorithms (machine learning), candidates are also searched for who only appear suitable at second glance, independently of the skills they themselves indicate on LinkedIn. For example, systems learn that people who have certain private preferences, attended certain schools, are unmarried and like to play handball are suitable for certain challenges—for whatever reason.
- *Employee referral.* Employees automatically receive job advertisements which, based on network information and other employee characteristics, are assumed to know suitable persons for the respective job. These so-called *recommendation systems*, which we are already familiar with from knowing platforms like Amazon, automatically provide the requested colleagues with suggestions about acquaintances from their network, and they can then decide whether they want to actively recommend them.

- *Candidate selection.* The same applies to the selection of candidates and applicants. Systems screen and evaluate incoming CVs. Here, too, they apply algorithms that optimize themselves autonomously and become better and better in their predictive validity. There is currently a controversial discussion here about whether machines are free of discrimination or whether they adopt human prejudices and biases from their human teachers.
- *Chatbots.* Applicants and candidates have the opportunity to communicate with so-called dialogue-based assistance systems. Because applicants and candidates increasingly expect real-time answers to questions, chatbots can be a great help. These systems access an almost infinite source of semantic knowledge and are increasingly able to adapt to the mood and preferred style of communication of their counterparts.
- *Performance and loyalty.* Based on transaction data, communication, presence and absence, timeliness of LinkedIn profiles, visits to job portals, etc., not only future performance but also voluntary turnover in the company are predicted. In this way, a so-called flight risk score can be determined for each employee, which expresses the turnover tendency of an employee. This has already been discussed in the context of employee retention (see Sect. 10.3).
- *Talent identification and promotion.* As already reported in Sect. 8.1, Google was able to develop an algorithm that can predict the internal promotion of employees in an amazingly valid way. This very example showed how little information needs to be used to achieve a comparatively high predictive validity.
- *Career options.* Employees automatically receive recommendations for next career steps in the company. Here, too, recommendation systems are used which are based on a comparison of opportunities with the personal profile. These opportunities can be jobs, projects or tasks. On the basis of the reactions of the employees, the system learns which options are interesting from the point of view of the person concerned and which are not.
- *Social networks.* Employees are encouraged to network with colleagues internally, similar to what is done on LinkedIn. These recommendations are based on the respective profiles.
- *Organization.* In sport, it is already possible to analyse movement, interaction and performance data and predict which team formation and which interplay within a team is the most promising for which opponent. Trainers who make intensive use of this technology are also called "laptop trainers", a term not intended as flattery. In the entrepreneurial context there are already approaches to calculate promising team constellations. Who should work with whom and on what, so that the greatest possible success can be achieved in which situation?

This list is anything but complete. It is only intended to outline the direction in which we think when we talk about Digital HR or *People Analytics*. This has hardly anything to do with the classical approaches of established HR information systems.

Human and Algorithmic Decisions

If you take a closer look at the above list and description of possible application scenarios of AI, you will notice that you should distinguish between two types of scenarios. Some scenarios describe activities that could be relevant for a centrally controlling instance and enable it to control them. The other scenarios address needs on the part of employees in the sense of people-centered enablement (see Fig. 11.8).

Let's first look at the left side in Fig. 11.8. These include the scenarios candidate selection, talent identification and promotion, performance and loyalty, and the organizational scenario. If one recalls the HR triangle described in Sect. 2.2 with its various types of HR outlined there, then these scenarios are located in the upper right corner (central planning and control). They support a higher-level instance, for example, the HR function in the central exercise of its responsibility. It is concerned with making the right decisions *about* employees, the human resource. This central instance is the actual user of AI. Armed with AI, it is able to assess who will perform best with whom, where and from whom, from which employee one should better distance oneself and which employees are particularly worthy of promotion. A centrally planning and controlling HR function has always thought and acted from this position. With AI, however, this type of HR reaches a new level.

When companies continuously collect data about their employees and systematically draw conclusions about their future, this must be threatening or even frightening for the employees concerned. This weakens their subjective conviction of control, their awareness of being the master of their own situation. In such scenarios, employees do not know what the company knows about them. And even the higher-level decision-makers can only understand their decisions to a limited extent because they are based on changing (learning) algorithms. You might be hiding behind the famous Black Box.

At so many People Analytic conferences one encounters self-proclaimed "evangelists" of this new development, who with an amazing euphoria project scenarios like the above onto the wall. It is comforting to see that not everyone in

The HR function ...	The employees (or applicants) ...
can identify suitable internal and external candidates for specific jobs	receive personalized learning opportunities based on their jobs, preferences, challenges and previous learning histories
can more validly judge which applicants are suitable for which jobs	
identifies early on who intends to leave the company voluntarily	use their external network more effectively to recommend suitable candidates for their own company
assesses internal talent for appropriate programs or upcoming promotions	receive real-time questions to almost any answer about jobs and career opportunities
recognizes which employees should work together in which teams.	receive personalized offers for next career steps (jobs, projects, etc.) in the company
	receive recommendations on who in the company they should connect with.

Fig. 11.8 Scenarios of central control versus people-centered enablement

the audience shares this euphoria. How could one not think of monitoring, manipulation and loss of control in these scenarios?

Even Google seems to have gone too far with these considerations in relation to its own HR. They distanced themselves from the idea of letting algorithms make decisions about people (cf. Sect. 8.1). The extent to which the development of AI can be halted in the HR context is difficult to assess. In the end, however, the strategic question arises as to whether people or machines make decisions about people. If trust in artificial intelligence (AI) is in the foreground, the following premise will be given priority:

> We rely as much as possible on artificial intelligence, big data and machine learning for people-related decisions. This leads to more reliable decisions and fewer prejudices. (2-1)

If, on the other hand, you rely on the human being as the ultimate decision maker of all HR-relevant decisions, then you are more likely to commit yourself to this strategic alignment:

> Decisions about people are made by people. Artificial intelligence can help, but never has the last word. (2-2)

The latter premise always assumes that behind a decision there is a person who should be able not only to justify his or her decision but also to take responsibility for it. Accordingly, the justification against a talent nomination can never be: "We did not nominate you into the talent program because our talent algorithm did not consider you suitable".

This thinking from a central authority in the sense of central planning and control seems astonishingly deeply anchored in the traditional understanding of HR. The application of technology has always been primarily concerned with making the lives of HR staff easier and even better ensuring that you end up with the right person in the right place at the right time. It is important to see that things can be different and that technology can take a different place. In the international HR community, this different way of thinking is increasingly associated with the term *Employee Experience*.

Employee Experience

The other half of the scenarios listed above describe activities that are designed to support employees in people-related issues and challenges. On the right side in Fig. 11.8 these are summarized. It is not about arming HR with new opportunities but about making the lives of employees, managers and teams easier.

> We use information technology to make the lives of employees, teams and managers in the business line easier. (1-2)

This strategy unmistakably reflects the HR type of people-centered enablement. By following this line one puts oneself in the perspective of the employees. One deals with their concerns, their needs, their questions and challenges and provides appropriate solutions. For several months there has been a new term *employee experience* for this view in connection with digital technology. This has nothing at all to do with the central approaches outlined above. So anyone who claims—and this is what you read and hear in abundance in poor presentations and blogs—that Digital HR strives to make better decisions *about* employees in order to ultimately achieve a better Employee Experience has probably not understood the contradiction between these two worlds.

People Over Systems

In an interview with the Frankfurter Allgemeine Zeitung on June 3, 2017, Stefan Ries, SAP Human Resources Director, commented on the changed conditions for performance assessment and feedback in his company. SAP has recently introduced an approach called "SAP Talk". It is about continuous feedback instead of the annual, classic performance appraisal. In concrete terms, he explains: "Through the use of technology, supervisors and employees are constantly in a position to discuss the development [individual achievement of objectives] and to store the results". Numerous companies that now organise so-called *check-ins* instead of annual performance appraisals report a similar situation (see Sect. 6.2). These are basically mini appraisals, which can take place once a quarter at the request of the employees.

This raises the crucial question of what technology is needed for this. In fact, I recently discussed this aspect intensively with a group of international training and development managers. In the end there was helplessness in the room and with it the realization that technology is hardly relevant here. Good employees constantly get feedback. You do not need an app or any other tracking tool. At SAP, too, it is not only since the introduction of a corresponding technology that we have been able to talk about project progress. I've been with the company for several years, talked thousands of times about project status and never put anything into an HR tool.

Many things require neither a process nor an IT tool. This view may seem backward-looking or even hostile to technology. However, it is also possible that this attitude is first and foremost pragmatic and realistic. Many HR professionals will be relieved to read this sentence. For companies, this results in two opposing strategic options. Either one tries to represent technically all that can be represented technically.

> What can be technically mapped does get technically mapped. This enables us to achieve efficiency and transparency. (3-1)

Or you can use technology more cautiously and adapt the agile principle "People over Processes"—"People over Systems". What can be handled interpersonally and informally should also take place at this level. Often this approach is characterized by higher effectiveness and speed.

Effectiveness and speed take precedence over efficiency. We do not automate everything that can be automated from a technical point of view, but focus above all on interpersonal exchange. (3-2)

If one has experienced enough product presentations of the numerous software providers, one can sometimes get the impression that inside-out might get considered by them from time to time. First, one develops numerous functionalities in quiet seclusion in order to convince the market afterwards. It is amazing what could be done technologically if only the employees and managers would use the functionalities in ways the software providers imagined it. That is why the most annoying thing you can do for the sales staff of these vendors is to ask them the question: "But which employees really use this function?"

What Is the Best HR Solution on the Market?

Recently I stumbled across a post on LinkedIn. There, an apparently inexperienced HR manager asked the following question: "We are currently thinking about implementing a new HR solution that we want to implement throughout the company. Which solution and which provider would you recommend?" Interesting were the numerous comments from the community. "Workday", "No, SuccessFactors", "Cornerstone I can recommend", " Umantis is good". It went on and on. The bottom line was that everyone was somehow right and wrong at the same time. But the simple, correct answer would have been: "It depends".

In the following it is less about things such as licensing costs, implementation effort, complexity, scope of functionality, integration, interfaces, usability or support, although all these may be critical factors to consider when deciding for or against a suite or solution. What is more important is the extent to which a solution can support the preferred type of HR and the associated HR strategy. No more, no less. If you focus on central planning and control with regard to the types of HR, you will prefer the solution that makes HR life easier. In the case of people-centered empowerment, a different solution will take precedence.

The book also covers a number of key issues, the selection and direction of which are the cornerstones of the HR strategy. In connection with each topic, corresponding strategic dimensions were discussed. Once a company has clarified these dimensions, it is also in a position to decide on the right IT solution, provided that the respective aspect is to be technologically supported. If talent identification takes place top-down according to the classical pattern and using the performance potential matrix, then the solution should support this. If, on the other hand, you opt for peer nomination, according to which a talent is a talent if the others also see it that way, then it would be good if the solution would rather reflect this strategic alignment. If you rely on passive strategies when searching for candidates, then the solution should support the placement of advertisements paired with a traditional ATS. If, however, the use of employee referrals or talent communities is prioritized for a number of target functions, it would certainly be advantageous for the solution to map this part accordingly.

The Hierarchical Heritage

As logical and simple as this advice may sound, in practice it leads to another dilemma. Do you rather rely on comprehensive overall solutions, so-called *suites*, which at the same time combine a wide range of functionalities, or rather on *best-of-breed*? The latter means putting together an IT landscape from the best solutions that appear suitable for the particular requirements. Complete solutions offer the great advantage of integration. You have everything under *one* single umbrella so to speak. In addition, they reflect the best practices of numerous companies over many years that are the state of the art.

> We prefer standard solutions as far as possible. This allows us to benefit from best practices and the established state-of-the-art of other companies. (4-1)

Best-of-breed, on the other hand, can lead to interface problems and increased overall complexity. In return, you get the solutions you really need. CIOs are seldom enthusiastic about this idea because they are particularly interested in reducing complexity. The decision for one or the other variant should not be a question for the CIO alone. This dilemma plays a decisive role, particularly with regard to the HR strategy. It is not so much a matter of integration or complexity as of the understanding of HR, which is implicit in most established overall solutions as a legacy from past years and decades. Because many large software vendors have rightly built what the big customers wanted in recent years, the HR understanding behind it is usually purely hierarchical. If you look at the strategic dimensions in this book, you will find that most software vendors have oriented themselves to the traditional, hierarchical side that strives for stability and predictability.

On the other hand, there are numerous niche providers with partly fantastic solutions for certain requirements in addition to the well-known, large software providers. Since start-ups are usually at work here, it is not surprising that their solutions are more suited to an agile understanding of leadership and organization, because these start-ups themselves have in most cases a more agile understanding.

> We're betting on best-of-breed. This gives us the flexibility to support our agile understanding of leadership and organization technologically where we want it to be. (4-2)

Of course, many large software providers are currently working at full speed on more agile functionalities. Recently, I found myself at an analyst meeting at Cornerstone, a leading provider of HR software. I asked the wonderful CEO Adam Miller how he intends to deal with the balancing act between stability and agility. He then moved to the flip chart and announced in his usual charismatic manner: "Our Strategy is ..." then he began to write in big letters "... OLD + NEW". In doing so, he summed up the situation of his company and its large competitors. While many customers still rely on traditional approaches and thus make the most money today (old), an increasingly large group of customers wants more agile solutions (new). Right now, you have to serve both of them. For this the term *ambidexterity* appeared. The situation is comparable in the automotive industry. Money is still earned primarily with traditional cars that are driven by human drivers and powered by combustion engines. Still only a small target group wants self-driving vehicles with electric drive. The question at the end of the day is with what momentum providers of traditional solutions create the turnaround.

Today, when I work with companies on their HR strategy, and when I consider a more agile, strategic direction, I often have concerns about whether the current software vendor whose solution the company is using can support that direction. In fact, it often cannot (yet) do so.

People Over Data and Analytics

It seems to me that there is a certain misunderstanding in the international HR community. It is argued, for example, that the primary premise in the course of digitization is the possibility of smart use of employee data in order to then be able to make smart decisions about employees. The opposite is true. Agility, as a prerequisite for being able to assert oneself in a world of digitization, relies primarily on interpersonal relationships. The principle "People over Processes" described in the agile manifesto applies here. This principle can be extended in the context of the strategic options discussed in this subchapter (see Fig. 11.9): *People over Data and*

Primary customer	1-1 *Employees in HR* We use information technology to make the lives of HR professionals easier.	1-2 *Employees and managers* We use information technology to make the lives of employees, teams and managers in the business line easier.
Role of Analytics	2-1 *Decision making* We rely as much as possible on artificial intelligence, big data and machine learning for people-related decisions. This leads to more reliable decisions and fewer prejudices.	2-2 *Decision support* Decisions about people are made for and made by people. Artificial intelligence can help, but never has the last word.
Technology versus people	3-1 *Maximum use of technology* What can be technically mapped is also technically mapped. This enables us to achieve efficiency and transparency.	3-2 *People over Systems* Effectiveness and speed take precedence over efficiency. We do not automate everything that can be automated from a technical point of view, but focus above all on interpersonal exchange.
Preferred solution	4-1 *Standard solutions & suits* We prefer standard solutions as far as possible. This allows us to benefit from best practices and the established state-of-the-art of other companies.	4-2 *Best-of-Breed* We're betting on best-of-breed. This gives us the flexibility to support our agile understanding of leadership and organization technologically where we want it to be.

Fig. 11.9 Overview of all strategic dimensions of Digital HR and people analytics

Analytics. In some ways, these considerations appear to be a paradox, similar to what has been argued in relation to metrics (Sect. 11.2)—more digitization requires more interpersonal interaction.

References

Augsdorfer P (2008) Managing the unmanageable. Res Technol Manag 51(4):41–47
Bartlett CA, Ghoshal S (1998) Managing across borders: the transnational solution. Harvard Business Press, Boston, MA
Brealey RA, Myers SC, Allen F (2007) Principles of corporate finance. McGraw-Hill, New York
Fitz-Enz J (2009) The ROI of human capital. Measuring the economic value of employee performance, 2. Aufl. Amacom, New York
Gadenne V (1984) Theorie und Erfahrung in der psychologischen Forschung. Mohr, Tübingen
Gigerenzer G (2008) Bauchentscheidungen. Die Intelligenz des Unbewussten und die Macht der Intuition. Goldmann, München
Gladwell M (2006) Blink: the power of thinking without thinking. Penguin, London
Janis IL (1982) Groupthink. Psychological studies of policy decisions and fiascoes. Houghton Mifflin, Oxford
Kahneman D (2011) Thinking, fast and slow. Macmillan, New York
Kaplan RS, Norton DP (1996) The balanced scorecard: translating strategy into action. Harvard Business School Press, Boston, MA
Lazear EP (2000) Performance pay and productivity. Am Econ Rev 90(5):1346–1361
Morrell K (2008) The narrative of 'evidence based' management: a polemic. J Manag Stud 45(3):613–635
Pfeffer J, Sutton RI (2006) Hard facts, dangerous half-truths, and total nonsense: profiting from evidence-based management. Harvard Business Review Press, Boston, MA
Simon HA (1947) Administrative behavior. A study of decision-making processes in administrative organizations. Macmillan, New York
Trost A (2014) Talent relationship management. Competitive recruiting strategies in times of talent shortage. Springer, Heidelberg
Ulrich D (1997) Human resource champions. The next agenda for adding value and delivering results. Harvard Business School Press, Boston, MA
van Dijk H, van Engen ML, van Knippenberg D (2012) Defying conventional wisdom: a meta-analytical examination of the differences between demographic and job-related diversity relationships with performance. Organ Behav Hum Decis Process 119(1):38–53

Managing Change and Transformation 12

In classical textbooks on personnel management, the subject of *change management* is usually looked for in vain. This is particularly surprising in view of the fact that coping with changes and transformations, some of which are extensive, is not only one of the greatest challenges facing many companies, but that they often fail, particularly because of the human factor. In this respect, this topic should not be missing from this book.

In the course of this chapter, it becomes clear that the classical understanding of change management, as found in numerous books on the subject, is becoming increasingly diffuse. Even the question of what is meant by "change" is becoming increasingly blurred. In this respect, a sort of delimitation and sorting will be carried out in the following. Subsequently, the question is examined how change and change management can be presented in an agile context.

12.1 Three Different Scenarios

We start this chapter with three different stories. The first story is as follows: In a medium-sized company, the executive board comes to the decision to restructure the entire organization comprehensively. Based on a function-oriented organization, the company is to be organized according to product families in the future. In concrete terms, this means that overarching functions such as marketing, R&D, sales, etc. will be dismantled and each product division will have its own independent functions of this kind in the future. The executive board sets up a project group, which—supported by an external management consultancy—starts planning. At the same time, change management activities are being initiated which, in addition to communication measures, also include measures for active involvement and targeted training. The transformation should be completed after 6 months, so that the organization as a whole can find its way back into a stable mode.

Let us now come to the second story. In one of several plants of a mechanical engineering company, a group of engineers are experimenting with an optimized form of *shop floor management*.[1] The successes are visible after a short time. Within an internal community, the engineers report on their successes. A few weeks later, they share their experiences with their colleagues from other plants in a comprehensive workshop in which all production managers, foremen and numerous specialists take part. The new ideas spread quickly in the other plants. Individual pioneers of this new development act as active companions and consultants during implementation. What began small became a comprehensive kind of movement within production. The Head of Production acted as a sponsor, but was largely out of the picture from a technical point of view. It seems as if this transformation has no real end but continuously experiences new steps of optimization. You are never done.

Now for the third story. A company is becoming increasingly disgruntled with its annual *budgeting process*. This process has always followed the classical hierarchical pattern with numerous vertical loops. Forecasts, market reports, reports on previous sales and costs, business plans etc. are carried out from bottom to top several times and adjusted from top to bottom. Countless, time-consuming coordination and negotiation rounds take place. At the same time, the managers concerned experience this process not only as extremely patronizing, time-consuming and nerve-racking, but sometimes even as nonsense. In the end things will always be different anyway—at least that is the perception of those affected. The new CEO and the new CFO jointly identify the problem and order a comprehensive reengineering of the process. The goal is to offer more room for personal responsibility and entrepreneurial thinking. Even the complete abolition of all forms of budgets and budgeting processes is seen as a serious option. In a meeting of all managers, a working group is elected to consider alternative possibilities. The task is to identify relevant, desirable benefit expectations and, taking into account the principles of personal responsibility, trust and flexibility, to outline approaches and solutions which are then to be carried back to the management circle and discussed there in larger circles.

Three Scenarios

All three stories are about change. If you have a closer look at these three stories, you will notice that they are fundamentally different from each other. The simple scheme in the Fig. 12.1 may help to illustrate the differences.

The first story (restructuring) describes a comprehensive change from state A (function-oriented organization) to state B (product-oriented organization) within a hierarchical, stable setting. The change is top-down and limited in time. After a large-scale transformation, which in a certain way comes over the organization—and is therefore accompanied by change management measures—one strives for a renewed state of stability after the transformation is finished.

---

[1] Shopfloor management is an approach in which employees discuss continuous improvement and current day-to-day issues directly at the point of value creation, for example in the shop floor, in short cycles (cf. Suzaki 1993).

12.1 Three Different Scenarios

Fig. 12.1 Four scenarios of possible changes

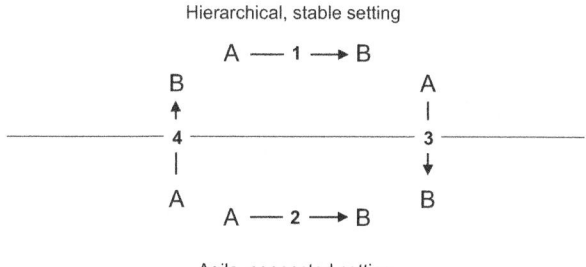

The second story (shopfloor management) describes a change within an agile context. It is initiated bottom-up, tested and laterally scaled step-by-step and independently via communities. Even though a transformation from one state (A) to another state (B) takes place here, this transformation has no defined end.

The third story takes place neither in a hierarchical nor in an agile context. It describes a transformation from a hierarchical state (A) to an agile state (B). As we will see, these forms of transformation often begin hierarchically because they are initiated and allowed top-down. The rest of the process, however, follows agile principles, because agility cannot be forced hierarchically—any more than peace can be achieved by military, aggressive means.

Two Levels

This book therefore deals with two levels of consideration. On the one level, the question of how the design of changes works in hierarchical versus agile worlds is examined. A comparison is made between scenario 1 and scenario 2. Basically, the topic "change" is treated in the same way as all other key HR topics in the previous parts of this book. In connection with the topic of talent development, for example, we also asked ourselves how this works differently in hierarchical, stable worlds than it does in agile worlds. But now we are talking about change and change management.

In addition, however, this book must also provide answers or at least suggestions to the long overdue question of how an originally hierarchically managed company succeeds in making the transition to greater agility. We're moving on a kind of meta-level here. After considering changes in the context of the agile or hierarchical operating system, the last Chap. 13 (Transformation into an agile future) will deal with the question of how to change the operating system itself. This is scenario 3, as outlined above. In a way, this is a specific issue that requires specific considerations.

At least academically, a fourth case is also conceivable (see scenario 4 in Fig. 12.1). This case describes a change from agile origin (A) to more hierarchy and stability (B). Companies that take this path want to move away from personal responsibility, networks, collaboration and teamwork. But they want more silo thinking and division of labour. They want conformity instead of previous diversity. Leaders in partnership make room for bosses etc. This case is not discussed further in this book. In the past months and years, I have simply not encountered any company that deliberately wanted to take this path, even though this development could be observed in some companies. In fact, this step is very simple and possible almost overnight, although in this case one has to expect an immediate decrease in motivation and performance and an increase in fluctuation.

12.2 Change Management: Classic Thinking

This subchapter first takes a look at the topic of change management as it is seen and practised in hierarchical, stable companies. We look at how change decisions are made, what changes are and what role change management plays in a hierarchical context.

From Stability to Stability

One of the common models cited in connection with change management is Kurt Lewin's (1947). At the time, Lewin was concerned with the question of how people in groups can change habits and behavioural patterns. What finally remained of this research in current management literature was a plausible three-step model according to which groups must be unfrozen first, for example through a process described as irritation in this book (see Sect. 7.3). Then there is a process of social learning and change (move) to finally return to a state of stability (refreeze) consisting of new but stable roles, values, behavioural patterns etc. Lewin spoke more of constancy than stability. Even though Lewin did not intend this to be the case, this model served as a perspective on organizations according to which they are seen as a kind of machine. We are also talking here about the machine metaphor. If a machine no longer functions as it should, it must be disassembled (unfreeze). Then it is newly constructed (move) and finally reassembled in a new state (refreeze), so that it works productively for an indefinite time and in an unchanged form. This is roughly how changes are seen in hierarchically managed organizations.

> Changes occur out of a state of stability. After a phase of upheaval, we are again striving for this stable state. (1-1)

You actually want to avoid changes of this kind, because a machine is not productive during the new design. In addition, changes always entail a risk of failure. Will the machine really work better afterwards? In this respect, it makes sense to make changes only when they can no longer be avoided. All this requires a certain perspective on what you see as change and what you don't.

Change in Hierarchical Organizations

John Kotter (1996) is certainly one of the most frequently quoted thought leaders on the subject of change management. His book "Leading Change" is regarded by many change managers as the bible of change management. But even Kotter's remarks still owe a clear definition of what is meant by "change". How he interprets this term can be seen from the actual applications that he describes for illustration purposes. It becomes clear that he subsumes change as exactly what one tends to understand by it in a hierarchical context, namely a comprehensive, large-scale change with strategic implications.

> By "change" we mean first and foremost a comprehensive change with strategic implications that affects many employees at the same time. (2-1)

We are talking about big, organizational restructuring, about large-scale adjustments and optimizations of processes in the sense of reengineering, about comprehensive (total) quality management programs, about mergers and acquisitions, about company-wide programs to achieve a profound and sustainable cultural change, about fundamental strategic changes of direction. Everything John Kotter describes is big and extensive. And this is not surprising, since it is precisely with these special transformations that the special need for special leadership becomes apparent. This obviously does not involve small-scale, short-term changes, such as personnel replacements, operational decisions or even singular optimizations in the sense of continuous improvement.

Top Management as the Driving Force

So, it is not surprising that change—as described above—is a matter for top management, which is why John Kotter speaks of "change leadership". His eight steps of a successful transformation begin with what can be named as suffering. Kotter (1996) refers to the so-called *sense of urgency* as a counterpart to complacency. In the end, it becomes clear that self-satisfaction can essentially be a dangerous characteristic of senior management—not employees. In the event of a change, it is, according to Kotter, the task of the management level to formulate a convincing vision, to communicate it and finally to set up a powerful management guiding coalition, as he names it. In an extremely hierarchical way, Kotter starts from the implicit assumption that changes are not only decided at the top of the company, but are also driven from there.

> Changes of strategic importance are always decided, planned and driven top-down. This is a central task of senior management. (3-1)

Hierarchically socialized readers are not surprised. From where else, one is inclined to ask. However, as we will see in the further course of this chapter, not only reforms from above but also revolutions from below are conceivable, as are comprehensive decisions on change that are taken by the corporate democracy.

As already explained in Sect. 11.2 in relation to the rationality and justification of investment decisions, companies try to make strategic decisions after careful analysis and consideration. Even before or at the time of the decision, there must be an explicit conviction that this decision will have the desired consequences. At least that is what we're assuming.

> Changes are only initiated if one is aware of their consequences at the highest decision-making level. Anything else would be irresponsible. (4-1)

Do we want to buy this company or not? Do we want to implement a new ERP system and if so, which one? Do we want to continue with the production of product X or do we prefer to invest in product Y?

Change Management from a Hierarchical Perspective

From this point of view the change is affecting the employees. It was decided on at a higher level and those affected are in some way the victims of the change. The change is also extensive and of strategic scope. At the same time, however, it is known that the initiated change would only be successful if the employees concerned were willing and able not only to support this change, but also to actively commit themselves to its success.

However, this cannot be assumed in principle (cf. Conner 1992). The probability is high that employees do not like the change at all or only in part. Above all, the decision at the top conveys a low level of subjective control. Employees feel externally controlled, patronized, and fear that they may emerge from the change as the losers. Once again it becomes clear from everyday business life that they themselves are only objects and not subjects of corporate events. The result can be open or hidden resistance, which at the end is detrimental for the change project. At this point, reference is usually made to the *emotion curve,* and stages based on the work of Elisabeth Kübler-Ross (1969). Accordingly, the objects of the changes initially fall into a dysfunctional shock rigidity, begin to rebel and then go through a painful phase of depression. Of course, management does not want all this. This is why change management comes into play at this point.

> Change management serves to keep resistance to a minimum and to ensure the necessary skills for the future state on the part of those affected. (5-1)

Change Management has therefore always dealt with the human side of change. This is less about financial, technical or planning aspects than about the behaviour and experience of employees in the context of comprehensive transformations. If one summarizes the extensive literature or the numerous consulting approaches around the topic change management, then one arrives at a quite simple, common denominator, which is shown in Fig. 12.2.

On the right side of this model change success is indicated, the goal of all efforts. The merger was a success. The new ERP software has been successfully implemented. The restructuring has turned into a good thing. The new processes

12.2 Change Management: Classic Thinking

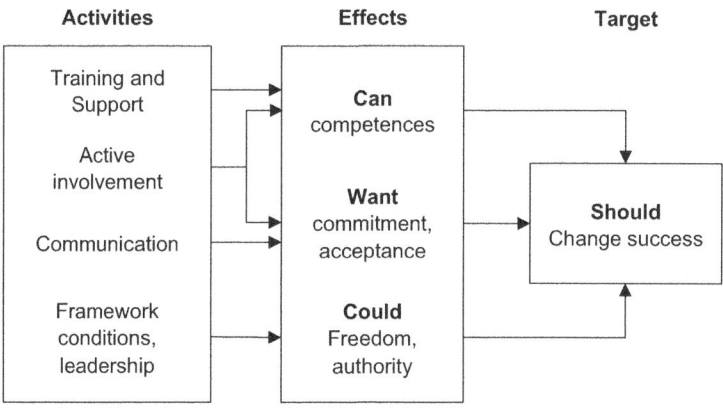

Fig. 12.2 The core of classical change management

after reengineering have stabilized. The change in strategy—for example, the change from producing combustion engine to electric motor at an automobile manufacturer—is bearing fruit. The changed values of the employees have been reflected effectively and sustainably in their daily behaviour. This successful change is what the company has been striving for from the very beginning. It reflects the *should*, the desired state after a successful change. For this success to be achieved, three simple and obvious factors are decisive on the part of the employees: they *can* contribute to the success, they *want* to and *could* do so. In the management language, all this is also referred to as commitment, acceptance, competence, authority, etc. For all this to be achieved, a number of targeted and planned activities are required, which together make up what is known as *change management*, indicated on the left side in Fig. 12.2.

Through *communication* not only the necessity of change but also a convincing vision of change is conveyed. A clearly defined communication strategy describes who is informed by whom, when, why and how. The desired result is the highest possible commitment on the part of the employees that the change will be beneficial for the company but also for themselves. *Training* measures and accompanying *support* ensure that colleagues not only want to contribute to change, but can also bear the consequences of change. Both can be strengthened through appropriate active *involvement*. Turning those affected into active players as a communication and development measure at one and the same time. Finally, it must be ensured that the employees also are able to live the change. This requires appropriate framework conditions, which often have to do with the type of leadership and organization.

This representation of a traditional change management is certainly very simplified. Nevertheless, it reflects what has been thought, practised, taught and written for many years in connection with this subject. The most frequently quoted books on this subject are by and large also include a description of this (cf. Kotter 1996; Cummings and Worley 2005). Basically it stands for a hierarchical view based on the assumption of stability as a normal and ideal state. At the top of the hierarchy it is decided to transform the company from a current situation to a target situation. In order for this to happen successfully from the top management's point of view, appropriate top-down change management measures are initiated. Once the change has taken place, one strives for a state of stability.

Communication: As Late as Possible

As described above, traditional change management cannot avoid communicating the comprehensive change to the affected employees. This is usually done according to a clear plan. This plan seems to follow certain principles, especially in hierarchically managed companies. A central principle is that communication takes place top-down. Middle managers learn about a change before their employees do. In addition, employees should be informed of a change before they hear about it from the press. This is not only a question of respect for colleagues, but also a question of control. Internal communication seems to be somewhat controllable, whereas information that reaches the public can develop a threatening dynamic of its own. All this leads to the following strategic orientation:

> The workforce is not informed until as many details as possible have been thought through and planned for a change. Anything else would lead to uncertainty and confusion. (6-1)

In a hierarchical context, the moment of broad communication will be delayed for as long as possible, because the mere announcement of a change on the part of those affected triggers questions. What does this mean for me? Will I lose my job? Will my job or environment change? Are my qualifications sufficient? A management team that thinks hierarchically wants to maintain control more than anything else. The inability to provide answers to numerous questions is tantamount to admitting that one does not know what one is doing.

12.3 Change in an Agile Setting

The traditional understanding of change and change management has always been comparatively clear. Most of what was written about change management or practised in relation to change management in the last century was more or less from the same mould. Well, in the context of agility the concepts of change and change management seem to be becoming increasingly diffuse.

The Diffusion of a Traditional Concept

If one observes the debate concerning change and change management in communities inspired by agility, one inevitably gets the impression that a Babylonian confusion of languages is at hand here. In contrast to the above, there is talk of

12.3 Change in an Agile Setting

continuous change, of many small changes driven by employees themselves, of earliest possible involvement, of experimentation, failure, continuous learning and of scaling the successful.

These alternative views on change and change management seem to leave little of what was previously associated with these concepts. At the same time they become more diffuse. What is a "change" at all and what is not, one tends to ask. Where does change management begin and where does it end? In the light of agile principles, this development should be taken very seriously. In this respect, the alternative points of view already mentioned will be discussed step by step in the following. Overall, they represent strategic antitheses to the traditional understanding.

Early Involvement

We start again with a quite traditional point of view. Accordingly, companies usually go through several phases when changes occur. At the beginning there is the initialization. This phase includes an active examination of a possible change and finally leads to a decision about it. Should this company be acquired or not? Do we want to introduce new software or not? Are we betting on a new product line? Do we want to relaunch our performance management? If the decision is positive, the scope of the project is determined. One describes a vision, gives the project a name and decides according to which strategic priorities the change should be made. Is it about speed or quality? Is there little or no involvement of those affected? Then the project is set up. A team is put together. The budget and the milestones are defined. This is followed by the extensive conception or design phase. In a reengineering project, for example, process charts are drawn. The future is anticipated in this phase. Finally, the actual change takes place in the sense of implementation. The new corporate structure goes live. The new product is now in production. The new brand is communicated and rolled out. And because all this never runs smoothly from the outset, a phase of stabilization is needed. Problems that arise here are cleared of the way, employees are supported, etc. An overview of these phases is shown in Fig. 12.3.

But now to the actual question: At what point should the affected employees be informed about the change or actively involved? At which stage do those affected play an active, decisive, creative role? There are two extreme answers to this question and any number of shades of grey in between. Hierarchically thinking companies will tend to communicate changes as late as possible, preferably after conception and planning, as argued in the previous section.

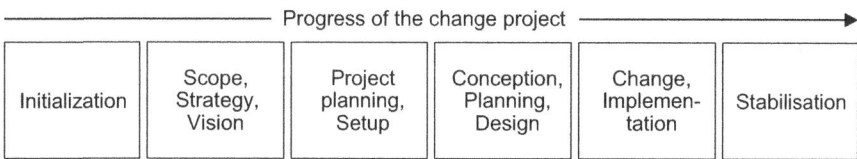

Fig. 12.3 Typical phases of a change project

In an agile context, however, the answer is based on agile principles: Employees should be involved as early as possible, if possible during initialization. For agile companies this answer is the basic attitude, a kind of default setting and only in justified exceptions is it deviated from.

> In the course of changes, employees take active responsibility as early as possible. Late communication creates victims, ignores the creativity of those affected and triggers dysfunctional resistance. (6-2)

Companies that think and act in this way justify this by the fact that later resistance can be avoided and that the intelligence and knowledge of the employees can be actively used at an early stage. Through this strategy, those affected embrace the change and will be more motivated than if they were later surprised by decisions made over their heads.

Corporate Democracy and Grassroots Movements

The idea of strategic and comprehensive decisions always being made by top management is probably kind of naive. If you leave the business world for a moment and look into the history of Europe, for example, you will quickly see that numerous, significant changes have been brought about by the citizens, the people. One thinks here of the French Revolution or the peaceful revolution that preceded the German reunification.

Are revolutions in companies conceivable? They are called differently in this context but the principles are quite comparable. Imagine what happens in a company when a single employee has an ingenious idea of strategic potential. Figure 12.4 shows two scenarios.

We'll start with scenario A. An employee has (1) an idea. In a hierarchical context, the employee will talk to his or her direct manager. If things go well, he or she talks to the next level manager and so on. Finally, if the top management (2) is

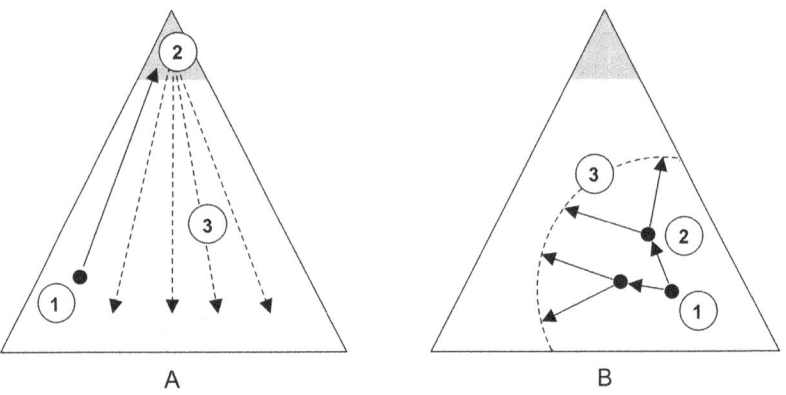

Fig. 12.4 What happens to a good idea with strategic potential?

12.3 Change in an Agile Setting

also convinced of this idea, there is a good chance that a strategic decision will emerge from the idea, which in the end (3) will have an impact on the entire company. In hierarchical companies, the idea only has an official chance through this path. The official lines of report and command must be followed.

Scenario *B* could take place in an agile context. An employee has (1) an idea. He or she may talk to colleagues from other areas about the idea and try to convince them about his or her idea. What starts as a small group (2) gradually becomes a larger, cross-functional community, which believes in this idea. In the meantime, the idea of joint exchange has developed and been improved. Possibly the first pilots have already taken place. All this happens beyond formal hierarchies and is either only tolerated or even desired by senior management. In the end, the idea and its implementation (3) find its way in large parts or even in the entire organization. This scenario is only conceivable in agile organizations. There, however, it is a self-evident principle.

> Where possible, it is the employees themselves who initiate, decide and drive change (bottom-up). (3-2)

With changes of this kind, the concept of the *grassroots movement* has become increasingly widespread in practice—changes that take place slowly, from below and increasingly across entire companies.

As I write this book, a concept that is not only capable of enabling grassroots movements but also of spreading in the form of such a movement is rapidly gaining acceptance, especially in large, formerly hierarchical companies. We are talking about *Working Out Loud*, a concept that takes up numerous principles of agile work (cf. Stepper 2015). Employees network on their own responsibility across department boundaries and meet weekly for a period of 12 weeks in so-called circles, which do not include more than five colleagues. Each circle participant not only pursues his or her personal, explicitly formulated goal, but also supports the other participants in achieving their respective goals. In the end, this concept is not only about building networks but also about increasing perceived self-efficacy and internal visibility. For more and more employees, this concept is the appropriate vehicle to stretch their heads out of the previously felt institutional limitations and meaninglessness.

Between the two scenarios described above there are, of course, mixed forms. Sometimes ideas and suggestions for change are addressed upwards by more and more employees until they become unmistakable. In other cases, companies hold large-scale *open space events* where very large groups of employees are involved at the same time and have the opportunity to articulate and accumulate the need for change. And when the decision is finally taken to change any size or scope, the employees are democratically involved in the decision-making process. You vote on whether a product should continue to be produced. You vote on restructuring, on changing an internal process, on selecting new business software, on the right cost-saving measure, etc. And if not all employees should always vote, then a group is chosen which takes over this task representatively for the majority. In this context, there is increasing talk of *corporate democracy*. For the hierarchically socialized observer this seems completely utopian. For more and more companies, on the other hand, this is the only viable way forward and the successful examples have been becoming more frequent and visible for several years now.

In principle, strictly hierarchical companies find it extremely difficult to develop and disseminate new ideas for change independently and on their own responsibility, because the necessary freedom for this is not provided for. Probably the biggest obstacle to concepts such as Working Out Loud is middle management. Employees who network on their own initiative, spend time with colleagues from other areas, develop their own ideas compete with their "actual task" (as is stated in their job descriptions) from middle manager's point of view. It is not uncommon for employees to hear from their direct superiors when they are doing work in the interests of the company: "What are you doing back in that circle? You do not seem to be working to your full capacity. How can you have so much time for new ideas and initiatives? And anyway, what do you actually have to do with the colleagues from the other departments? Are you looking for a new job? If something does not suit you here, just talk to me".

Iterative Change

As already described previously in this chapter, large-scale changes in hierarchically managed companies always go through the phases of conception and planning before starting into the well-prepared phase of implementation. The better the conception and planning, the more successful the implementation. In a stable setting, this approach might be appropriate. Often the resources of external consultants with many years of experience in comparable change projects are engaged. They are then happy to bring their semi-finished blueprints from other projects with them (the customer's name is changed in the footers of the PowerPoint slides).

However, for more and more companies the situation is different. Particularly in the context of digitization, they are breaking new ground and other companies hardly have any experience that can be transferred directly to their own case. You go, so to speak, on a journey to a country for which there is no map available yet. In this case it is better to do what the explorers have done before: drive on sight. In the management language, this is referred to as an iterative procedure (see also Sect. 4.3). Instead of first planning and then acting, planning and acting become blurred in short-term cycles. Things are tried out, hypotheses are formed, pilots are started, prototypes are tested. Progress is characterised by early failure, simultaneous learning and rapid optimization. What proves itself is finally scaled up.

> Changes are always fraught with uncertainty. Therefore, they take place continuously through protected experimentation, learning, failure and scaling up the successful. (4-2)

Of course, this does not apply to all forms of change. For example, it is difficult to test the full scope of the merger of two companies. For agile companies, however, the iterative approach is the basic attitude and not the exception.

Evolution or Revolution

Several years ago I asked the following question in an exam: "What is a change in the context of change management?" Only years later did I realize how difficult it was to answer this particular question. At that time, I conveyed the traditional understanding of change management described above, according to which a change is always comprehensive, of strategic importance and many employees are equally affected. In my opinion, that would have been the right answer at the time.

When I now sit together with HR professionals, organizational consultants, agility bloggers or other clever representatives of the agile thinking community, I occasionally dare to ask the above question: "Hey, what do you actually understand by a change?" What follows is always amazing. It can be observed how experienced, educated, intelligent, reflected professionals from the relevant scene are far from finding a common denominator. The statements range from a traditional understanding—which tends to get rejected by the progressive faction—to the statement that change is somehow everything that goes along with a change in thinking and behaviour. In contrast, the view that change in the context of change management is all that change management requires, seems intelligent, although somewhat tautological. This includes small and comprehensive changes. There is the traditional view that change management is about big change only. We then like to talk about revolution, a real upheaval, a reform. This view is contrasted with the view that change is an evolution consisting of many small adaptations. Both perspectives are justified.

> Change is evolution rather than revolution. We consider even comprehensive changes to be the sum of many small changes. (2-2)

Whether now changes in the sense of a revolution or reform fit more to a hierarchical world and the evolution more into an agile world, cannot be answered in general terms.

Internal and External Locus of Control

As already explained in the previous section, change management always had the intention to keep a change under control despite human, dysfunctional reactions. It was primarily a matter of avoiding resistance as far as possible on the one hand (want) and at the same time ensuring change-relevant abilities on the part of those affected (can) on the other. And when we talk about control in this context, we mean explicitly and implicitly the control of senior management (cf. Kotter 1996). But you do not have to see things that way. Not only management aims for control, the employees do so too.

This consideration touches on the psychological concept of *locus of control*, which originally goes back to the humanist psychologist Carl Rogers (1961) and was further developed by Rotter (1966). To illustrate this concept in an organizational context, two fictitious employees—we call them Anne and Ben—are juxtaposed. First to Anne:

> Anne is convinced of what she does every day in terms of content. She recognizes the meaning in her work. Her actions are driven by intrinsic motivation. She does what she does because she not only thinks it is right, but also because she believes she can do it herself. She can attribute success to her own effort and ability. She tackles new challenges and changes when she is convinced of her potential to learn new things. She takes responsibility for failures and feels strengthened in her self-esteem when she achieves success.

Obviously Anne possesses a strong belief in her being in control. In psychology we refer to this as *internal* locus of control. This is quite different in our second fictitious case, Ben:

> Ben either does what he is told or what he is allowed to do. Ben may or should only tackle new challenges and changes if his supervisor believes he can. The meaningfulness experienced in his work is secondary, after all he is paid appropriately for what he does. He does not recognize successes as his own successes. Finally, he merely followed the (apparently) correct instructions. The same goes for failures.

Obviously Ben has an *external* locus control. He experiences himself as the object of an environment that determines him. People like Ben tend to often ask: "What am I supposed to do now?" or "Am I doing it the right way?"

The crucial question now is how individuals with internal or external locus of control react to changes in their environment or how they deal with them. If one distinguishes between external and self-determined changes in the case of changes, the four quadrants in Fig. 12.5 result. By externally controlled changes we mean those that occur without the active intervention of the employees or are decided over their heads. Self-determined changes, on the other hand, are those changes that were initiated or even decided by the employees themselves.

If employees with external locus of control become victims of a change that passively happens to them (B), they rightly react with uncertainty. What will this

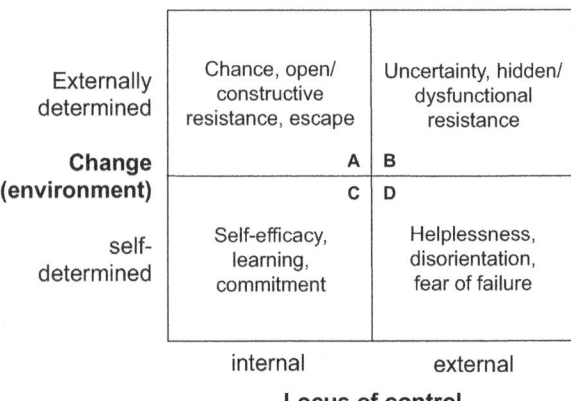

Fig. 12.5 Reactions with different environmental-individual constellations

12.3 Change in an Agile Setting

mean for me? Will I be able to meet the new, changed requirements? Do they think I can do that? What if I don't? Especially for people with an external locus of control, such a collapse of stability conveys a feeling of losing control. They experience themselves as the toys of a superordinate system (cf. Conner 1992). Because you know that you can't do anything about it, resistances tend to be concealed and possibly lead to becoming dysfunctional, even destructive behavioural patterns (e.g. sabotage, inner resignation, service by the book).

But even for employees with an internal locus of control, externally determined changes are difficult to endure (A). They are reluctant to respond to changes decided over their heads. Such changes remind these employees that they too are dependent on a system in which others have more power than themselves. Any resistance is articulated openly and constructively, because one never wants to give the impression that one is really only a victim. Nevertheless, they see an opportunity in change: "If that is the case, we'll make the most of it now".

If employees with external locus of control are enabled to initiate and promote self-determined changes (D), they react with helplessness and disorientation. They look at their managers with helpless eyes and ask: "And what exactly are we supposed to do now?" Answer from above: "Please think for yourself". Reaction of the employees: "And how do we do this in concrete terms?" People with external locus of control on the one hand and an environment that demands self-determination on the other are simply incompatible. However, if those affected try to take their own steps, they do so in disorientation and with an overwhelming fear of failure—cycling without support wheels. Effects of this kind can also be observed in society when people are released from a totalitarian system into the personal responsibility of a democracy. Sooner or later the call for a strong ruler becomes loud.

People with an internal locus of control feel most comfortable in a self-determined environment (C). Through autonomous thinking and design, they experience what the great psychologist Albert Bandura (1997) refers to as *self-efficacy*. He sees it as an essential source for continuous learning, meaningfulness and identification with one's own work.

What do these considerations mean for change management? The conclusions are comparatively simple. Traditional change management is based on case *B*, according to which dependent people with an external locus of control must be guided by an externally determined change. The challenge is not so much to keep employees in control—which they have never experienced anyway—but to maintain control on the part of senior decision-makers who initiated the change. The aim is to reduce uncertainties and keep dysfunctional resistances at a minimum. In hierarchically managed companies this is the normal case.

In agile companies, on the other hand, the opposite case *C* in the bottom left corner is aimed at as the default setting, although the neighbouring cases are not excluded. But if exactly this case *C* occurs, then change management is simply obsolete. The principle applies:

> As long as employees drive change themselves (could), we do not have to worry about competence (can) and acceptance (want). (5-2)

If employees do what they think makes sense in a self-determined way, then resistance is not to be expected. Of course, especially in agile settings, there are sometimes intense conflicts and disputes. But these are part of daily normality. There are also challenges and sometimes the feeling of being overwhelmed. But that, too, is normal. As explained in detail in Sect. 7.3 (Continuous learning), agile companies speak of irritations here, which in turn are assumed to be essential prerequisites for continuous learning and professional development.

I have got to know agile companies again and again that have their own change management team. But if you take a closer look at what these teams do day in, day out, their work includes organizing bar camps, open space events, design thinking workshops or arranging training to teach agile working techniques. All this has nothing to do with classical change management at all.

Change as a Normal State

If, for example, a process is reengineered in a hierarchically managed company that is designed for stability, then at some point there will be a document describing the new process. This document then probably has a special sounding name like "ProcessDescription08-15_final_final_absolutfinal.doc", or something similar. If then something is really "final", then nothing more is supposed to be changed in the process. Now it is valid for an indefinite period of time. There used to be an old process that was valid for many years. Then this process was put to the test and redefined under pain. Finally, the new process was adopted and now it is all fine. Unfreeze, move, and then above all: refreeze.

In the course of increasing priority towards more agility, however, this logic is more and more being called into question. With reference to Kurt Lewin, it is often postulated that in agile settings there is no longer a refreeze, but only a move within the constant state of both unfreeze and move. This idea goes hand in hand with the already mentioned consideration that there are no more big changes in agile settings but only many small ones. Change and transformation become normal. Everything flows. Nothing is more constant than change.

> We regard continuous change as a normal state. Changes are never complete, nor should they be. (1-2)

I myself am not ready to accept this idea completely, but assume that even in agile companies there are comprehensive changes that will eventually be completed. It would go too far to claim that this does not exist in such a setting. A single case would be sufficient to refute this assertion—as Karl Popper would rightly object. Nevertheless, the tendency behind this consideration is to be taken seriously at least theoretically. It goes hand in hand with a strategic dimension in which change is either seen as one-off or as part of a continuous, never-ending process of change.

In the preceding sections, a number of facets of change and change management were examined, where a view that deviated from the traditional viewpoint led to change and change management being questioned or seen in a different light. Understanding change now as part of a continuous, never-ending process finally calls traditional change management into question. Now, at the latest, the boundaries between change management and *continuous improvement processes* (CIP) are blurring. Where does change management begin and where do daily operational decisions stop as part of regular business management?

Change and Change Management in an Agile Context

In this chapter we have assumed a traditional understanding of change and change management. Accordingly, a change is a one-off process in which a comprehensive transformation is made. This change is initiated, planned and controlled by senior management. Extensive analyses, risk assessments and rational decision-making processes precede this initiation. They usually take place without the employees. During implementation, appropriate change management measures are required to overcome uncertainties and resistance on the part of the affected employees. After the change has been completed, one is anxious to return to a stable state.

In the preceding sections, this traditional understanding was successively taken apart. Each facet of change and change management was compared with possible alternatives. It became clear that these alternatives are most conceivable in agile companies. Employees decide for themselves about changes that are ultimately driven by themselves. Unique, comprehensive changes give way to continuous change, consisting of many small changes. Therefore the threat of resistance loses importance. Rational planning and control make room for experimentation, failure and continuous learning (see Fig. 12.6).

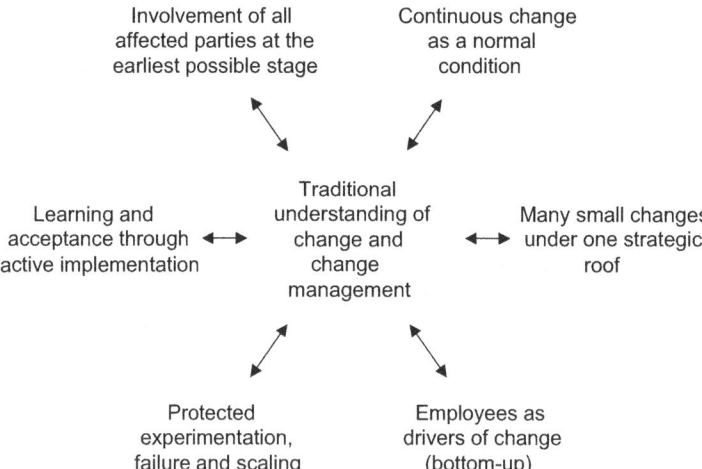

Fig. 12.6 Alternative characteristics of change and change management in an agile setting

Nevertheless, it should not be assumed that in a hierarchical setting only one, traditional side is possible, while agile companies distinguish themselves by the other side. Reality is by far more complex and the perspectives usually mix. The bottom line, however, is that it is unmistakable that the significance of change itself seems to be changing and with it the relevance of what has been understood as change management for many years. At the same time it can be stated that in the course of agilization the terms change and change management lose their clarity. In a way, they seem to be diffusing. If there had been only agile companies in the history of mankind, the discipline of change management would probably not exist and John Kotter would have had to turn to another topic.

All in all the dimensions presented in this chapter are less strategic than descriptive (see Fig. 12.7). They serve less to strategically align the handling of change than to outline how changes and their management can be understood in different ways.

Desired normal condition	**1-1 Stability** Changes occur out of a state of stability. After a phase of upheaval, we are again striving for this stable state.	**1-2 Change** We regard continuous change as a normal state. Changes are never complete, nor should they be.
Meaning of "Change"	**2-1 Strategic change** By "change" we mean first and foremost a comprehensive change with strategic implications that affects many employees at the same time.	**2-2 Evolution in small steps** Change is evolution rather than revolution. We consider even comprehensive changes to be the sum of many small changes.
Drivers for changes	**3-1 Senior Management (top-down)** Changes of strategic importance are always decided, planned and driven top-down. This is a central task of senior management.	**3-2 All employees (bottom-up)** Wherever possible, it is the employees themselves who initiate, decide and drive change
Decision-making processes	**4-1 Rational** Changes are only initiated if one is aware of their consequences at the highest decision-making level. Anything else would be irresponsible.	**4-2 Explorative** Changes are always fraught with uncertainty. Therefore, they take place continuously through protected experimentation, learning, failure and scaling up the successful.
Objective of change management	**5-1 Acceptance and competence** Change management serves to keep resistance to a minimum and to ensure the necessary skills for the future state on the part of those affected.	**5-2 No necessity** As long as employees drive change themselves (could), we do not have to worry about competence (can) and acceptance (want).
Communication to employees	**6-1 Late communication if possible** The workforce is not informed until as many details as possible have been thought through and planned for a change. Anything else would lead to uncertainty and confusion.	**6-2 Early involvement as possible** In the course of changes, employees take active responsibility as early as possible. Late communication creates victims, ignores the creativity of those affected and triggers dysfunctional resistance.

Fig. 12.7 Overview of all strategic dimensions for managing change and transformations

References

Bandura A (1997) Self-efficacy. The exercise of control. Freeman, New York

Conner DR (1992) Managing at the speed of change. How resilient managers succeed and prosper where others fail. Villard, New York

Cummings TG, Worley CG (2005) Organization development and change. Thomson/South-Western, Mason, OH

Kotter JP (1996) Leading change. Harvard Business School Press, Boston

Kübler-Ross E (1969) On death and dying. Routledge, London

Lewin K (1947) Frontiers in group dynamics. In: Cartwright D (ed) Field theory in social science, S 5–41

Rogers CR (1961) On becoming a person: a therapist's view of psychotherapy. Houghton Mifflin, New York

Rotter J (1966) Generalized expectancies for internal versus external control of reinforcement. Psychol Monogr 80(1):1–28

Stepper J (2015) Working out loud. For a better career and life. Ikigai Press, New York

Suzaki K (1993) The new shopfloor management. Empowering people for continuous improvement. The Free Press, New York

Transformation into an Agile Future 13

Almost always when I have given a lecture on modern, agile HR strategies, the question that follows is how one would manage to move as a company from a hierarchical, stable world in the direction of higher agility. As a reader of this book you might have thought of a similar question while reading it. In fact, we can see an overall trend towards higher agility. I have not met a single company in recent years that has claimed that it wants to move more towards silos in the coming years, reduce lateral cooperation, standardize jobs and take responsibility away from employees. The development seems to be exactly the other way around. Anyway, I will take the liberty of making a personal statement first.

A Personal Statement
If I had a solution to the question of how the agile transformation actually could succeed, I would probably be a future candidate for the Nobel Prize in Economics. After every keynote I am downright afraid of the above question, because I find myself again in the situation of having to say to a large audience: "I do not know how this can work in your case". Maybe I do not have to have an answer to the question either, because after all I am just an HR professor and not an expert on agile transformation. And also this book deals with relevant questions around HR and not primarily with agility itself. Nevertheless, this problem touches and occupies me every day. And so for many years I have been moving from one irritation to another, from one insight and observation to the next. My learning process and my approach to this topic are also somewhat agile. I am never at the end just like nobody ever will be. We can only learn continuously. Therefore, everything I write in the following merely reflects a current state of my point of view. I do this with the tantalizing hunch that in 5 or 10 years I would see things differently and more maturely. Books are static and always a snapshot. The change we are currently experiencing is not.

I would therefore first like to address the difficulties and major hurdles of an agile transformation. This is followed by a series of principles of successful agile transformation, of which I am convinced at least today. The reader may take all this not as the ultimate truth, but as a source of stimulation and inspiration.

13.1 Challenges and Hurdles

Turning a hierarchical company striving for stability and predictability into an agile company is a challenge that many companies have taken up. But to master this transformation successfully is close to the limit of impossibility. You should be aware of that. The reasons for this are manifold and sometimes only a few of them are enough to see a project of this kind fail.

Integration and Interfaces

Large corporations in particular operate on the basis of numerous integrated and interfaced processes. This is not only the case in HR—think of the numerous interfaces between performance management, remuneration, talent management, etc.—but also in purchasing, logistics and accounting. Here it is rarely possible to remove or rebuild isolated processes, because all the rest is connected with it. Either you change everything somehow or nothing at all.

Internalized Thinking and Acting

Hierarchical thinking and acting in hierarchical companies is deeply internalized in the subconscious of all players and explicitly hardly accessible. This thinking is reflected in almost every micro-situation. One acts according to a hierarchical pattern without being aware of it. This can be felt in communication, in language—how e-mails are written and answered, how meetings take place, etc.—in architecture, in the form of even the smallest decision-making processes, in clothing, in almost everything. Behaviour is shaped by culture and, conversely, behaviour strengthens culture. How to find the exit from this cycle?

Proven Behavioral Patterns in Difficult Times

Particularly in difficult situations, people tend to fall back on proven behavioural patterns. If it then becomes even more threatening, behaviours related to childhood appear (e.g. hysterical screaming). Then follow archaic patterns, escape or attack. If the weather is fine, an agile transformation could succeed. But do not let the weather change for the worse. Then at the latest, a firm grip will be taken from above. Then there is an end to self-direction and informal networking. Not only does Laloux (2014) report such cases. In fact, a number of companies, Laloux referred to in his ground-breaking book "Reinventing Organizations", have fallen back into old hierarchical behaviour patterns in the wake of a crisis. Developments of this kind take place amazingly fast.

Reproduction of the Same

Systems, whether hierarchical or agile in nature, naturally try to reproduce themselves. In systems theory we also speak of the process of *autopoiesis* (Luhmann 1984). In organizations, for example, there is a tendency to select or promote people who are similar to the decision-makers themselves. Bureaucrats support bureaucrats or hire them. Bureaucrats apply to companies in which they expect to be allowed to be bureaucrats. In contrast, those people who do not fit into the system (lateral thinkers) tend to be thrown out.

Hierarchization of Agile Efforts

When a delicate, agile seed grows in any unit within a company—this is usually the case in the IT function—its agile thinking and acting is literally eaten up by a hierarchically dominated superior power. What begins agile is gradually hierarchized top-down. Working Out Loud, for example, begins self-directed (cf. Stepper 2015). However, from the day on which the HR Director adopts this topic in a well-meaning manner, KPIs or Working Out Loud representatives are called in. At some point circles will no longer take place because the people want it, but because they have to, which certainly means the end of this beautiful concept.

External Regulation

Companies, too, are integrated into overarching systems whose dynamics and functionality they depend on. Banks are subject to banking supervision. Suppliers must endure quality management audits because they are not accepted without the appropriate certificates. Trade unions demand certain regulations. And then there's the legislator. The demands of these bodies are often anything but compatible with agile principles. They are often based on mistrust and a traditional understanding of business management. All this leads to complex reporting structures and rigid documentation based on mostly rigid rules. "We'd like to operate in a more agile manner, but we're simply not allowed to."

When Employees Request the Boss

And then there are the employees. Even when an executive undergoes a wondrous Saulus-Paulus-like transformation from boss to coach, that executive is pushed every hour or even every minute into the boss role that his or her employees are accustomed to and still request. "Is that convenient for you?" "How exactly are we supposed to do this now?" it is hard to turn a boss into a coach. After all, the boss became the boss because he or she is who he or she is. However, the real challenge only begins when the boss decides to be coach from now on. His or her team won't always thank him or her. And the coach's danger of falling back into the boss role lurks in every second.

13.2 Principles of Agile Transformation

These points outlined in the previous section could be extended at will. They are anything but complete, but they give an impression of how extremely difficult it is to change the nature of an entire company or just parts of it. The principles of successful transformation discussed later in this chapter take up some aspects or supplement them. The following principles are discussed in detail:

- Agility is not an end in itself. It requires convincing reasons why agility strengthens the company's competitiveness.
- One should know where one stands in the sense of a self-critical status view and develop realistic expectations of the future.
- The CEO must really want the agile transformation
- It requires coaching by externals with experience. You cannot reinvent yourself or pull yourself out of the swamp.
- An agile transformation should take place as early as possible according to agile principles. Agility cannot be forced in a hierarchical manner.
- You do not change the culture by changing the culture. Rather, one should always start by changing the structural framework conditions first.
- The personal experience of relevant players is more important than a theoretical communication of a possible, agile future.
- Especially in large companies, agile transformation is more evolutionary and step-by-step than in the form of revolution or reform.
- You have to allow failure to happen and learn collectively from it.
- Often there is nothing else left to do but to restart completely on the green field.
- As an individual employee you should show courage, not be too impressed by the hierarchical environment, but be right in the end.

Agility Is Not an End in Itself

No company becomes agile because it only wants to become agile. To become really agile you need solid business reasons. Several reasons were already discussed in the first chapter of this book. At this point John Kotter is certainly right when he repeatedly refers to the importance of a "Sense of Urgency". Ultimately, the issues at stake are competitiveness, the resilience needed to adapt to new market conditions at an appropriate pace, employer attractiveness and innovation. These reasons must be clear and evident.

Self-Critical Status Review and Realistic Expectations of the Future

An agile transformation always presupposes an intensive, honest, structured and moderated confrontation with the question of where one currently stands and where one wants to go. What is our current, dominant understanding of leadership like? Do our employees and teams tend to be committed to higher authorities or to their colleagues and customers? How much personal responsibility and self-control is currently given? All these aspects have already been explained in detail in Chaps. 2–4 in this book.

According to my own experiences, there are two traps here. The tendency is to overestimate the current status with regard to its agility character. "We are actually quite agile in many respects". On closer inspection, however, the expectations are extremely low. I have done this exercise many times before and hear statements of this kind again and again. Then it is argued, for example, that the employees actually already have a great deal of creative freedom. If I then ask what this assessment is based on, I hear things like "We have an employee suggestion system where every employee has the opportunity to contribute ideas". Employees of really agile companies would laugh themselves to death. They are used to simply implementing good ideas. In the light of low expectations, many things seem incredibly agile. It is therefore important to reflect critically on assessments of the current situation. External monitoring is therefore very helpful.

The second trap is to overestimate the possibility of what can be achieved in the medium and long term. Several months ago, when I carried out this exercise with executives from federal ministries, those present initially thought that they could bring their organizations to a start-up-like level in a few years. After more intense discussion and a confrontation with reality in genuinely agile companies, it quickly became clear that this would never be the case.

The CEO Must Really Want it

There is a simple truth that agile transformation will never succeed if the CEO does not want it out of deep conviction (see also Laloux 2014). Readers who want to contribute to an agile transformation in their company but at the same time find that their CEO is not committed to this topic can close this book at this point. It just does not make any sense. You have to see things in this clarity and toughness, even if the high importance of the CEO seems somewhat hierarchical at first glance.

Why is that? The agile thinking and operating *product owner* in the sense of Scrum, for example, will have a difficult life if his next level manager acts as a boss. The product owner bears the responsibility for the development of a product but acts from a moderating role. He's more a coach and a partner than a boss. While he and his team have nothing but the customer's needs in mind, the boss expects reports and gives instructions for things of which he has only limited knowledge. In constellations like these, the superior boss becomes the greatest obstacle. Conversely, product owners in such a setting will have hard times in protecting their team and its work from the boss. To put it even more vividly, here is a typical dialogue between a Product Owner (PO) and a higher-level Head of Department (HoD):

HoD: Will you please send me a status report of all your projects by the end of the month? You know, nicely, with traffic lights and the like.
PO: Why?
HoD: The Head of Division [the manager of HoD] has asked for it.
PO: Why?
HoD: He didn't say. He wants it and that is why he is getting it. That is the way it works.
PO: What if I do not see that?
HoD: Then I have a problem. And you do not want that, do you?
PO: At least ask him why he needs the reports. And take the opportunity to tell him that our clients neither expect nor pay us for writing damn reports.
HoD: I am not questioning my supervisor's instructions.
PO: Then let me talk to him.
HoD: That makes me look bad. So, you won't be doing that.
PO: OK, then tell him that we would be very pleased about his interest in our projects and that he is always welcome to participate in one of our upcoming sprints.
HoD: He won't have time for that.
PO: Then he obviously does not care about what we do. You can tell him that, please.

And it goes on and on and on this way, day in, day out. The ultimate solution to this problem can only be that the CEO either protects the company as a whole or individual divisions or pilots from hierarchical mechanisms. Especially in hierarchical companies, but also in agile organizations, the CEO simply has the power for it. When he stands in front of the team and clearly announces that certain things will no longer take place, then these things are usually over.

Coaching by Externals with Experience

When hierarchically socialized employees and managers begin to set up agile structures, there is a constant danger that they will fall back into hierarchical thinking. As a consultant, I've experienced this a hundred times. "If the employees do not want to work on their own responsibility, then we make this part of their target agreement with corresponding KPIs, etc.". And there it is again, the hierarchical ghost. A wrong decision in a weak moment and things go in the wrong direction again. External coaches with experience can make a valuable contribution here. "Objection. We had actually agreed that we didn't want this anymore. So, let's discuss this again, please". External coaches can give practical impulses. "Why do not we just do this?" "That is right. Why not? We hadn't thought of that at all". Of course, they didn't think of it. You never have experienced it.

Internal coaches are also conceivable. It is not unusual for colleagues who have already had intensive experience with agile work to help those in other areas that are still in their infancy. In this sense, it is conceivable to build internal pools of coaches and set up a multiplier system.

Agile Principles in Transformation

In a way, an agile transformation is a multi-layered problem that seems insoluble on closer inspection. A company wants to reinvent itself from a current, hierarchical origin and become somehow agile. It is clear that something needs to be done about this. A transformation does not just fall from the sky. But how do you do the things you do? A hierarchical company acts hierarchically. An agile company, on the other hand, acts according to agile principles. But how does a company act in the course of a transformation if it wants to become agile, but is still hierarchical and can only be hierarchical? A thought experiment can help here. We imagine two extreme scenarios. First, the hierarchical scenario.

> During a closed meeting, the company management decides on an agile transformation. For this purpose, a steering committee is first set up and then the project group is defined. After a clear objective has been developed with the help of an external consultant, a detailed roadmap is drawn up - milestones, project phases, work packages, sub-projects, timelines - the usual. After that the thing always gets carried out. What was initially planned is now being worked through step by step. The project leader (Head of Agile Transformation) may regularly report to the Steering Committee to report and to collect strategic instructions.

Those who are already used to agile working will feel instant pain in this scenario. This is an agile transformation according to hierarchical principles. This can't be good. Now to the other extreme:

> The starting point is a two-day blend of bar camp and conference on the topic of "Agile Future", to which managers and employees are invited at the same time. This event was preceded by an extensive reflection on the current situation and the conceivable future (as described above). Impulses were given by external speakers, who created a high degree of irritation. Supported by external coaches, all those involved are working on sketching an agile future. Pilot areas will then be found on a voluntary basis. In these pilot areas, work is then carried out on the future iteratively and with the constant involvement of those concerned.

From an agile point of view, this approach sounds much more likeable. The problem with this, however, is that a hierarchical company with such a setting finds it extremely difficult. You try to be agile while you are still hierarchical. This creates a series of leaders who participate in the Bar Camp (because the CEO wants it) without really participating—"what is all this monkey business about?"

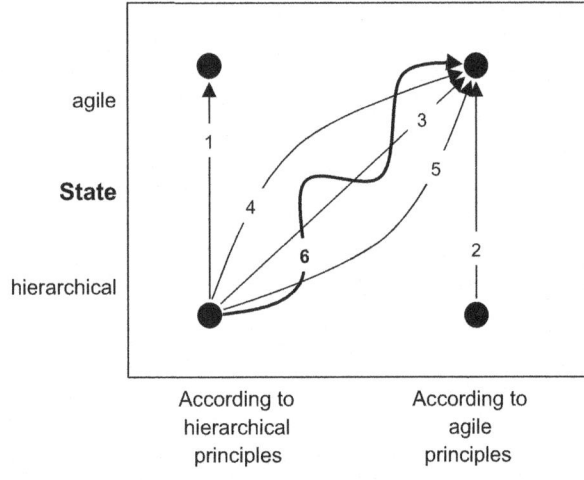

Fig. 13.1 Agile versus hierarchical principles in an agile transformation

You can neither transform a company into an agile state with hierarchical mechanisms nor act according to agile principles right from the start. The first strategy is indicated by arrow 1 in the Fig. 13.1, the second by arrow 2.

If one considers the range of possible strategies in a structured and somewhat academic way, the possibilities 3 to 6 indicated in the Fig. 13.1 remain. Option 3 shows a direct transition from hierarchical principles to agile principles. Approach 4 is based on the assumption that one first starts hierarchically and then in the course of the transformation turns the curve to agile principles, while 5 is the appropriate counterpart. Probably strategy 6 is the most likely. It assumes that the path to an agile state is a kind of adventure, a never-ending journey, paved with surprises and continuous fluctuations between hierarchical and agile principles. At some point, agile principles must dominate. An initially planned blueprint does not exist. Then all the features described in the previous chapter on the agile page will probably come into play. This has comparatively little to do with classical change management.

You Do Not Change the Culture by Changing the Culture

An agile transformation always also means a cultural change in the company. Now we know how in the past decades there have been repeated attempts to carry out cultural change projects. Their approach always has been comparatively simple. First, you decide how you want to be. The result is then what is usually referred to as *corporate value statements*. They state, for example, that in the future you want to treat each other with trust, place the customer at the centre, teamwork is more important than individual combat and that you want to treat each other with respect. Afterwards, workshops will be held throughout the company to consider what these

13.2 Principles of Agile Transformation

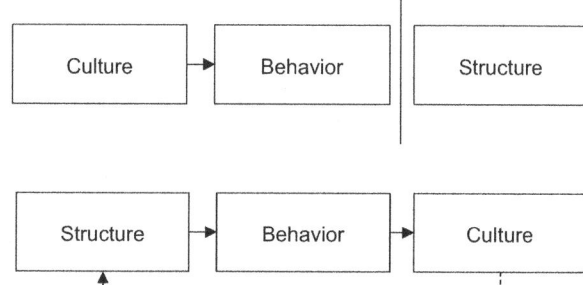

Fig. 13.2 Culture as a starting point for cultural change

Fig. 13.3 Structure as a starting point for cultural change

official corporate values mean for everyday life. From time to time, the matter is tracked by an employee survey to see to what extent these values have already had a noticeable impact. If you put so much effort into this project, then it has to work somehow. That is how you deliberately think.

The central assumption behind this standard is the belief that by defining desired values one can cause behaviour without affecting the structural context (cf. Fig. 13.2). "Once all employees have understood and internalized the values, they will act accordingly".

We can safely say today that this approach does not work because formal structures are ignored. One cannot expect a culture of trust to develop in a company as long as the employees require the approval of the divisional board member to purchase a pen. Teamwork will not take place as long as the formal performance review is competitive. There will be no eye level between employees and managers as long as managers decide one-sidedly about the salary and career of their employees. This entire book deals with the question of how to adapt HR structures—processes, systems, responsibilities, etc.—in order not only to make agility possible but also to promote it. A CEO can stand up to his or her team and proclaim "trust, respect and openness" as the new values. But whether the CEO is taken seriously by the employees depends on what is actually done in the company and how the structures fit in. "Aha, trust, nice. Then you can immediately switch off the tracking of working hours, right?"

The logic behind cultural change must be different. It assumes that you can't change culture by changing culture. That sounds paradoxical at first. The starting point must always be structures (see Fig. 13.3). The definition of structural framework conditions is of course based on the desired culture (dotted arrow), but the latter is not directly applied.

For decades there has been a scientific debate in social psychology about how attitudes and behaviour are related. Usually there are only small correlations between the two variables. A respondent's attitude to driving a bus does not correlate with the actual behaviour of preferring the bus to one's own car. Numerous studies now suggest the assumption that attitude does not determine behaviour, but that vice versa it does (cf. Dillard 1993). When people are induced to behave in a certain way (bus driving)—due to structural conditions—they will adapt their attitudes accordingly in the long run. One can transfer these considerations to the organizational context. Accordingly, rules, processes or systems must first be used to enforce a certain behaviour. As soon as those affected behave accordingly, one no longer has to worry about their attitude.

Personal Experience Instead of Only Theoretical Teaching

In my lectures on agile leadership, I always get two opposing reactions from different groups of people. Some ask themselves, from which strange star I probably come or from which strange world I have sprung. From others I again get one hundred per cent approval—"exactly the way you presented it, is how it works". The difference between the one and the other group is usually that the second group has already personally experienced or came into contact with what I represent.

Often hierarchically socialized managers develop a rather diffuse picture of what agility means in everyday life. As soon as they have heard terms like diversity, self-responsibility, networking paired with strange words like "Scrum", "Squads", "Sprints", "Coach", "Co-Working-Space" several times, they think of agility as chaos, anarchy, a colourful bunch of crackpots, where everyone somehow swoops away, does what he or she wants, without any purpose and direction. This point of view suddenly vanishes when these managers have concrete insights into agile work or even experience them directly. In the end, they realize that agile work is only for adults, and that it is the opposite of hierarchically managed kindergartens. Agility, as it quickly becomes clear, means a higher degree of speed, commitment, transparency, coordination. Above all, one learns that, for example, Scrum does *not* follow no rules but different rules and that the mutual obligation to deliver quickly and close to the customer is more pronounced than many hierarchically thinking managers could ever have imagined.

This is another reason why more and more companies are carrying out so-called *learning journeys* in the course of their agile transformation. It is not always necessary for the entire management team to make a pilgrimage to Silicon Valley. Sometimes a visit to one of the many start-ups in the home country, a visit to a co-working space or an internal internship in the already agile IT department within your own company is enough.

One Stone at a Time

Large companies in particular will find it extremely difficult to reinvent themselves completely overnight. The reasons for this have already been sufficiently addressed in the previous sub-chapter. What we observe, on the other hand, is usually a procedure that reminds us of the beautiful game Jenga. The challenge of this game is to gradually move wooden stones from a tower without it collapsing. Over the years, many companies have built bureaucratic towers consisting of rules, policies, reports and reporting paths, decision paths, target cascades, control systems—not to say "systems of mistrust". Usually these stones are interlocked in a company. With some stones, however, you can see the possibility of changing them in isolation or even removing them completely.

If a company comes up with the idea of extensively easing the travel expense policy in the course of its agilization in order to place responsibility in the hands of its employees—in the sense of Netflix: "Act in Netflix's best interest"—then many managers will become afraid. "If we do this, costs will explode." Then you pull the stone out of the tower with trembling hands and after some time you can see that the tower has even gained stability. The costs did not explode but were even reduced. The downturn of working hours tracking has not meant that nobody shows up to work anymore. On the contrary, since the teams themselves take care of their holidays, we have fewer bottlenecks. The abolition of the objective setting did not cause chaos but resulted in more reliable coordination. A step-by-step approach holds the chance of learning and increases the belief of all participants in the feasibility of change as a whole.

Allowing Failure and Learning from it

The last thing managers in hierarchically managed companies want are surprises. Surprises are the opposite of what you actually aim for, namely control, predictability and stability. Negative surprises are particularly tragic. As long as one assumes that failure was not consciously intended, every form of failure holds something unforeseen. However, as explained at several points in this book, failure is part of agile development. In this respect, failure is always an integral part of any agile transformation.

Now, especially in hierarchically thinking companies, there is a phenomenon that has long been known in management and communication theory. It describes the risk of having to bear personal, negative consequences when communicating bad news "upwards". One also speaks here of the "killing the messenger of bad news phenomenon" (Harris and Nelson 2008). The bearer of the bad news is in some way associated with the bad news itself. It is better to eliminate this phenomenon within the framework of an agile transformation, because it makes any open, constructive approach to instructive and bitterly necessary experiences impossible.

A successful institutional opportunity to deal with failure openly and with a twinkle in the eye does exist, for example, in so-called *fuck-up events*. At such events, employees and teams report on their own efforts, which they ultimately had to admit had failed. The purpose of such meetings, of course, is not to make a public mockery of oneself, but to offer an opportunity to learn from mistakes. Here a corresponding moderation helps, which usually refers to the following questions:

– What did we intend to do and what did we actually (not) achieve?
– What were the assumptions on which our approach was based?
– What did the failure finally manifest itself in?
– What were the main causes of failure?

– What have we learned from this and what would we do differently in the future?

This is not just a matter of discussing the content. Fuckup events signal the positive meaning and importance of failure—failure is fine in principle as long as there was a serious effort behind it and one is willing to learn from it. Measures of this kind give failure a stage and not just success. Failed people become heroes, people who have dared something but do not take themselves too seriously.

Green Meadow as an Option

Finally, one important option should not go unmentioned, namely the creation of a corporate division that functions according to its own agile rules alongside the original hierarchical part of the company. This option does not necessarily require change or transformation. Rather, one makes a kind of new beginning on the much-quoted green meadow. At least the following ways of doing so have to be distinguished:

- A new division will be separated from the existing company, which will now operate according to agile principles. Within this new area, the reset button is pressed. Together with external coaches, completely new structures are defined according to agile principles.
- A division in which agile principles prevail from the outset will be completely redeveloped. In a way, companies are trying to build their own innovative start-up garages.
- Almost all large corporations now operate their own incubator or accelerator programs, in which they support start-ups with financial support and expertise, benefit from them and create long-term candidates for acquisition.
- A formerly independent company (e.g. a start-up) that is used to working according to agile principles is acquired. After the acquisition, care will be taken to ensure that this company continues to adhere to its management and organizational philosophy.

If independent corporate divisions or units are separated, rebuilt or acquired, two characteristic challenges must be expected: firstly, too much integration or, secondly, too little integration.

Too much integration means that the hierarchical superior power dominates the new business area, which then is gradually crushed by its understanding of leadership and organization. The hierarchical—mostly bigger—part of the company does not do this out of malice. It only follows its natural, well-intentioned way of doing things. And those who are eagerly at work here are simply in the majority. Too little integration, on the other hand, is reflected in the fact that there is not only no exchange between the company divisions, but that they actively avoid each other. The hierarchically socialized Dr. Pfeffer (with suit and tie) finds no common ground with the agile thinking Jordan, who wears a T-shirt even in winter. The right degree of integration can probably only be achieved through interpersonal dialogue, in which representatives of the old and new worlds meet in person and discuss the rules of the game and measures for closing ranks together.

Be Bold, Be Right

I do not want to close this chapter without answering one last question that is asked second most often: "What can I do as an individual if I want to work in an agile way but find myself in a deeply hierarchical and stable context?" It is primarily fear that prevents people from doing what they are convinced of. So the first counter-question must be, "What are you afraid of?" Is it the fear of losing one's job, of damaging one's career, of being worse off at the next pay rise? Here it is helpful to first become aware of one's own position in the company or in the team. How easy is it really to be replaced? At the end of the day, many employees will find that a non-compliant use for the interests of the company cannot really harm them. Before you get fired as a (rare) software developer, a lot has to happen.

At this point I could tell great stories of wonderful people who have achieved great things in hierarchical companies against strong resistance from top. Their stories are usually similar. First, they have an idea they deeply believe in. They work on this idea because they can't do anything else but take their job seriously. In the beginning it is important to develop the idea further, to find internal supporters and to achieve first small successes. It can be an advantage if this idea does not appear on the radar of superiors. Already in Sect. 12.3 this approach was presented as bootlegging. Many of the people I am thinking of here remember situations where they were requested to meet an executive board member. "What are you doing? I do not remember asking you to do this." After that, they just kept going because they couldn't help it. Not infrequently experiences of this kind motivate and the inner rebel comes to bear. What is more motivating than the inner obligation to want to prove to others that you are right? I also count myself as this kind of a person and can understand this feeling only too well. Very often—and this is the interesting thing about these stories—these rebels end up as heroes, particularly when a superior leader sees causes to decorate him or her with an award. "Look here. You can achieve this if you show initiative with courage and perseverance". And so, the troublemakers suddenly become intrapreneurs, who one likes to put on the pedestal as role models for others.

The prerequisite for this is adherence to a principle that the wonderful CEO of Microsoft Satya Nadella has summed up in a few words: *be bold, be right*. Be bold, but make sure you end up right. If you are not bold, you have no future. If you are not right, you are done.

References

Dillard JP (1993) Persuasion past and present: attitudes aren't what they used to be. Commun Monogr 60:90–97

Harris TE, Nelson MD (2008) Applied organizational communication. Theory and practice in a global environment. Lawrence Erlbaum, New York

Laloux F (2014) Reinventing organizations: a guide to creating organizations inspired by the next stage in human consciousness. Nelson Parker, Brussels

Luhmann N (1984) Soziale Systeme. Grundriss einer allgemeinen Theorie. Suhrkamp, Frankfurt am Main

Stepper J (2015) Working out loud. For a better career and life. Ikigai Press, New York

Index

A
Accelerator programs, 360
Acquisition, 9, 38, 81, 84, 97, 100, 115, 147, 187, 226, 235, 241, 333, 360
Acquisitive function, 235
Action learning, 157, 204, 205, 210, 211
Active sourcing, 1, 37, 40, 43, 81, 93, 94, 96–99, 101, 311
Agile manifesto, 297, 326
Agility, viii, 4, 23, 25, 27, 29, 33, 47, 53, 55, 56, 78, 81, 121, 126, 275, 315, 325, 326, 331, 336, 341, 344, 349, 352, 353, 357, 358
Agilization, 1–3, 33, 69, 111, 119, 301, 346, 359
Alpha error, 101, 304, 306
Alumni network, 282
Ambidexterity, 66, 325
Ambiguity, 159, 161
Annual performance appraisal, 138, 142, 143, 174, 290, 293, 323
Applicant tracking systems (ATS), vii, 2, 104, 296, 317
Aptitude diagnostics, 106, 112
Architecture, 5, 75, 259, 297, 350
Artificial intelligence (AI), 14, 23, 67, 105, 109, 112, 180, 195–197, 280, 284, 296, 318–320, 322, 326
Attitude, vii, viii, 15, 22, 23, 33, 57–59, 69, 84, 109, 129, 132, 133, 137, 147, 152, 192, 202, 207, 208, 224, 235, 240, 266, 276, 277, 280, 281, 283, 297, 316, 317, 323, 338, 340, 357
Autonomy, 56, 63, 73–75, 230, 258, 259, 262, 266
Autopoiesis, 351

B
Balanced scorecard, 12, 303
Base pay, 5, 138, 223, 231, 235–243, 307
Behavioural anchors, 18
Behavioural patterns, 170, 178, 332, 343, 350
Best-of-breed, 325, 326
Beta error, 101, 105, 106
Big data, 318–320
Bonuses, 28, 44, 77, 142, 234, 246–248, 250, 282, 283, 300, 304, 310, 314
Boomerang hiring, 282
Bootlegging, 315, 361
Boss, 10, 13, 34, 54, 59, 63, 67, 70–73, 76, 79, 113, 116, 120, 122, 123, 131, 139, 160, 161, 171, 216–218, 223, 233, 262, 274, 278, 284, 290, 292, 332, 351, 353
Bottleneck functions, 27, 37, 38, 43, 84, 94, 96–98, 103, 105, 108, 192, 242
Brand ambassadors, 88
Branded house, 85
Breathing company, 248
Bring Your Own Device (BYOD), 317, 318
Broadbanding, 239, 240, 312
Buddy programs, 152
Budgeting process, 330
Bureaucracy model, 11
Business context, 113, 154, 157, 158, 207, 232, 243, 294, 318
Business models, 14, 32, 33, 65, 173, 316
Business purpose, 30, 35
Buyer behaviour, 32

C
Candidate approach, 82, 90–101
Candidate experience, 1, 81, 87, 91, 98, 106–108, 304

Candidate focus, 82, 90, 94, 100, 101
Candidate journey, 107
Candidate retention, 5, 90, 95, 100
Candidate search, 90, 94, 95, 97–100, 319
Candidate selection, 320, 321
Career, vii, 37, 40, 82, 83, 95, 102, 107, 111, 147, 163, 187–219, 238, 268, 269, 276, 283–285, 305, 320, 321, 357, 361
Career coaching, 203
Career networks, 88, 93
Career paths, 19, 198–200, 211, 213, 215
Career planning, 19
Career website, 59, 83
Causality, 267, 310
Center of Expertise (CoE), 289, 296–298
Central planning and control, 15–17, 20, 21, 27, 45, 116, 164, 165, 198, 199, 207, 210, 321, 322, 324
Certainty of outcome, 66, 244
Certainty of process, 66, 244
Change, 8, 62, 81, 121, 180, 195, 223, 294, 329, 349
Change management, vii, 5, 10, 329–336, 341, 343–346, 356
Chatbots, 320
Check-in, 114, 117, 134, 135, 323
Chief executive officer (CEO), 3, 7, 12, 16, 23, 31–33, 35, 47, 51, 58–61, 83, 86, 100, 114, 132, 140, 141, 149, 159, 162, 163, 166, 172, 178, 183, 190, 198, 212, 214, 216, 220, 230, 240, 261, 264, 267, 268, 270, 273–275, 278, 281, 282, 296, 305, 309, 310, 325, 330, 352–355, 357, 361
CHRO, 35, 42, 292, 299, 301, 313
Clinical judgements, 109, 208–210
Cloud solutions, 291, 318
Coach, 20, 34, 56, 71, 73, 122, 123, 126, 131, 133, 139, 140, 160, 161, 164, 190, 203, 223, 233, 290, 296, 351, 353–355, 358
Coaching, 124, 144, 154, 165, 166, 172, 190, 193, 352, 354
Cognitive dissonance, 244, 245
Cognitive heuristics, 313
Collect approach, 182–184
Communication, 13, 18, 33, 55, 63, 86–91, 107, 125, 127, 128, 135, 140, 156, 158, 169, 176, 197, 214, 232, 259, 260, 262, 268, 269, 271, 280, 300, 317, 318, 320, 329, 335, 336, 338, 346, 350, 352, 359
Communities of practice, 78, 176

Compensation, 47, 54, 223, 224, 226–228, 233, 234, 237, 239–241, 243, 249, 275, 288, 289, 293, 294, 301
Compensation policy, 223–235
Competence, vii, 10, 18, 21, 103, 112, 127, 130, 155, 156, 167, 168, 171, 172, 179, 207, 210, 219, 220, 292, 293, 297, 312, 335, 343, 346
Competence assessments, 18, 21
Competency models, 18, 155, 156, 192, 209
Competitive advantage, 27, 29, 31, 34, 35, 315
Connect approach, 182–184
Connectivity, 1, 14, 174, 318
Contingent pay, 47, 244
Continuous improvement processes (CIP), 64, 345
Continuous learning, 44, 138, 147, 162, 166–180, 183, 314, 337, 343–345
Control, 8–10, 14, 21, 22, 34, 47, 55, 65, 67, 69, 71, 73, 79, 90, 124, 156, 164, 169, 171, 179, 207, 208, 239, 258, 264, 266, 302–315, 321, 322, 334, 336, 341–343, 345, 358, 359
Control loop, 303
Core competencies, 27, 31, 64
Corporate culture, 8, 13, 22, 156, 184, 192, 230, 276
Corporate democracy, 333, 338–340
Corporate strategy, 26, 27, 29, 34, 35, 38, 154, 155, 159, 166
Corporate value statements, 356
Cost-per-hire, 105, 112, 304, 305, 307
Critical functions, 38
Critical leadership situations, 161
Crowdsourcing, 63
Cultural change, 333, 356, 357

D

Decision theory, 313
Descriptive career paths, 199, 200
Design thinking, 173, 344
Development dialogue, 167, 174
Development goal, 120, 122
Development planning, 18, 19, 168
Development program, 19, 49, 153–155, 157–159, 189, 194, 300
Dialogue-based assistance systems, 320
Difficult mass hiring, 96–98
Digital HR, 196, 287, 315–327

Index

Digital transformation, 2, 3, 14, 21, 33, 54
Digitization, 23, 32, 41, 64, 67, 69, 81, 84, 119, 175, 204, 207, 272, 280, 315, 326, 340
Discrimination, 210, 320
Disruption, 32, 56, 64, 65, 262
Diversity, 10, 21, 23, 56, 58, 86, 91, 148, 163, 192, 228, 255, 264, 265, 311, 332, 358
Division of labour, 75–78

E
Effectiveness strategy, 105
Efficiency strategy, 104, 105
Elected Salary Commission, 234
Emotion curve, 334
Empirical test construction, 109
Employee engagement, 253, 266
Employee experience, 322
Employee profiles, 18
Employee recognition system, 234
Employee referral programs, 93, 98, 299, 304, 314, 318
Employee retention, 5, 40, 44, 253, 275–285, 320
Employee satisfaction, 14, 229, 268, 308
Employee Self Services (ESS), 2, 317
Employee stock ownership, 247
Employee surveys, vii, 5, 18, 39, 44, 48, 131, 132, 253, 266–276, 293, 300, 308, 312, 357
Employee value proposition (EVP), 82, 83, 85–87, 91, 97–100, 108
Employer attractiveness, 44, 88, 253–266, 352
Employer brand, 16, 28, 39, 40, 43, 81–87, 90, 97–99, 108, 288, 300, 301, 304, 309–311
Employer branding, viii, 1, 5, 18, 27, 37, 39, 40, 43, 81–91, 101, 254, 275, 289, 300, 304, 312, 313
Employer branding strategy, 90
Employer positioning, 83, 88, 91, 290, 300, 301
Enablers, 2, 3, 71–73, 79, 126, 139, 160, 164, 174, 216, 223, 233, 240, 290, 301, 302
Enterprise social networks, 176, 182, 193, 201, 318
Equal pay, 229, 240
Equity, 224, 226, 227, 247
Ethnocentric world view, 49
Evidence-based management, 310–311, 313
Executive development, 44, 48–50, 153–166, 170, 289, 291, 301
Executive search, 92

Exit interview, 278, 279, 281
Expatriation, 19, 194, 201, 289, 290, 295
Expert, 5, 18, 39, 69, 96, 161, 187, 234, 255, 288, 349
Expert careers, 5, 39, 187, 212–220, 234
Explicit knowledge, 175
Externalization, 175, 176, 183
Extrinsic motivation, 231–233, 236, 239, 245

F
Facebook, 88, 89, 177, 304
Factual complexity, 294, 295
Fear, 33, 116, 129, 139, 161, 204, 239, 283, 293, 309, 334, 343, 361
Feedback, 5, 12, 71, 107, 119, 158, 267, 306
Feedback app, 134, 135, 318
Feedback processes, 128, 134
Feedback providers, 129–133, 135–137
Feedback rules, 128, 129, 131
Filter bubble, 177
Flexible grading, 237, 238
Flexible work arrangements, 257, 259
Flexitime, 257, 263, 266
Flight risk, 280, 320
Follow-up processes, 269, 274, 276
Forced distribution, 139–141, 144, 234, 246
Forced ranking, 54, 140, 246
Formal, 18, 73, 77, 110, 113, 120, 127, 129, 135–144, 147, 165, 167, 169, 173, 200, 202, 207–210, 212, 217–219, 239, 280, 339
Formal assessments, 138, 139, 141–144, 168, 179, 207, 211, 246
Fuck-up events, 359, 360

G
Gallup, 266, 274
Gamification, 184
Gender diversity, 265
Generation Y, 1, 255, 256
Generation Z, 255
Gini coefficient, 240
Global integration, 50, 290, 291, 300
Goals, vii, 22, 58, 119–144, 158, 215, 217, 226, 228, 248, 250, 283, 303, 306, 308, 330, 334, 339
Goal Setting Theory, 123
Grassroots movement, 338–340
Groupthink, 312
Guerrilla recruiting, 93

H

Hay system, 237
Hierarchization, 351
Hierarchy, 10, 11, 29, 55, 59, 69, 79, 121, 126, 135, 187, 212, 215, 217, 234, 331, 335
High potentials, 19, 189, 191–196, 201, 202, 204–207, 210, 211
Hire & pay, 15, 16, 20, 22, 88, 188, 190, 198, 199, 210, 290
Home office, 257
House of brands, 86
HR amplitude, 16
HR analytics, 316
HR business partners, 1, 92, 99, 102, 105, 241, 289, 291, 294, 296, 297, 315
HR curator, 296
HR department, 17, 20–22, 92, 93, 95, 99, 100, 110, 120, 138, 158, 159, 164, 168, 216, 288, 292, 296, 298, 299, 302, 305, 314, 317
HR factory, 296, 299
HR information system (HRIS), 19, 120, 296, 316, 320
HR marketing, 18, 84, 89, 95, 292, 313
HR network of expert, 296
HR organization (HR Org), 5, 19, 48, 92, 111, 287–302, 306
HR planning, 18
HR playing field, 15, 19, 53
HR triangle, 15, 29, 53, 198, 321
Human Capital Value Added (HCVA), 309
Human resource (HR) requirements, 98, 99
Human resource (HR) strategy, 4, 5, 7, 51, 53, 66, 116, 131, 324–326

I

Idea of man, 60, 61
Ignorance, 4, 21, 170, 171, 294
Implicit knowledge, 175
Incidental, 167, 175, 177
Incubators, 65, 360
Informal feedback, 135
Informal learning, 151, 169, 173, 174, 179
Innovator's dilemma, 65
Instagram, 88
Instant surveys, 273
Institutionalization, 9, 10, 13, 15, 16, 42, 65, 232, 276
Integration, 81, 113, 116, 117, 220, 263, 300, 324, 325, 360
Internalization, 9, 175
Internal mobility, 202

Internal talent market, 201
Internet of Things, 319
Intrinsic motivation, 225, 226, 231–233, 236, 245–247, 250, 282, 342
Intuition, 109, 208, 311, 313
Inverted pyramid, 59, 60, 72, 79, 240
Investment calculations, 309, 312, 313, 315, 316
Involvement, 94, 97, 98, 101, 107, 174, 210, 249, 268, 272, 276, 298, 329, 335, 337, 346, 355
Irritation, viii, 162, 163, 170–172, 176, 177, 314, 332, 344, 349, 355

J

Job advertisements, 36, 38, 81, 82, 91, 92, 97, 102, 103, 107, 254, 293, 294, 304, 319
Job architecture, 18, 297
Job descriptions, 18, 125, 168, 179, 275, 340
Job evaluation, 18, 237, 243
Job planning, 18
Job posting, 18
Job profiles, 18, 103, 109, 168
Job rotation, 78, 178
Job-sharing, 257, 260, 265
Job value, 237

K

Key functions, 27, 35–38, 103, 181, 192, 228, 242
Key HR topics, 5, 26–29, 33, 34, 48, 53, 55, 66, 75, 223, 287, 331
Key performance indicators (KPIs), 12, 19, 45, 93, 303, 351, 354
Key roles, viii, 35
Knowledge, 20, 21, 34, 49, 56, 69–71, 140, 147–184, 187, 201, 216, 262, 267, 270, 289, 299, 306, 318, 320, 338, 353
Knowledge database, 181, 182
Knowledge management, 5, 44, 147, 180–184, 318

L

Lateral scoring, 234
Leadership, 1, 7, 26, 53, 109, 119, 153, 189, 223, 253, 290, 333, 353
Leadership assessment, 164, 165
Leadership competency, 155, 156, 163, 166, 192

Leadership development, 5, 48–50, 155–157, 159, 160, 162, 192
Leadership feedback, 164–165
Leadership model, 156, 192
Leadership role, 27, 71–73, 139, 158, 160, 233, 265, 290
Leadership styles, 53, 56, 158
Leadership theories, 158, 160
Leadership understanding, 119, 120, 126, 132, 139
Learning, 5, 9, 25, 54, 104, 138, 147, 187, 277, 290, 332, 349
Learning context, 151, 154, 156, 158, 159
Learning journeys, 171, 358
Learning needs, 21, 157, 167, 168, 172, 177, 179, 180, 300
Learning objectives, 154, 156
Learning on demand, 167, 177, 179
Learning projects, 204–207, 211
Learning resources, 176, 177, 319
Learning transfer, 154, 156, 158, 169
Life plans, 55, 58, 79, 264–266
Life tasks, 188
LinkedIn, 2, 88, 93, 98, 109, 278, 280, 304, 318–320, 324
Local differentiation, 49, 50, 290, 300, 301
Locus of control, 341–344
Long-Term Incentives (LTI), 283
Lorenz curve, 240, 241

M
Machine learning, 23, 109, 195, 197, 280, 319, 322, 326
Machine metaphor, 102, 332
Management, 1, 9, 25, 54, 81, 119, 147, 187, 223, 254, 288, 329, 350
Management by objectives, 124
Management systems, 15–17, 19, 21–23, 54, 193, 288, 290
Manager Self Services (MSS), 317
Massive Open Online Courses (MOOCs), 176
Matching, 172, 203, 208–210
MBA programs, 155
Mentors, 152, 157, 166, 187, 196, 200, 202, 203, 205, 211
Mergers, 333, 334, 340
Merit increases, 232, 234
Micro-learning, 175
Minimal Viable Products, 69
Mobile learning, 177

Motivation, 13, 21, 60, 65, 77, 102, 104, 110, 112, 129, 131, 141, 149, 150, 153, 172, 179, 180, 184, 192, 213, 226, 230–233, 235, 236, 243–245, 267, 304, 305, 332
Multiplier system, 355

N
Nerds, 218–220, 297
Networks, 10, 16, 20, 22, 29, 43, 63, 65, 68, 78, 93, 95, 99, 100, 102, 124, 126, 155, 159, 174, 177, 193, 198, 200, 201, 203, 205, 206, 218, 246, 280, 296, 299, 302, 314, 318–320, 331, 339, 340

O
Objective setting, 5, 18, 44, 117, 119–127, 156, 215, 220, 359
Onboarding, 5, 44, 81, 111–117, 178, 201, 230
One-time bonuses, 246, 247, 250
Ontogeny, 188
Open space events, 148, 149, 339, 344
Organization, 1, 7, 26, 53, 92, 119, 156, 196, 223, 259, 329, 350
Organizational development, 174, 268
Overjustification effect, 245

P
Paradoxical interventions, 282
Partner, 71–73, 79, 123, 124, 126, 127, 139, 140, 160, 164, 223, 233, 265, 275, 282, 284, 289, 290, 292, 296, 353
Pay bands, 224, 237–240, 243
Pay differences, 238–240, 243
Pay differentiation, 228, 229
Pay grades, 224, 237–241, 243, 282
Pay transparency, 229–230, 236
Peer counselling, 162, 163, 206
Peer nomination, 193, 218, 324
People analytics, 5, 23, 109, 194–196, 207, 277, 280, 287, 315–327
People-centered enablement, 15, 16, 20–22, 25, 27, 45, 117, 198, 199, 210, 321, 322
People over Processes, 208, 297, 323, 326
Performance appraisal, vii, viii, 1, 12, 16, 18, 20, 21, 34, 39, 42, 54, 55, 67, 77, 119, 124, 128, 131, 133–135, 142, 143, 167, 174, 198, 233, 290, 293, 310, 323
Performance assessment, 323
Performance community, 248

Performance evaluation, 18, 44, 67, 73, 129, 139, 143
Performance expectations, 44, 119–127, 133, 141, 144, 174
Performance management, 10, 54, 119, 297, 298, 337, 350
Performance potential matrix, 189, 275, 324
Performance review, 5, 54, 71, 142, 156, 233, 234, 357
Performance standards, 121, 124, 126, 295
Persona, 84
Personnel department, 100, 287, 298, 302
Personnel deployment planning, 18
Personnel selection, 18, 81, 101, 104–109, 112
Positioning of, 31
Potential, 9, 35, 40, 43, 47, 55, 59, 69, 71, 72, 78, 82, 87, 90, 93, 99, 103, 104, 106–108, 111, 112, 133, 136, 138, 161, 162, 165, 166, 187, 189–191, 201, 203–205, 237–239, 244, 256, 275, 282, 338, 342
Potential assessments, 19, 198
Predictive analytics, 109, 316
P90/P50 relation, 241
Pre-mortem analysis, 311, 312
Priorities, 8, 10, 29, 31, 32, 34, 35, 38, 40, 66, 85, 103, 106, 121, 124, 142, 144, 155, 166, 220, 228, 230, 256, 266, 268, 270, 271, 276, 322, 337, 344
Product owner (PO), 353
Profiling, 84
Profit sharing, 247, 248
Project management, 68, 149, 153, 169, 171, 173, 174
Psychological contract, 62, 77, 277
Pulse surveys, 271, 272, 274

Q
Q12, 274

R
Rapid prototyping, 69
Recommendation systems, 319, 320
Recruitment, 22, 36–38, 43, 45, 81, 90, 91, 93, 96, 98, 102, 290, 298, 299, 304, 309, 317
Reengineering, 330, 333, 335, 337
Reflection, 8, 14, 15, 83, 88, 119, 128, 133, 143, 144, 153, 158, 160, 162, 164, 166, 173–175, 178, 179, 190, 311, 314, 355
Regulation, 9, 32, 33, 127, 223, 257, 258, 260, 261, 266, 291, 351

Remuneration, 5, 18, 20, 25, 38, 42, 44–47, 62, 117, 126, 142, 144, 217, 223–250
Restructuring, 330, 333, 334, 339
Reversed mentoring, 152, 203, 210
Right potentials, 191, 192
Role of HR, 46
Rules, 4, 8–14, 16, 18, 23, 55, 59, 63, 65, 73, 103, 104, 120, 124, 125, 127, 128, 134, 165, 178, 200, 203, 208, 209, 234, 247, 260, 261, 263, 265, 288, 291, 313, 351, 358, 360, 361

S
Sabbaticals, 263
Salary differences, 240, 241, 243
Scarcity of resources, 32
Scientific management, 244, 310
Scrum, 13, 68, 144, 173, 358
Search strategies, 93, 96, 100
Selection decision, 81, 102, 109–112, 299
Self-efficacy, 63, 72, 77, 230, 339, 343
Self-regulation, 47, 56, 133, 141, 230
Semi-autonomous working group, 261
Sense of urgency, 333, 352
70-20-10 rule, 200–202
Shared service center, 289, 295
Shared service organizations, 105
Shop floor management, 330
Situational performance dialogue, 141
SMART rule, 120, 121
Social dynamics, 136, 174, 226, 233–235, 249, 292–298, 302, 306, 314
Social feedback, 128
Socialization, 178
Social judgment, 137, 193
Social learning, 78, 174
Social media, 83, 88–91, 113, 134, 152, 176, 177, 184, 217
Sourcing strategies, 95
Specialist careers, 213
Specialist hiring, 96, 97, 99
Spill-over effects, 263
Stability, 4, 23, 27–29, 47, 55, 61, 65, 81, 102, 126, 165, 167, 196, 199, 287, 325, 330–332, 335, 343, 344, 350, 359
Start-ups, 65, 171, 325, 358, 360
Statistical judgement, 109, 208–210
Stock options, 247, 248
Strategic management systems, 10, 17, 23
Strategic search, 96, 97, 99, 100
Strategy development, 25, 28, 29, 159
Stretch jobs, 201, 206
Stretch roles, 201, 211

Index

Structures, 9, 10, 12–14, 16–18, 23, 53, 59, 65–68, 100, 150, 153, 199, 223, 225, 234, 236, 239–241, 260, 263, 265, 275, 337, 351, 354, 357
Succession planning, 19, 297, 298
Suites, 325
Survey feedback method, 268

T

Talent, 1, 10, 25, 54, 81, 138, 150, 187, 237, 254, 288, 331, 350
Talent acquisition, 38, 40, 41, 47, 62, 81–117, 187, 238, 291, 299
Talent acquisition strategy, 90, 101
Talent community, 1, 43, 94, 95, 97–99, 324
Talent development, 45, 46, 157, 187, 189, 196–211, 331
Talent identification, 5, 19, 27, 44, 104, 117, 138, 187–197, 218, 312, 320, 321, 324
Talent management, vii, 1, 10, 16, 21, 25, 42, 47, 54, 187, 191–194, 198, 201, 204–210, 288, 290, 293, 297–299, 301, 350
Talent managers, 190, 208
Talent nominations, 138, 194–197, 322
Talent promotion, 209, 211, 320, 321
Talent relationship management, viii, 10, 38, 81, 98, 309
Talent review, 19, 189
Target commitment, 123
Target functions, 26, 27, 29, 38, 40, 84, 86, 91, 96, 98, 114, 181, 192, 291, 324
Target transparency, 125
Task dynamics, 47, 56, 75, 76, 121, 244, 246
Task uncertainty, 70, 121
T-concept, 69, 132, 151, 212, 289
Teleworking, 257
Theory X, viii, 60, 61, 73, 151, 223, 225, 234, 258
Theory Y, viii, 60, 61, 151, 223, 225
360-degree assessment, 198, 271
360-degree feedback, 19, 20, 164
Three-pillar model, 288, 289, 294, 296, 297
Time-to-fill, 105, 112, 306, 308
Total compensation, 224
Touchpoints, 87, 91, 108
Trainee programs, 153, 178
Training, vii, 5, 16, 18, 20, 21, 38, 39, 41, 42, 45, 57, 113, 116, 117, 128, 134, 147–153, 155–158, 168, 173, 176, 187, 198, 200, 204, 205, 207, 230, 275, 281, 283, 292, 295, 299, 304, 308, 323, 329, 335, 344
Training maturity, 152
Transformation, 2, 5, 14, 21, 22, 155, 250, 271, 294, 329–346, 349–361
Trust, 8, 10, 23, 54–56, 73–75, 79, 89, 115, 148, 150, 162, 172, 190, 202, 208–211, 274, 277, 280, 305, 306, 310, 322, 330, 356, 357
Trust-based working hours, 74, 257, 258, 260, 263
Turnover costs, 277, 281
Turnover intention, 280
Turnover rates, 48, 281, 282, 284, 307
Twitter, 88, 109, 193, 217

U

Understanding of leadership, 3, 7, 26–29, 33, 48, 53, 54, 60, 67, 69–75, 119, 120, 126, 132, 139, 161, 223, 235, 259, 265, 269, 274, 275, 325, 326, 353, 360
Upward appraisals, 164

V

Vacancy focus, 92, 100
Variable pay, 5, 16, 27, 138, 223, 232, 243, 250
Varieties of HR, 4, 15
Variety, 22, 29, 55, 58, 84, 114, 116, 149, 207, 224, 247, 271, 280, 295
Vocational training, 44, 147–153, 155
Voluntary turnover, 16, 254, 275, 276, 279–281, 283, 284, 320

W

Waterfall model, 68
Working conditions, 41, 44, 63, 74, 216, 253–266, 269, 271, 276, 279
Working hours flexibility, 258
Working hours models, 257, 258
Working Out Loud, 78, 206, 339, 340, 351
Working time accounts, 257
Working time flexibility, 253, 257, 261
Work-life balance, 1, 57–59, 256, 263–264, 266
Work location flexibility, 5, 243, 253, 257, 261
Workplace, 74, 75, 257–259

Y

Yellow Pages, 2, 176, 182, 318

Made in the USA
Las Vegas, NV
01 September 2022